Architectural Management

Architectural Management

M.P. Nicholson

Director of Architectural Management
University of Nottingham

E & FN SPON

An Imprint of Chapman & Hall

London · New York · Tokyo · Melbourne · Madras

Published by
E & FN Spon, an imprint of Chapman & Hall, 2–6 Boundary Row,
London SE1 8HN

Chapman & Hall, 2–6 Boundary Row, London SE1 8HN, UK

Van Nostrand Reinhold Inc., 115 5th Avenue, New York NY10003, USA

Chapman & Hall Japan, Thomson Publishing Japan, Hirakawacho Nemoto Building, 6F, 1-7-11 Hirakawa-cho, Chiyoda-ku, Tokyo 102, Japan

Chapman & Hall Australia, Thomas Nelson Australia, 102 Dodds Street, South Melbourne, Victoria 3205, Australia

Chapman & Hall India, R. Seshadri, 32 Second Main Road, CIT East, Madras 600 035, India

First edition 1992

© 1992 M.P. Nicholson

Printed in Great Britain at The University Press, Cambridge

ISBN 0 419 17780 9   0 442 31598 8 (USA)

A catalogue record for this book is available from the British Library

Library of Congress Cataloging-in-Publication data available

This book is dedicated to
All those brave young men and women
who survived an
Insight into Architectural Management
course and still wanted more.

Contents

CHAPTER ONE

*'Running a business calls for all characteristics
we admire in our folklore heroes, and yet it
never occurs to us that they are to be found in
the leaders of our small companies. Courage
and compassion, vision and imagination,
determination, persistence against adversity,
creativity and wisdom are all called upon. Yet
we persist in thinking of this occupation,
which still employs one in five of our working
population, as being dull, bureaucratic and for
lesser mortals.'*

John Harvey-Jones

Architects in a changing environment

M. Paul Nicholson
Visiting Professor, University of Bio Bio, Chile
Professor W.B. Jepson
Emeritus Professor, University of Aston, UK

Abstract
The profession of Architecture and the services which its provides
have gone full circle. The early close relationship with the building
process was curtailed for about one hundred years. It has only been
during the last decade that designers and builders have been allowed
(by lifting their self-imposed constraints) to come closer together.
This has encouraged the Design and Build contracts and the Management
Fee contract procedures to flourish and come into common use.
Keywords: Architectural Management, Professional Development,
Architect's Appointment.

During the past 250 years the nature of demand for the products of the
building industry has changed dramatically, and that for architectural
services has come almost full circle. It has come from the master
builder informed in the classical styles of architecture, or some
dialect of them, to that of the master builder capable of delivering a
building at a price whose performance equates with a user-need (which
may be commercial, industrial, monumental or domestic).

The industrial revolution expanded the building market. It
introduced new clients - developers, industrialists, the investors in
docks, harbours and railways, public corporations and many more. At
first the work called only for the traditional craft skills with which
architects were familiar, but as new techniques and materials came
into use and called for engineering design skills in order to fit them
for construction, new professional associates entered the field.

Occupations which were formerly the province of the upper streams
of society began to expand to meet burgeoning opportunity.
Professional institutions and new centres of learning expanded the
scope for those with ability to serve society. Architects faced a
situation in which the demand-led expansion created scope for
exploitation by unscrupulous developers and builders. In an attempt
to maintain their image as a profession they debated whether to
retain in their number the measurers, developers, contractors and
others, some of whom also offered design services (see Architectural
Magazine, Vol.1 1834). They decided on exclusion. The role of the
architect as the independent, educated, gentleman designer became the
model of the 19th century. It eschewed speculation and fee competition, and claimed the independent status permitting action as an
impartial arbitor between client and contractor.

There were consequences. Associated professions, which also had concern for status, identified their own professional role and the standards to fulfil. Their expertise developed in isolation. Its exploitation was their justification as a practice. The pace and pressure of technology, spurred by concern for economy, exacerbated the process of fragmentation. Undergraduate studies were later to reflect the patterns of professionalism.

It was Philibert De l'Orme in the 16th century who felt that during his time the profession of architecture was becoming more specialised, that it was more clearly defining its responsibilities and privileges (A. Blunt). It is interesting that De l'Orme critic- ised the patrons of his time for choosing master masons and carpenters and even painters to design their buildings, rather than architects.

It took such people as Paladio, Michelangelo and Bramante to create awareness of the distinction between designers and craftsmen/ constructors so that, by the end of the 16th century, Alberti was able to write "the craftsman is merely an instrument of the architect." (Campbell).

No clear pattern had emerged by the 18th century. In 1747 Campbell wrote of architects as either agreeing with the client to build for a fixed price, or to be paid for supervising tradesmen who were to be selected by the architect. In both cases, the architect (who may have been a master tradesman) was responsible for the employment and dismissal of the workforce.

It seems that during the 19th century also, the role and definition of an architect was undefined. Many architects acted as developers and designed, constructed and financed vast areas of new housing in the industrial cities. Men such as Cubitt (1785-1861) in London, and Watson Fothergill (1844-1928) in Nottingham, proved that the architect could retain his stature as a designer whilst involving himself in the business of construction. Many fine examples of their work exist to this day.

Being at the sharp end of the construction process must have allow- ed the contemporary 19th century architect to observe at first hand the activities of the construction operatives. They would have seen the individual craft lodges develop into united single-trade unions, and in 1831 or 1832 (Place MSS) the formation of a General Union (Houldsworth). The formation of The Builders' Society in 1834 must have further isolated the architects from the rest of the construction industry, and in 1835 the RIBA was founded.

Whilst the early builders' associations were essentially 'reactive' institutions which were formed in hurried response to crises in industrial relations, the RIBA appears from the outset to have had crusading motivations. It imposed constraints on the professional standing of the Institute. Restrictions from practicing all activities outside the confines of the design and supervision of that design were imposed. No more the Master Builder; no more the Developer; no longer a natural involvement in the construction process. In short, architects isolated the design function from the very products of their own efforts - buildings.

The early RIBA addressed itself to the full comforts of protectionism. A mandatory fee system was imposed on the members. The numbers of young men and women entering the profession were monitored and controlled through the Institute's entry procedures. Codes of conduct of the members and conditions of engagement were cheerfully accepted by the architectural fraternity. The architect's unique position within standard building contracts was established, which allowed him to be an agent of the employer whilst at the same time he could be the arbitrator of disputes between the contractor and the employer.

The pattern was set for architects to devote their energies to the production of fine architecture. Work was plentiful, particularly between the wars. All of this amounted to a situation where British architects did not have to concern themselves with commercial matters, with finance, organisation and management. Their profits were assured and their future appeared healthy.

There was an error in the reasoning. In the 20th century the centres of largely labour-intensive industry extended to accommodate a larger and more mobile population. The distribution of electicity and the availability of the motor car gave flexibility for the development of land which had, hitherto, not commended itself. The road network grew and did not suffer the limitations of the rail systems and canals that preceded it as the principal arteries. Again, the architect allowed other parts of the industry to exploit the opportunity, and the acres of semi-detached houses, the council house estates and much industrial and commercial development proceeded without their influence.

Ribbon development, the control of which abuse led to the creation of housing estates, was the only planning constraint on the random development of urban facilities to accommodate the new communities. The product has been much criticised. At the end of the Second World War the need was expressed to introduce a system of town planning. In the event the nature of the legislation was bureaucratic, it gave little if any scope for a creative approach to the architectural treatment of towns and cities. Its structures were dictated more by the traffic pattern and the client's return on investment than future townscapes. Yet another profession (that of Town Planning) emerged.

The manner in which architects dealt with the individual commissions, particularly in the building boom of the late '60s and early '70s, gained few plaudits. Failure to establish their influence at the pinnacle of public need led to its decline to the point when associated professions believed that their training and experience was more nearly aligned to the principal components of client demand. The aesthetics of building had become subsidiary to its site occupancy and its technical economy. Much of the investment was public. Concern led to criticism.

This concern about the construction industry in general and the design professions in particular, has been shown by a number of British governments. The Emmerson Report was the first to notice the gap between those who design and those who actually build and who recommended, in order to improve efficiency, that ways should be found which might bring the two processes closer together.

In 1964 a further Government committee under the chairmanship of Sir Harold Banwell stated:

(a) As the complexity of construction work increases, the need for a design team at the outset, with all those participating in the design as full members, is vital.
(b) Restrictions on the activities of members of the professional institutions needs to be re-examined.
(c) The use of unorthodox methods of contract procedures has advantages which should not be lost to members of the Public Sector through rigid adherence to outmoded procedures.

It appears that the RIBA (which was the main target of the Banwell Report, found little cause to pursue the recommendations. In an act of further concern the UK Government published a follow-up report in 1967 mistitled 'Action on Banwell.' This spelt out the inaction arising from the 1964 recommendations.

Change, nevertheless, was inevitable. During the following twenty years local authorities (such as Nottinghamshire, which pioneered the CLASP system) experimented with new techniques and management systems. Contractors undertook Design and Build responsibilities. Project Management was applied to major construction processes. Management of works for a fee by a management contractor became acceptable; indeed, it was welcomed by the large chain stores, commercialists and industrial clients. The architect's role consequently shifted with each new opportunity.

The architects began not only to lose their traditional position as leader of the construction team, but to find that they were faced with competition from outside as well as from within their ranks. Building surveyors, construction technicians and many others offered design skills to the public for a low fee. The RIBA could no longer impose its recommended scale of fees and the cold wind of competition began to erode the vestiges of comfort and security.

The decline of the economy in the late 1970s and the accession to power of a government with a harsher view of social responsibility and practices in restriction of trade led to a severe building slump. The industry sought new fields. The oil-rich countries had little patience with the idea of client participation in the minutiae of the building process; they wanted a satisfactory functioning building at a price and on time. The architect and patron model was dismissed for that of the designer and supplier of a product. The climate was ripe for the development of project management extending from inception to completion.

It has only been during the past few years that social and economic pressures have created a climate in which Banwell could flourish. In an act of unprecedented courage, the RIBA abolished, in 1983, the scale of mandatory fees. This, it must be said, followed a criticism from the Office of Fair Trading and also a Monopolies Commission Report on advertising by solicitors, vets and accountants.

The fee scale was not the only thing to go; restrictions on advertising were lifted; the 'directors rule' was also abolished. Architects could again practice the art of building as well as the skill of design. Architecture as a profession had returned (if it wanted) to the status of a Master Builder and could, after a lapse of one hundred years, be totally involved in the full production of buildings.

During 1983 two important publications were produced: 'Faster Buildings' and the 'Manual of the BPF System', both illustrating the degree of experimentation which was taking place at that time. The former analysed the differing management techniques on five thousand industrial contracts with a variety of roles for the architect. The latter suggested an unorthodox approach to the management of both the design and construction processes.

Not only were dramatic changes taking place in the UK, but other countries were also involved in this revolution. The main conclusion of the 1984 Conference of Architects in the Commonwealth Countries was that architects were performing management functions which were beyond their basic architectural education and experience. Architectural education was, and still is, design-centred with little regard for the management of the design process. Furthermore, few schools of architecture take seriously the whole subject of 'Architectural Management.'

John Carter in the Architects Journal, was one of the first commentators on the new roles of architects - he said "that the new-found (1981) freedom of architects to initiate speculation or to direct building or component companies, must be used to broaden and deepen the profession's educational base." Regrettably the RIBA, whilst allowing the practitioners to have freedom of operations, has not yet revised its traditional thinking on educational parameters for future architects.

The full circle therefore has been turned - practice and educational training need to rethink the traditional values and look towards a new and vital industry. Alan Meikle, the former County Architect of Hereford and Worcester County Council, in supporting the then proposed Code of Conduct said, "So, if we are to retain the initiative in our affairs, we must react to these changes in our work, the building industry and the society in which we live."

References

Architectural Magazine. (1834) 1, pp. 12-16.
Banwell, Sir Harold. (1964) **Report of the Committee on the Placing and Management of Contracts for Building and Civil Engineering Work.** London, HMSO.
Blunt, A. (1958) **Philibert De l'Orme.** Zwemmer, London.
Building Economic Development Council. (1983) **Faster Building for Industry.** London, HMSO.
British Property Federation. (1983) **The British Property Federation System for Building Design and Construction.** Manual of the BPF System, London.
Campbell, R. (1747) **The London Tradesman.** London, p. 155.
Carter, J. (1981) **The Code is Dead: Long Live the Code.** Architect's Journal, 194(43), pp. 282-83.
Emmerson, Sir Harold. (1962)**Survey of Problems before the Construction Industries,** Report prepared for the Minister of Works. London, HMSO.
Houldsworth, K. H. (1983) **Building Industry Employers and Trades Associations 1833-1884.** M.Phil. Thesis, University of Nottingham.

National Economic Development Office. (1967) **Action After the Banwell Report.** London, HMSO.

Meikle, A. **RIBA Code of Conduct - FOR the Proposed Changes.** Architect's Journal, 171(26), p. 1228.

Place MSS.27, Brit. Lib., 799, p. 124.

Data on the managerial tasks and needs of architects

R.E. Finnigan, R.F. De La Mare and S.H. Wearne
Technological Management Unit, University of Bradford, UK

Keywords: Architects, RIBA, Practice Management, Project Management, Construction Management, Future Careers, Education, Training, Survey Method.

1. Introduction

A survey of members of the Royal Institute of British Architects carried out in 1986 indicated that architects of all ages recognised that they had a great need for 'managerial' knowledge and skills (Finnigan et al, 1986). In this survey data was obtained by sending a questionnaire to 1 in 20 members in the UK, and some were also interviewed.

The data obtained indicated that architects of all ages have a great need for managerial knowledge and skills, and that most of them believe they have been insufficiently prepared, by way of formal education and training, in many of these, particularly in the human relations, financial, organization and contractual skills.

The detailed results indicated the relative importance of expertise in estimating, planning, marketing, organization, contracts, law, safety, work study and other managerial subjects. The data showed how the use and need of this expertise varied with age, level of responsibility, type of employer and size of organization, and whether the members sampled had received any training in the subjects needed, what training they saw as needed, and what were their problems in construction management.

The survey provided a basis for policies on how much tuition and guidance on managerial subjects should be included in courses and training at various stages in architects' careers. This paper recommends that the profession should consider repeating such surveys regularly in order to provide up-to-date data and to be able to identify trends in the profession's needs.

2. Survey management

The 1986 survey was carried out by the Technological Management Unit of the University of Bradford with assistance and advice from senior members and staff of the RIBA.

The costs of employing research staff to prepare the questionnaire, supervise its distribution, prepare the answered questionnaires for data processing, analyze the results, interview some respondents and help draft this report were met by a grant from the Science and Engineering Research Council under their specially promoted programme for research in construction management. The RIBA undertook the work of selecting a sample of their members, provided postal labels addressed to them, and gave comments on the results and drafts for this report. The University met the costs of coordinating the survey and of the data processing.

3. Purpose

The survey was designed to obtain data on:

- The relative importance of expertise in estimating, planning, marketing, motivating, organizational and contractual relationships, law, safety, work study and other managerial subjects.

- How these needs vary with age, level of responsibility, type of employer and size of organization.

- Whether training had been obtained in the subjects needed, either initially or later in careers, and what training was needed for future responsibilities.

- What were their problems in construction management.

- What were their comments on such a survey.

4. Survey method

Posting a questionnaire to a random sample of the RIBA members was chosen as the main method of obtaining data, followed by interviewing of a few respondents. This choice of method was based upon experience gained by us in a series of surveys of the managerial needs of engineers and builders (See the reports listed at the end of the paper).

4.1 The questionnaire
The scope and wording of the questions appropriate for RIBA members were decided as a result of exchanges of drafts and two meetings with the Institute's staff. In particular we agreed that we should obtain data and comments from those in small practices and be able to compare their needs with the larger organizations.

Our questionnaire asked for detailed data on the skills and experience listed in the table attached as an Appendix at the end of this paper. Respondents were asked to indicate whether each was required in their present post, whether required in future career, and whether instruction in them had been received up to qualifying as an architect or in subsequent training.

The questionnaire included specific questions requiring 'Yes' or 'No' replies and open questions requesting respondents to write in their own answers. They were also invited to end by adding any general comments.

A specimen copy of the questionnaire is reproduced in the report.

The RIBA runs surveys to obtain data on employment and earnings, and these are sent to 1 in 5 of architects on the Registration Council's register. Our questions duplicated them only to the extent of asking for data on type of employer and age. For our purposes this data provided a basis for assessing whether the respondents to our survey were comparable to the larger number of architects covered by their employment and earnings survey.

4.2 Questionnaire response rate
Number of usable questionnaires received: 382
Number sent out: 1,104
Net response rate: 35%

67 of the questionnaires received were not usable because they were from retired members or the answers were not complete.

4.3 Interviewing
The purpose of interviewing some respondents was to explore their perceptions of their work and ascertain whether they felt that the questions we had asked had enabled them to give an accurate description of their managerial needs. It was limited to those who indicated in replying to the questionnaire that they were willing to be interviewed.

The interviewing was semi-structured, covering the following points:-

Thanks to the respondent for helping with the survey.

Statement of the purpose of the interview.

Discussion of their answers to some questions.

Discussion of any general comments added at the end of the questionnaire.

An invitation to respondent to give views on the survey and its purpose.

Any other points.

4.4 Presentation of data
The data obtained in the survey was presented in five sections in the report, as follows:

Qualifications, ages, employment and place of work. This was 'demographic' information on who responded.

Managerial content of the respondents' jobs, most difficult or demanding aspect of job, autonomy, coordination and solution of problems.

Relevant training and future training needs.

More detailed data on the managerial contents of jobs compared with level of responsibility, age, type of employer and size of firm.

A summary of the results of the interviewing.

A review of general comments from respondents.

5. Data obtained

20 pages of the report display the data obtained. Here we have space for extracts and the main conclusions.

5.1 Employment
The range of ages of respondents had a median value between 40 and 49. Office employment predominated, as would be expected. There was quite an even spread of size of employing organizations, but with less respondents in those employing 10 to 199 people. Approximately half the respondents had been in the same organization or post for ten or more years.

5.2 Managerial extent of posts
As indicated by the detail shown in the Appendix to this paper, the questionnaire was designed to obtain data on the extent that the respondents' present posts required managerial skills and experience.

The answers showed that aspects of project and office management were considered to be much more difficult or demanding than design. As stated in an interview, the items listed do not necessarily create insurmountable problems. Also they may not be dominant in the respondents' work. The answers indicate that expertise in professional and contractual relationships, personnel, finance, commercial management and obtaining new work may be vital if only occasional needs.

The work of a quarter of the respondents was predominantly architectural or technical. On the other hand, the answers to this question show that the majority of respondents' work was partly or predominantly administrative or managerial. The data indicated that 75% or more of members required expertise in:

> Negotiate with other professions
> Negotiate with contractors
> Establish feasibility (of job or project)
> Plan and control preparation of brief, sketch
>   plans, scheme design & detailed design
> Direct supervision of others
> Negotiate with clients
> Negotiate with public authorities (not as clients)
> Review project costs

Establish viability (of job or project)
Motivation of others
Review construction performance
Plan and control budgets (of office or practice)
Nominate sub-contractors

and that 50% or more required expertise in:

Establish cost ceiling/range (of job or project)
Negotiate with others
Establish needs and resource availability
Select personnel
Draft contracts
Plan manpower requirements
Business planning
Plan construction
Evaluate project viability
Marketing of services
Establish policy on fee payments
Taking responsibility for planning matters
Identify potential projects
Negotiate with employees
Train employees - professional
Advise on organizing building procurement
Accounting

In the above and later lists the items appear here in descending order of the percentages of respondents stating that they required them.

It should be noted that at least 50% of the respondents required expertise in all the items listed under 'Traditional Job or Practice Management' except Computing/I.T.

As might be expected, less than 25% of the respondents required expertise in:

Use company law
Programming, design and construction
   in relation to sales
Trading as property developers
Trading in land/buildings
Trading as contractors/sub-contractors
Acting as house or estate agents
Trading as manufacturers/suppliers to the
   construction industry
Acting as auctioneers

5.3 Training received
Discussions in the interviews showed that the answers on training given in the questionnaire might not be as accurate as we would have wished because of varying interpretations of what training and experience was relevant. Also there could be duplication in the content of instruction received by individuals before or after qualifying, or the instruction received might not be appropriate for

the working needs. Allowing for these doubts, the respondents as a whole indicated that they were inadequately trained.

Considering the items noted earlier as required by at least 75% of the respondents, the data indicated less than half that percentage were trained in:

> Negotiate with other professions
> Negotiate with contractors
> Establish feasibility
> Direct supervision of others .
> Negotiate with clients
> Negotiate with public authorities
> Review project costs
> Establish viability
> Motivation of others
> Review construction performance
> Plan and control budgets
> Nominate sub-contractors

and similarly with most of the expertise required in their present posts by at least 50% of the respondents.

Generalizing from these results it appears that they were least well prepared in the following categories of expertise:

- Personal skills of motivation and supervision
- Formal skills of negotiating
- Project identification, evaluation and selection
- Manpower planning and selection
- Business planning and marketing
- Budgeting, fee policy and accounting
- Project costing, planning, reviewing costs and
    construction performance

and relatively well prepared in:

- Planning and controlling preparation of briefs, design, etc
- Drafting contracts and nominating sub-contractors

Generalizing even further, the survey showed that the greatest need may be for skills in managing people, as has been observed to be a common need in the construction industry (Fryer & Fryer, 1986).

5.4 Most difficult or demanding aspect of job

Professional/Contractual relationships	15%
Personnel management	14
Commercial management/development;	
obtaining new work	13
Financial management	11
Self-management	9
Public relations; politics/bureaucracy	9
Design	4
Updating	2
Miscellaneous	13
None..	12

Note: The items listed are our classifications of the statements made by respondents.

5.5 Management courses and formal qualifications

None of the respondents had gained the MBA or DMS levels of formal study for management, and that only 3% had taken any management courses. These were less than figures for other construction industry groups (Faulkner & Wearne, 1984; Finnigan et al, 1986). This result was consistent with the much criticised UK reliance on responsibility for generating competence (Coopers, 1986).

5.6 Needs for future careers

In contrast to this last result, the data obtained showed that the respondents to the survey expected to require a wide range of items of additional expertise for their future careers. Most required were the following:

> Computing/I.T.
> Develop entrepreneurial expertise
> Marketing of services
> Plan and control budgets
> Research into market conditions
> Identify sources of funding
> Identify potential customers
> Analyze project risk
> Evaluate project viability
> Data processing
> Accounting
> Use company law
> Trading as property developers
> Select personnel
> Use employment law

The above were those stated as future requirements by at least 20% of the respondents. Most of these and the other items stated as more required are not what is called traditional job or project management.

5.7 Variations with type of employing organization

The respondents' statements of the most difficult or demanding aspects of their jobs varied between categories of employer.

The detail indicated that professional and contractual relationships were easier in multi-profession organizations, a result to be expected if most or all the specialists required by projects can work together in these firms. Other results to be expected were that commercial and financial matters were less significant in public organizations, but their public relations or political and bureaucratic problems were greater.

Multi-professional organizations appeared to achieve less complexity in architectural and technical matters, but correspondingly more administratively and managerially, as might be expected. Items such as business planning, accounting and negotiating with clients etc. mostly involve respondents in private practice. Those in multi-disciplinary organizations were more involved in organization & methods, computing, funding and sales, but less in project feasibility and viability, drafting contracts, planning and negotiating. Those in public services show generally less involvement in many items, particularly in office or practice management, advising on building procurement, contracts, construction, negotiating, and in non-traditional areas of work such as entrepreneurial and marketing skills, as would be expected.

The least differences between these three main categories of employment were in the items of job or project management, though in public service there was clearly less involvement

5.8 Variations with size of organization
There were some differences in the most difficult or demanding aspects of jobs in different sizes of organization.

Professional and contractual relationships seemed to be less difficult or demanding in organizations employing between 20 and 99 people. This may be because this size of firm is large enough to make specialization possible without relationships having to be predominantly formal, but it should be noted that in the data there was no clear change in the significance of personnel management over the range of sizes of organization shown except that it was insignificant in the smallest ones.

Commercial management, development and obtaining new work appeared to be relatively more difficult or demanding for the organizations employing less than 20 people. If anything the data indicated the same for financial management, but both the above results may have been influenced by the respondents' lesser involvement in those matters in the public offices that were likely to be amongst the larger organizations.

Public relations, politics and bureaucracy appeared to be most difficult or demanding in the smaller and in the larger organizations, but it seems likely that they were demanding in very different ways. In the smallest this result may be related to obtaining new work, but in the larger offices may be related to political control.

Only 4% of all respondents stated that design was the most difficult or demanding aspect of their jobs, but this was particularly demanding in the larger offices.

5.9 Variations with level of responsibility
The detail indicated that the respondents in the more senior posts had the greater needs for managerial expertise. This trend was least in the 'Traditional Job or Practice Management' items. It was more marked in the other sets of items, but it should be noted that the following were required by more than 50% of respondents whatever their level of responsibility:

> Direct supervision of others
> Motivation of others

and most of the 'Traditional' items.

5.10 Variations with age

Overall the peak of needs for managerial skills and experience in their current posts occurred to respondents aged about 40 years. There was a drop in the total of difficult or demanding problems after a peak in the age range of 40 to 49.

Considerable variations were found in how the respondents' statements of the most difficult or demanding aspect of job varied with their age. Professional and contractual relationships and self-management were more dominant in the statements of the younger respondents. Personnel management, commercial management development, obtaining new work, financial management and public relations, politics and bureaucracy were more dominant in the middle ranges of age.

Many of the items listed were shown to be needed by most at all ages. Including the youngest respondents more than 50% of *all* ages needed expertise in the following:

> Negotiate with other professions
> Negotiate with contractors
> Establish feasibility
> Plan and control preparation of brief, etc
> Direct supervision of others
> Negotiate with clients
> Negotiate with public authorities
> Review project costs
> Establish viability
> Review construction performance
> Nominate sub-contractors
> Establish cost ceiling/range
> Negotiate with others
> Establish needs and resource availability
> Plan manpower requirements
> Plan construction

Most of these were items listed under 'Traditional Job or Practice Management'.

Only the following items in the table were most required by respondents aged over 50:

> Accounting
> Negotiate with employees
> Review project costs

but as noted above this last item was required by at least half of those at all ages.

One item was most required by the youngest age group:

> Negotiate with clients

but again was required greatly by all ages.

5.11 Variations in future requirements with age

Respondents' statements of the expertise required for their future careers varied with their age at the time of answering. Their views of requirements decreased generally with age. This is to be expected

16

as expertise will have been acquired with experience. The greatest future needs were overwhelmingly those of the respondents not yet 35. This may indicate that they perceived that the greatest requirements come around the age of 40, as noted above. A decrease in further requirements after that age would therefore be expected for this reason alone.

6 Results of the interviewing

A large number of respondents (199) indicated in answering the questionnaire that they were willing to be interviewed to help with the survey. We were therefore able to select 18 drawn from the main categories of employment, size of firm and ages of respondents who were located in different regions of the country. No one approached by us declined an interview. All were interviewed at their place of work.

Discussing the respondent's present post and type of organization was often a convenient way of starting the interview. Some amplified what they had written. None stated that their written answer needed correction, except one minor correction from one respondent.

Two had changed to different posts. In these cases we discussed the needs of their posts at the time of answering the questionnaire.

Interviewing was the opportunity to ask respondents about their description of the most difficult or demanding aspect of their post, as a means of checking what we thought was meant by their written answers to this open question. None of their replies in the interviews showed that we had misunderstood them. Two respondents stated that the most difficult or demanding aspect of their work was not necessarily typical or frequent. Another commented that his statement about settling the final account for a contract was the most demanding aspect of his post did not mean that it was not done well. One in teaching remarked that administration was a growing and the most demanding aspect of his work in a technical college because staff were not recruited, trained or rewarded for it.

Managing one's own time was stated or implied in several answers discussed in the interviews, but the main problems mentioned were: contractual and professional relationships, personnel management, getting new work, business planning and financial control.

The majority of the respondents interviewed stated that many of their answers about training received indicated that skills, etc had been acquired by experience or through informal guidance at work. Some had obtained instruction in formal in-company seminars, but more at external short courses. One respondent commented that he had learnt much by part-time lecturing.

One respondent who had indicated no training needs in the questionnaire stated that he expects he will require non-traditional skills such as entrepreneurship for his future career.

7 General comments from respondents

7.1 The survey
Several respondents stated that the survey was welcome as it showed that the RIBA were interested in their members' needs and was potentially valuable in indicating what was happening to the profession. One stated that he had replied to the questionnaire because it wasn't selling anything.

One respondent suggested that the questionnaire should perhaps have been sent to a sample of all architects on the Register, particularly as the younger ones may therefore be under-represented, but appreciated that it is the RIBA who can use the results to initiate actions. One commented that he thought the questionnaire reflected a bias in the RIBA towards the larger practices.

Several respondents gave the view that architects need to be more business-like and entrepreneurial, especially to take the lead in conceiving and promoting new projects, rather than leave these to other professions and less qualified groups. One stated that the profession should concentrate on design conception and the coordination of projects, but others supported the view that they needed to be better managers.

Two commented that it was important to note that much of the work now available consisted of small jobs, conversions, refurbishment and interior cosmetic detail, and that financial limits demand 'more for less' from architects and contractors.

Several respondents commented that relationships and the scope for speculative work were much more formal or limited in public organizations compared to private practice, but were more predictable. Two in public organizations anticipated that their future may be to go into practice on their own.

7.2 Training
Training up to qualifying was criticized by several as being limited by the experience of teachers and attitudes of senior architects, resulting in 'gaping holes' compared to working needs. They recommended that students should at the least be introduced to accountancy, contracts and job and practice management, when at Schools of Architecture, and two commented that courses they had taken in social sciences and motivation were very useful.

All who expressed a view on this stated that learning by experience alone was narrow and inadequate, and that mistakes due to this were expensive compared with formal training. Postgraduate courses were not considered to be the remedy, because of their cost, but one respondent stated that he was planning to take a part-time MBA.

The use of short courses as run by the Institute for Advanced Architecture Studies was mentioned favourably by three respondents, but with comments that more was needed and that local courses were needed to limit their expense. Several respondents commented that short courses run by various organizations had been too elementary or not in terms recognized as relevant to the profession.

7.3 Role of the RIBA

The interviews indicated that members expect the RIBA to be more than a club, to take the lead in action on all the results of the survey, and particularly to help those in private small practice and distant from London or other major centres.

Actions to raise standards and to protect the profession were also expected, to give individuals more benefit than obtained by being on the Register, for instance by lobbying Parliament and actively representing members. In one country abroad the state guarantees the payment of fees due.

8. Conclusions

8.1 Survey method

The use of a postal questionnaire enabled us to obtain a large amount of data in a relatively short period of time. This method has limitations in producing qualitative information and certainty about the meaning of words used, but the interviews though few in number had the value of indicating that the results obtained from the questionnaire were not misleading.

From an inspection of the data obtained we have no reason to doubt that the sample of RIBA Members was representative, and many of the answers accord with what would be expected. One might conjecture that the Members with more managerial jobs or aspirations might tend to be those who answered the questionnaire. The few respondents who were interviewed did not confirm this. We hope therefore that the high rate of response achieved may mean that the membership was represented sufficiently well for our purposes, although the possibilities of error or bias should be borne in mind when using these results.

8.2 Need for managerial professionalism

The data indicated that the work of the majority of RIBA members requires expertise in personal skills, negotiating and many other aspects of job, project and office management for which they were not trained formally and are thus expected to learn by experience. This conclusion is consistent with the lack of concern for professionalism in training in the skills and knowledge required for managers in the UK which has been so severely criticised.

Although data obtained from current employment should not be taken as entirely relevant to future needs, it does provide a start to discussing what may be needed. The data obtained in this survey may be most relevant in indicating what is needed by the youngest members. Expertise in many of the items listed in the Appendix to this paper is clearly needed early in careers, before being in a post that is predominantly managerial. In discussing the actions needed in the qualifications of architects, a distinction can therefore be made between the instruction initially required in these 'managerial' subjects and the further training required as a manager.

The data obtained indicated that most training for management needs to be completed by about the age of 40, if it is to be of most use. The detail indicated that many of the subjects listed were required, but we think that the content of skills and experience required in them will be different from those required early in careers. The data obtained also indicated that the needs which respondents thought they required varied with size and type of employment, but it should be noted that those interviewed in private and public offices stated that the needs were now broader than the traditional ones and demanded that personal skills and business expertise should be gained faster and better than by experience alone.

8.3 Repeating the survey

A repeat of the survey would produce up-to-date data on architects to provide a guide to their needs in their jobs and careers. If repeated it would also indicate trends, and so help make predictions. We do not have the resources to undertake another survey, but we would be willing to assist with planning any further work. The questionnaire is freely available for re-use and all the data obtained is accessible for further analysis.

9 References

Coopers & Lybrand Associates (1986) **A Challenge to Complacency: Changing Attitudes to Training**. Report to the Manpower Services Commission and The National Economic Development Office.

A C Faulkner & S H Wearne (1979) **Professional Engineers' Needs for Managerial Skills and Expertise**. Report TMR 15A, Technological Management, University of Bradford.

A C Faulkner & S H Wearne (1984) **Civil Engineers' Needs in Construction Management - Report of 1984 Survey**. Report TMR 153, Technological Management, University of Bradford.

R E Finnigan, R F de la Mare & S H Wearne (1986) **Managerial Needs of Chartered Builders**. Report TMR 154, Technological Management, University of Bradford.

R E Finnigan, R F de la Mare & S H Wearne (1987) **Managerial Needs of Architects**. Report TMR 155, Technological Management, University of Bradford.

B and M Fryer (1986) Managing people in the construction industry. **Int. Journal of Construction Management & Technology**, 1, 1, 5-20.

Royal Institute of British Architects (1986) **Architects' Employment and Earnings**.

S H Wearne (1981) Engineers' managerial tasks. **Journal of European Industrial Training**, 5, 6, 22-24.

S H Wearne et al (1984) **Managerial Skills and Expertise Used by Samples of Engineers in Britain, Australia, Western Canada, Japan, The Netherlands and Norway**. Report TMR 152, Technological Management, University of Bradford.

* Copies of reports TMR 152, 153, 154 and 155 are available at £10 each (including postage) from the Technological Management Unit, University of Bradford, Bradford BD7 1DP.

In the questionnaire respondents were asked to indicate whether skill and expertise in any of the following were required in their present post, whether any were required in future careers, whether instruction in them had been received up to qualifying as an architect, and whether in subsequent training:

OFFICE or PRACTICE MANAGEMENT
Business planning
Marketing of services
Plan and control budgets
Accounting
Negotiate with employees
Work Study (method study)
Data processing
Organization & methods (O & M)
Plan manpower requirements
Select personnel
Direct supervision of others
Motivation of others
Use employment law
Use company law
Train employees - clerical
Train employees - professional
Train employees - managerial
Computing/I.T.

TRADITIONAL JOB OR PROJECT MANAGEMENT
Establish needs and resource availability
Establish cost ceilings/range
Establish feasibility
Establish viability

Plan and control the preparation of:	Brief
	Sketch Plans
	Scheme Design
	Detailed Design

Advise on organizing building procurement
Draft contracts
Plan construction
Plan maintenance
Negotiate with clients
Negotiate with public authorities (not as clients)
Negotiate with other professions
Negotiate with contractors
Negotiate with others
Nominate sub-contractors
Review project costs
Review construction performance
Computing/I.T.

OTHER AREAS OF PRACTICE
Develop entrepreneurial expertise
Research into market conditions
Identify potential projects
Identify potential customers
Evaluate project viability
Analyse project risk
Establish policy on fee payments
Identify sources of funding
Taking responsibility for planning matters

Programming, design and construction in relation to:	funding
	marketing
	sales

Acting as auctioneers
Acting as house or estate agents

OTHER ACTIVITIES
Trading in land/buildings
Trading as property developers
Trading as contractors/sub-contractors
Trading as manufacturers/suppliers to the construction industry

Communication and clarification between designer and client: good practice and legal obligation

A.P. Lavers
Oxford Polytechnic, Oxford, UK

Abstract
The author considers the relevance of communication between designer and client at the design stage to the avoidance of failures which may lead to disputes and, ultimately, claims. The benefits of clarification of the design brief are examined. It is concluded that such clarification constitutes good practice. It is further contended that it is part of the legal obligation normally undertaken between architect and client where the former is the principal designer and the latter the building owner. The author's general conclusion is that insufficient attention is often given to improved communication as a means of eliminating disputes and potential claims.
Keywords: Law, Legal Obligations, Professional Negligence, Design Liability, Clarification of Design Brief.

1 Introduction

Disputes arising from building failure often derive wholly or partly from a mismatch of knowledge and expectation between building owner/client and professional designer. Even the term 'building failure' is a loaded one, since the perception of non-performance or under-performance may not be shared. The mismatch may derive from a number of factors. There may be disparate degrees of experience and expertise between client and designer. Given that there is a wide range of experience and expertise as between categories of client, this disparity is very likely. Chiefly, this will consist of an inexpert client, an individual or a non-property company undertaking a project (or one of the type in question) for the first time, working with an experienced and knowledgeable architect. The mismatch could be the converse, although it is suggested that this would be comparatively rare, viz. an expert client and an incompetent designer. Related to, but not always co-extensive with, the question of knowledge is that of expectation. Clients form expectations which are either inconsistent with those of the designer or even inconsistent with what any designer might accept as realistic. Some of these expectations are formed in good faith but grounded in ignorance. This may be ignorance of what this designer can do, ignorance of what any designer can do, ignorance of the relationship between cost and quality, ignorance of the relationship between time and quality, ignorance of the properties and life of materials. Other expectations may be grounded in greed or self-deception; a belief that something can be had for nothing or very little, or that designers can be expected to find 'miracle' solutions to insoluble problems.

Designers, too, on the other side of the equation form expectations. They may expect too much of clients, especially inexpert clients. This is particularly so when it comes to limitations of products or design solutions. Where the design is severely constrained by the client's budget, it may be self-evident to the designer that lower standards of performance and/or life are the natural sequitur. The architect has a better chance than most clients of making an accurate prediction of the life of any product or building. The same is true of risk. Architects, while they are not building scientists or chemists, are still better placed than most clients to advise of the degree of risk in specifying a product.

There is nothing inherently wrong in the existence of such a mismatch. Initially, at least, it must be a common phenomenon. But it is the role of communication to reduce the disparity in knowledge by diffusion, i.e. from where there is more to where there is less. It is the role of communication to bring closer together the expectations of the parties, so that the designer better understands the client's aspirations and beliefs and can respond to them in what he produces or can seek to modify them if they cannot be met.

If that communication does not take place, or is significantly imperfect, the mismatch of expectation, of purpose, even, is likely to persist through and after the project. The consequences of this continuation are considered below.

2. Increased risk exposure through mismatch of expectations as between client and designer.

Paradoxically, the greater the ignorance and/or inexperience of the client, the greater is the trust likely to be placed in the designer and the less is likely to be the client's appreciation of the need for efficient communication to articulate design objectives. Trust, while generally positive, may here have the negative consequence of encouraging the designer to make assumptions or even decisions which are not compatible with and are increasingly divergent from the client's badly explained wishes and beliefs. The designer does this by no means always because of the arrogant belief that he knows better than the client what the client wants. The reason may be a (superficially well-intended) desire to give the client the benefit of superior knowledge/experience. It my be a desire to improve efficiency by avoiding frequent reference back. The consequence, however, is nearly always divergence between the understanding and position of the respective parties, exacerbated by the fact that the inexpert client may not know enough to be pro-active. They may not ask the right questions.

The divergence of the perceptions of the parties may come sooner rather than later, as the design is implemented. While the effect of this may be an unwelcome altercation and the need for reappraisal and perhaps improvisation, an early realisation of differences is preferable, while they can still be reconciled or at least modified. Put crudely, the problem may still be acute, and arguments may develop about money, but while the contractor is still on site, much may be achieved.

The divergence is not, however, always discovered sooner rather than later. Clients may only become aware of the performance capabilities of a building when they try to use it, or try to use it fully. In the recent contractors' negligence case of Department of Environment v Thomas Bates[1], the office building was quite capable of bearing its imposed loading despite the deficient cube strength (bearing capacity) of the concrete. It was when the tenants proposed using it to full capacity that a problem became apparent, because the inadequate concrete was not capable of bearing its design load. It is axiomatic that many defects in buldings are latent. In the case of Pirelli General v Oscar Faber and Partners[2] the deficient product specified by the defendant consultant engineers caused damage shortly after completion of the industrial chimney in 1969. But the damage was only discovered upon a routine inspection in 1977.

Designers would be ill-advised to derive much comfort from the successful running of the limitation defence in the Pirelli case. The reality is that appearance of damage arising from latent defects, or the discovery of damage which is itself latent, will result in the opening up of disputes and (potentially) claims in projects which have long since been completed. The same is especially true of deficiency which consists in what the client regards as a product or building failing to achieve its expected life. The commencement of acrimonious contact and the issue of proceedings is delayed, not avoided.

Thus far, discussion has been centred upon the client's ignorance and its consequences. But there may be circumstances where the designer's inadequacies are the source of dispute.

Designers have limitations, like all other professionals. They may be inhibited from discussing those limitations with their clients, especially in times when competition for work is such as to encourage the most positive portrayal of the expertise available. Yet failure to make clear the limits of competence, may have the most serious consequences, in terms of the achievement of the desired result and in terms of potential liability. The client is encouraged, explicitly or implicitly, to place confidence in one who cannot justify it. Clients are likely to feel betrayed and resentful. It need not be risk of failure on the part of designers working at and beyond the limits of their competence which is the cause of dispute. It may be risk of failure, rather, of the design or some element of it. That design or element may be seen by the designer as 'client-led', in the sense that the client has encouraged or even sought to insist upon its use. The failure of communication lies in the failure to spell out the degree of risk and the potential consequences of failure.

It is a feature of the phenomenon of disputes arising some time after performance that the respective memories of the parties differs sharply as to what was agreed, in the absence of formal record. This is partly attributable, no doubt, to defective recall, but also partly to a form of wishful thinking, a selective recall which imbues the remembered events with a character favourable to the party in question and to the version of truth for which they are now contending. It will be suggested below that improved communication only helps to avoid this consequence if it is reliably recorded in writing. It is sufficient here to suggest that a divergence in expectation between the parties is likely to be exacerbated by a divergence in recall as to what was agreed.

3. The obligations of communication and clarification

Thus far, the question of good communication has been discussed implicitly as a matter of good practice, in that absence of it is identified as one of the factors which is productive of disputes and claims. There are comparatively well-documented cases where it is contended that proper communication between client and designer could have avoided the problem which was the subject of the dispute. Delegation of design by the principal designer is a feature found commonly in such cases. It is axiomatic that designers in a complex project will be unable physically to undertake the design of every element personally. This encourages the use of procurement systems which anticipate the delegation of design tasks of different elements of the building. But where an architect or other consultant undertakes the role of principal designer (lead consultant), delegation of parts of that role becomes more problematic. In Moresk Cleaners v Hicks[3] the plaintiff cleaning company employed the defendant architect to draw up plans and specifications for building a laundry extension. The architect, who was unused to working with reinforced concrete, delegated part of the design task to the contractor. When the structure suffered damage due to an error in design, the client sued the architect. The Official Referee criticised the architect's decision to delegate unilaterally saying that "If he wished to take that course, it was essential that he should obtain the permission of the building owner before that was done". Similarly in the Canadian case of District of Surrey v Carroll-Hatch and Associates[4], the British Columbia Court of Appeal held both an architect and a consultant structural engineer liable to their client, a municipal authority, following serious subsidence caused by negligent foundation design. The engineer, conscious of the volatile soil conditions, advised the architect of the need for a proper soil investigation. The architect replied that the client would not pay for such work. Crucially, this request by the engineer was not communicated by the architect to the client. This omission to communicate such a vital request ensured that the architect would be held liable. It may be observed that the engineer also held laible because he allowed his very limited notes to be transmitted to the client without clearly warning of their inadequacy. Again, a duty to be pro-active in communication had been neglected with disastrous consequences.

Indeed, the duty to be pro-active in communication is a recurring theme in design liability cases. Perhaps this duty is most acute where the designer is working at the upper limits of his knowledge or knowledge generally. In EDAC v William Moss[5] consultant architects were held liable to their clients for failure to address obvious ongoing problems in the design of curtain walling of an office block. The principal deficiency in the architect's work was, in the words of Judge John Newey QC that " Morgan (the firm) should have informed EDAC fully of the position and advised what was needed". The Judge had no doubt that the client "would have accepted advice frankly given; in any event EDAC would have had no alternative but to agree to fundamental changes if they were ever to obtain a satisfactory building. EDAC would, of course, have been put to very considerable expense, but still a good deal less than they are likely now to incur". The cause of this deficiency was perhaps two-fold. First, the architects concerned were working at the limits of their knowledge of curtain walling. Second, Mr Rae, the project architect, "lacked the firmness of purpose and the assertiveness required for effective supervision of a large project". Forthright communication, however unwelcome, to the client, would unquestionably have avoided the litigation in this case.

It is important that the designer 'takes the client with him' in the sense of explaining the degree of risk in alternative options and advising on choice. In Victoria University of Manchester v Hugh Wilson[6], the design called for a reinforced concrete extension to be clad in red brick and ceramic tiles, to achieve aesthetic consistency with the existing University building. The tiling adhesive failed and the clients sued the architects (inter alia). Judge Newey, giving judgment against the architects emphasised that "Architects who are venturing into the untried or little tried would be wise to warn their clients specifically of what they are doing and to obtain their express approval". It needs only to be added that the warning and approval should be written, as in an exchange of correspondence. This will remind both parties of what was said and help to avoid a dispute arising from what has been called euphemistically 'selective amnesia'.

4. Conclusions: the duty of clarification

The examples of communication failure in this paper are specific. but there is authority for the proposition that there are general legal obligations upon designers to take the initiative in clarifying the client's objectives and thus the design brief. The duty to be positive and pro-active in informing the client was examined in the important decision of Richard Roberts Holdings v Douglas Smith Stimson Partnership[7] where an architect was held liable in negligence in failing to advise of the unsuitability of the material used for the lining of an effluent cooling tank. Again there was the feature of reticence in expressing a lack of expertise. As the judge commented "If the architects felt that they could not form a reliable judgment about the lining for the tank, they should have informed (the clients) of that fact and advised them to take other advice, possibly from a chemist". The value of this case, though, particularly lies in the court's perception of a pro-active and interpretative function of the architect. The defence was that the architects had forwarded much trade information from potential suppliers to the clients. but the judge noted that this information was given without analysis and virtually without comment. His somewhat severe observation was that the architects "were not a secretarial agency for the clients". In other words, the architect was guilty of neglect of professional duty in failing to communicate his assessment of the information. It was not enough to sit back and allow the client to make decisions on materials unaided.

The most powerful exposition of the obligation to clarify the design brief is to be found in <u>Stormont Main Working Mens Club</u> v <u>Roscoe Milne Partnership</u>[8]. The Stormont Main case should dispel any doubt as to the existence of a positive duty on the part of designers to clarify the design brief. The factual background of the case is explored by the author in his 1989 Architect's Liability article.[9] The nub of the dispute between client (club) and architect was whether a games room was intended to be for recreational games only or to be suitable for top-class competitive and exhibition snooker, which proved impossible in the finished building because of space constraints. Judge Bowsher was unequivocal in his view of the architect's duty (although Mr. Milne was exonerated from a finding of negligence on the facts): "In making his design, an architect has a duty to exercise due care to ensure that the design should be reasonably effective to achieve the client's purpose". This, of course, demands that the designer should clearly understand 'the client's purpose'. To that end, Judge Bowsher stated that "if the client has expressed his instructions in terms which leave the architect in doubt as to what his purpose is, the architect has a duty to ascertain what is the purpose he is instructed to achieve". It would be difficult to improve upon this statement as an explanation both of good practice and of legal obligation. The designer who is unclear as to the client's objectives as they appear from the brief can only protect his interests and those of the client by seeking and obtaining written clarification. The Stormont Main litigation could also have been avoided by greater adherence to this point. It is submitted in conclusion that good practice and legal obligation converge to demand greater attention to positive communication as between designer and client.

5. References

1   (1990) 3 Weekly Law Reports 457
2   (1983) 2 Appeal Cases 1
3   (1966) 2 Lloyds Reports 338
4   (1979) 101 Dominion Law Reports 3d 218
5   (1984) 2 Construction Law Reports 1
6   (1985) 2 Construction Law Reports 43
7   (1988) CILL 444
8   (1988) Construction Law Reports
9   Lavers A.P. (1989) Architects Liability 1-3

Learning from Detroit: architecture, mass production and the car re-visited

T. Clelford
Architect: Tutor, Thames Polytechnic, London, UK

Abstract
This paper reconsiders the analogy frequently made between
buildings and the mass production of automobiles. It accepts
weaknesses in the comparison which have already been noted,
but suggests that the analogy may instead have relevance for
architectural practice as a model for managing the design and
construction processes and for marketing architectural
services to the public.
Keywords: Mass production, Design, Mechanisation, Systems,
Marketing, Architectural Practice, Automobiles.

1 Introduction

When I trained in the 1970s, I attended a school of
architecture that prided itself on being at the forefront of
architectural education. Consequently we did actually have
management lectures. These were somewhat simplistic to say
the least. The first lecture identified a few large-scale
organisations that had been successfully managed through
history: the armed services (not surprising, given the
military background of the management tutor), the roman
catholic church and, from the twentieth century, the
management of American early mass production plants for
automobiles, where, we were told, Henry Ford had a lot to
answer for.

The mention of Ford may have been misleading. There was
volume production of automobiles by others before him - by
Ransom E Olds (presumably of Oldsmobile fame) in America and
by others in Europe - but it does at least indicate the
fascination that cars and the manufacturing process that
produces them has had for architects throughout this century.

2 Mass production, Automobiles & Architecture Then

Those early mass production plants were geared (as the name
implies) towards making more of the same thing. But
immediately that concern was extended to making that item
quicker, cheaper and with less resources. This, though
obvious, needs to be said because it was precisely these
interests which were considered to be so fascinating to many
of the architectural theorists of the early twentieth
century. Those preoccupations, as some of the papers here
show, are still with us today.

Let's briefly look at some examples of lessons leading
architects took from the automobile plant and mass production
generally and consider what they did with them. I suggest
that these ideas were important to architectural theorists in
three ways.

Firstly the plants were seen as a paradigm for the mass
production of buildings and architectural components or
products. The attraction was that if an item could only be
made efficiently and in sufficient quantity then it would be
cheap and accessible to all. An obvious example here is Le
Corbusier's 1920 project for the Citrohan House, a simple
house intended for mass production where even the name is a
pun on the name of the french automobile manufacturer Andre
Citroen. (As further evidence of Corbusier's fascination with
the automobile, it's worthwhile bearing in mind that his
scheme for Paris a few years later was named after another
car manufacturer, Voisin.)

Secondly the cars themselves were thought of as examples
architecture could aspire to. They were seen as ergonomically
and efficiently designed, engineered rather than just
constructed, to much finer tolerances, using components built
elsewhere rather than built on site. An extreme example of
architecture following this model would be Buckminster
Fuller's Dymaxion House.

Running in parallel with that was the idea of
standardisation. In buildings this became the theme of
modular construction from standard components which were
easily and rapidly put together. As Russell (1981) points
out, this idea was pioneered by Albert Bemis in the USA in
the 1930s. He took his inspiration from car construction and
some of his illustrations make the parallel explicit. In the
UK production line buildings using industrial processes took
off after World War Two when plants such as those used for
aeroplanes were turned over to making buildings. The Bristol
Aeroplane Company provides a good example: after the war it
built AIROH houses and medium-rise school buildings. (As an
aside it's worth mentioning that the aeroplane industry had
already started to experiment with other types of technology

and construction during the war: the use of timber in the Mosquito and Barnes Wallis's work on bomber fuselages are examples. Mass production is a moving target and mainstream architecture seems to lag a little behind the ideas as well as the practice.)

So far this has been a fairly conventional overview of the architect's love affair with the car and the manufacturing system that produced it. Love affair is a good phrase for the interest because what architects seem to have felt was essentially a passion, based on an image, rather than a detailed knowledge of how things were put together. That ignorance shows in the projects. The manifestations of this interest that come closest to success and are the most convincing work because of detailed knowledge rather than an interest in the superficial. For example, Charles and Ray Eames produced an elegant house from mass produced components that was still being praised and used as a model a quarter of a century later. And one of Norman Foster's former partners, Michael Hopkins, more recently developed his own steel framed building system, the Patera building, having studied the historic system of vernacular timber framed construction while at the Architectural Association. But while these two prototypes are elegant and eminently feasible, they didn't go into mass production. Much of the Eames furniture did, a tribute to their manufacturer and to the passion with which the Eames understood the manufacturing process and pursued an understanding of detailed components or technologies such as the jointing systems used.

The third and final influence of the automobile plant on architects is less obvious but far more interesting from the point of view of this conference because it focuses on how the results were achieved rather than the plant or the products themselves. The management ideas - typically Taylorism - used to run the plants were seen as a model that could be applied to other forms of production, including construction. The hope was that if you planned production carefully enough you could break the project down into easy, repetitive tasks, each of which could be handled at high speed by a worker who learned to specialise in that task. An early example of this transfer, Russell noted in 1981, was the great interest shown by the constructivists after the Russian revolution, who were influenced by these ideas precisely because they had to rapidly reorganise the labour force and rebuild a society as well as buildings. They were searching for manufacturing and management ideas that promised to be modern, fast and efficient, compared to conventional craft-based construction which was considered inefficient, slow and out-moded. That transfer of ideas from America to revolutionary Russia after World War One was mirrored by the transfer that took place from America to Japan after World War Two. We'll briefly look at a result of

that, one of the modern products of the Japanese auto
industry, later on.

3 Architectural Practice In The UK Today

The influences mentioned above tend to be based on an
idealized and sometimes historic view and have been in
circulation for at least fifty years. Before I go on to look
at lessons which I think can be learned today from the
automobile industry I'd like to give a brief, personal and
jaundiced view of current architectural practice in England.

There's not enough work: indeed we haven't had last year,s
economic upturn yet, let alone this years. People don't want
to buy what we have to sell. Yet we live in a country where
the building stock and infrastructure is old, often of poor
quality or badly maintained or stretched beyond endurance.
Maybe that statement should be rephrased as a shortage of
clients, will and money.

It's still a time of high unemployment in the profession
yet more and more student architects are passing through our
schools of architecture. To get work there's intense fee
competition between architects, making us a very cheap
profession to employ. Yet people seem to manage quite well
without us - or to at least be ignorant of the benefits of
employing architects.

Job costing is often still scrappily done, usually on the
basis of putting a notional percentage fee against a job then
working out what resources can be spent against it rather
than having a detailed costing of what has to be done. That's
not surprising when each building is seen as a one-time
solution to a one-off problem.

There's increasing doubts about the protection we have
from the law or insurance to do our jobs yet we find
ourselves taking on more and more responsibilities we didn't
look for about work we have less and less control over.
Arguments about companies versus partnerships, collateral
warranties, supervision versus site visits, even registering
as an architect, typify this.

There's limited standardisation in our work and in the
products that go into it. Some use 'standard details' which
somehow never quite are standard, lifting a drawing rather
than the expertise that went into it. Meanwhile many
architects rush to obtain QAQC, quality assurance under the
British Standard, with systems they're evolving as they go
along.

Consequently many architects often end up unwittingly cutting their own professional, legal and particularly financial throats. Many projects make a loss more often than architects would care to admit, particularly if they take into account interest charges while they wait to get paid.

Meanwhile some architects are busy. They are in demand because they have something people want. There are architects of signature buildings who don't need to cut fees. They can instead charge more. There are architects with specialist skills or know-how that make them essential: for example one practice has a promise of a commission from five of the six applicants for a broadcasting franchise. And there are architects who have built up a relationship - and I hope expertise - with a particular client that is carrying them through the trough of this market.

4 Mass Production, Automobiles & Architecture Now

So if it can help with at least some of the problems outlined above maybe there's still scope for architects to learn more from automobile production. Maybe it can tell us something about how we manage the design process; how we handle construction; and how we can market our services and sell our buildings to the public. Let's look at some examples.

It seems to me that automobile design is a paradigm for a design process that is both evolutionary and carefully researched; that is tried and tested, carefully engineered and functional in the best sense of the word. Corbusier and Ozenfant's idea of the 'objet type' seems to be a good if unconscious and rather touching example of this: the belief that a product can evolve to fulfil its' function and in doing so become beautiful in its' own right.

In the world of real products perhaps the approach is best summed up by Wally Byams, the man behind the Airstream caravan, or (as he referred to it) the Airstream Land Yacht. Byams said 'We don't make changes - only improvements.' His background was in aircraft manufacture and design and he then applied this know-how to trailer production. The result is a true 'machine a habiter' that has evolved over forty years, changing slightly with each successive model as advances become possible.

The effect of this approach on architectural practice can be a concentration on developing expertise with certain components, suppliers or systems to the extent that the architect is able to become fluent and skilled in them and able to have a constructive technical and creative dialogue with the manufacturer. The architect is in turn then able to give the client a better and faster response. For example,

Foster Associates' expertise from their Newport School competition entry enabled them to make a rapid response to IBM's needs when they had to quickly produce a pilot headquarters office at Cosham.

Value engineering techniques to reduce costs, time or resources without reducing performance also become more useful when designs evolve. They are embodied in the architectural urge to do more with less. Foster Associates again provide an example, although the story may be apocryphal, with their first Sainsbury Centre commission at the University of East Anglia. At the time it represented the height of skin panel and gasket technology and Norman Foster allegedly sent an illustration of the building to his one-time collaborator and guru Buckminster Fuller. Bucky's reputed response sums up the next improvement needed: 'Yes Norman, but how much does it weigh?'

Automobile manufacturing continues to be used as a model for building construction. The idea of the manufactured building is still with us. It offers a seductive image but also offers the architect more control if he has the necessary know-how. Richard Rogers has been quoted as favouring it precisely because the standards of management, manufacturing and control were potentially much higher off site than on: the traditional construction, management and supervision process on site let him down in buildings early in his career and he's avoided it since.

Another aspect is how the car is manufactured. There's been a swing in automobile production to the use of teams who make a complete car and who are responsible for its quality. The use of group assembly has enabled ideas like quality circles to take off, breaking down barriers between different departments, subcontractors and suppliers. That could be mirrored in building construction - but examples are rare. One reason why construction project teams function so badly is because at present they're sort-lived, limited to the duration of the project.

Finally the automobile industry can be used as a paradigm for the marketing and selling of architectural services and buildings. In the early years of the century we should note that there was little or no concern with using the management know-how available to harness the power of the plants to make a greater range of products or products more closely geared to the desires of the the customer. Henry Ford's famous quote 'Any customer can have a car painted any colour that he wants so long as it's black' was in fact an admonition to his salesmen, who in an attempt to sell more cars had been guilty of catering to the whims of potential customers. But as more manufacturers have come into the market it's become increasingly important to find ways of making the product

more desirable or attractive to the customer so that you can
sell more or charge more.

One way of achieving this is by differentiating between
otherwise similar products. That's done by creating a range:
X, XL, GL, GTi, XR3: we all despise it but we all succumb.
And increasingly it's taken further, allowing the customer to
select options from a range for a particular model: not just
the colour of the bodywork. BMW is a prime example of this.
The firm is famous for its tendency to provide so many
optional extras that it's now reputed that you'd need to
compare fifty BMWs leaving their plant before finding two
that were identical. The result is that the customer has a
more personalised product, better suited to his or her wants,
which hasn't sacrificed the image of engineering excellence.
The customer has welcomed the opportunity to inflate the
product's price and the company's profit and has done so
without disrupting the manufacturer in the slightest.
Wouldn't it be nice if architecture was like that?

In building the response is less clear but there are
examples. Within the public housing sector it can still be
adventurous to let tenants chose the colour of their front
doors - although there were attempts in Camden through
PHASSAK (following Habraken's ideas) to offer tenants a
choice of internal layout. In the private sector the whole
DIY industry has grown up, supported by owner occupiers
differentiating themselves from their neighbours. Not by a
lot, but by enough to show that 'I'm the same as you but
better'. The commercial sector has responded more directly
with the concept of shell and core construction. That doesn't
have to mean a decrease in quality, as Arup Associates
buildings at Finsbury Avenue and Broadgate in London show. It
meant tenants got their buildings sooner and were then able
to employ their own architects to design the interiors for
them. Those architects have been pleasantly surprised when
they've found that, per square metre, the fitting-out budget
has exceeded the initial building cost.

The final lesson on marketing from the automobile industry
is Nissan's S-Cargo Van. You may not have heard of it or seen
it: that in itself is interesting for a production car from a
multinational manufacturer. The only one I know of in this
country was exhibited in 1991 in London's Design Museum. It's
unusual and interesting because it pushes the flexibility of
production techniques to the limit. It was produced for a
limited market - the youth market; it was produced for a
limited period (from 1989 to 1990) and by only one plant -
Nissan's Pike factory. It was only sold in one, comparatively
small market - Japan itself. In its' looks it's an emulation
of a competitor: the name is a pun on escargot, after the
snail-like shape (and possibly the snail-like pace) of
Citroen's 2CV, itself one of the most long-lived production

models in the world. The 2CV was itself a product of a tight and rigourous design specification and (it must be said) is still a favourite architect's car. The S-Cargo emulates it in the most complimentary way and shows that a short production, carefully targeted product can still be successful even if it emulates a fifty year old competitor - if you market it correctly. Better management means mass production increasingly does not mean a mass product. The expertise is being applied at a smaller and smaller scale. Soon it could reach the level of building.

5 The Architect's Response

Having noted lessons that could help design, construction and marketing we should look at the architect's traditional reply: that he's designing a tailored, one-off solution. The one-off design takes time, money and all too often produces one-off problems. Yet the results often aren't distinctive. In those cases the client can be forgiven if he or she can't perceive what value's been added by the architect. The architect's seen as the person who 'only did the drawings'. The building doesn't bear a architect's distinctive signature and the client in turn has difficulty seeing how it's different. Yet most architects still re-invent the wheel with every building. That's not, surprisingly, often a feature of great architects: we can trace through an oeuvre the same preoccupations, the use of identical materials, components from the same supplier, subtle variants on the same plan. Frank Lloyd Wright's houses are a good example. Few things are right first time: species evolve and the fit survive. Why not designs?

As a profession we need to recognise architecture as the product of particular technologies and know-how that it pays to master. I've already cited the transfer of design expertise from Foster's Newport School Competition to IBM Cosham. Too often we persist in being jacks of all trades and masters of none - without even the virtues of a supermarket low-cost piled high 'me too' brand.

We need to build up relationships with particular suppliers, subcontractors and manufacturers that will extend beyond the 'one site stand' of a single building contract. Relationships can then be built up between companies and between individuals which can become dialogues. There's scope for feed-back and the gradual improvement of the product and the building in the light of the architect's use. And during this process the architect develops a special expertise in particular materials or technologies - like the Eames' interest in patented joint technologies we saw earlier or their skill with moulded ply that gave the World War Two leg splint, a post-war sculpture by Ray Eames and eventually the classic Eames armchair for Herman Miller. Together these start to give the architect more control over the project and enable a faster response. And architect, client and contractor are exposed to less risk because there's less ignorance. And the knowledge gives us more economic control because we have an understanding and an influence over more than one contract. Maybe it'll even give more of us the confidence to become contractors.

For example, we could develop an expertise in energy efficiency related to a particular building type: as has happened with the Hampshire school programme. We might concentrate on compatible component systems like the SCSD schools system in California, where an attempt to produce a flexible system for school building resulted in a shifted focus on whether different combinations of sub-systems fitted together, enabling a greater variety of buildings to be created with a wider range of fittings and fixtures.

One reason to adopt the systems approach to buildings is that because of the varying life-spans of different systems, identified in offices for example by Frank Duffy, important changes to the building have to be made after completion at increasingly short intervals. The interaction of different sub-systems has since become an important factor with the occupants of sophisticated buildings: hence the rise of facilities management. And as the scale of those changes increases architects will be more useful if they have the know-how and the flexibility,

6 A Last Example

As I reach the end of this paper I'm aware that many of my examples have come from the hi-tech school of British architects and projects with large professional teams, even larger budgets and wealthy clients. Some might be tempted to dismiss the points because of that. But that's not essential: the evolution of expertise and therefore control over the design and construction process is there in elements of the work of Shalev and Evans for example. But to prove my point I'll take an example from the opposite end of the spectrum: the work of the late Walter Segal.

Segal once told me that he had developed his system because he wanted to have more control over the design and construction process. He proceeded to describe the extent of control he had. It was total. With his system he could do his own structural calculations. He could work without a quantity surveyor yet was still able to cost his buildings accurately. He could correctly predict the amount of work he had to do and knew exactly what limited overheads would be involved. Some specification clauses and calculations could be standardised. For years he didn't need an assistant and his drawing style consisted of A4 bank paper traced over a tartan grid and Xeroxed as necessary.

He remarked that any architect who used the standard JCT form of building contract should be sued by his client with professional negligence. In his system roles were simple and well-defined: he preferred to use the same team again and again and the contractual mentality of a World War One sniper was avoided. Because the projects were well understood, with a minimum of uncertainty in virtually every area, the architect and the contractor could work economically, quickly and profitably. Just as important, the uncertainties that faced the client in terms of completion date, costs, appearance, were minimised. And finally Segal's system was a unique service - that gave him all the work he ever needed.

REFERENCES

Armes, Andrew (1991) **The Wally Byam Paradigm** - lecture, Thames Polytechnic
Appleyard, B (1986) **Richard Rogers** Faber, London.
Clelford, A (1974) **Interview With Walter Segal**
Clelford, A (1983) **Flexibility and Change in Two Buildings by Foster Associates** MSc dissertation, Bartlett School of Architecture, London.
Duffy, F; Cave C; Worthington, J (1976) **Planning Office Space** Architectural Press, London
Russell, B (1981) **Building Systems Industrialization And Architecture** Wiley, London

CHAPTER TWO

*' Design management may be regarded as a
vogue phrase, but whatever title is thought to
be most appropriate, the underlying philosophy
and the use of appropriate management
techniques should not be disregarded.'*

J. F. Drage.

The price of the independent design

A.G. Doree
University Twente, Enschede, The Netherlands

Abstract
This paper discusses the cost consequences when professional clients use different modes of contracting out
design activities. Three basic modes of design production
are compared: in house design department, contracting out
to an independent design firm and the design/construct
scheme. The question stated is: "Which should be used
regarding overal efficiency?" Tentative answers point to
the conclusion that either in house design or the design/-
construct scheme should be used. Contracting out to an
independent design firm is not expected to deliver the best
solution.
Keywords: Design process, Design procurement systems,
Transaction costs economics, Life cycle costs.

1 Introduction

Now a days only very few clients construct their own
builded facilities themselfs. In the whole of the construction industry "construction" has become a separate trade.
When a client needs a building, contracting out of the pure
manufacturing is in general inevitably. As a result many of
the known procurement systems focus on client-contractor
relations.

The division between the roles to be performed, and subsequently knowledge and profession, is clear as far as the
roles of the client and the constructor are concerned. However, this is not so clear for the role and the profession
of the designer. Many professional clients still have their
in house design departments; some construction firms have
their own design department; independents design firms
operate on the market.

In the past decade in most organizations many management
positions are taken up by lawyers and economists. This
trend also occurred in organizations who operate as "professional clients". This development often brings about a
financial radioscopy of the organization. Questions are

studied such as: "What should the organization do itself, and what should be procured from suppliers?" The answer regarding construction work is clear, but what about design activities? Should clients do their own design work or should the design be procured outside the company? This question puzzles many professional clients. Often the lawyers and the economists act in a rigid manner. Design is no "core-business" and should be disposed of.

This paper investigates three fundamental different modes of design acquisition: in house design, contracting out to independent design firms and the design/construct scheme. The query is which of the three considered schemes looks best seen from the viewpoint of overall efficiency.

2 A general description of the situation

In the Netherlands much of design and engineering of public facilities is traditionally carried out by the local and (sub)national public authorities themselves. Up till now the most apployed procurement method is the general con-tractor approach.

At this moment however, due to budgetary problems of the national and local administrations, politicians promote and stimulate reduction of the (national and local) governmen-tal apparatus. This results in experiments with other types of procurement methods, such as design and construct, and contracting out design work to independent design firms. The mayor reason for adopting this new approach is to economize on public expenses. The main tendency is towards more and more contracting out of design activities, which is supposed to result efficiency improvement due to savings on the total sum of designers salaries.

The prime underlying supposition is that public agencies are operating less efficient than private firms. A design acquired from the market is perceived as less expensive as a design acquired in house. Since public agencies tend to be more bureaucratic than privately owned firms the former statement is commonly accepted[1]. Subsequently many see the contracting out of design activities as a positive contri-bution in the reduction of public expenses.

---

[1] Williamson [1985] argues that internal production lacks competition. Internal production needs another incentive structure. This alternative incentive structure is less effective as the outside competition incentive. As a result internal production has to be less efficient (c.p.). Bokkes [1989] supplies this argument. He states that public production has more than just a strait for-ward financial objective. In pursuit of this multiform objectives concessions on efficiency have to be made.

3 The perceived problem

If economizing on public expenses is the main purpose, the question arises whether design should still be done out "in house" or whether it should be partially or completely commissioned out. The main problem can be stated as:

- Regarding the point of efficiency, when should the design be produced in house and when should the production of the design be contracted out?

4 Answers found in literature

When we look for answers in the established procurement systems literature, especially to those books and essays which compare different procurement systems, the next insights emerge.

Franks (1984) compares six types of management systems and uses five performance requirements. Although contracting out of design activities is obvious in case of package deal and design/construct, none of six described management systems refers to in house design. Furthermore Franks only uses one financial criterium called "economy", which should be interpreted as project costs.

The EDC publication "thinking about building" compares nine alternative procurement systems (in four classes) and uses nine criteria. Also no distinctive difference is given concerning the design procurement system, and one financial criterium "price certainty". The questionnaire makes notice of "controllable variation". When variation is not controllable they advice not to use design and construct.

The NEDO publication (1974) describes both the consultant approach and the design and construct approach. Little attention is given to in house design acquisition.

Walker (1984) states in his book that in analyzing and designing organizational structures relationships of people in the organization are of importance. He mentions the roles of the people, the decisions they (are allowed to) take, and their relations in arriving at decisions. Knowing that the design process is a decision making process, than the points Walker addresses underline the importance of evaluating the distinction between "in house design" and "contracting out".

Rougvie (1987) also makes no distinction between in house design acquisition and contracting out to independent design firms. He compares nine procurement systems on seven criteria. Design and construct score best on the lowest overall cost (project costs) and worst on flexibility.

Singh (1990) presented a paper on the last CIB W92 meeting, which showed a selection tool for procurement systems developed on the basis of an elegant research project. Nine procurement systems are compared on eight criteria. But he also does not distinguish between in house design acquisition and design from a independent design firm.

Bennett (1985) distinguishes three types of organization: programmed, professional and problem-solving. These types are respectively suited for standard constructions, traditional constructions and innovative constructions. Although he does not differentiate regarding in house versus contracting out of design activities, he emphasises the role of the client and the decisions the client has to make. "When the client does not carry them out (the essential aspects of his role), another team within the project organization will do so but not necessarily, or indeed not even probably, in the way which meets client's needs".

This overview shows it is hard to find answers to the stated question. Most of the literature refers to procurement systems without distinguishing between in house design acquisition and acquisition of design from independent design firms. The authors often implicitly suppose the participation of independent design consultants. Furthermore seldom is looked beyond the horizon of the project. Most criteria used to evaluate the different procurement systems concern the project itself. Although we probably all know the proof of the pudding is in the eating, little attention is given to the use aspects of the building (such as value and costs).

5 Working towards an answer

Since literature gives no strait answers a more theoretical approach is needed. In general, selecting among alternatives cannot be done without measuring relevant aspects of the individual alternatives, and comparing the individual scores per alternative with the specified targets. This approach will also be followed for the stated problem concerning the contracting out of design activities.

Comparing in house design with contracting out, in the context of efficiency of public expenses, can be done on several levels of observation. The fundamental layer of comparison is production efficiency: which is more efficient, in house production or the production of the supplier.

But it would be wrong to decide on matter of contracting out on the basis of production efficiency only. On top of the layer of production costs is a layer of transaction costs: contracting out may save on production costs, but additional costs have to be made. These are costs such as the costs of finding and selecting a suitable contract partner, negotiating, drafting the contract, and last but not least monitoring and assuring the progress and the result of the design. These costs of contracting out have to be included in the evaluation of the different design procurement systems.

In the evaluation concerning contracting out the two mentioned financial layers are mostly considered, but one other aspect is often overlooked. When financial effects of contracting out are analyzed, consideration has to be given also to opportunity costs and opportunity losses. These are the expected costs and value parameters of the building (when realized) when it is designed in the alternative design procurement situations. These opportunity costs and losses should be included in the consideration.

Ergo for the choice between in house design versus contracting out, three financial aspects have to be considered:
- production costs (for producing the design).
- contracting costs (costs of the contracting).
- opportunity costs (costs which are unnecessary, and which could have been prevented).

Through their design-decisions designers directly and indirectly influence these three cost categories.

As being part of the production system which has to be paid for, their wages directly influence the production costs of the building. Since designers decide on form and substance of the building, which has to be manufactured they indirectly influence the production costs of the building. Furthermore, by not making the right decisions the may cause opportunity costs and losses. The next paragraph extends this notions.

5.1 The role of the designers

Designers play a crucial role in the building development process. They operate in between the client and the manufacturer. Designers combine two specific sets of knowledge: (1) knowledge of the way building characteristics support certain client-processes, and (2) knowledge of constructing buildings. Each time they make a design they do it for a specific situation. The specific situation is described by the client in a program of requirements and wishes, supplemented with constraints on time and money[2]. For the designers this document identifies the design problem. During the design process (intermediate) solutions are sought and the problem is restated (all in a cyclical manner). Alternative solutions will be generated, and will be evaluated and selected regarding the stated program of requirements (various authors).

Designers are professionals who can operate independent

---

[2] referring to the project management literature which promotes the control parameters: Money, Time, Quality, Organisation and Information [various authors].

or who can operate together[3]. The main function of the designers is to translate client's requirements and wishes into a buildable design and (even more important) usable building. Ideally designers communicate, on the one side with the client over his requirements, wishes and constraints, and on the other side with constructors over practical solutions. As professionals they diagnose the problem and select a program leading to solutions. It is expected that the solution will be more optimal as the designer has more insight in the needs and wishes of the client and more insight in the possibilities of construction technology. The further the knowledge base of the designer stretches towards the client side as well as to the construction side, the more balanced and appropriate the design and the building will be.

The designers determine several value and cost parameters which can be attributed to the building. These parameters are:
- characteristics of the building, which effect:
  . the costs of construction; the main part of the total project costs (often referred to as investment costs).
  . the potential use-ability and value of the building.
  . the operational characteristics of the building, and thus the use-costs (operation, heating, maintenance, security etc.).
- costs of the design: designers have to be paid, so their activities directly influence the costs of the project. Since designers are part of an organisation, parts of the bureau costs may be attributed to the operational costs of the "mother"-organization.

The first category contains the product costs (in literature often referred to as life cycle costs[4]). The second category contains the production costs of the design. The categories are interrelated. Ultimately category two costs flow into category one[5]. The relations between the several costs are illustrated in the figure 1.

When we realize that design costs vary from 5 to 15 percent of the total project costs, and that the total projectcosts, calculated as depreciation and interest, vary between 25 and 75 percent of life cycle costs, then design

---

[3] "professionals" as in Mintzberg [1979] and Bennett [1985].

[4] see also Flanagan cs 1989.

[5] category two "design costs" financed out of project budget, are part of the investment in the building and will subsequently be part of the life cycle cost (as depreciation and interest).

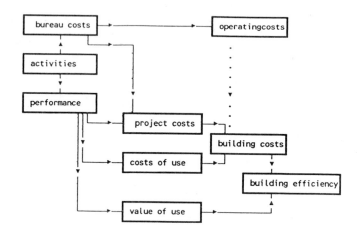

figure 1. designer's influence on several cost parameters

costs amount from 2 up to 11 percent of the life cycle costs. The average value of the design cost percentage is approximately 5 percent. So design contributes a small por- tion of the life cycle costs, but it strongly influences the other 89 to 98 percent of the total costs.

Contracting out of design work may lead to lower design costs, but since design cost are a fraction the project costs the savings can be no more than a fraction of a small portion of the total life cycle costs.

Knowing that it seems justified to re-state the former posed question. The question must not be, if and when contracting out of design activities leads to savings on design costs. More relevant is the question if and when contracting out of design activities leads to better and/or cheaper objects. The parameters to be taken into evaluation are the project costs, the use related costs, the life cycle costs, and last but not least the use value of the object.

5.2 Management of the design process
If the design process is regarded as a production process it is obvious that management is necessary. For executing effective management an explicit objective is a necessary

condition[6]. In practice of governing the design activities
the three financial objectives are usually considered:
1.   design production costs (minimize).
2.   project costs (minimize investment).
3.   life cycle costs (minimize).

The mentioned objectives are not complementary. During the
design process trade-offs between the objectives have to be
made: for example initial investment vs. maintenance costs.
Because the objectives are semi-competitive, priority has
to be stated[7]. Otherwise, due to the unclear objective,
effective steering of the design activities will be impossible.
    When the design process is regarded as a decision making
process, then it seems plausible that different priorities
regarding the financial objectives imply different decisions during the design process, and thus lead to different
designs and buildings. The priorities regarding financial
objectives are related with the organizational context of
the design production team. If the design is done on a lump
sum basis by an independent design firm the main objective
will be to minimize design production costs. That is the
only way to make a profit (especially in case of price
competition).
    So it seems plausible that different design procurement
systems, lead to different priorities concerning financial
objectives, lead to different management of the design
process, lead to different designs and buildings (even when
the designers are completely the same, the organizational
context forces their decision making process in a certain
direction).

5.3 Comparison of design acquisition options
The analysis will be restricted to three principal modes of
design acquisition. The former introduced dichotomy in
house versus contracting out is elaborated through dividing
the last in contracting out to an independent design firm,
and contracting out to a construction firm. Thus the three

---

[6] according to de Leeuw (1988) six conditions have to be
    fulfilled before effective steering of a system is
    possible. The first condition concerns a stated
    objective; A model of the production process is needed;
    Information about state of the system and information
    out of the environment are needed; furthermore the
    management should have sufficient steering variability
    and information processing capacity.

[7] Ideally object efficiency should have the highest
    priority. Up till now seldom a financial utility
    function is given in a building development project.

47

modes taken into consideration are:
- acquisition of design in house.
- acquisition of design as design/construct scheme.
- acquisition of design from a independent design firm.

The key-question is:
. How do the three modes of design acquisition differ
  regarding the pursued financial objectives, and how does
  the difference in priority declaration effect the cost
  and value parameters of the building.

design acquisition in house
The design is made by a specialized department of the
client organization. In house design acquisition often
leads to the traditional project organization. This is
general contractor or separate trades with ex-ante competition, contracts are preferably lump sum, otherwise unit
rate, seldom cost plus.
   The internal design department has the potential for the
best integration of use-, operation- and maintenance data
into the design. The intense relation with the client
organization creates a strong learning potential through
feedback of user experience to the designers. This process
results in a strong knowledge base concerning the client/-
use aspects of the building. The intense relation guarantees client-designer communication. This facilitates the
start of the design activities on the basis of unstable and
incomplete programs of requirements.
   The advantages of this structure are: maximum flexibility during design, insight in the client organization, and
insight in the requirements and wishes of the client/users.
   The mayor complaint about this structure is that the
internal design department tends to bureaucratize, tends to
risk avoidance, and forces design details into the design
which are "over-done" and subsequently to expensive (hobby-
horses). Through the absence of the market and the
inevitable survival, the designers experience little to no
incentive to innovate.
   In day to day practice the design department often is
responsible for delivering a project on budget. Other
departments are charged to operate the building. This leads
to emphasis on the project costs objective for steering the
design activities. But through the intensive relation with
the client organization to much emphasis on project costs
at the costs of higher life cycle costs is often anticipated.
   Conclusion: Although the design efficiency is not as
high as in the other types of design procurement, the
"inside" knowledge of internal design department, and the
long term relation with the client/user secures that use-
value and use-costs are taken into consideration during
design activities.

design acquisition through design and construct

Design and construction are executed by one organization. The client formulates a program of requirements, wishes and constraints. This document forms the basis for the design/-construct contract. The contract can be obtained by nego-tiation as well as by competition. The pay structure may be lump sum, unit price or a combination of both.

Characteristic of design construct is the clear division of responsibilities between client and contractor. This structure facilitates design-construction communication. The advantage concerning the product is the integration of construction technology knowledge into the design phase. The designers may built a knowledge base on matters con-cerning as buildability. The potential improvement of buildability may lead to substantial project costs savings.

As a consequence of the temporary character of client-contractor relation the designers have limited knowledge concerning the client organization and the use aspects of the contemplated use-process. This makes it more difficult to design a building for typical use aspects. Through the choice of contract the client-designer relation is forma-lized. The client-designer communication on matters of design is often difficult. Late or extra specifications often have substantial cost consequences. The client has often no opportunities, or at high expenses, to influence the design activities. This causes severe problems in complex projects which are carried out in a political context.

Through strong emphasis on price competition, project costs savings may be pursued at the risk of more life cycle costs[8]. The designers are aware that their relation to the client is a temporary one. They are more concerned in costs saving regarding their chance of getting the construction contract then in savings regarding the expenses of the client.

Conclusion: Through the emphasis on project costs, design and construct offers an opportunity for extending buildability efforts, and may lead to savings on project costs. But through the distance in the relation between user/client and designers less use-value and/or more use costs may be the consequences[9].

---

[8] This can partially be countered by extending the design/construct schema to an design/construct and operate scheme. Although it is expected that this results in giving more consideration to use-aspects of the building, this scheme up till now is rarely used.

[9] When the life cycle costs consist mainly of capital costs, and a clear and complete requirements program can be formulated, design/construct may be a considerable

design acquisition from a independent design firm

The client drafts a program of requirements, wishes and constraints. The independent design firm designs the building. A contractor constructs the building.

As far as the terminology of procurement systems concerns this scheme looks very much like the in house design department situation. But there are three fundamental differences.

- Independent design firms combine limited client specific knowledge on use-aspects of the building with limited specific knowledge on construction technology. In sense of their knowledge base they are isolated. Furthermore they seldom receive feedback from the use phase. Also they often exclude quality guarantees and they limit their liability, which transfers risks to other project participants.
- Acquisition of design from an independent design firm implies introducing a third party into the project. The clients has a contract with the designers and has a contract with the construction contractors, but for the flow of work between design and construction no formal contract is drafted. In case of imperfect or incomplete drawings often conflicts arise between client, designers and contractor over who is to blame and who has to pay the damage.
- The design firm is often a commercial enterprise which has to make a profit. In order to do so it will pursue savings on design production costs. The ultimate goal is to deliver more designs with less costs made, in stead of delivering better designs (measured in terms of life cycle costs and use-value)[10].

There seem to be two typical situations for contracting out design to independent design firms. One is when the own capacity of the client is temporary insufficient. The other is when the independent design firm has specific expertise which the client lacks.

Conclusion: Independent design firms tend to emphasize design effort efficiency. They will settle for a design which is acceptable for the client in stead of a design which is optimal for the client (in terms of use-value and life cycle costs).

---

alternative for the traditional procurement systems.

[10] Unless reputational effect are effects are considered. In that case they may anticipate that delivering better designs, lead to a better reputation, which may result in obtaining more orders and contracts, and subsequently profit and continuity in the long run.

6 A tentative answer

Now back to our central problem. There are three fundamental modes in obtaining designs. Which is best regarding savings on public expenses:

- acquisition of design in house.
- acquisition of design through design/construct.
- acquisition of design from independent design firms.

When the alternative design procurement modes are compared on the financial parameters as stated in figure 1. The next table appears:

In this table the traditional mode, in house design is given as reference. The scores in the other columns are relative to the traditional mode. Most important are the two bottom rows. They show the effect of the design procurement system on life cycle costs and life cycle value.

	trad	indp	D&C
des.cost	0	–	–
prj.cost	0	+	–
use cost	0	+	+
lifecycle	0	+	–/+
value	0	–	–

The scores in the column of the independent design firm show no financial advantages compared to the traditional way. The last column shows possible savings on project costs, and possible savings on life cycle costs. In both the columns a reduction of value is expected. The table suggest, that when the objective is to improve on the overall efficiency, considerable thought should be given to the consequences of contracting out of design activities before the design procurement systems is selected.

The table gives some insight in the effects of contracting out design activities. But, as shown in the previous paragraphs up till now there is no consistent theoretical framework which explains the effects of different procurement systems on use and cost parameters of the building. This makes it difficult to give strait answers in the matter of design procurement systems, so the best that can be done is stating some tentative answers and indulge in some speculation.

Some tentative answers:
. In house design gives the client maximum flexibility for change orders during the design process, and gives the client maximum possibility for integration of use related data in design. Although design departments tend to be less efficient internally, they seem to offer the best opportunities for controlling and steering on use value and life cycle costs of the building. Through the absence of competition these design departments lack a

innovation incentive.

- Design and construct offers the least in flexibility towards the client, but offers most concerning buildability and project costs and time control. Design and construct makes it possible to integrate specific construction technology knowledge and information into the design.

  Maximum use of design and construct advantages requires clear, complete and stable programs of requirements. Furthermore it must be possible for the client to measure and evaluate the life cycle cost before construction actually starts.

  When the portion of capital costs in the total of life cycle costs increases the favour for design/construct increases.

- Independent design firms probably do best in design efficiency, but they tend to opt for proven design. They have no direct short cut to information of the client or the construction contractor. Given the intention to save on public expenses, there are no arguments supporting design acquisition from independent design firms.

What may happen in the future regarding acquisition of design; A speculation on possible developments (supposing saving on the public expenses is the aim):

- The public apparatus still is responsible for making their own designs. Especially when it is difficult to make a clear, complete and stable program of requirements the best solutions seems to be the traditional way; in house design.

  The public design agencies have reorganized their internal process. They employ high educated technicians and operate at a higher efficiency level than up till to day.

- But when it is possible to draft a clear and complete program of (measurable) requirements, and their are expected little amendments on that program, design and construct may be a good alternative (when possible then set up in competition).

- In case of complex buildings or building processes in complex (political) environment, the client will take care of the design. In more standard situations design and construct offers good opportunities.

- The independent design firms are hired more by the contractors than by the clients. The clients hire people from independent design firms only for advise on specific technological matters and for temporary enlargement of their own apparatus.

- Some cautious experiments will be executed with the most far reaching form of contracting out, design/construct and operate.

7 Conclusions

Looking back at the arguments used to support extending contracting out of design activities, we can conclude that promoting contracting out exclusive on the basis of design production efficiency is indeed defendable. Independent design firms probably have the best design efficiency. But, it is not enough to look at design production efficiency only. Contracting out results in transaction costs. The more difficult it is to draw up a contract and to live up to it, the more transaction costs have to be expected. And last but not least delegating design activities to other organisations may result in designs where opportunities to make them better, lower life cycle costs or even more value are set aside.

Up till now there is no theoretical frame work which describes and predicts the effects of contracting out design activities on the cost- and value parameters of the building in a valid way. In this paper I presented some parameters which have to be regarded when contracting out of design is considered. I made some tentative remarks, comparing three fundamental design procurement systems: in house, through design/construct and from independent design firm. As it looks now there are no strait answers to the question which is the best design procurement system. But it seems plausible that either the design should be made in house, or the design should be contracted out in a design/-construct scheme. It is expected that for contracting out design to independent design firms a higher price has to be paid.

references

Bennett, J. (1985) **construction project management,** Butterworths, London.
Bokkes, W.Th.M. (1989) **privatisering belicht vanuit de transactiekostenbenadering,** Faculty of public policy, University Twente, Enschede (NL).
Building EDC. **thinking about building,** Building EDC.
Eldin, N.N. (1988) constructability improvement of project designs, **journal of construction engineering and management,** ASCE, vol. 114(4), pag.631-640.
Flanagan, R., Norman, G., Meadows, J. & Robinson, G. (1989) **life cycle costing,** BSP professional books, Oxford.
Frankel, E.G. (1990) **project management in engineering services and development,** Butterworths, London.
Franks, J. (1984) **building procurement systems,** Chartered institute of building; Ascot.
Haselhoff, F. (1988) **het kan best anders in de bouw,** Stichting Bouw Research publicatie no 166; Rotterdam.
Leeuw, A.C.J. de. (1988) **organisaties: management, analyse,**

ontwerp en verandering, Van Gorcum, Assen.

NEDO. (1974) before you build, nat. economic development office; London.

Rougvie, A. (1988) project evaluation and development, The Mitchell Publishing Company Limited, London.

Singh, S. (1990) a rational procedure for the selection of appropriate procurement system, CIB publication 132, CIB, Rotterdam.

Walker, A. (1984) project management in construction, BSP professional books, London.

Williamson, O.E. (1985) the economic institutions of capitalism (firms, markets, relational contracting), The Free Press, New York.

Planning and estimating design work – a review of British practice

D.J. Blackwood and S. Sarkar
Department of Civil Engineering, Surveying and Building, Dundee Institute of Technology, Dundee, UK
A.D.F. Price
Department of Civil Engineering, University of Technology, Loughborough, UK

Abstract
This paper deals with the methods adopted by Architects and Engineers to plan and estimate the cost of their professional services and reviews techniques used by design managers to predict and plan the staff resources which are necessary for effective and efficient design work. The paper considers the significant trend towards fee competition amongst design professionals shows that there is a growing need for practices to more accurately assess and realistically programme their staff resource requirements. The paper also considers the extent to which cost control systems adopted by design managers are used to predict the cost of future design work and will describes a comprehensive survey which is currently being undertaken to investigate these issues.
Keywords: Design Management, Planning, Estimating, Cost Control, Questionnaire Survey Design.

1 Introduction

In recent years the environment in which Architectural and Civil Engineering design organisations operate has changed dramatically, partly as a result of changes within the construction industry. There is evidence of a marked shift from traditional contractual arrangements towards, in particular, design and build arrangements (RICS, 1991) which radically alters the role of the designer. Design and build arrangements require a different range of design services from those required under traditional arrangements; for example, the designer, being employed by the contractor, may be required to produce fewer drawings and may not be required to be directly involved in contract administration (Architects Journal, 1991a). Additionally, professional practices which are heavily involved in design and build syndicates may, through unsuccessful bids, encounter an increased amount of work which generates no revenue for the practice and expenditure on this work must be absorbed elsewhere. Consequently, designers require methods other than recommended fee scales to determine the value of their services.

The relationship between clients and their professional advisors has been fundamentally altered by external pressures, with the philosophy behind scales of professional fees having been under review by the Monopolies and Mergers commission since 1967 (Rowdon et al, 1988), and vigorously attacked by the Office Of Fair Trading (New Builder, 1991). Although the Restrictive Practices Bill which would have banned fee scales was not included in the 1991 Queen's speech, the industry has in reality adopted fee competition (Architects Journal, 1991b) despite widespread opposition from the construction industry design professions, (RIBA Journal, 1991 New Civil Engineer, 1991a).

The imposition of greater competition amongst design organisations has also occurred in the public sector with the new Local Government Bill extending compulsory competitive tendering to professional services. A further development affecting Civil Engineers was the privatisation of the Water Industry in England and Wales which resulted in many Local Authority Agency agreements being critically reviewed and re-defined.

However, the risks associated with allocating design work on a least cost basis alone appears to be recognised in the recently produced "Guidelines for the Design of Government Buildings" (Delafons et al 1991), which noted that "good design can achieve benefits in terms of operational efficiency and quality of product that are much more significant than a marginal difference in fees". Furthermore, in November 1991 a consultation document was published by the Government which proposes a two envelope system for compulsory competitive tenders for design work whereby financial bids would only be accepted if they conformed to predetermined quality standards. (New Civil Engineer, 1991b).

The effects of increased fee competition, either through traditional contractual arrangements or through design and build arrangements, against a background of the need for compliance with predetermined quality criteria, will inevitably require a higher degree of accuracy in the selection of necessary design resources and the estimation of design fees for fee bids than had been required under recommended scales of fees. There can however be no certainty that design organisations' planning and estimating systems, which have been developed over many years during which fees were rigorously controlled by recommended scales, will be adequate for the new competitive environment. It is therefore possible that the inherent quality of construction projects will be influenced as much by the effectiveness of design managers' planning and estimating systems as by the technical expertise of the designers.

Consequently, a programme of research has been initiated by Dundee Institute of Technology in conjunction with Loughborough University of Technology to identify, and consider the adequacy of, existing practice with regard to planning design work and estimating design fees as adopted by design managers in Architecture and Civil Engineering in the UK. This work is being supported financially by Tayside Regional Council, Water Services Department. The remainder of this paper is concerned with part of that research programme which constitutes a survey of planning and estimating practice in the context of design work.

2 Literature review of existing practice in planning and estimating design work

Literature on planning and estimating design work is scarce with the emphasis mainly on planning and cost control functions rather than the estimating process. A study of Consulting Engineers in the UK (Rowdon et al, 1989) suggested that "many professional practices earn substantially less than they should, due in large measure to ineffective planning and control", and furthermore "many managers and supervisors do not plan because they consider their type of work does not lend itself to planning" Rowdons paper suggested that a work-package approach should be adopted for design work and that the planned design resources required for each package should be estimated, in consultation with the staff involved in the design work. Significantly, no methodology was suggested for estimating these resources. Another study of a multi-disciplinary practice (Davis et al, 1987) proposed a simulation approach to determine the overall manpower requirements for such practices but again omitted to describe the means of identifying the resources required for the various design activities. Standard guide books for design professions, whilst again emphasising the planning and cost control functions of design managers, contain only an outline of the estimating methods which can be adopted by design managers.   The RIBA Handbook of Professional Practice and Management (RIBA, 1991b), Section A1.3 makes reference to the fact that architects should be competitive, competent and adaptable, and Section A4.5 acknowledges that commissions for professional services will be let through competitive bidding and negotiation. However, the only apparent reference to assessing resources, which would be a necessary stage in developing a fee bid occurs in Section A8 of the Architects Job Book (RIBA 1988). The approach described would seem to relate to design work let on a percentage of the value of the project, presumably on a fee scale basis. In the context of fee competition, such an approach would not be desirable since design resources would then be allocated to design work in response to the "market value" of the commission. A more appropriate approach would be to determine the fee bid as a result of a careful consideration of the resources which would be necessary to provide an adequate level of professional service.

Considering Civil Engineering practice, a guide on the management of design offices (Rutter et al, 1991) identified the following four methods of estimating design resources which were based on:

  (i) projected income from the project;
 (ii) historic cost data of schemes which are broadly similar;
(iii) process-related data expressed in terms of required design input for likely quantities of reinforced concrete, weights of connections in relation to the tonnage of structural steelwork etc, which could be taken as measures of the complexity of a project; and
 (iv) the number of drawings required together with an estimate of the necessary man-hours to produce a drawing.

However, this text did not deal specifically with the means of collection, manipulation and application of data to produce cost estimates although limitations affecting the accuracy of data collected through time-sheets was discussed.

3. Survey of existing practice in planning and estimating design work.

In order to gain more information on the techniques used by design managers and their frequency of application, a comprehensive survey of UK design professionals is currently being undertaken. This work has been divided into three stages:

(i) a series of interviews with practicing design managers in order to verify whether the approaches suggested by the literature review are being adopted by design managers to plan and estimate design work. This enabled an appropriate questionnaire to be developed;

(ii) a postal survey of suppliers and producers of software to determine the availability of commercial software to assist design managers in these functions;

(iii) a postal questionnaire survey of three hundred design managers to test any conclusions drawn as a result of the series of interviews.

3.1 Interviews with design managers.

Eight organisations, six of whom had previously expressed an interest in the research work were selected as being representative of a range of construction industry design offices. The sample comprised:

the head office of a large firm of consulting engineers (800 Staff);

three regional offices of consulting engineers (100 to 20 staff);

the head office of a multi-disciplinary design organisation (200 staff;

the regional office of a medium sized architectural practice (100 staff);

the office of a small architectural practice (20 staff);

a local authority water services department design section (80 staff)

An outline pilot questionnaire was developed consisting of;

(i) a section relating to the type of work carried out by that office;

(ii) a section relating to planning and estimating procedures;

(iii) a section relating to the influence of fee competition on planning and estimating procedures; and

(iv) a section concerning quality management procedures and the relationship between this and planning and estimating.

This questionnaire was sent to senior staff in the selected design organisations in advance of visits to their offices where the senior staff were interviewed using a semi-structured interview based on the pilot questionnaire. Whilst these interviews gave only an overview of current practice in design management, a remarkably consistent approach to planning and estimating design work emerged. In discussing the outline pilot questionnaire, a model of the planning and the planning and estimating process was developed as shown in

Figure 1 and this model was consistently adopted by all organisation. There are several features of interest in this figure which are highlighted below.

It was found that the responsibility for developing an initial estimate of the design resource requirements and the initial programme of design work was delegated entirely or partially to the Engineer or Architect responsible for the design of project. It also transpired that a range of techniques were adopted to estimate resources, and that these were similar to the techniques identified in the literature review. The techniques mentioned during the interviews were:

    a) to make a broad comparison with previous projects of a similar nature with the estimates of the necessary man-hours of the various grades of engineer being derived by the engineer on the basis of experience rather than from "hard data";

    b) to estimate, based on experience of projects of a similar nature, of the number of drawings required for a project and the man-hours associated with a drawing;

    c) to make a broad estimate of the cost of the completed works and, through consideration of recommended scales of fees (with suitable adjustment), determine required man-hours of the various grades;

    d) to apply a central data-base containing data on the necessary resources for specific activities. Only one of the organisations claimed to to have such a system but admitted that it was not widely used and that completed projects were not always appraised and therefore the central data-base was not always up to date and reliable.

All of the organisations interviewed used most of the above planning techniques at some time and also at some stage of a projects development although technique (d) was considered to be impracticable by some of the organisations.

The significance of the "commercial decision", which is an unavoidable element in the process of bid formulation was discussed at length in relation to fee competition. All organisations currently consider that the cost of design work is predominantly estimated as result of a broad estimate of the necessary resources required to adequately design the project in a professional manner and that this estimate is then compared to the recommended fee scales as a check on its validity. Furthermore, the level of the fee bid would be considered against commercial criteria but this would not greatly influence the bid. If an organisation considered they could not win a project and adequately resource its design they would decline to submit a bid for the work.

The role of the organisations' cost control system was discussed at length. It was generally agreed that traditionally the cost control systems was the main management function since estimates had been based on fee scales and resources could be selected to match the given fee. However, as a result of the increasing trend toward fee competition, the organisations conceded that the data currently used for cost control could be utilised further for estimating future projects. Some were considering the development of more formal links between the cost control and estimating functions but there was no

Figure 1 : Model of the planning, estimating and cost control sequence for design work under competitive conditions.

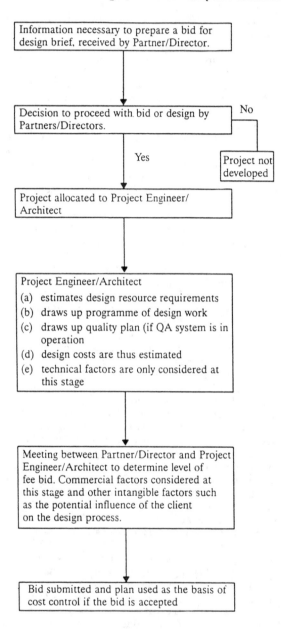

Information necessary to prepare a bid for design brief, received by Partner/Director.

Decision to proceed with bid or design by Partners/Directors.

No

Yes

Project not developed

Project allocated to Project Engineer/ Architect

Project Engineer/Architect
(a) estimates design resource requirements
(b) draws up programme of design work
(c) draws up quality plan (if QA system is in operation
(d) design costs are thus estimated
(e) technical factors are only considered at this stage

Meeting between Partner/Director and Project Engineer/Architect to determine level of fee bid. Commercial factors considered at this stage and other intangible factors such as the potential influence of the client on the design process.

Bid submitted and plan used as the basis of cost control if the bid is accepted evidence of any such links currently in operation.

The concept of quality of design under fee competition arrangements was discussed and most organisations considered that some form of Quality Assurance would be required to ensure that high standards were maintained. Not surprisingly, all organisations considered that their current Quality Assurance procedures were adequate but two firms had additionally sought and received third party certification in accordance with BS5750. Most organisations did not readily perceive a link between Quality Assurance system and their planning procedures although one company did develop a quality plan for each project as part of the planning and estimating process.

In general, the interviews provided a useful overview of planning and estimating practice and at this stage some preliminary conclusions can be drawn which are:

1. because of the widespread application of recommended fee scales, design managers were traditionally able to work from a known fee to identify permissible resource requirements and ensured profitability through the application of comprehensive cost control systems.

2. Planning and estimating of design work is still perceived by design professionals to be a "flying by the seat of the pants" activity and consequently empirical methods not supported by specific data, such as an estimate of the number of drawings or a broad comparison based on experience of similar projects have been adopted to estimate design resources.

3. Whilst most consultants recognised that, in the current competitive environment, a more rational approach should be adopted to planning and estimating resources for design work and were considering changes, none of the companies were actively reviewing their estimating systems.

4. The design managers agreed that the data in their cost control system was not used directly to assist estimating but most considered that the information would be of value.

Clearly, in view of the size of the sample of design organisations, no definite conclusions could be drawn at this stage and therefore two postal surveys were developed to investigate further the initial conclusions.

3.2 Survey of software developers and suppliers

It was apparent at a recent construction industry computer exhibition that a number of software companies were offering office management packages for professional practices. These included modules which would deal with contract administration, accounts systems including the issue of fee notices and sophisticated staff time recording and cost control. In addition, many companies offered sophisticated estimating packages for contracting organisations but in contrast none of the companies had an established system for estimating consultants fee bids. As software development is market-led it can be concluded that the absence of fee estimating systems is indicative of a lack of demand amongst professional practices for this facility which tends to confirm the preliminary conclusion above. A survey of software developers and suppliers was therefore initiated and a list of 30 companies who claimed to provide management support software to the construction industry was compiled. A letter was sent to each company explaining the overall objectives of the research project and requesting information on any appropriate software which could be used by professional design organisations for planning and estimating design work fees. At the time of writing, responses have been received from twelve companies and the breakdown of software packages on offer was as follows:

4 general planning packages;
3 professional office management packages, each with cost control modules but excluding an established fee estimating system;
4 contractors estimating systems;
1 contractors accounting system.

The response to date from software companies indicates that cost control software for design practices is available but fee estimating software is not. This tends to support the preliminary conclusion that design management is biased toward a cost control approach.

3.3 Questionnaire survey of design offices

In order to further test the initial conclusions drawn from the series of interviews, a questionnaire survey of design offices has recently been sent out to obtain information from a larger and hence more reliable sample. Response rates from postal surveys can be be as low as 25% (Oppenheim, 1986) but a previous survey by Dundee Institute of Technology (Jack, 1989) on contractors' planning systems demonstrated that if initial telephone contact was made prior to the dispatch of the survey a response rate of 78% could be achieved. A total sample size of three hundred was adopted and telephone contact was made with the majority of the recipients. The sample consists of:

100 Architectural Practices;
100 Consulting Civil Engineering Practices;
100 Others, consisting of a combination of Building Services
    Engineers, Local Authority departments and Water Companies.

The questionnaires were targeted at individual offices of firms rather than head offices since the interviews suggested that individual offices would be responsible for their own fee estimating and cost control. The offices were selected at random but firms with less than 20 employees were excluded from the survey. The questionnaire was designed to further test the initial conclusions from the interviews, and the layout generally corresponded to the outline pilot questionnaire. The first section was designed to gain general information on the respondents office and areas of work. The second section was designed to determine the frequency of use of the various planning, estimating and cost control techniques which were identified during the interviews. Three questions in the second section were specifically designed to establish if there was any formal link between design managers' cost control and estimating functions. The third section of the report deals the role of quality assurance procedures in the planning and estimating process, and the final section seeks to verify the accuracy of the planning and estimating process model as shown in Figure 1. Unfortunately, data from the questionnaire survey is not available at the date of publication of this paper but should be available at the conference.

4. Conclusions and outline of future work.

Despite widespread opposition from design professions, the construction industry has adopted fee competition for professional services. This move away from recommended scales is likely to increase the need for the application of more accurate planning and estimating techniques by design managers. Whilst final conclusions can not yet be drawn from the survey described in this paper, initial indications are that design management is generally achieved through the application of cost control systems which are intended to ensure that design resource input for a given project does not exceed a pre-determined level. However, the survey suggests that an empirical approach based on qualitative judgement is generally used in the determination of the required design resource input. Furthermore, there is little evidence of the application of cost control data to predict the design resource requirements for future design work.

This must raise doubts about the practicality of accurately assessing the necessary levels of design resource input and therefore this gives rise to concern about the quality of design work in an increasingly competitive environment, particulary in times of recession when fee bids are likely to be particularly keen.

The survey described in this paper forms part of a larger programme of research on the suitability of design management planning and estimating techniques in competitive conditions. Future work in this programme aims to both measure the effectiveness of existing management techniques to develop a planning and estimating system for design work based on data from a cost control system. This work will be case study based, initially in one sector of the construction industry, namely the design section of Tayside Regional Council, Water Services Department who are collaborating with and sponsoring the research programme. It is anticipated that this work will be extended to other sectors of the industry and the authors would welcome any comments and suggestions from the Architectural Profession.

5. References

Architects Journal (1991a) Design and build, Architects
    Journal, 3 July 1991, 51-53.
Architects Journal (1991b) Recession survey, Architects
    Journal, 24 July 1991, 9.
Davis C and Cochrane S R (1987) Optimisation of future
    manpower requirements in a multi-discipline consultancy,
    Construction Management and Economics, 5, 45-56.
Delafons J and Jefferson B (1991), Guidelines for the
    design of Government buildings, HMSO, London.
Jack W (1989) The extent of use of microcomputers in
    contractors planning, Unpublished BEng (Hons) Project,
    Dundee Institute of Technology.
New Builder (1991) OFT renews war on professional scales,
    New Builder, 24 Jan 1991, 8.
New Civil Engineer (1991a) ACE gathers fee bid evidence,
    New Civil Engineer, 17 Oct 1991, 6.
New Civil Engineer (1991b) Quality beats cost as government
    standard, New Civil Engineer, 7 Nov 1991, 7.
Oppenhiem A N (1986) Questionnaire design and attitude
    measurement, Glover, London.
RIBA (1988) Architects job book: volume 1 5th edition, RIBA
    Publications, London.
RIBA (1991) Handbook of professional practice and
    management 5th edition, RIBA Publications Ltd, London
RIBA Journal (1991) Practice, RIBA Journal, June 1991, 25.
RICS (1991) Quantity Surveying 2000, RICS, London.
Rowdon I J and Mansfield N R (1988) What price
    professionalism? Proc. Instn. Civ. Engs, Part 1, 84,
    Feb., 85-93.
Rowdon I J and Mansfield N R (1989) Controlling design
    practice, Proc. Instn. Civ. Engs, Part 1, 86, Feb,
    189-205.
Rutter P A and Martin A S (1990) Management of design
    offices, Thomas Telford Ltd, London.

The management of building flexibility in the design process: a design decision support model for optimisation of building flexibility in relation to life-cycle costs

M. Prins
Eindhoven University of Technology, Eindhoven, The Netherlands

Abstract
Considering the long life span of buildings, it may be assumed that the usage will change as time progresses. Different usages require different spatial and material properties of a building. Therefore, buildings need a certain degree of flexibility. This paper describes a model of a building which makes it possible to specify the flexibility of buildings in relation to their life-cycle costs. The model can be used as a design decision support tool to assist in making decisions about flexibility and life-cycle costs in the different stages of design processes for new buildings and also in making decisions about the rehabilitation of buildings. The model supports decisions about the number and kinds of building components, their connections, and their life spans. A case-study is used to demonstrate the possibilities for practical implementation.
Keywords: Flexibility, Cost Control, Building Economics, Life-Cycle Costing, Financial Economical Optimisation, Life Span of Building Components, Design Decision Support Model, Design Methodology.

1 Introduction

1.1 Flexibility

In this context, flexibility is the capacity of a building object to respond to certain events by means of functional, spatial or material changes. These are events that one can expect to occur, but to what extent and when is not sure (Brinkman, 1989; Prins, 1989).

In order to specify the demand for building flexibility, a flexibility scenario is required. This flexibility scenario will be used to make prognoses about social, economical and cultural events that one expects will cause changes in the use of a building. In the case of a specific building, a flexibility scenario can specify a flexibility demand.

The flexibility demand contains a specification of the required functional, spatial and material changes of a building during its life span at certain moments, according to the prognoses in the flexibility scenario, and within the limits of a specified budget. The flexiblity demand is articulated as a set of physical design variants.

The flexibility supply of a building is determined by physical and financial aspects. Flexibility supply and flexibility demand have to be fitted together, within the context of the flexibility scenario.

1.2 Changes

According to systems theory, a building may be considered as a collection of interrelated elements. The subject of this study is the flexibility to be realised by changing the material elements of a building.

Thus, multifunctionality as a specific form of flexiblity is not discussed here. The diversity in the supply of building types with its capacity to respond to a changing demand on the building market is also omitted from this discussion (Tempelmans Plat 1991).

All types of flexibility can be expressed by combinations of six types of change of physical elements within a building:

- A building element, after its installation in the building, undergoes no further changes during the whole life span;
- A building element is due to one or more equivalent substitutions;
- A building element is due to one or more non-equivalent substitutions;
- A building element is replaced once or more often within the building;
- A new building element is added;
- A building element is removed without replacement.

It is assumed that the degree of flexibility of a building depends on the number of building elements to be distinguished. The more elements present, the higher the degree of flexibility.

Another important factor determining the degree of flexibility is how these elements are technically connected together. The more effort is required to disconnect elements from the building, the lower the degree of flexibility.

A third factor which influences building flexibility is the life span of the elements which compose the building. The longer the life span of the elements, the less moments there are to adapt the building to a changing context, without losing money by demolishing elements which are not yet written off.

1.3 Building economics
The flexibility demand of a building is formulated in such a way that every building element has to be specified by the given types of changes, occurring during the life span of the building.

As a building is composed of parts with different life spans, it is incorrect to depreciate the building as whole. Each element has its own depreciation period (Tempelmans Plat, 1982). All costs which have to be made for the investment in a building element, its maintenance, its assembly, for its removal and also all the costs for repairing the surrounding elements where relevant, have to be calculated as costs of the building element. It is important to distinguish maintenance costs from costs for replacement and other kind of changes (Bon, 1989). In an ideal situation, depreciation periods are divided by decision moments.

In order to calculate building costs over the life span of the building, all the costs have to be allocated to relevant elements and decision periods. An element has to be written off (depreciated) as soon as it no longer supplies the services demanded of it.

Since the appearance of the building will change, it is necessary to relate the costs calculated to the actual form. The building has to be used (rented) on a monthly or yearly basis, which means that the costs have to be known over the same period. Therefore, calculations have to be made on the basis of the annuity calculation. By discounting and accumulating all expenditures of all building elements during their life span, it is possible to acquire an insight into the real total period costs. This type of cost calculation is known as "costs in use analysis" or "life-cycle costing" (Flanagan, 1989; Stone, 1975).

1.4 Designing flexible buildings
A designer who wants to offer a building with sufficient flexibility supply, according to a specific flexibility demand, has to make decisions about the number, kind, life span and use of building elements and about the relationships between them. If the designer is also given the constraint that the building must have minimum life-cycle costs, the problem

becomes even more complicated. In this case, solutions have to be found about, for instance, the following types of questions:

- Will an investment in the life span quality of an element yield lower life-cycle costs?
- Will another composition of elements (for instance some large or several small elements) result in lower life-cycle costs?
- What extent of investments should be made in lowering assembling and demolishing costs of a building element, considering the expected frequency of change?
- What is the optimum choice between investment costs and maintenance costs for a certain building element?
- If the expected price increase in labour is greater than the price increase for material (or vice versa), which combination of technical quality and life span quality of an element will give the lowest life-cycle costs, considering the maintenance costs and the expected frequency of change?

The following paragraphs introduce a building model and a design model which make it possible to facilitate all these types of questions in the design process.

2. Complex Integral - Building - Object Model (CIOM)

2.1 Order systems
A building object is a system comprising several elements, interrelated in a specific way.

An object analysed with just one specific purpose in mind and described in elements and relations between them, according to Domain Theory (Trum, 1990; Bax, 1979) may be considered an order system. Orders are general categories of material and immaterial means for the achievement of goals and can be seen as a conceptual, purposeful ordering of reality, within which partial plans can be made. These plans are to be integrated in a total plan and are referred to as order systems.

Sub-systems are hierarchically ordered elements of an order system, distinguished when an object is analysed within a certain order. The ordering in sub-systems (e.g. the number of sub-systems) is specific for every order system.

For the purpose of studying flexibility, four orders are distinguished in the building sector: a social order, a time order, a use order and a technical order. As spatial material or physical elements are always concerned in a building object, it is adequate to introduce composed order systems: a physical-social order sytem, a physical-time order system, etc.

Each order system is set of elements whose simultaneous change can be initiated by a common cause; the nature of the cause, a decision or action, determines the name of the system. Hence, in a physical-social order system the cause of the change is of a social nature: e.g. a decision about the division of responsibilities over parts of the building. The four order systems are hierarchically ordered in aggregation levels: a lower level- (e.g. physical-technical) order system can be aggregated to a higher level (e.g. physical-use) order system, etc. This means that decisions made on the use order system are based on the technical order system, etc. Thus, this ordering in levels is relevant for the phases in a decision making or design process.

In the case of a dwelling the following order systems are described. (Prins, 1991):

- **Physical-social order system:** The division of a building into elements which are fully paid by the inhabitant and for which he is held responsible, and into elements about which the community (city or town council etc.) has responsibility (support and infill structure according to the original definitions by Habraken, 1985) are characteristic for this order system. Within this order system, categories of elements can be discerned according to the categories of responsibility. This distinction of elements is especially suited for dwellings. With, for instance, an office building a distinction of an unchangeable long-term structure and a changeable short-term structure is meaningful.

- **Physical-time order system:** elements of a building within this order are categorised according to the time they are expected to be of economic use.
- **Physical-use order system:** elements of a building within this order are categorised according to specific use.
- **Physical-technical order system:** elements of a building within this order are categorised according to how they are technically connected, and the technical life span.

2.2 Building object model

Thus, a building is considered to be a composition of order systems. (Because all these order systems are physical in nature, this adjective will no longer be used in the name of the systems). Order systems are complex within themselves. Figure 1 shows a graphical representation of a theoretical analysis of an object, described as a set of order systems; the highest level order system consists of five sub-systems.

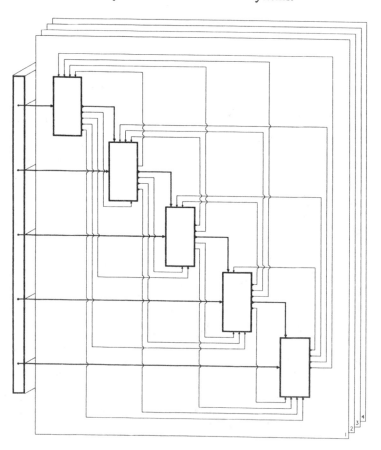

Figure 1: Scheme of an order system.

In this figure, the box-like base-line on the left represents the object as a whole in all its complexity. The rectangles represent the various sub-systems. The lines between the rectangles are all the theoretically possible relations between the sub-systems.

The short lines between the rectangles determine the hierarchy within the order system. These types of relations are of a conceptual nature. The other lines represent the operational relations. These types of relations can be divided into top-down and bottom-up relations. Operational relations are of a causal nature. Most of the top-down and bottom-up relations, as far as they have relevance, are tied to how the sub-systems are technically connected in lower level order systems. These relations are not discussed in this paper.

The four layers in the scheme represent the four order systems. Together, they compose the building object model in terms of flexibility. The scheme shows all the theoretically possible relations. Analysis of a practical situation always results in a selection according to the properties of the object. The scheme may also be used to describe a set of requirements as a starting-point in a design process (Prins, 1989).

2.3 A building as a composition of order systems

The composition of a building in terms of order systems is expressed according to the rules governing the aggregation process, a process restricted by the way the order-systems or levels are matched. There are three options for this matching: 'full-unity', 'unity' and 'woven'. Figure 2 shows an example of these three matching types for two order systems.

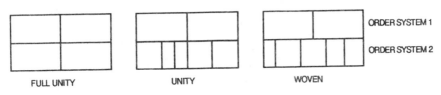

Figure 2: Matching between sub-systems for two order systems.

When this match is characterised by 'full unity', a set of physical elements (sub-systems) is defined which is relevant (is equivalent) to all the distinguished order systems.

When the match between order systems is characterised by 'unity', a sub-system defined in one order system corresponds with a number of sub-systems in the other order systems. In this situation the description of an object in order systems corresponds with descriptions of this object at several aggregation levels.

When the match between order systems is characterised by 'woven', sub-systems defined in one order system do not correspond with the sub-systems defined in the other order systems.

Analysing reality almost always yields situations of the woven type. With design processes however, the other matching types are more convenient. In order to structure design processes, order systems are made to correspond with aggregation levels. Aggregation levels in turn are made to correspond with phases in the design processes.

The model for an integral description of a building object as composed of elements (sub-systems) in all relevant orders is called a "Complex Integral (building) Object Model" (CIOM). According to this model, the integral description of the building itself is called a "Complex Integral (building) Object System" (CIOS).

In order to make the potentials of an object system operational a new notion is introduced: chains.

3 Chains

3.1 A building as a tree structure of chains

A chain is a set of physical elements of an object, changing at the same moment, according to a specific flexibility demand. A chain is also defined as a set of sub-systems within an order system (see fig. 1 and 2), because these changes can be initiated by the same cause (happening at the same moment).

Chains are discerned according to the order system to which they belong and receive the name of that system. The content of a chain on the adjacent lower level of a CIOS consists unequivocally of chains again, when the match between order systems is characterised by "unity" or "full unity". Thus, a chain in a social order system is an agglomeration of chains in the time order system, and so on. Parts of chains are sometimes referred as units; they are always defined on a level lower than that of the chain itself. The life span of a chain is determined by the shortest life span of its constituing units.

Figure 3 gives a scheme of a CIOS which corresponds to figure 2. In this scheme, the composition of an object is shown, represented in a tree structure, in which two order systems are discerned. The boxes in the scheme represent chains or subsystems.

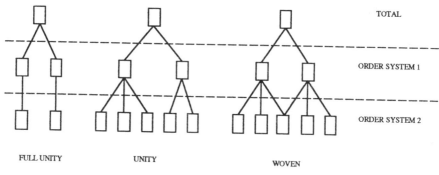

Figure 3: Scheme of a CIOS as a tree structure of chains.

3.2 Types of chains

According to the CIOM defined in paragraph 2, four types of chains can be defined: 'social chains', 'time chains', 'use chains' and 'technical chains'. Short descriptions of the four types of chains are given below:

- **Technical Chain:** The coherence of the chain is determined by the technically inseparable mutual connection of its elements. An inseparable technical connection means that, when one part is disconnected, the remaining parts are technically not repairable, or that the required financial investment to disconnect a part and repair the remaining parts, is higher than the economic value of the whole. The units of technical chains are components, which are technically inseparable elements that arrive on the building site as a whole; they are units of production.
  It can be concluded that the technical chain is the smallest chainging part in an object.
- **Use Chain:** The coherence of the elements is determined by its use and by the technical chains which are part of the use chain. As a technical chain is the smallest element of change, a use chain must be composed of at least one technical chain.
- **Time Chain:** The coherence of the chain is determined by its life span and by the use-chains and technical chains which are part of the time chain.

70

- **Social Chain:** The coherence of the chain is determined by categories of responsibility, its life span and by the time chains, use chains and technical chains which are part of the social chain. According to the pre-assumptions of this study, only two social chains can be distinguished, namely infill and support structure. For the same reason, the infill elements are the only elements which change within reasonable periods of time. Thus, the division into infill and support elements determines the border lines for this research.

4 Calculation Model for period costs (CMPC)

4.1 Calculating a CIOS
Given a required flexibility demand (derived from a flexibility scenario), in the building model (CIOM) presented, the main entrances for optimising the life-cycle costs are formed by the number, life span and kind of elements of which a building is composed, and the technical connections between them. In order to calculate the life-cycle costs of a building in a scenario, all cost data of a building has to be allocated to sub-systems of the CIOS and to the relevant decision periods. This means that the input for life-cycle cost calculations is structured according to the CIOM. As a consequence, the calculation model has the same structure as the CIOM

4.2 Levels in the calculation model
The smallest element of change in a CIOS is defined as a technical chain. Thus, in the calculation model this technical chain is the lowest input level of cost data.

In the calculation model, four levels of aggregation of input and output are possible, according to the four types of chains defined in paragraph 3.2. However, in a design process, only real cost data on the technical level is available at this moment.

In the calculation model, it is assumed that all levels can be expressed in terms of mutual aggregation. Thus there must be at least 'unity' for the match between the order systems. In the case of 'woven' matches, problems would show up with the division of costs. This problem often occurs when modelling existing buildings according to the calculation model. In practice, this situation always means that, with a change of a specific chain, parts of other chains which are not yet at the end of their life span and are probably also not written off, have to be demolished. This always causes loss of capital.

4.3 Input and output data in the calculation model
Although energy and other types of running costs can initiate a change process, they do not influence the flexibility, and are therefore not implemented in the model. For the same reason, all types of government taxes, insurances etc. are not implemented. Also, price developments are not taken into account; they do not influence decisions because the cost-benefit relation is assumed to remain constant and, in most cases, no valid decision calculations for total average period costs can be made with this parameter.

If the cost data of technical chains is specified, the costs for all the other chains and for the building as a whole can simply be calculated by accumulation. Higher level input is possible when cost data on these levels is generated by previous calculations, using the model. The input of the model on the technical chain level consists of (Prins, 1990):

- Life span of the building as a whole and of its various elements, the chains according to CIOM;
- Investment in the chains, composed of the costs of materials, equipment and of labour at the times of investment;
- Maintenance expenditures of the chains;
- Demolishing expenditures and residual value of the chains.

The output of the calculation model gives the total average period costs for the building. Design variants, modelled as a CIOS, meeting the same flexiblity demand and the same quality criteria can be compared. The variant with the lowest total average period costs is the optimum one. The output of the model is always generated on the highest (social chain) level. Additional output can be generated on all other CIOM levels. Also, real period costs can be generated on all levels.

5 Flexibility and costs in the design process

5.1 General remarks
The main aim of the presented theory is to enable the design of an instrumental model which can support decisions at different stages in a design process, concerning life-cycle costs in relation to flexibility demand. In design processes, the flexibility demand has to be derived from a flexibility scenario. Each specific flexibility demand can be worked out in design variants for the various moments during the life span of a building, which express the change of its physical elements. For a building modelled as a CIOS, these elements can be defined as chains. The flexibility supply is determined by the properties of the building and can also be expressed in chains.

Decisions on design variants can be taken on all aggregation levels of the CIOS. In each case, one simply has to calculate the average total periodical costs of a variant and compare these to another variant. The cheapest variant is the best in terms of costs and flexibility. By analysing how the costs accumulate on the lower CIOS levels, the designer can try to find inducements for lowering the costs in a new design variant.

In the research project, the calculation model described in paragraph 4 is developed as a user-friendly, fully interactive and menu-guided computer program called 'Calculation Model Period Costs' (CMPC).

5.2 Common design strategy
The first thing that has to be done before one can starts designing a flexible building is to formulate a relevant flexibility scenario.

After the flexibility scenario is written, one can choose for a bottom-up or a top-down strategy (Tempelmans Plat & Prins, 1990). A mix of these two strategies is also possible.

In the case of a bottom-up process, the financial input of the CMPC exists of real estimated expenditures of the technical chains.

In the case of a top-down process, the financial input of the CMPC exists of experienced rated input for a higher level chain, as generated by the CMPC in previous design processes. The more the CMPC is used in the design process, the more data is generated and the more data is available for the other CIOM levels.

We now have a common strategy for a design process of a CIOS in which an attempt is made to optimise building flexibility, and to minimise life-cycle costs, with the aid of the CMPC. The ten steps of this common strategy are:

1 Write a flexibility scenario in which assumptions are made about all relevant social, political and cultural events which may influence the use of the building. Write also a financial-economical scenario in which the expected developments of the relevant parameters are specified.
2 Design a spatial variant which is the basis for the further design of the building.
3 Choose a CIOM level for further design.
4 Write the flexibility demand for the chosen level and specify the chains, their measure, place, quality and connections.
5 Estimate the expenditures.
6 Calculate the costs with the aid of the CMPC.

7 Generate CMPC output on all relevant CIOM levels and decide whether the variant is acceptable or not, depending on the value of the total average period costs.
8 If the variant fits the norm, then decide whether how to continue the design process or stop. If the variant does not fit the norm, then analyse how the costs accumulate and try to find clues for lowering the costs in a new variant.
9 Proceed to the next level, generate a new variant and repeat steps 1 to 9.
10 Select the collection of design variants of chains, which together have the lowest total average period costs.

Figure 4 depicts this common design strategy in flow chart form.

This procedure can be carried out both in the design process for a new building and for existing buildings, and is valid for the building as a whole as well as for its composing elements. The repeated use of this procedure, in combination with the aggregation of cost data to the higher levels in the CIOM, delivers general cost data on these levels. This data can be applied in procedures which are restricted to the higher levels giving a quick insight into the costs related to flexibility in the early stages of the design process.

6 Case-study

6.1 The object of study and the methodology
The CIOM and the CMPC have been successfully implemented in two case-studies. The subject of the first case-study was a dwelling project in the Netherlands, in which the complete infill structure was replaced by a new flexible one in 1991.

Both infill structures, the original and the new one, are seen as variants in a design process. Total exploitation period is assumed to be 45 years, with a discount rate of 5%. Both infill structures were modelled as a CIOS and the expenditure data was estimated on the level of the technical chain, using the commercial Dutch cost data sheets. It was assumed was that only equivalent replacement would take place, initiated by technical obsolescence.

The subject of the second case-study was a new dwelling situation, for which three variants were worked out for the realisation of an inside wall in terms of its material and connections. These three situations were: a wall made of brickwork, a flexible system wall ("Metalstud"), and a wall made of gasconcrete. The flexibility demand was specified as: a wall in year 0, a removal without replacement in year 15 and reconstruction of this wall again in year 30. Total exploitation period is assumed to be 45 years, with a discount rate of 5%.

6.2 Results
Case 1.
The initial investment for both infill packages was estimated to be approximately 40,500 Dutch guilders (approx. US $ 20,250 dollar).

The total average yearly period costs for the old infill were calculated at 2,647 guilders. The total average yearly period costs for the new infill were calculated at 2,423 guilders.

An analysis on the level of the life span chains makes clear that this difference can partly be explained by the fact that the investment in the short-term structure (life span less than 20 years) is lower in the case of the new infill structure. Analysis on the level of the technical chain shows that labour costs for replacements are also lower in the case of the new infill structure.
Case 2.
By analysing the cost data of the three inside walls, there appaered to be surprisingly only very small differences in the total average period costs. Due to the relative high initial

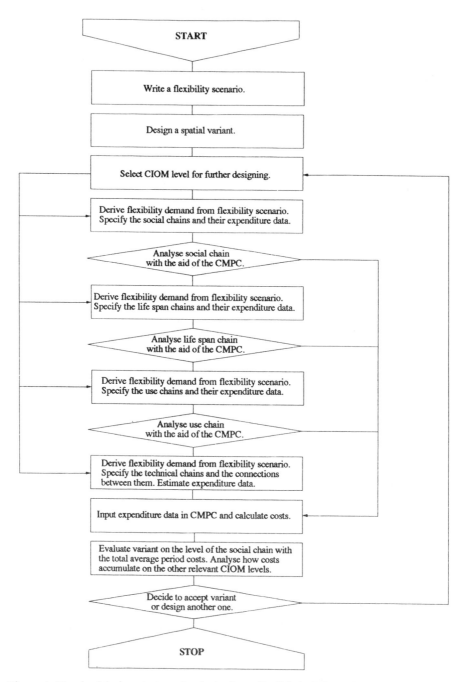

Figure 4: Standard design strategy for designing a flexible building with minimum life-cycle costs with the aid of the CMPC

investment, the system wall appeared to be the most expensive at 119.02 guilders yearly. The brick wall had total yearly average period costs of 109.35 guilders, and for the wall of gasconcrete this was 108.73 guilders. The initial investment for both of these walls was almost the same. The very small differences can be explained by the low frequency of change. As only two change moments were modelled, and because these moments were both in the far future (15 and 30 years), the differences in demolishing costs and labour costs for the two other flexible solutions, compared to the brick wall, do not result in really lower period costs.

6.3 Conclusions
The theory of the CIOM and CMPC appeared to be practically applicable for both a full infill structure and for isolated building elements, and could be used as design decision support tool in the design process.

Modelling a building dynamically with only replacements according to technical obsolescence, without using a flexibility scenario gives in itself a good insight in the life-cycle costs of building variants and their flexibility.

The level concept of the CIOM gives a sufficient insight into the breakdown of the life-cycle costs, and can be seen as a good tool for generating ideas for new, cheaper design variants. Due to the level concept of the CIOM in all phases of the design process, decisions can be made, based on real estimated cost data, calculated to according life-cycle costs, with relatively little effort from the designer or cost expert for analysing, compared to the existing models.

Acknowledgements

This research is supported by the Netherlands Technology Foundation (STW).

References

Bax, M.F.Th. (1979) Domain Theory, **Open House International**, vol.4 no. 2.
Bon, R. (1989) **Building as an Economic Process**. Prentice Hall, Englewood Cliffs, New Jersey.
Brinkman, S. (1989) Flexibiliteit; beheersprocessen en proces beheersing, (**Flexibility; Controlprocesses and Process Control**), dissertation Eindhoven University of Technology, Eindhoven.
Flanagan, R., Norman, G., Meadows, J., Robinson, G. (1989) **Life-Cycle Costing, Theory and Practice**. Blackwell Scientific Publications Ltd, Oxford.
Habraken, N.J. (1985) **Supports - an alternative to mass housing**. Architectural Press, London.
Prins, M., Bax, M.F.Th. (1991) An Integral Relational Design Decision Support Model to Optimize the Flexibility of Buildings in Relation to Life- Cycle Costs, in **Organization and Management in Construction** (eds. Zaja, M.), Gradevinski Institute, Zagreb.
Prins, M., Tempelmans Plat. H. (1990) A Design Decision Support System Based on Different Lives of Components, in **Proceedings CIB Conference on Building Economics and Construction Management** (eds. Ireland, V.), Sydney University of Technology, Sydney .
Prins, M. (1989) Decision making and Flexibility; an Integral Design Decision Support System, **Proceedings CARDO Symposium Quality in the Built Environment** (eds. Wilkinson, N.) Open house International, New Castle Upon Tyne.

Stone, P.A. (1975) **Building Design Evaluation, Costs-in-Use.** E. & F.N. Spon Ltd., London.

Tempelmans Plat, H., Prins, M.(1991) Reverse Planning of the Built Environment, **Open House International**, vol. 16 no. 1.

Tempelmans Plat, H. (1991) Cost-optimal flexibility of housing supply, in **Management, Quality and Economics in Building** (eds. Belzega, A., Brandon, P.) E. & F.N. Spon Ltd., London.

Tempelmans Plat, H. (1982) Micro Economic Analysis of the Process of Design, Construction and Operation of Houses, **IABSE Journal** J-14/82, Zurich.

Trum, H.M.G.J., Bax, M.F.Th. (1990) The applicability of domain theory in technological design, in **Design in Engineering Educating** (eds McCabe, V.J.), Dublin.

Planning building design work

E.J. Coles
Department of Architectural Services, West Lothian District Council, Scotland, UK

Abstract
This paper discusses an approach to planning and monitoring the work of building design consultants.

Various factors may increase or decrease the need for the close planning and control of work. Design team leaders must be involved in planning, but the majority of design tasks need not be planned formally.

Measures of progress and efficiency are discussed, since these can help managers to decide how to use the time and man-hours which remain to be spent on a project. Progress cannot easily be assessed by drawn output. Information inputs, key design decisions and the coordination of design information should also be taken into account.

Where planning and control systems are introduced or modified, a planner and data analyst might be needed, together with a "champion" who ensures that everyone contributes effectively to setting up and using the system.
Keywords: Building, Control, Design, Monitoring, Planning.

1   Introduction

Clients, design practices and construction companies are presently seeking closer control over design work, to ensure that information produced is adapted to the needs of construction and is timely, coordinated and provided as cheaply as possible. However, the planning and control techniques which are applied to construction may be too rigid for design work, where the definition of tasks, their sequence and the time required to do them, can all be very fluid.

This paper describes how the traditional approach taken by design professionals to planning and expediting their work, can be reconciled with the techniques of work-breakdown, network analysis and work-measurement. It condenses material prepared by the author for the Chartered Institute of Building and the Universities of Reading and Bath.

2   Control of Progress

2.1 Self Regulation

The greatest value of planning is probably not in the
close control it offers to practice and project managers,
but in the way it enables teams to get on with their work
in a coordinated way, with a minimum of outside
intervention. By asking team leaders to consider what has
to be done, by whom and in what sequence:
a) agreement can be reached which commits everyone to a
   timetable,
b) designers understand when and how others are dependent
   on their work,
c) problems which threaten the programme are more likely
   to be recognised and dealt with "on the shop floor".

2.2 Management Information

However competent the design team may be, clients,
practice managers and project managers have legitimate
reasons to seek information about progress. If work is
not proceeding productively and efficiently, they must
take action.

The degree of detail needed to plan a design project
and report progress can vary according to several factors,
as below.

2.3 Complexity and unfamiliarity

It is more difficult to plan complex and unfamiliar work
and devise accurate measures of progress. Work can also
be harder to control where the client or project
organisations are large or complicated. In general, the
more difficult work is to plan, the more important that
the work content, sequence, roles and responsibilities
should be discussed in detail and close control of work
exercised subsequently.

2.4 Haste

If design time is compressed, especially if fee bidding is
low or there is an overlap with construction operations,
then it is important to be sure that work is done in the
right sequence (without rework) and at the right time (so
that no-one waits for information).

2.5 Risk

Competition and fee bids increase the risks of (a)
financial loss for design practices and (b) shortfalls in
the quality of the buildings produced. The propensity to
ignore or control risk may be influenced by the
organisation culture: whether it is accustomed to running
as a well-oiled machine, or happier as "organised chaos".

3   Mechanisms of Planning and Control

3.1   The Work Planning Process
While simple design jobs can literally be planned on the back of an envelope, sophisticated computing is commonly used on large and complex projects, with a team of people to gather and analyse data. At either extreme, there is an underlying process of (a) work breakdown, (b) formulating the duration and sequence of activities and (c) defining how to measure and report progress.

3.2   Work Breakdown
The complexity of buildings requires that design work is divided "horizontally" between specialists, "temporally" between design stages and "vertically" into the detailed tasks of design development. The vertical division of work depends on the actual design which emerges, how it is documented and the need for specialised advice. This dimension of the breakdown therefore has to be reconsidered at each stage of the project.

3.3   Sequence of Activities
During design work, information is exchanged between the designers, the client and others, in a complex pattern of formal and informal communication. The detail of task definitions and sequences tends to follow rather than dictate this pattern. Clearly, work can proceed faster if design options are developed and evaluated simultaneously, rather than sequentially, but this necessitates strict control over the "status" of designs, i.e. it should be clear whether they are merely ideas or to be the basis of work by others.

3.4   Duration of Activities
Schedules of drawings have been used for a long time to estimate the man-hours needed for the detail design and production drawing stages. However, production drawings and specifications represent only the output of design work; more than half of a design process is spent gathering information, developing preliminary designs and verifying the consistency of work (at all stages). In scheduling the entire process, this "silent majority" of the workload must be taken into account.

3.5   Progress Monitoring Points
By adding up the amount of work done on each defined task (research, sketching, calculating, drawing, specifying, checking etc.), an overview of progress can be obtained. To avoid false claims, careful attention must be given to the quality of coordination between drawings, specifications and the cost plan, and the tasks that are not mentioned on the work schedule.

Before there is significant output, other features of the design process can be used to measure progress. At the beginning of each stage, when the team discuss their programme, each discipline should describe the information they require from others and a schedule of dates should be agreed. In some cases, it may be relevant to include tasks in the planning such as agreeing: the format of drawings, computing protocols, quality management procedures and so forth.

3.6 Base Plans
Because the detailed analysis of tasks can only be done stage by stage, initial project programmes appears only in outline. This "master plan" may need to be updated as work progresses, but the original version, or "base plan" is retained for comparison.

3.7 Network Analysis
Attention should focus on chains of activity that threaten to exceed the time allowed for any one stage. Either the duration or the dependency of tasks on this "critical path" can be adjusted to reduce its length. Planning software offers the advantages of quick calculation and clear graphical presentation. This assists discussions about the need for resources and simultaneous working. Sometimes, amendments to the actual design are appropriate, for example, adjustable fixing systems enable structural design work to proceed independently from the design of services and finishes.

3.8 Presentation of Work Planning
Staff will only work to a plan which is easy to understand and bears a clear relationship with what is happening. Excessive detail is confusing and rapidly gets out of date. It is therefore important to pin up clear, simple plans where people can scribble amendments on them.

4 Progress

4.1 Key Information
Managers need to ensure that enough time, resources and enthusiasm remain to complete a job. Timesheet systems have long been used by practice managers to calculate how much of their fee has been consumed and how much remains. While these systems could often benefit from being speeded up, the difficult part of monitoring is to produce clear and succinct measurements of progress and productivity.

4.2 Productivity
This can be expressed as:

$$\frac{\text{Actual value of work done to date}}{\text{Planned value of work to be done by this date}} \quad (1)$$

Where the "value" is a percentage of the work in a project or stage of the project. Separate figures can be produced for each discipline in the design team (as described in 3.5, above).

4.3 Efficiency
This can be expressed as:

$$\frac{\text{Actual cost of work}}{\text{Planned cost of work done}} \quad (2)$$

Again, clear definitions of tasks are the basis of measurement, with due allowance for unplanned work.

4.4 The Need for Corrective Action
This can be highlighted by comparing:
a) productivity so far, against the productivity required to complete outstanding work within the time remaining;
b) the efficiency of a team so far, against the efficiency required to complete the job within the planned man-hours.

These calculations are similar. Taking (b), the efficiency needed to complete within budget is:

$$\frac{\text{Money remaining to complete}}{\text{Planned cost of outstanding work}} \quad (3)$$

If the prevailing efficiency is poor, e.g. 1.1, the efficiency needed to complete the design work within budget will be less than unity, say 0.9. In this case, the required change in efficiency is 1.1 / 0.9 = 1.22, i.e. a 22% higher output. Practical responses to this might include closer supervision, unpaid overtime or putting more productive individuals into the team.

5 Setting up a Planning and Monitoring System

5.1 Impediments
Obstacles to setting up a planning and monitoring system include:
a) the common belief that design work cannot be planned;
b) the belief that designers are impeded by factors beyond their control;

c) resistance by designers (especially architects) to having their working methods forced into a mould which inhibits creativity;
d) the "mystique" of network analysis;
e) the fear that data collection and analysis will consume more time and energy than it is worth.

5.2 Counter Arguments

Answers such as the following can be advanced:
a) Insist that each design stage is signed off, and staff will find that they have no alternative but to plan ahead.
b) Progress monitoring shows clients and managers where designers are in fact delayed by others, and they can do something about it.
c) If designers are helped to plan work for themselves, they are free to maximise the time available for creativity.
d) Network analysis only tests logic by calculation, the theory is simple to pick up. While software gets more sophisticated, it is also becoming more user-friendly.
e) Planning helps to avoid time-consuming problems and monitoring brings timely help from managers when it is needed.

5.3 Time for Change

Project managers are skilled at imposing planning and monitoring systems very quickly. Where planning systems are introduced "internally" by a practice, many months may be needed to define roles and set up a trial system, before applying it generally.

5.4 New Roles

The introduction of a work planning and monitoring system, or amendments to an existing system may requires:

a) A champion:
   The staff all the design disciplines, who are often in different companies, may need to be encouraged and cajoled into spending time on analysing and agreeing what they need to do, at every stage of the job.
b) Planner and report formatter:
   It is better if there is someone who understands the logic of network analysis and can stimulate designers (and constructors) to analyse their work, define tasks, recognise dependencies between these and guage (staff) resource requirements.
c) Data collector and analyst:
   Team leaders may need prompting to produce figures for the (percentage) completeness of defined activities under their control. Knowledge of design work and the individuals is essential if these figures are to be

interpreted intelligently. There may be a need to relate the timesheet accounting system more closely with the work breakdown used for progress monitoring.

6   Conclusions

Factors such as the project type, scale, complexity, and level of risk should be considered when deciding how closely to plan and monitor design work. In setting up a planning and monitoring system, roles, responsibilities, systems and procedures have to be agreed. Software selection may be influenced by the quality of graphics and ease of use in an interactive way, e.g. to assist discussion.

To monitor progress, a base-plan must be defined. This requires a breakdown of work into principal stages and design disciplines. More detailed tasks should be identified at each stage of work, together with critical sequences, which might overrun the time allowed.

It is vital that team leaders participate in detailed planning and agree to "deliver" output according to the resulting timetable. Adjustments to the design itself can disassociate tasks so that more work can proceed simultaneously and with less need for coordination.

In the early stages of design work, there may be little output to measure objectively. The establishment of quality systems, information inputs, key design decisions and so forth, can then be used to assess progress.

It is unlikely that a high proportion of work will appear on design work schedules. Undefined tasks must always be taken into account when assessing progress.

Key ratios can sharpen the reporting of progress. These focus on the comparison of previous productivity and efficiency with the productivity and efficiency necessary to complete a design project on time and within budgeted man-hours.

The management of the design process

B. Sawczuk
DGI Group plc, Kenilworth, Warwickshire, UK

Abstract
This paper describes how the approach to managing design develops with the age
and growth of an architectural practice. It explains how layers of design
management are introduced within an organisation and how two styles of approach
may develop; that of 'conveyor belt' design or 'project designer' with back up skills.
The paper goes on to discuss the fundamental ingredients of managing the design
process and the importance of managing the client and contractor as part of a larger
team.
Key words: Company Management, Design Management, Client Management,
Integrating Skills.

1 Introduction

The approach to Managing Design within an architectural private practice, be it a
Partnership or Company, develops with the age and growth of the organisation. In
the early years, the Founder has a 'hands on' approach and lives with the project on
a day-to-day basis: often he will maintain direct contact with the client and carry out
the drawings and contract administration (Fig. 1A). As the organisation grows and
matures, the Founder or his Partners/Directors will not be able to handle each
project personally throughout. There becomes a split in workload, with the Partner
taking the initial brief and communicating internally to the Project Architect or
Technician to put in hand drawings and contract documentation (Fig. 1B).
Depending on the workload of the Partner and his own personal skills, he may have
a key role within the concept drawing stage but will break away once the project
concept design has been established.

With further growth and maturity, the design organisation will be handling more
and more work and therefore the Partner may take on a marketing and sales role,
with less and less input into the design process and its management. It is at this
stage that a new role develops - that of Design Manager - which becomes the link
between the Partners and the drawing office. This role may carry the title of
Associate or may not even have a specific title but the role is developed by those
within the organisation who show managerial skills and can handle organisational
problems (Fig. 1C).

Within some organisations, the Partners have mixed skills: some are primarily in
Marketing/Sales whilst others are in design management or even remain on the

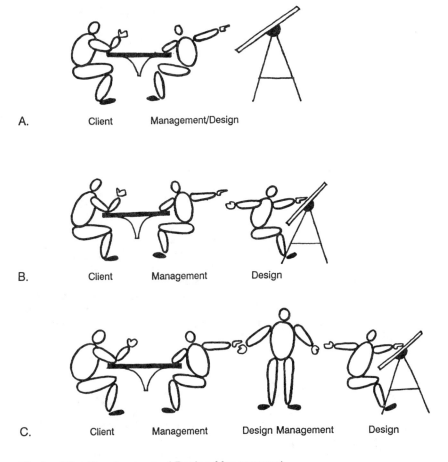

A.   Client   Management/Design

B.   Client   Management   Design

C.   Client   Management   Design Management   Design

Fig.1.   The Development of Design Management

drawing board as concept designers. Therefore, within some organisations, titles
may mislead function and may be more a sign of status than functional role.

It is evident, therefore, that three distinct layers of management are created:
within some organisations they will be distinct roles, whilst within others the roles will
possibly change with workload, individual preferences or company policy. These
layers of management are:

Company Management   Addresses corporate matters, resources, finance,
                         policy, design strategy and external influences.
Design Management   Tends to supervise the services in an organisation and
                         will co-ordinate and control design briefings and design
                         reviews.

Design Projects   Responsibility for individual projects and services.

To make these layers of management work, there needs to be a degree of overlap; therefore company management contains some design management which, in turn, contains some project design skills.

2 The integration of skills

A totally balanced Designer, with equal strengths in management and design, is rare and, it could be argued, not ideal because there may be a requirement for star performers in both camps working alongside each other for mutual benefit. This view can be taken to its extreme and 'conveyor belt' design can develop within organisations where individuals are pigeonholed into key stages of the design process (Fig. 2).

Alternatively, the organisation may develop key members with specific skills that can serve a number of projects on an 'as and when' basis and may include contractual advice, graphics for presentations or programming skills (Fig. 3). For the smaller organisation, which could not accommodate a back up service of 'experts', team work is important, with cross-fertilization of ideas and expertise from one project team to another and feedback from one project relayed to all members of the various teams. Another way to achieve this is to mix or change the team members from time to time, so that knowledge is shared: this would also prevent 'islands' of knowledge building up within the organisation.

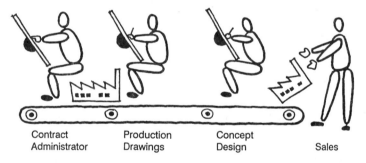

| Contract | Production | Concept | |
| Administrator | Drawings | Design | Sales |

Fig.2.   Conveyor belt design

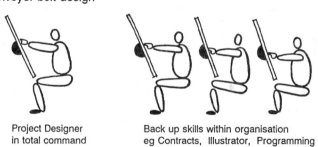

Project Designer   Back up skills within organisation
in total command   eg Contracts, Illustrator, Programming

Fig.3.   Project Design with back up facilities

Some organisations will import a manager who is not a trained designer but is a trained manager; this may have some distinct advantages but the disadvantages may be greater. For success, there needs to be commitment from the top down, with clear thinking and clear policy and company approach. Therefore, how can the non-designer manager be committed to something he does not understand or, indeed, value?

3 Fundamental ingredients to managing the design process

No matter how complex the project or how big the project team or, indeed, how fast the project will develop, there are four basic ingredients to the management of the design process, these being:

Plan	There must be a plan of action. It might follow the RIBA work stages or another in-house approach. Each work stage will also have its own plan of action.
Action	The plan must be actioned in accordance with the plan.
Review	At regular intervals during the action process, the action must be reviewed and compared to the original plan.
Feedback	If the action is not going according to plan, there must be feedback to modify the plan to take into account deviations in the action. Also, the action must be put back on course.

This Plan, Action, Review and Feedback process is a continuous process and vital for a successful project (Fig. 4).

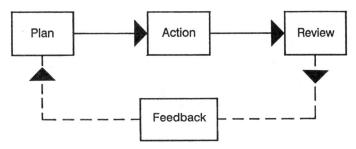

Fig.4.   Fundamental ingredients to managing the design process

4 Objectives

The objectives of a designer are different to those of a manager and it is the harmonious existence within one team of these diverse objectives that make a successful design organisation. If one were to pick three key objectives for designer and manager, they may well be:

Designer   Ideas/innovation
                    Recognition by peer group
                    Achievement

Managers   Business Plans/strategy
                       Profits/growth
                       Stability

5 Managing the client

The design process revolves around the client's needs and therefore the client should be part of the team and obviously requires managing. Up to now, we have considered the internal management process. This needs to be widened to bring in the client's contribution, which must be controlled and timed to suit the design process, so that the correct information is received on time and variations (which are quite often due to the lack of proper consideration at the appropriate time) are reduced to a minimum.

At the outset of the project, the interface within the client organisation must be identified, whose main task is to pass on the brief and sufficient information at the right time to the design organisation, to enable the design process to proceed. The interface must have a degree of authority within the client organisation, to enable him to obtain information from other parts of the organisation and to overcome any obstacles or resistance to the release of such information. Although not a requirement, it would be beneficial if the interface had previous exposure to the construction industry and is aware of the need for information at the correct time. If the client nominee has not previously been involved with the design process or construction, it would be well worth the investment for the design organisation to spend some time with the client interface to explain the process and the input required of the client body within that process. The client interface must feel part of the team, should be involved in regular design review meetings and have an input and, indeed, agree to the programme and all proposed client actions.

The design process will go through various stages, whether it be the RIBA work stages or a variant. To give confidence to the designers and the client, it is important to seek acceptance of the proposals, at each major stage, from the client body. Probably the most important stage in the design process for all those within the client body to give their acceptance is at the conclusion of scheme design (RIBA work stage D) and prior to the commencement of detail design and production information (RIBA work stages E, F, G). At this stage, the design is frozen and the drawings and specifications produced provide the springboard for the remaining workload.

In an ideal world, all design information is complete prior to construction but when time is of the essence, design and construction overlap, with design ideally sufficiently ahead of construction so as not to cause delay. It is very rare that modifications are not required during the construction period, be it to improve 'buildability', to overcome a design oversight or to react and overcome on site difficulties. It is therefore important during the construction stage to have good communication not only with the contractor but also with the client, so that the need for modifications can be identified early, redesigned and endorsed by the client without disrupting on site operations. Furthermore, the client and contractor should be considered as potential members of the design team during the construction stage.

In conclusion, it is important to emphasise that the success of a project is greatly influenced by its management and the maximisation of the team members' talents, together with the managed and co-ordinated input from the client and building contractor.

6 References

Royal Institute of British Architects, (1990) **Architects Appointment**. RIBA Publications Ltd., London.

Sharp, D. (1986) **The Business of Architectural Practice**. Williams Collins Sons & Co. Ltd., London.

Walker, D. Oakley, M. and Roy, R. (1988) **Managing Design**. The Open University Press, Milton Keynes.

Managing the construction process through a framework of decisions

M. Loosemore

Department of Civil Engineering and Building, The Polytechnic of Wales, Pontypridd, Mid Glamorgan, UK

The purpose of this paper is to propose a Universal framework of decisions that is common to all construction projects. An awareness of a universal framework simplifies the task of management by focussing upon the most important activities within the construction project organisation.

The following conclusions are drawn:

1) To aid the management of the construction process there is a need to identify common elements that characterise all construction project organisations.

2) Although construction projects are unique there is an identifiable pattern of decision processes that is common to them all.

3) There is one type of decision but different types of decision process.

4) There are Technical and Organisational decisions processes and Organisational decision processes can be classified hierarchically into four levels by the nature of their output.

Key words: Decision, Typology, Systems, Hierarchy.

Managing the construction process:

Managers of construction project organisations are faced with unique problems. The variability of the Client's requirements and of the final product means that each project poses wholey different challenges. In addition to this, Bennett (1985) maintains that the need for a wide range of knowledge and skills within the construction process creates a complex organisation. Since it is the manager's task to create and control this organisational structure, his task becomes arduous. In addition to the variation of skills, Walker (1989) recognised that project participants can also be highly differentiated in terms of location, timing, employer and profession. Walker (1989) maintained that the level of differentiation is directly related to problems of information flow within the project organisation. The environment of the construction project organisation also creates special problems because as Hughes (1989) showed, every construction project is faced with a uniquely diverse complex and uncertain environment. Since Lawrence and Lorsch (1967) concluded that "organisation is a function of the nature of the task to be performed and its environment" it follows that each project should have a different organisational structure. Finally, the temporary and dynamic nature of the construction process creates problems of motivation and control and as Lansley (1984) states "the throwing together of consultants who are not all familiar with each others work methods and weaknesses, has rarely been challenged".

The need for a universal framework of decisions:

Hughes' (1989) work illustrated that effective management is partially achieved through the creation of appropriate organisation structures. Faced with an increasingly complex environment brought about by economic and technological changes, the traditional methods of organisation have proved ineffective and in recent years this has led to a frantic search for new methods of organising and administering construction projects. Bennett (1991) provides a reason for this recent activity maintaining that the construction industry has been much slower than other industries in adapting to the changing world. This proliferation of standard organisational approaches has been accompanied by general confusion and this has been highlighted by NEDO (1988) which states "the proliferation of new organisations has aggravated the existing problems of coordination, communication and motivation both within the industry itself and in its relations with its customer". To counter the adverse effects of this increasing complexity there is a need to simplify the manager's task by creating a simple conceptual picture of the project organisation. This can be achieved by identifying and highlighting common elements that run through all construction project organisations and which are an important influence upon it.

It is proposed that there is a universal pattern of decisions that is common to all construction project organisations and that the identification of such a pattern is the key to simplifying the Construction Manager's arduous task.

The importance of decisions to organisations:

Philosophy, Economics, Mathematics and the Social Sciences have all contributed to the better understanding of how decisions are made and this reflects its importance as an issue. Walker (1984) highlights its importance to the construction process when he makes the statement that "the decision making system is the mechanism through which the whole construction process moves forward".

Considering its importance it attracts relatively little attention as an area of interest within Construction industry research activity. Even in the Social Sciences where most effort has been devoted to the study of decisions, it is still a relatively young and emerging area. Decision making is commonly tackled very superficially as an integral part of studies that concern other issues. Where it is tackled as a subject in its own right the approach is either highly scientific or very general. There is no doubt that its importance to the effectiveness of organisations merits some rigorous attention in an industry which is attempting to improve its performance.

What is a decision?

Emory and Niland (1968) see a decision as " a point of selection and commitment". In contrast to this, Simon (1960) considers decision making as something wider than just a point of commitment maintaining that it is a process consisting of three principal phases: finding occasions for making a decision; finding possible courses of action; and choosing among courses of action.

The essential difference between these definitions is that one regards decision making as a process which occurs over a period of time and the other sees it as a single point in time. This distinction between the decision itself and the process that surrounds it, is a very important one which is seldom made.

Types of decisions:

Thompson and Tuden (1963) saw the value of a typology of decisions. They maintained that "the identification of a typology enables the sorting out of:

1) Aspects of decisions situations that confront decision makers.

2) Actions that decision makers may take in those situations."

Furthermore, Cooke and Slack (1991) state that "to understand decision making and so to hopefully make better decisions one must be able to recognise different types of decisions".

There have been many attempts to classify decisions. The most notable of these was that of Simon (1960) who classified decisions by the extent to which the stages involved in solving the problem could be structured. The resulting typology referred to Programmable and Non programmable decisions. Gore (1962) arrived at a three point classification of decisions referred to as Routine, Adaptive and Innovative decisions. The classification was different to Simon's (1960) being based upon the nature of the problem faced. Drucker (1967) made the same distinction as Simon (1960) classifying them as Generic and Unique decisions respectively. Like Gore (1962), Delbecq (1967) developed a three point classification comprising Routine, Creative and Negotiated decisions. This typology was based on the degree of congruence between the values of the contributors to the decision process. Thompson (1967) suggested four decision strategies each determined by the uncertainty of information which the decision maker is faced with. The typology was composed of Computational, Judgemental, Compromise and Inspirational decisions. In recent years Mintzberg has arguably contributed most to this area. Mintzberg (1973) produced a typology which comprised of Entrepreneurial, Adaptive and Planning decisions differentiated by the level of uncertainty in the decision making environment. More recently Mintzberg et al (1976) changed the basis of classification by concentrating upon the difference in time between the appearance of the problem and the point at which the decision was made. The resulting typology consisted on Opportunity, Problem and Crisis decisions. Walker (1980) developed a typology of decisions for the construction process and this has subsequently been taken further by Hughes (1989). Hughes (1989) developed a four point classification of Policy, Strategic, Tactical and Operational decisions being differentiated by environment, sub system and organisational position. The most recent and novel approach to the study of decision making within construction project organisations has been developed by Bennett (1991). In a natural extension of Systems Theory Bennett (1991) used the analogy of the human nervous system as a basis for developing a model. The model developed resulted in a three point classification of decisions based upon hierarchical positioning within the organisational structure.

Every one of the above typologies fails to make the critical distinction between the decision itself and the process which surrounds it. Each typology classifies decisions by referring to the nature of the process which surrounds it and all fail to consider what a decision actually is. In making the distinction between decisions and the activity that surrounds them both Hughes (1989) and Emory and Niland (1968) reinforce the opinion that decisions represent points which occupy no time, resources or space and thus effectively do not materially exist.

Thus decisions are essentially the same in what ever context they are taken, it is the surrounding decision process that differs, not in its structure but rather in the nature of the information which flows through it. The conclusion must therefore be that there is only one type of decision but different types of decision process. The different types of decision process can be classified by the nature of information that flows around and through them.

Classification of decision processes:

Decision output can be used as a basis of classification and this view is supported by Mintzberg (1973) who holds that there is essentially no difference between the jobs of top and bottom managers, "the only difference is orientation and in the ends to which the managerial activities are directed".

Eilon (1971) maintains that "the decision making process is an evolving one which involves the gradual narrowing down of options" he goes on to identify three types of decision outputs in all organisations, those that relate to goals, those that relate to measures and resources and those that relate to means. This universal classification of decision outputs is used as the basis of categorisation in the new typology proposed within this paper. Hughes (1989) identified an additional type of decision output which exists within temporary organisations, starting and terminating them.

The resulting typology is shown below;

POLICY DECISION PROCESS: Start and terminate the construction project

STRATEGIC DECISION PROCESS: Establish the organisational goals

TACTICAL DECISION PROCESS: Devise measures needed to attain those goals set at Strategic level and then select the resources needed to carry out those measures.

OPERATIONAL DECISION PROCESS: Devise the means to enable those resources selected at Tactical level to attain the goals set at Strategic level.

The arrangement of decision types:

Knowledge of types of decision process is to some extent useful in itself to those studying construction project organisations. However by relating types of decision process to each other patterns can be revealed which could be used as a framework to understand and classify organisational structures in construction projects. Walker (1989) suggests a similar advantage of such a framework when he states "the essential determinant of the structure of an organisation for the design and construction of a project is the arrangement of decision points and the way in which the contributors need to be integrated in order to produce material upon which decisions can be made".

When an organisation is faced with a complex problem such as the procurement of a building it copes by fragmentation. In order to reduce its complexity the problem is initially dissected incrementally in to its component parts. In terms of the building procurement problem these will be the project stages. Each Stage represents a sub problem which is then solved individually by further fragmentation. The fragmentation of each sub problem is achieved through the hierarchy of the organisational structure, its function, as Cooke and Slack (1991) state being to "maintain the focus of the organisation as it grows and becomes more complex". It is within the hierarchy that specialist roles develop and it these specialist roles that incrementally solve each sub problem.

Thus problems are tackled by organisations through both horizontal and vertical fragmentation and this is illustrated in figure 1.

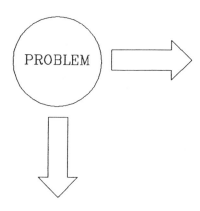

Figure 1 Horizontal and vertical components of problem solving

Since decisions exist to solve problems it is likely that the pattern of decision making within construction organisations will have both vertical and horizontal components. It is proposed that each type of decision process is associated with a particular hierarchical level and the arrangement of the decision processes within that hierarchy will depend upon the nature of the dependency between them. The Policy decision process must come both first and last since they initiate and terminate the whole construction project. To have any purpose and to allow progression from Inception to Completion, the organisation must have goals and the Strategic decision process sets these down. The goals can only be attained by deciding upon measures and by selecting resources to carry them out, this will be decided within the Tactical decision process. Finally, the resources must be coordinated in order to achieve the goals set at Strategic level by devising the means of production and this is established within the Operational decision process. The pattern of decision making that incorporates both vertical and horizontal components is illustrated in Figure 2. Each decision process in the hierarchy restricts the one below it. Thus the Strategic decision process must operate within the constraints set down by the Policy decision process, Tactical decision processes must be made within the constraints set down by the Strategic decision processes and Operational decision processes must be made within the constraints set down by the Tactical decision processes.

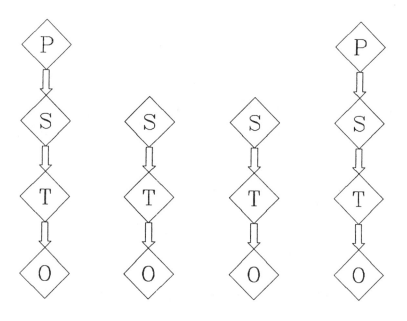

Figure 2   Patterns of decision making processes

Systems and Sub systems:

The model presented above can be developed further by using systems theory which is based largely upon the pioneering work of Lawrence and Lorsch (1967) which developed relationships between organisational structure and environmental conditions. The systems approach is useful in that it is essentially a way of analysing complex processes so that the interrelationships of its component parts and their influence upon the total process can be better understood. Berrien (1976) defines a system as a " set of interacting components distinguished by a boundary which selects the kind and rate of flow of inputs from and outputs to the environment". A thorough analysis of the literature in this area reveals that sub systems have clear barriers and are differentiated on the basis of task, contributors, nature of internal exchanges and environment. Thus by the use of systems theory one is able to identify the component parts of the construction project organisation.

The construction project organisation in the context of systems and sub systems:

The work of Morris (1972), Walker (1980) and Hughes (1989) represent the most recent and successful, attempts to apply systems theory to the construction process. They see the construction organisation as a system comprised of a number of interdependent sub systems whose boundaries are defined by decisions.

The project organisation, which is a temporary one, is created and terminated by the policy decision processes and thus it is between them that the project system exists. Although the project is a temporary sub system of the Client's organisation, for reference purposes this paper refers to the project as the system. Within the project system there are sub systems which are the project Stages and these are created and terminated by Strategic decision processes. Strategic decision processes are responsible for setting goals and thus these Stages will be differentiated on this basis. Each Stage is comprised of its own sub systems which are referred to as Activities which are created and terminated by Tactical decision processes. Since Tactical decision processes are responsible for devising measures and selecting resources the Activities will be differentiated on this basis. Each Activity is comprised of sub systems which are referred to as Operations and created and terminated by Operational decision processes. Since Operational decisions are responsible for devising means these Operations will be differentiated on this basis. Thus the construction project is made up of a series of Stages, the Stages are made up of a number of Activities and the Activities are made up of a number of Operations.

Sub system junctions:

At the junctions between the sub systems there are two decision points, one which terminates the previous sub system and one which triggers the next. Like all decisions they occur in an instant and occupy no resources time or space. Hughes (1989) referred to these as Trigger and Terminal decisions and maintained that they occur simultaneously , that is that the decision to terminate instantaneously initiates the next sub system. This paper contends that because every decision is preceded by the convergence stages there can be a time difference between the two decisions. Furthermore the Terminal and Trigger may be made by different organisational members.This awareness of systems allows a final expansion of the decision making pattern and in its full complexity it is illustrated in figure 3.

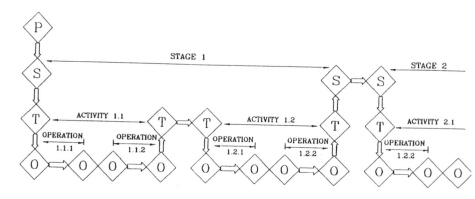

Figure 3 Patterns of decision making in the construction organisation and sub systems.

Figure 3 presents a very linear picture of decision making within the construction process but in reality it is not linear because at any point in time there may be many overlapping Stages, Activities and operations. The degree of overlapping will vary from project to project and NEDO (1983) suggests that the degree of overlapping will depend upon the duration of the project in relation to its size and complexity. Furthermore, the model assumes for simplicity sake that all decisions are sequentially interdependent but in reality Walker (1989) maintains that there is pooled and reciprocal interdependency to consider.

Organisational and Technical decision processes:

Policy, Strategic, Tactical and Operational Decisions collectively determine the structure of the construction project organisation and thus are referred to as Organisational Decisions. The collective result of these decisions is organisational work which occurs within the Operations at Operational level. It is the Operations that collectively produce the product which satisfies the goals set at Strategic level. The Operations do this by using the resources selected at Tactical level in the manner prescribed at Operational level. As the Operations proceed there is the need for decisions that determine the nature of that product that is being produced and these decisions are essentially technical in nature.

Examples of such decisions in the Scheme Design Stage of the construction process would include the decision to use a certain type of roof tile or the decision to use a Steel rather than concrete frame or a decision to use cladding rather than brickwork. In the Detail Design Stage they would include decisions to use a cladding profile and colour or decisions relating to the detailed location of internal services. These decisions do not influence the structure of the organisation and thus cannot be referred to as Organisational Decisions and are referred to as Technical Decisions because of their technical nature. All Technical Decisions such as deciding the nature of a building's structural frame will have a major influence upon the costs, time, quality and functionality of the final building. Since Strategic Decisions set down organisational goals they could be construed as being Strategic Decisions. However they are not Strategic Decisions because whilst the building is the final product is not the only product of the construction project organisation. Each Stage of the construction process has a product and the Strategic Decision within that Stage relates to the Quality, costs, time and functionality of that Stage's product.

This paper is primarily interested in the patterns of Organisational Decision processes rather than Technical Decision processes that can be revealed within construction project organisations. However any comprehensive model of decision making must recognise the existence of such important decisions.

The difference in the emphasis of Technical and Organisational Decisions is illustrated in figure 4.

	TECHNICAL DECISIONS	ORGANISATIONAL DECISIONS
ORGANISATIONAL STRUCTURE	INDIRECTLY	DIRECTLY
PRODUCT NATURE	DIRECTLY	INDIRECTLY

Figure 4   The influence of Organisational and Technical decision making

Although not important organisationally Technical Decisions do influence the nature of the final product produced and thus are very important since it is this product upon which the success of the organisation is often judged. The Technical decisions are more glamorous than Organisational Decisions and as a result have a much higher profile within project organisations. In contrast to the less prominent Organisational Decisions successful Technical Decisions are often rewarded by high profile prizes, awards and prestige. This may be a reason why other models of decision making within construction project organisations have neglected to consider them as a special case. Although it is true that without Technical Decisions the product of the organisation would not be produced, it is also true that without Organisational Decisions the Technical Decisions could not be made. This is because without Organisational decisions there would be no organisational member to make them. Consequently Organisational Decisions do merit special attention.

The final typology of Organisational Decision processes:

This paper defines a decision as a focal point for information within an organisation which occupies no time, resources or space and where an opportunity for change exists. Knowledge of the component sub systems within the project system permits an expansion of the typology of decision processes offered earlier in this paper.

POLICY DECISION PROCESS: The highest level of decision making process and represent the boundary of the project system.

STRATEGIC DECISION PROCESS: Establish goals and define the boundaries of the Stages.

TACTICAL DECISION PROCESS: Devise measures and select resources to attain the Stages goals. They define the boundary of the Activities within each Stage.

OPERATIONAL DECISION PROCESS: Devise the means by which the resources selected at Tactical level will be used to attain the goals set at Strategic level. They define the boundaries of the operations.

REFERENCES:

Bennett J (1985) "Construction Project Management" Butterworths; Cambridge.

Bennett J (1991) "International Construction Project Management: General Theory and Practice" Butterworth - Heineman Ltd, London

Berrien F K (1976) (late) "A general systems approach to organisations" in "handbook of Industrial organisational psychology" Dunnette M D (ed) , Rand McNally College Publishing Company pp7

Cooke S and Slack N (1991) " Making management decisions" Prentice Hall, London

Delbecq A L (1967) "The management of decision making within the firm: three strategies for three types of decision making" Academy of Management Journal Dec pp 329 - 339

Drucker P F (1967) "The effective executive" Harper and Row , New York pp 122 - 125

Eilon, S (1971) "Management Control " McMillan, London

Emory W C and Niland P (1968) "making management decisions", Houghton Mifflin, Boston pp12

Gore W J (1962) "Decision making research: some prospects and limitations" in "Concepts and issues in Administrative behaviour" ed Mailick S and Van Ness E H , Englewood Cliffs, N J Prentice Hall pp49 - 65

Hughes W P (1989) " Organisational analysis of Building projects" PhD thesis, Department of Surveying; Liverpool Polytechnic,

Lawrence P R and Lorsch J W (1967) "Organisation and Environment: Managing Differentiation and Integration" Havard University Press,

Mintzberg H (1973) " Strategy Making in three models" California Management review, Winter pp 44 - 53

Mintzberg H (1973) " The nature of managerial work" Harper and Row

Mintzberg H, Raisinghani D and Theoret A (1976) "The structure of unstructured decision processes" Administrative science quarterly, Vol 21, No. 2, pp 246 - 275

Morris P W G (1972) "A study of selected building projects in the context of the theories of organisations" PhD thesis: department of Building, UMIST.

NEDO (1988) "Faster building for Commerce" HMSO , London

Simon H A (1960) "The new science of management decision", Harper and row, New York

Thompson J D (1967) "Organisations in action" Mc Graw Hill , New York, pp134 - 135

Thompson J D and Tuden A (1963) "Strategies, Structure and processes of organisational decision" in Comparative Studies in Administration" Thompson J D et al (1963) University of Pittsburgh Press.

Walker A (1980) " A model for the design of project management structures for Building Projects" PhD thesis, Department of Surveying, Liverpool Polytechnic,

Walker A (1984) "Project Management in Construction" Grananda; London

Walker A (1989) "Project Management in Construction" BSP Professional Books

Constructability evaluation during detailed design phase

S. Alkass
Centre for Building Studies, Concordia University, Montreal, Canada
G. Jergeas
Revay and Associate, Calgary, Canada
A. Tyler
Civil Engineering Department, Loughborough University, UK

Abstract

The traditional system of construction, separates the the two main disciplines of design and construction. Normally the design is carried be a consultant and the construction is carried out by a contractor and rarely they communicate before the starting of the construction phase of the project. Designers in most cases lacks construction experiences, and construction expert knowledge is not available for junior designers, therefore they do not take into account the construction methods during the design stage of the project. As a result of this the construction industry is suffering from design complexity, increasing costs and longer construction durations. To overcome this problem, it is necessary to incorporate construction knowledge as part of process of design. Artificial intelligence (AI) and expert system techniques can be applied to make the construction knowledge available to assist the design engineer in evaluating the constructability of a selected design detail. The use of Expert Systems in construction is not new. These systems have been developed either as stand alone modules or integrated with commercially available algorithmic software systems. This paper focuses on integrating construction expertise with the design process at the detail design phase. It also describes the development of a PC-based expert system for the assessment of the constructability of a design detail. Knowledge for this particular domain was gained from design engineers, architects, and field practitioners such as site and planning engineers. The development of the appropriate knowledge acquisition and integration techniques are covered. The system is tested with practitioners and novices and the concept of consultation is validated.
Keywords: Constructability, Buildability, Expert systems, Design details

Introduction

Constructability/Buildability is a relatively new term in the jargon of the construction industry, but the concept of constructability, however, goes back many years.

The study of constructability suggest that the traditional separation of the design and construction processes is primarily responsible for the less efficient performance at current construction projects.

It also suggests new approaches for the design and construction processes and that the achievement of good constructability depends upon both designers and contractors being able to see the whole construction process through each others' eyes (CIRIA[1]).

Constructability is generating good interest within the construction practitioners, even though it is a relatively new term in the jargon of construction industry. The concept of constructability however, goes back many years.

Construction techniques have evolved over the centuries relying mainly on labour-intensive methods, material and equipment. As construction techniques have become more sophisticated so the separation of design and construction has increased.

In the traditional approach typically design is carried out first by a consultant and is constructed later by a contractor. Normally these two parties do not communicate prior to the construction stage of the project, despite the fact that most design engineers lack adequate construction experience (Gray[2]). As a result, important construction knowledge are missing during the design stage, leading to impractical, complex and costly design.

Constructability planning pursues the optimum integration of construction knowledge and experience with the engineering design to achieve the overall project objectives (O'Conner et al.[3]). In practice, this knowledge is generally held by few experienced practitioners and therefore accessible only in piecemeal manner.

Although the study of constructability highlights the inherent problems arising from the separation of design and construction processes, there has not been a clear understanding of how to formally incorporate the construction expertise as part of the design process (Jergeas[4]). A development of an expert system in this domain is an attempt to overcome these problems by acquiring construction knowledge, storing it in a computer system structured in a manner that facilitates-system consultation process in an environment that is largely judgment dependent.

In recent years, Expert Systems have been used in the construction industry. They have been developed either as stand alone modules or integrated with commercially available algorithmic software systems, performing various functions including: scheduling, estimating, cost control, database management, accounting, drafting, and word processing. This paper describes the development of an integrated prototype system that combines design procedures with the selection of design details. It is called Constructability Assessment for a Design Detail System (CADDS). The system integrates both data and knowledge gained from experience in designing and constructing different projects. Knowledge is first gathered from a number of experienced design and planning engineers and then structured and coded in a form suitable for manipulation and processing by the various functions within CADDS. The approach relies on well founded principles and experience-based knowledge collected from literature and field surveys. An example application of a retaining wall design selection is presented to illustrate the features of the system. The system will assist the architects and structural engineers in selecting the most appropriate and easy to construct design details. This enables owners and contractors to save time and money and avoid costly legal disputes. This paper focuses on Contractor's design difficulties experienced on construction sites. It explores contractor's viewpoints and identifies specific problem areas, specifically drawings, foundations, structural frames, floors, reinforcement and formwork.

Definitions of Constructability

In 1979, The Construction Industry Research and Information Association (CIRIA) started a research program aimed at investigating the major problems of current U.K. construction practice. This renewed interest in the concern for the interrelationship between design and construction which had followed previous reports since the early 1960's. Interest focused on the concept of buildability and suggestions that present designs were not providing value for money in terms of the efficiency with which the construction process is executed.

Constructability/buildability was defined for the first time in the U.K. by (CIRIA[1]) in 1970 as:
"The extent to which the design of the building facilitates ease of construction, subject to the overall requirements for the completed building".

CIRIA's somewhat simplistic definition inherently suggests careful consideration of design detailing to present a design solution assisting the construction phase whilst meeting desired performance and quality requirements within planned cost parameters.

Whilst CIRIA appreciates that ease of construction may be influenced by many organizational, technical, managerial and environmental considerations, the major contribution was thought to lie in those factors which fall within the influence or control of the design team.(Griffith[5])

It is wrong to associate constructability purely with the aspect of design, as there is increasing recognition for the contractors role and contribution of other parties in promoting ease of construction.

CIRIA states that the problem of constructability exists, and puts it down to:

".... the comparative isolation of many designers from the practical construction process. The shortcomings as seen by the builders were not the personal shortcomings of particular people, but of the separation of the design and construction functions ....."

For the purpose of this paper, the following definition of constructability produced by the Constructability Task Force of the Construction Industry Institute at the University of Texas is adopted.(3)

"Constructability is the optimum use of construction knowledge and experience in planning, engineering, procurement and field operations to achieve overall objective."

DESIGN DETAILS AND CONSTRUCTABILITY

Important factors such as easy to construct design details and functionality must be carefully considered during the design details stage of a project. Both functional and constructional aspects of detailing influence its overall performance. For example, different forms of exterior wall construction must fulfil basic requirements pertaining to aesthetics, durability, energy, fire resistance, acoustic and structural strength. In addition, compatibility with surrounding components, and installation, time and cost should be considered. It is not sufficient to have details which are aesthetically pleasing, functionally satisfactory but not thought out in terms of the construction-related aspects, including feasibility, and impact on cost and schedule.

In spite of the apparent importance of constructability on design, it is often ignored. As a result, problems arise during the project's construction phase causing schedule disruption and leading to costly legal disputes. This means that the extent to which the design of details facilitates ease of construction should be carefully considered. Furthermore the implications of using a specific design detail have to be identified for future improvement to obtain full performance satisfaction.

Constructability as a concept is not new in the construction field (Eldin[6], Tatum[7]). The importance of its improvement has been emphasized in project plan, site plan and major construction methods. Data collection for performing constructability improvement data collection techniques is well documented (O'Connor et al.[8]). Although constructability concepts have been identified to be a major factor in evaluating design alternatives, there have been no significant efforts made to devise a systematic approach to assess and catalogue construction details. Computer technology may be used to capture and code field experience to be presented later to design engineers in an easy to use computer programs will contribute to devise such an approach. This is an area where Knowledge Based Systems can be applied.

Data collection and surveys

Having established that a problem existed, a serious of actions were undertaken to identify the problem including: review of literature, interviews and postal survey with 26 contracting organizations and 30 consulting engineering practices within the construction industry in United Kingdom. A review of the literature on constructability of the

American experience was also under taken. Based on the survey the following point of views were concluded:

Contractor's Views

It was stated several times by some of the contractors interviewed during the research at the that generally they have no complaints about the concept of a design, but rather the details that it incorporates. Design detail difficulties, however, are prevalent, and, according to the contractors interviewed, are present on every contract. The nature of the difficulties are as follows:

1. Design details seem to be drawn in isolation with little thought given to the incorporation of the details in the construction process.
2. Over complex designs which are often costly in construction time and cause disruption.
3. Poor quality information provided for construction - from site investigations to construction drawings.
4. Not enough consideration is given to the practicality of details, nor to the effect they may have on the construction as a whole.
5. Superficially economic designs are often more costly due to their complex shapes or processes of construction.
6. The contractors often choose to give away some material costs in order to save on plant and labour costs.
7. Poor sequencing of operations forced upon the contractor by the design.
   Design detail difficulties have been grouped under the following categories (Jergeas[4]).

1. Drawings

Drawings were considered by some of those interviewed as not always being suitable for site operatives. Drawings were frequently criticized for poor quality which generally meant a lack of clarity and content.
Some of the examples given included the following:

i. Conflicting information and lack of coordination which produced contradictory information from different design sources such as Architects, Engineers, and Mechanical and Electrical consultants.
ii. Unfinished details; the designers completing part of the design and leaving the contractor to finish it.
iii. Information not being sent to site but available at the design office.
iv. Dimensions scattered over several drawings. The Architects' dimensions are frequently not tied in.
v. No grid lines or datum levels making setting out difficult.
vi. Minor details included with other unrelated details.
vii. Wrong bar bending schedule on the drawings.
viii. Poor information, often making it difficult to understand how the job should go together.

2. Foundations

Difficulties regarding foundation design arose due to:
i. Contractor's method of working not being taken into account at design stage, specifically on excavations such as stripping the site to a reduced level in one operation rather than individual areas excavated in isolation.

ii.   The use of small quantities of materials at the expense of additional labour and plant time such as small concrete details requiring extra formwork and labour for fixing, striking and placing concrete.
An example of this is that individual pad foundations, especially if closely spaced and numerous, are not necessarily a cost saving if individual areas are excavated in isolation, rather than stripping the site to a reduced level in one operation.
A similar principal applies in constructing a service reservoir, for instance, where additional thickening of ground slab may be required at the column positions.
iii. Over-complex shapes, such as where the foundation is designed as piles supporting very heavy ground beams between which spans the ground slab.

3. Structural Frames

The main areas of difficulty regarding frame design were identified as:
i.   The mixing of trades within the structural elements and poor sequence of operations.
A ground slab detail is presented as an example of poor operational sequences. The blockwork was detailed as overhanging the floor slabs. Therefore, the floor slab had to be constructed before a start could be made on the inner blockwork.
ii.   Little consideration given to speed of erection by the designers when detailing frame related structures, such as the use of insitu staircases and making openings through structural elements. There are several problems with openings in concrete walls:
      a) Reinforcement fixing is less straightforward.
      b) The fixing of the box-out sections to the formwork take extra time and cost more.
      c) Compaction of concrete under a square box-out is difficult to achieve and often leads to a poor finish requiring remedial work. If a hole is required, a circular one lends itself to a better finish.

4. Reinforcement

The difficulties with reinforcement commonly arising from the need to allow prefabrication. Steel reinforcement for beam and slab floors lend themselves to prefabrication. The beam cages can be fabricated at ground level, then lifted and dropped into place, with continuity and splice bars placed insitu through the column and beam junctions.

There is one important aspect to prefabricating such reinforcement and that is to allow generous cover, particularly end covers.

It is no good prefabricating cages if, when they are placed, there is insufficient cover so that the cage has to be taken out and prefabricated again. Tolerances must take account of the variations which might occur.

5. Formwork

The main areas of difficulty with regard to formwork were identified as:
i.   Difficulties in the re-use and repetition of design.
Many consultants design the lift shafts of buildings as the bracing. However, as a temporary works designer will point out, that becomes the critical item on the construction of the floors. The four walls of the shaft form a nice box, but boxes are not easy to build. The construction is slower, access is difficult for men and materials, and the next floor cannot be started until the walls (lift shaft) are completed.
Considering the shutters themselves, the main difficulty is that the inner shutters all have to be cut to the correct lengths.

ii. Not designing for the maximum use of mechanization to reduce labour costs. An example of that is where the formwork designer could not recommend a Table form or Flying form because the columns on the outskirts of the building were larger than the inner columns.

iii. Complex shapes seem to arise out of the belief that the minimum amount of material means the minimum cost. When dealing with concrete this is rarely the case.

EXPERT SYSTEMS AND CONSTRUCTIBILITY

Expert systems and their application in construction in general have been extensively described in the literature, (Mohan[9] ; Alkass[10] ; Alkass et al.[11]). Their application to evaluate design details for building projects and evaluation of design alternatives have been also considered (Cornick et al.[12], Maver[13]).

While ease of construction may be influenced by many organizational, technical, managerial and environmental considerations, the major contribution is thought to lie in those factors which fall within the influence or control of the design team. Therefore, the emphasis is better implemented on integrating construction experience during design.

Because of their attributes of combining factual knowledge with judgment, including the ability to handle incomplete and uncertain data, and communicate with their users in a language like English, such systems could have a special appeal to the construction profession. Expert systems however, are not a total substitute for experts, but they do help to conserve construction related expertise including information on constructability and are used to make expertise more widely, easily and quickly available for assistance in the decision-making process.

Constructability assessment when considered as a part of the design process is partially subjective and seems to rely mainly on personal knowledge and experience. The rules of constructability are based upon the construction ease and performance implications of the detail components and how these satisfy various functional criteria. The assessment input could be a partially or completely specified detail design and the result is usually a recommendation for improvement. Two main problems promptly arise in developing knowledge-based systems to assess constructability. The first lies in the formalization of the assessment criteria and the second in developing the interface between a syntactic approach of the graphical representation of the given design detail and the semantic representation of a knowledge-based system (Gero et al.[14]). This means that an approach to translate design description in the form of graphical representation into appropriate form of knowledge base description (i.e. from syntactic to semantic representation) is necessary to facilitates the development of an integrated system. The integration is most suited for the construction industry, where much appropriate software already exist to aid the personnel involved in decision making process for example design, drafting, scheduling, estimating, cost control, database management, electronic accounting, and word processing which could usefully be incorporated in any future new system and so possibly avoid some of the additional retraining of staff and new equipment when introducing a new system and also help counter the negative momentum generally engendered with the introduction of new technology. An integrated system might also include an Expert System containing experimental knowledge and engineering judgment to facilitate the decision making process. Clearly a successful outcome would depend on the economic integration with existing systems.

A PROPOSED INTEGRATED SYSTEM

The proposed system is designed to demonstrate how construction knowledge and experience may be most effectively presented and used during the detailed design phase of the project. CADDS is designed in an integration environment. It combines design procedures with construction methods to arrive at the selection of appropriate design details for a specific case based on ease of construction at optimum cost. The system comprises the integration of expert system with existing management software tools.

The knowledge-base of CADDS is build by first eliciting related knowledge from architects, structural engineers and construction practitioners through lengthy consultation with with known facts on construction methods, weather conditions and cost data. The knowledge is then organized, structured and coded to facilitate its use by non-expert considering that the inference mechanism being forward-chaining and knowledge being represented as rules. The mode of operation consists of series of questions linked by IF THEN logic, the logic tree being set of rules arranged to reflect the reasoning of the expert practitioner. The approach relies on well founded principles requiring the constructability of the design be carefully evaluated after which the appropriate design details are selected using rules of thumb ie. type of knowledge acquired from domain experts and stored in an expert system. Data base information, graphical knowledge representation and algorithms for making routine calculations are linked to the system, to enable comprehensive consultation.

CADDS is divided into three main modules, the *first* deals with the selection of a detail to conform with the user particular requirements stated during the query session whilst the second assess the constructability performance of a selected detail. This is done based upon the detail characteristics and its construction requirements, the system rules and the user preference of a set of goals. The third module identifies the cost implication of using the selected detail. Fig.1, illustrates the system's architecture and Fig.2, depicts the integration of the expert system with external programs.

During the selection criteria of a detail (a retaining wall in this case), attention is paid to set of characteristics pertaining to performance, construction aspects and constructability which may include :

1. The retaining wall system self weight .
2. Resistance to lateral loads.
3. Deterioration of the retaining wall components.
4. Installation of all the services' components within the wall
5. Dependence of the wall construction on weather conditions.
6. Degree of inspection required.
7. Type and complexity of the formwork used.

Designers first specify the characteristics of the desired wall system and according to their preferences with respect to previously mentioned selection criteria, CADDS then will advise on the selection of the best wall system. Once the user is satisfied with the decision, he or she may acquire more information on the system generated detail by selecting an icon from a menu. CADDS will then provide the user with the following informations:

1. The outline geometry of the detail
2. The position, shape, size of each component in the assembly.
3. The attachment type of each component.
4. The cost of each type.

This information is held in a file within the system's data base and the syntactic representation of the drawing is converted to semantic representation to enable processing of the expert system. This approach minimize the number of question posed by the system. Information attached to each stored detail may include:

1. Number of components.
2. The attachment description of each component.
3. Number of trades involved in construction of the detail assembly
4. Type of required site supervision and inspection effort.
5. Number of key features in the detail which become quickly hidden behind other layers of construction.

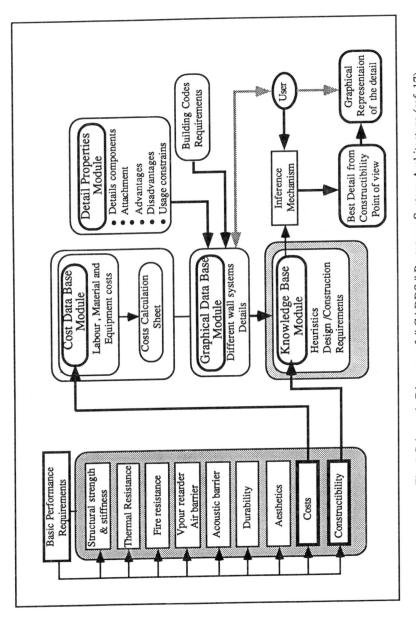

Fig. 1 Schematic Diagram of "CADDS" Prototype System Architecture (ref. 17)

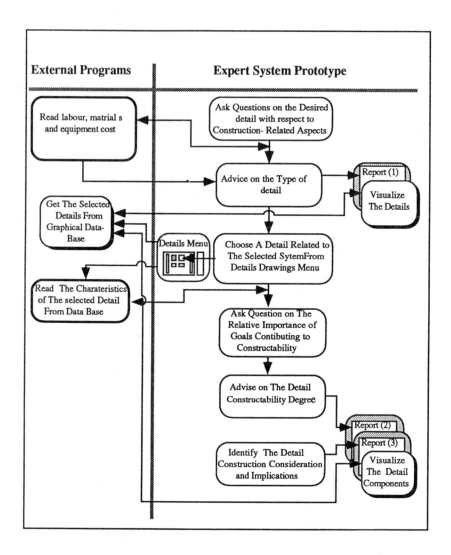

Fig. 2 The Interaction of The Expert System With External Programs

6. Advantageous and disadvantageous characteristics of the detail.
7. Total costs of construction (i.e. labour, material and equipment costs).

The user is requested to input his or her relative importance of the attributes associated with a particular design by assigning numerical values to or selecting from multiple-attributed criteria presented by the system in the form of *Great Importance, Fair, Moderate, Minor and, Not at all* . Fig.3 illustrates the constructability assessment for a wall system.

At the end of the consultation, advice on a selected detail is presented to the user followed by three explanation reports. The first deals with the detail selection, in this case a wall system, the second report deals with constructability assessment of a given detail which is presented as a ratio of the total relative importance input by the user for all attributes considered. The third report shows the implications of the selected detail design.

EXAMPLE APPLICATION

To illustrate the manner in which construction details can influence constructability and performance, the following example [adapted form (Jergeas[15])] a retaining wall section is shown in Fig. 4a. Presumably this detail was designed in this way to take advantage of reducing earth pressures higher up the wall. It was detailed to be cast in five separate pours. The system compares this detail with the one shown in Fig. 4b which meets the designing requirements of that of the first one except the later is different in shape and could be cast in three pours making it easy and quick process. Even though detail B needs more concrete, there has been a saving of 17% in cost that is not to mention the time saved in the process. Table 1 shows cost caparison between the two details.

Another illustration of the manner in which construction details can influence constructability and performance, is shown in the following second example [adapted form (Drysdale et al.[16])] of designing a simple detail is presented. In this example a major decision in the design of the shelf angle carrying the brick veneer in a cavity wall system is to what extent its position should be made adjustable. If the shelf angle is fixed in position at the time of concrete placement of the structural frame, its location both vertically and horizontally is tied to the construction tolerances of the frame. Such a method of shelf angle attachment presents some advantages and disadvantages with respect to constructability and required performance. On one hand, attachment to the frame usually by means of a cast in strap anchor is secure (i.e.performance). Also the construction is simple and straight forward and hence can proceed with a minimum of potential slipups and a minimum of site supervision and inspection effort (i.e. satisfying constructability requirements).

On the other hand variation in the vertical position of the shelf angle can result in either too large or too small a gap for the joint movement beneath the angle and thus, violating the structural requirements for joints movement. Such variation in the horizontal position of the shelf angle can be accommodated by varying the bearing area of the brick on the shelf angle from one floor to another which in turn, is constrained by a limited projection equals to 1/3 brick width (Building Codes requirements). In addition it is important that existing construction be measured up (e.g. Concrete slabs edges, Alignment and Spacing) and problems resulted be resolved before actual construction of the wall system begins (i.e. constructability).

Alternatively, an adjustable shelf angle attachment is possible by means of cast in or drilled-in anchors. By using this method vertical adjustment is possible by means of slots in the shelf angle and horizontal adjustment is achievable by means of shims. Cast-in anchor bolt location may not however, match the shelf angle slots (i.e.constructability). Consequently, greater construction care and inspection effort are required to ensure proper alignment of the shelf angle, proper use of shim plates and proper torque of

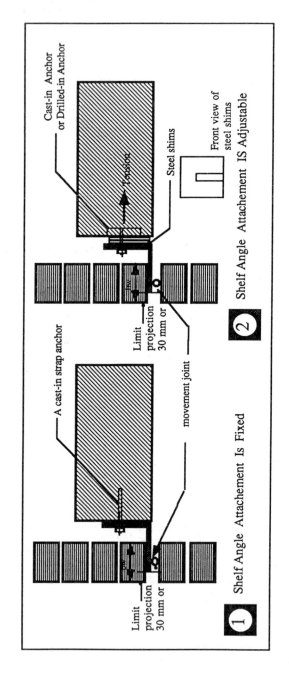

Fig. 3 The Detail Alternatives for The Shelf Angle Attachment

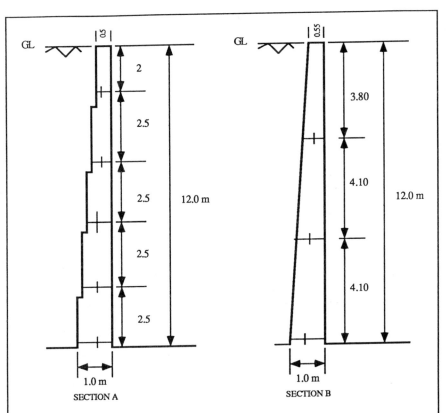

Fig. 4a Example Application a Reataining wall (ref.15)

Item	Detail A	Detail B	%Different
Formwork	$6072.94	$3799.48	37.40
Concrete	$5477.68	$5755.18	4.82
Stop Bar	$1226.35	$835.16	3.10
Kicker	$1117.46	$0.00	0
Reinforcement	$11889.10	$11338.03	4.6
Scabbling	$701.40	$465.16	33.6
Extra Tanking	$403.20	$0.00	0
Total	$26887.14	$22193.03	17.445

Fig. 4b Cost Comparison Between Details A & B (ref. 15)

friction connection created by tightening the nuts on the anchor bolts (i.e. constructability).

The example considered has demonstrated how the selection of the type of attachment should be performed with respect to constructability and performance, considering several aspects or attributes based on design and construction knowledge. Therefore it is quite beneficial to base the selection on a thoughtful assessment. A consultation will advise on the best alternatives and the results are presented within three reports present the detail graphically as illustrated in Fig.3.

CONCLUSIONS

Design details for construction projects depends largely on skilled judgment that accounts all likely variables. Much of this knowledge is held by experienced practitioners and is unlikely available to inexperienced personnel.

The most optimal for improvement comes from exploring alternatives to the construction techniques dictated by the engineer. Also the timely engineering information availability is a more serious problem than understandability.

Constructability improvement in a project appears in the form of of construction-sensitive designs, effective communication of engineering information, optimal constructor-originated techniques, effective construction management standards and construction input to design.

Constructability improvement of a design detail in a project can be achieved by effective design and construction integration. This requires either either the involvement of the construction experts from the outset, with or making their knowledge available for design engineers. CADDS attempts to provide the later alternative, capturing the knowledge and representing it in an efficient graphical form to the user.

The potential uses of the prototype system for design detail assessment and selection are clearly manifold, but most importantly, results of trails with users indicate that the concept provides a disciplined method of transferring knowledge and expertise to young design engineers.

REFERENCES

1. Construction Industry Research and Information Association (CIRIA), "Buildability: An Assessment", Special Publication 26, 1983. UK.
2. Gray, C. "Buildability - the construction contribution. Occasional paper No. 29, The Chartered Institute of Building 1983, England.
3. O'Connor J. and Tucker R., " Industrial Project Constructability Improvement", Journal of Construction Engineering and Management, vol. 112 1986.
4. Jergeas, G. " Detailed Design and Constructability" a   Ph.D thesis, Civil Engineering Department, Loughborough University, 1989, England.
5. Griffith, A., "A Critical Investigation of Factors Influencing Buildability and Productivity", A Ph. D Thesis, Heriot-Watt University, Department of Building, 1984, UK.
6. Eldin, N., " Constructability Improvement of Project Designs " , Journal of Construction Engineering and Management , vol 114 No. 4. Dec. 1988.
7. Clyde B. Tatum ," Improving Constructability During Conceptual Planning", Journal of Construction Engineering and Management , vol 113 No. 2. June 1987.
8. O'Connor J. Larimore M., and Tucker R., " Collecting Constructability Improvement Ideas", Journal of Construction Engineering and Management, vol 112 No. 4. Dec. 1986.

9. Mohan S " Expert Systems Applications in Construction Management and Engineering ",Journal of Construction Engineering and Management , vol 116 No. 1990.

10. Alkass S " An Expert System for Earthmoving Equipment Selection in Road Construction" a Ph.D thesis, Civil Engineering Department, Loughborough University, 1988, England.

11. Alkass S and Harris F " An Expert System for Earthmoving Equipment Selection in Road Construction"Journal of Construction Engineering and Management, vol 114 No.3 1988.

12. Cornick , T. and Bull, S.," Expert Systems for Detail Design in Building ", CAAD Futures '87, Eindhoven, The Netherlands,1987.

13. Maver, T.," Software Tools for the Technical Evaluation of Design alternatives", CAAD Futures 87, Eindhoven, The Netherlands, 1987.

14. Gero, J., and Maher, M., " Future Roles of Knowledge-based Systems in the design process " CAAD Futures '87, Eindhoven, The Netherlands, 1987.

15. Jergeas, G. " Constructability: Definitions, Concepts and Principals" an internal report, Revay & Associates, 1990, Canada.

16. Drysdale, R.G., Suter, G.T., Advisory Document , part 2 " Seminar on Brick Veneer Wall systems ", sponsored by CMHC CCRB, ABGC, MBEC, OBEC, June 12-14, 1989.

17. Alkass S., Moselhi O and Abdou A." An Integrated system to Aid Design Engineers in Selecting Easy to Construct Design Details",Civil-Comp 91, the Second International Conference of Artificial Intelligence and Civil Engineering Oxford UK.

A total cost performance index for buildings

M.J. Packham
Managing Associate, BWA Project Services, Bromley, Kent, UK

Abstract

This paper examines the concept of total cost in buildings and investigates the feasibility of producing a Total Cost Performance Index. To do so it:

- Identifies the components of total cost and examines their units of measurement to ascertain compatibility
- Investigates existing sources of information for each component
- Investigates the relative importance of the components one to another

The paper closes with an examination of outside factors impinging on total cost for which allowance should be made in any model.

Keywords: Total Cost, Total Cost Performance Index, Initial Cost, Renewals Cost, Occupancy Cost, Functional Use Efficiency/Cost.

1 Introduction

This paper is based on research originally carried out as part of a masters degree dissertation submission. The original aim of the study was to examine the concept of 'value' in buildings with a view to establishing an objective method for its assessment. Examination of various definitions of 'value' quickly established that to ascertain 'value' one must first be able to measure 'cost'. The whole emphasis of the study therefore changed direction such that it became an investigation of the practicality and methodology of compiling what has, for the purposes of this exercise, been termed a Total Cost Performance Index (TCPI) for buildings.

Having established the direction that the study was to take, the next task was to set parameters for its

execution.   Thus it was decided that so far as was
practical, existing bodies of information and techniques
familiar to the majority of property professionals should
be utilised.   By minimising development costs and making
'user friendly' it was envisaged that any systems
suggested by the research would be more readily adopted
by the industry than might otherwise be the case.
    Finally, the methodology of carrying out the
study itself was identified in stages as follows:

a) Definition of total cost
b) Identification of the components of total
   cost and examination of their units of measurement to
   ascertain compatibility.
c) Investigation of existing information sources with
   regard to each of the components.
d) Investigation of the relative importance of the
   components one to another.
e) Investigation of the practicality of producing a model
   combining each of the components into an overall
   measure of a building's total cost.
f) Examination of outside factors impinging on the
   components

The remainder of this paper is presented broadly in line
with this sequence.

2 Definition of Total Cost

Traditionally a building's cost was thought of as the
summation of land acquisition, construction and finance
charges together with the associated legal, agency and
design fees.   During the 1960's and 70's this definition
was widened to include what came to be termed 'life cycle
costs';   these include such regularly recurring items as
fuel costs as well as intermittent costs for the
replacement of building elements at the end of their
useful lives.
    Subsequently the definition was broadened still further
with Fuller, for example, [see Fuller R, 1982] suggesting
in the early 1980's, that a more comprehensive approach'
also considers the organisational costs of the users of a
building and assesses the effectiveness and economic
efficiency of the facilities related to the functions of
the user body'.   This definition was endorsed in 1987 by
Ward [Ward R, 1987 b] who stated that the 'one category
of cost.....notably absent from most life cycle analysis
(was) the costs associated with performing intended
occupancy functions and activities within the facility'.
    In a subsequent paper, Ward [1987 a] went on to define
total cost as follows:

$$TLCC = I + O + FU \qquad (1)$$

Where the Total Life Cycle Cost (TLCC) is equated to
the sum of

a) Initial (I) cost (eg: land, construction etc)
b) Operating (O) cost (eg: fuel, maintenance, renewals
   etc)
c) Functional Use (FU) cost (eg: the cost of
   organisational activity functions which are in essence
   an organisation's overheads or administration costs)

This definition forms the basis of the study although for
discussion purposes the 'O' cost component has been split to
differentiate between renewals costs and occupancy costs.

3. Initial cost

When considering the cost of any article, the first thing
that comes to mind is its purchase price which is almost
always expressed in terms of a lump sum. In the case of a
building this remains basically true. The purchase price is
made up of four elements: land acquisition, construction,
finance and fees and it is not unusual for both land
acquisition and construction to be expressed as lump sums.
They are however by their nature readily convertible into
costs per unit of superficial area, in the case of land
usually per acre or hectare and for construction per square
metre of built area.

Finance charges and professional fees are applicable to
both land acquisition and building cost. However, for the
purposes of this study, they can be ignored as under the
suggested method of total cost computation (see Section 7),
they would appear on both sides of the equation and by so
doing cancel each other out.

The cost of land varies considerably and depends on
demand/supply, location and use. It can also be highly
volatile and thus information can quickly become dated.
This is the biggest problem to assembling a land value
database. However, the Property Market Report [see Property
Market Report 1990] has already gone some way towards
providing such by publishing at six monthly intervals a
range of land values for different uses.

The information is however, regionalised rather than
localised and would need to be updated more frequently to be
of use in this context. One suspects that the leading
estate agencies already have such information to hand, and
the requirement is simply for it to be made more freely
available.

With regards a construction cost database, the Building
Cost Information Service (BCIS) has now been in existence
for more than twenty years. Over this time sufficient
information has been received for them to publish at three
monthly intervals a Study of Average Building Prices

(Section KB).   The information provided covers a wide range
of building types and sub-types and these costs can be
easily updated to take account of inflation, wage increases
and the like using the Building Cost Indices which are also
published regularly by the BCIS.   Similarly, regional
variations can be catered for by using their location
factors and as an added refinement, it is also possible,
knowing the quality of the building required, to assess its
cost against, for example, an upper percentile rather than
the mean.

4. Renewals Cost

The term 'renewals' is used here to describe those
intermittently recurring costs associated with the
replacement of items at the end of their useful lives.   The
number of components subject to such deterioration is quite
considerable particularly if the measure is over physical as
opposed to functional life.   Indeed, the only items not
likely to require replacing are the foundations and the
structural shell.
   Valuation of the cost of renewals is an integral part of
life cycle costing and has therefore been known in this
country for over twenty years.   The technique has not
however, been so widely adopted in this country as it has in
the United States and consequently there is a shortage of
suitable published information.
   The procedure involves the summation of the present
values of the replacement costs of each component over a
building's life.   Thus, for example, taking a component
with an average life of fifteen years and a replacement cost
of £10,000 in a building with a physical life of sixty
years, the renewals costs would be calculated as follows.

Year	Present Value Factor at a Discount Rate of 10%	Replacement cost £	Present Value £
15	0.2394	10,000	2,394
30	0.0573	10,000	573
45	0.0137	10,000	137
		Renewals Cost	£3,104

   For a particular building, derivation of the information
required to carry out this exercise is relatively simple.
The replacement costs can be extracted from the estimate
prepared to arrive at the 'construction' cost whilst the
component lives can be derived from any one of a number of

published sources [for example see 'Life Cycle Costing' Dell Isola A J and Kirk S J 1983].

To arrive at the overall renewals cost this exercise is repeated for each item that will require replacement over the building's life.

Renewals cost is therefore, as with initial cost, normally expressed as a lump sum at to-day's date and is similarly easily convertible to a cost per superficial unit usually per square metre of built area.

5 Occupancy Cost

In his book 'Premises Audits' Bernard Williams [Williams B, 1988] describes occupancy costs as 'the total cost of running, maintaining and modifying the fabric and services of a building excluding rent, building rates and major works for fitting out and replacement of components'. From this it is clear that occupancy cost is a term used to describe items which recur regularly throughout the life of a building as a result of its use; these include

(a) Energy - eg: for heating, lighting etc,
(b) Cleaning - eg: daily office cleaning, window cleaning etc.
(c) Maintenance - costs associated with maintaining the building at its current standard
(d) Service Charge - this cost centre relates primarily to leasehold premises and varies considerably from building to building, and from landlord to landlord. Items allocated to it typically include, for example, cleaning of common areas such as staircases and toilets.
(e) Security - again highly variable being dependent on individual organisations and their security requirements which can range from a simple door answer phone system through to sophisticated anti-intruder devices.
(f) Insurance - cost varies according to type of cover required
(g) Fitting out - this cost centre does not usually appear on the list of occupancy cost categories. It is included here to cover those minor enhancements which every building occupier carried out (eg: minor partition alterations) but that do not readily fall into either the maintenance or renewals categories.

Once allocation between cost centre has been decided it is a relatively easy exercise to calculate annual costs for each of them and derive the total occupancy cost for the building. If required this can then be converted to an annual cost per superficial unit of built area.

Several databases of occupancy cost are published but probably the best known is that produced by Building Maintenance Information Ltd (BMI) in the form of their

'Study of Average Occupancy Costs'. Whilst not as detailed as the Average Building Prices published by BCIS, they do form an adequate benchmark against which comparison can be made if required. There is also the added advantage that update indices are published at regular intervals.

Other databases are published by leading estate agencies (eg: Savills and Jones Lang Wootton) but these primarily relate to office occupancy costs.

6 Functional Use Cost

Functional use costs are essentially human costs ie: staff salaries, but they also include the materials and other items required to perform the function of an organisation using a building. They constitute in most instances the largest component of total cost as was strikingly demonstrated by R. Ward [1987 b] in his paper 'Office Building Systems Performance and Functional Use Costs' which shows that they can outweigh the combined total of initial, renewal and occupancy cost by a ratio as high as 9:1. Despite this very little cost information has been published on this subject primarily owing to major difficulties in devising a system for its assessment.

Measurement of functional use efficiency (and hence cost) is highly problematic as it requires the analysis and assessment of subjective or intangible concepts which cover a wide spectrum of different topics; some examples of these would include:

(a) Increased productivity arising from better lighting

(b) A poor location which makes it harder to get suitable staff unless premium salaries are paid

Methods have been devised that suggest such assessment is possible and one such is contained in the ORBIT-2 report.

This looked at trends in organisational change, information technology and building design and technology. It identified seventeen key issues relating to them and then devised a points system (ie: 1-9 with 9 being the highest rating) to enable an organisation to objectively and consistently rate a building in terms of how well it performs in resolving these issues. It went on to identify six aspects from which each of these issues should be viewed.

This resulted in a matrix arrangement which, it is suggested, could be modified to provide a method of assessing functional use cost. The suggested modified matrix structure is shown overleaf. It attempts to demonstrate that the relative importance of each 'aspect' within an 'issue' varies and that in some instances a particular aspect is not relevant to a specific issue. Additionally, it should be recognised that any calculation of Functional Use Cost must also provide for a 'weighting' of the 'issues' one to another.

Issue \ Aspect	Location & Tenure	Bldg Shell +Form	Major Bldg. Serv.	Local Dist'bn of Serv.	Fit Out	Office Furn
Organisational Issues:						
.Change of Staff size	*	*	*	+	+	+
.Attract/ Retain	*	*	N	N	*	+
.Communication of Status	N	*	+	N	*	*
.Relocation of Staff	N	+	*	*	*	*
.Informal Interaction	*	*	N	N	*	*
.Human Factors	N	N	*	*	+	+
.Outside Image	*	*	N	N	*	*
.Security	*	*	+	+	*	*
IT Flexibility	+	+	*	*	+	+

.Key: * Important
       + Of less importance
       N Not applicable

(Note: The ORBIT-2 study was sponsored by eighteen major North American organisations and was carried out by representatives of three consultant firms: Facilities Research Associates, Ithaca, New York, DEGW, London and the Harbinger Group, Norwalk, Connecticut - Summaries of these reports' findings can be found in 'Growing Concerns [Duffy F and Stansall P, 1985] and 'ORBIT-2 Know Your Buildings IQ' [Duffy F, 1985]).

.7 Computation of Total Cost

In summation of Sections 3-6, it can be seen that as one progresses from Initial through to Functional Use cost the body of information available reduces dramatically such that, for the latter, there is no recognised method of calculating quantum. Section 6 does however demonstrate the feasibility of producing a suitable method of measurement.

The following table lists each component of total cost and the units by which they can be measured. In so doing it clearly shows the lack of compatibility between them.

Component	Unit of Measure
Initial Cost	[£/hectare (Land) [£/m2 (Building)
Renewals Cost	£/m2
Occupancy Cost	£/m2 per annum
Functional Use Cost	Points rating

To overcome this it is suggested that each component could be converted to an index. For Initial, Renewals and Occupancy cost this can be done by comparison with a base derived from published data. Thus, for the land acquisition element of Initial Cost the price paid for the site would be converted to a cost per hectare. This would then be divided by a current average price per hectare extracted from a database of localised land values and multiplied by 100 to give a Land Index ie:

Actual price per hectare   x 100 = Land Index
Current Average price per hectare

(An Index of less than 100 would therefore indicate that in terms of the Land component of its total cost the building performed better than the average).

A similar exercise could then be undertaken to derive a Construction Index for the building element of Initial Cost using the Study of Average Building Costs and adjustment indices published by BCIS as demonstrated below.

Actual/Estimate Construction Cost/m2 x 100 = Construction
Average Construction   Index
Cost x Latest Index x Location
      Base Index   Factor

The Land and Construction Indices would then be combined using a weighting to produce the overall Initial Cost Index.

Land Index x Weighting =

                                                    +

Construction Index x Weighting =

            Initial Cost Index
                                          _____

                                          _____

For Renewals and Occupancy Costs similar procedures could be adopted to convert them to Indices. However, for renewals costs, there are no published averages with which to make comparison and it would be necessary to create a 'designer' average for the type of building being examined. This could be done by selecting a representative sample of say ten buildings from the cost analysis also published by BCIS. This would be a relatively quick exercise once a standard spreadsheet had been set up on a computer although in some instances the cost centres contained in the analyses require further splitting down to get to the pure renewals costs. For example, the roof element combines the cost for both the roof structure and roof finishes and whilst the latter will require renewal, the former will not.

With regards functional use cost the position is different in that it has been suggested, in the absence of published information, that it should be measured against a points rating system. A pro forma similar to that shown below could therefore be used to convert it to an index using the criteria for scoring and weighting as already briefly discussed in Section 6.

Issue	(a) *Average Score (1-9)	(b) Actual Score (1-9)	(c) Issue Weighting	(d) (a)x(c)	(e) (b)x(c)
Staff Size Change	5				
Attract/Retain Workforce	5				
Comm. of Hierarchy	5				
Relocation of Staff	5				
Informal Interaction	5				
Ambient Environment	5				
Image to Outside	5				
Security	5				
IT Flexibility	5				

$$\underline{\hspace{2cm}} \div \underline{\hspace{2cm}}$$

$$= \frac{\underline{\hspace{2cm}}}{x \ 100}$$

Functional Use Cost Index value   ======

(* On a points rating system of 1-9 this will always be 5)

The indices derived for each of the four components of total cost would then need to be combined to produce the Total Cost Performance Index that is the subject of this paper. Again, it is suggested that this would best be carried out using a weighting system and the somewhat sketchy information currently available seems to indicate an average ratio, for example, for offices of I (Construction cost only?):O:FU of 5:5:90. A suitable pro forma is shown below.

TCPI Pro Forma

Component	Index		Weighting		
Initial Cost	_____	x	_____	=	_____
					+
Renewals Cost	_____	x	_____	=	_____
					+
Occupancy Cost	_____	x	_____	=	_____
					+
Functional Use Cost	_____	x	_____	=	_____
					=
	Total Cost Performance Index				_____

The procedures proposed in this Section may appear cumbersome. It is believed however that they are far more difficult to describe than to actually carry out. No complicated mathematics are involved and the use of a computerised pro forma would drastically cut calculation time.

8 Other Factors to be Considered

Any model must make allowance for all outside factors which can impinge on the components from which it is derived. In the case of the TCPI these can be grouped under three main headings:
- Client Type
- Taxation and Grants
- Depreciation/Obsolescence

8.1 Client Type

In their report 'The Performance Evaluation of Office Buildings', G. Williams and B. Middleton [1987] identify four major client groupings:

Client Types   -   Developer/Trader
            -   Investor
            -   Owner/Occupier
            -   Tenant

Each of these groups clearly have different expectations from a building and the same building will therefore in all probability have four different Performance Indices.

To the developer/trader buildings are simply merchandise and he is primarily interested in the difference between acquisition cost and the anticipated market value. Traditionally this type of client has paid little attention to the occupancy costs of his buildings and none to their functional use costs.

The investor judges a building against different criteria and looks to long term security rather than short term profit. He is therefore primarily interested in long term performance both as a means of providing some protection against inflation and as a method of increasing capital value through rental growth. To achieve the desired high levels of rental growth the property must therefore be capable of attracting and keeping tenants.

Of the four client types identified, the owner-occupier is the one most likely to be interested in all of the components which go to make up total cost. His interest is not limited to his initial expenditure but extends to the use to which the building can be put and its functional efficiency in executing that use.

The tenant takes a radically different view from his counterparts. In this case initial cost is of no importance and the model must be flexible enough to reflect the switch of interest to rental levels. Many of the countries leading agencies publish information on rental levels and thus the compilation of a database to enable inclusion of rental in any model would not be too difficult.

In addition to the four main client groupings, it is suggested that further client classification should be incorporated into the model to distinguish between the public and private sectors which it is felt can sometimes take differing viewpoints.

8.2 Taxation and Grants

The world of taxation is a complex one. Fortunately, the working of the system itself simplifies matters considerably as it is geared primarily to the status of the individual or company rather than to that of any building which they might own. On this basis the aspects of taxation that do need to be considered can be limited to Capital Allowances and Value Added Tax.

Capital allowances only apply on new buildings in a small number of strictly limited instances. More importantly however, they are also claimable in a large proportion of cases on 'plant and equipment' which, because it can amount to a considerable portion of a buildings initial cost, can be highly valuable.

For most organisations VAT is simply a book-keeping exercise, however some organisations, eg: charities and institutions are either partially or completely exempt from the VAT system and thus any VAT paid cannot be reclaimed. Another factor for consideration is that under the current VAT system, listed buildings are zero-rated; as existing buildings they would normally attract VAT at the standard rate. More recently new legislation has introduced the concept of the 'Option to Tax' which gives the right, subject to certain exemptions, to elect to waive exemption from VAT on otherwise exempt supplies of interests, etc in land. This has complicated the matter quite considerably and makes the inclusion of VAT in any model that much more difficult.

So far discussion has essentially been limited to the effect of taxation on 'initial' cost but as will be realised it is equally applicable to both 'renewals' and 'occupancy' cost. With regard to the latter, amounts spent on maintenance, repairs, heating, lighting and the like are regarded as business expenses and as such are deductible from profits before the application of tax. They are, therefore, effectively tax free. For 'renewals' costs, capital allowances are available for the replacement of plant and equipment, on a similar basis to that outlined above.

These comments are made in relation to standard rate tax payers. There are of course many variations primarily dependent upon the tax status of the organisation concerned and any model must be flexible enough to incorporate all permutations.

Whereas the world of taxation confuses by its complexity that of grants can bewilder by its sheer variety. This is demonstrated by a quick look at FRED (Financial Resources for Economic Development) [Institute of Local Government Studies, 1983-88], which shows that not only is there a wide variety of assistance on offer, but that it is available from a number of different sources.

Despite the number of grants available, the majority of projects go ahead without any assistance, even so it is suggested that it would be prudent to make provision for them in any model.

8.3 Depreciation and Obsolescence

As buildings grow older they depreciate and as a consequence do not perform so well financially. Thus, as buildings age rental growth slows and the increased requirement for repairs leads to unexpected capital costs. It can be seen therefore that depreciation is as much part of a building's total cost as its construction or occupancy cost.

Depreciation and obsolescence are sometimes regarded as being synonymous, however, more correctly, depreciation of an asset arises directly out of its use over the passage of time, whereas obsolescence results from changes external to the asset itself. Thus, an asset may not have depreciated but it could have been rendered obsolete by, for example, technological change.

The study 'Obsolescence - The Financial Impact on Property Performance' [Jones Lang Wootton 1988 a] dramatically demonstrates the effect of obsolescence by suggesting that the rate at which an ageing property's equivalent rental value falls behind full market rates can be as much as 2.7% per annum.

When considering depreciation and obsolescence it is important to remember that we are dealing with two assets. For the building any model must take cognisance of its propensity for:

(a)   Physical deterioration
(b)   Obsolescence - Economic
                       Functional
                       Aesthetic/Visual
                       Legal
                       Social
                       Environmental

For land, the factors to be considered are more complex and could include, for example, the effect of:

(a)   A relaxation of planning controls
(b)   Tax changes and incentives or grants
(c)   Population changes
(d)   Changes in levels of economic activity
(e)   Changes in industrial operational methods
(f)   Social change
(f)   Infrastructure change

From the above it should be clear that the majority of factors affecting depreciation and obsolescence are subjective or intangible and as such are difficult to measure for inclusion in any model.

However rates of physical deterioration can be controlled by use initially of a high standard of materials and regular and thorough maintenance procedures. These measures would almost inevitably lead to higher initial, renewals and occupancy costs and would therefore be catered for by the mechanisms described in Section 7 for these components of total cost.

Similarly buildings with an in-built high degree of flexibility will be able to accommodate change more readily and as such will be more resistant to becoming obsolete. Flexibility is of course a key component in the assessment of functional use cost as demonstrated by Section 6.

9.0 Conclusion

As stated in the introduction to this paper, its contents are based on research originally carried out as part of a masters degree dissertation. Obviously this original document was much longer and I am conscious that, in attempting to abbreviate it, certain areas may appear to have been dealt with superficially. Hopefully however it has been clearly demonstrated that production of a means of measuring a buildings total cost is feasible.

It is suggested that the most appropriate method of deriving such is by means of a weighted index, primarily as this overcomes the problem of compatibility between the units of measure of the four identified components of total cost.

Finally, whilst the paper ascertains that the production of a model to calculate total cost is possible it also identifies areas where further major research is required if it is to become a reality; these relate specifically to:

(a)   Measurement of functional use cost
(b)   The weighting of the components of total cost one
       to another

References

Building Cost Information Service [1988.a] Study of Average
    Building Prices, Building Cost Information Service,
    Kingston-upon-Thames
Building Cost Information Service [1988b] Regional Trends,
    Building Cost Information Service, Kingston-upon-Thames
Building Maintenance Information [1985] Study of Average
    Occupancy Costs, Building Maintenance Information Ltd,
    Kingston-upon-Thames
Dell Isola A J & Kirk S J [1983] Life Cycle Cost Data,
    McGraw Hill book Company Inc. USA
Duffy F [1985] ORBIT 2 - Know Your Building's IQ. Facilities
    (Volume 3 No.12) December 1985 pp 12-15
Duffy F & Stansall P [1985] Growing Concerns, Designers
    Journal, Octoner 1985
Fuller R [1982] - Life Cycle Costing, A Comprehensive
    Approach, in P S Brandon, editor Building Cost
    Techniques: New Directions, E&FN Spon Ltd, London
Institute of Local Government Studies [1983-1988] Financial
    Resources for Economics Department, Institute of Local
    Government Studies, Birmingham
Jones Lang Wootton Papers [1988a] Obsolescence, the
    Financial Impact on Property Performance, Jones Lang
    Wootton, London
Property Market Report [1990] Property Market Report Autumn
    1987, Valuation Office Inland Revenue Surveyors
    Publications, London
Savills [1987] Property Management Cost, Savills, London
Ward R [1987a] an Economic Framework of Total Functional
    Value for Advanced Comfort Systems, Massachusetts
    Institute of Technology USA
Ward R [1987b] Office Building Systems Performance and
    Functional Use Costs, Paper All Proceedings of the Fourth
    International Symposium on Building Economics, Danish
    Building Research Institute, Copenhagen, Denmark
Williams B [1988] Premises Audits, Bulstrode Press, London

CHAPTER THREE

*'Project Management today must operate in a
complex constraining, and uncertain
environment. As a result, the project
management task is itself more difficult and
complex. In this more complex environment
control is today treated in its broader context
of the planning and monitoring of the total
project process.'*

P. W. G. Morris

Construction contracts and risk

R.F. Gibson
Department of Civil Engineering, Paisley College, Scotland, UK

Abstract
This paper examines traditional contract approaches to
risk apportionment. The ideas of risk management are
examined leading to a discussion of an approach to
determine an expected value for the contract sum and the
contract duration based on frequency distribution.
Keywords Risk management, Contract Risk Simulation

1 INTRODUCTION

The construction of a building to a defined price, time
and quality is a complex risk activity, requiring
organisational skills, knowledge, time and resources
outwith the possession of the average person or
organisation ie the "promoter" or "employer" who requires
the building. Thus, the promoter requires a builder or a
"contractor". However, by relying on a builder to
deliver the building to cost, time and quality the
promoter requires a contract to protect his objectives.
Likewise, the builder requires a contract to ensure
payment.

It is perhaps worthwhile considering the uniqueness of
a construction project. Even if the superstructure is
identical to previous projects the substructure may well
be different. The logistics involved with acquiring
resources to time, price and quality will be different.
The climatic, political and economic regimes may be
different. Finally, the contractors organisational team
and sub-contractors may also be different. But of
course superstructures are rarely identical, so in
addition to the above risk factors can be added all the
risks associated with the construction of a prototype. A
thorough analysis of the distinctiveness of construction
projects can be found in Hillebrandt (1974).

2 Building procurement models

Due to the technical complexity of both building design and construction the delivery of a building requires three distinct rôles, a promoter, a designer and a builder. However, these rôles may be separate or combined. From this five procurement relationships result as shown in figure 1:

    Traditional
    Design and Build
    Self Build
    Employer Designs
    Kit Build

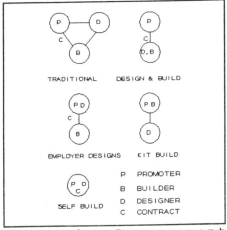

Figure 1   Procurement
Relationships

However, it should be noted that not all yield contracts between a promoter and builder. For example, Self Build generates no contracts while Kit Build involves a sale of goods. Interestingly, if the delivery of a building is considered as an organisational process a fourth factor, management, is required. This in turn yields procurement types such as:

    Project Management
    Management Contracting
    Construction Management

These procurement models with their emphasis on ideas such as the management of the construction process and the need for single point responsibility are thought to be more suited to the achievement of the goals of cost, time and quality (Franks 1990).

3 Contract type and the determination of the contract sum

The law of contract suggests that the price to be paid is agreed between the contracting parties at the time of contract. However, because of the difficulty in determining, even in the most carefully planned project, either the quantity or quality of work actually to be undertaken or because construction must commence prior to completion of design, the contract sum to be paid may be either unknown or different to that agreed at the time of contract signing. Because of the difficulty of the promoter and his design team being able accurately to determine the quality and quantity of the contract works at the time of contract signing a number of contract types have been designed to address this problem:

Fixed price contracts

> Lump sum: This is the only contract which yields the final contract cost at time of signing. Once signed such contracts do not permit design changes. Normally, these are only suited for small works.
> Measurement: This is a fixed rate based on items in the bill of quantities and thus produces a contract sum. However as the total quantity of work as built is usually different to that in the contract documents the contract sum incurred by the employer may well be different from that produced at the contract signing. These contracts permit variations in bill items and thus offer a mechanism for design changes.
> Schedule of rates: This is a fixed rate for what at the time of contract signing are undetermined items and quantities. Associated with this type of contract is an approximate quantities contract. These contracts can be used for maintenance where the scope of the works will often be very uncertain. Neither of these produce a contract sum.

Cost reimbursement contracts

> Cost + fixed fee: This is the reimbursement of all the prime costs for labour, plant and materials incurred by the contractor plus a fixed management fee for overheads and profit.
> Cost + % fee: As above except the management fee is a percentage of contract costs.
> Cost + fluctuating fee: As above except the management fee varies with performance. The fee becomes a target increasing inversely with contract

costs.

Cost reimbursement contracts enable construction to commence in parallel with design (Griffis, 1988). However this demands that the employer must sanction the use of cost, time, resources by the contractor. In such contracts the employer has an adminisrative burden and carries considerable risk. Nevertheless, cost reimbursement contracts when used in conjuction with construction management enable 'Fast Track' construction (Sabbagh, 1989).

Bill of Quantities contracts extend project times and costs by placing design and construction in series, and construction costs are further increased by the production of a bill. Furthermore, all contractors competing for a tender incur estimating costs, thus, as a result, national construction costs are increased. Nevertheless, this traditional type of building contract is popular with employers as they feel it offers a rational basis for competitive comparison of tenders and minimises contract risk. However, because contractors often have to produce tight margins to win contracts they then attempt to augment the contract sum by subsequent claims; for example, loss and expense on the inevitable variations (Horgan & Roulston, 1988). The British Property Federation (BPF) in the manual to their own contract form produce a powerful critique of this traditional contract form. The BPF say that traditional procurement methods result in poor design, inadequate supervision, insufficient choice of materials and increased costs and time delays. Furthermore, the use of a bill of quantities apart from being time consuming may even dictate the design. Finally, the BPF claim that traditional methods lead to a confrontational attitude between employer and contractor. Later in this paper, an alternative approach to fixed price contracts will be considered. This new approach, which is based on the uncertainty of the construction process, will develop expected values for contract sum and contract duration.

4 Risk and 'Consensus in Idem'

A fundamental principle of the law of contract is that of 'consensus in idem' ie both parties must understand and agree to the same terms (Burns,1966). This should mean both parties agreeing to the same price, time and quality. However, when drawing up the contract the potential risk should be identified and apportioned between builder and employer. If this can be done it will be an important safeguard as it prevents the employer from resorting to expensive arbitration or litigation and enables the builder to produce a

competitive yet profitable contract sum. The contract
sum determined by a contractor is priced on the basis of
resources (labour, materials, plant) overheads, profit
and a margin for risk. Standard contract forms do much
to state risks and to state which party is liable for
carrying the risk. For example, contract forms state
what procedures are to followed if antiquities are
encountered or war is declared. In addition, the
Standard Method of Measurement in conjunction with the
Common Arrangement of Work Sections provides a risk
reduction rôle; for example, excavation rates are based
on a particular soil type and ground water level. Thus
all contractors pricing a contract can in theory do so
with a much clearer idea of the construction liability to
which they are exposing themselves. Likewise, the
employer will get a better idea as to the financial
liability to which he will be exposed.

It is worth noting that this reliance on legal
obligations for building delivery is not universal. For
example, Japan, with a population about twenty five times
greater than that of Scotland and with a construction
output which is about thirty four times greater than
Scottish construction output, is reputed to have roughly
the same number of lawyers as there are in Scotland and
no quantity surveyors!

5 Types of contract risk

Contract risk has been classified by Jones (1980) into
four useful categories:
    Fundamental Risk - catastrophes affecting society eg
War damage, Nuclear fall out, supersonic bang damage.
JCT 80 Clause 21.3 defines risks such as Nuclear fall out
as 'excepted risks'. These risks are not borne by the
contractor. In these cases the promoter would presumably
seek recompense from the government.
    Pure Risk - these are risks related to projects eg
fire, lightning, storm. As with fundamental risk the
probability of occurrence is slight. JCT 80 Clause 22
deals with these by requiring either party to fully
insure against their occurring. Such risks are readily
and cheaply insured commercially.
    Particular Risk - These are associated with specific
construction activities eg collapse, subsidence,
vibration, lowering of ground water level. Again this is
a risk which is a potential loss to the contractor. JCT
80 Clause 21.2 requires the contractor to formally
maintain insurances in the joint names of the parties.
    Speculative Risks - eg ground conditions, weather,
inflation, material supplies, technical risks. These are
risks which offer the possibility of profit rather that
just loss to the contractor. Thus a skilful contractor

should be able to use this risk to his advantage. These risks are best dealt with by careful pre-contract planning and the production of clearly thought out method statements.

6 Principles of Risk Management

This is a relatively new aspect of construction management but it offers considerable potential to the construction industry. Traditional tendering procedures by contractors have concentrated on determining the cost, time and resources of a project. With Risk Management rather than pricing the cost of putting a nail into a wall the potential liability and associated probability of risk, of the task must be identified. Such an exercise might well identify possible risks such as, power cuts, damaged plaster, burst pipes or even death. It can be seen from these simplistic examples that the establishment of Health and Safety requirements for a safe system of working is merely a subset of risk management. The production of a successful method statement by a contractor may well depend on the conscious or subconscious application of risk management principles. It can be seen that if risk management is important to successful new build it may also be crucial to other building activities such as refurbishment.
The principles of risk management were summarised by Perry (1986) as follows:

    Identify risk sources
    Identify risk effects
    Identify risk probabilities
    Minimise risk

Of these the minimisation of risk is the approach which develops a risk reduction strategy. If the risk of winter building operations is considered, a risk reduction strategy would have three options:

    avoid risk, eg no winter building;
    carry risk, eg invest in winter building equipment;
    contract out risk, eg engage a subcontractor for all winter building activities thus transferring winter building risk to the subcontractor

In essence, the greater the risk borne by the contractor, the greater the required financial return by the contractor. For example, in the world of business, the lowest commercial return is that obtained on UK gilt edged stocks. Because of their certainty of income payment they are considered as risk free investments. Thus no construction project should have a yield which is

less than that obtainable from a gilt which will be
redeemed by the end of the contract period. However, as
most projects have risk, the return sought by a
contractor should be considerably in excess of that of
gilts. The establishment of a risk/return relationship
is a worthwhile exercise for all involved with the
construction process. The simple interpretation of this
is that the greater the contract risk the greater the
margin of safety in pricing the tender by the contractor.
Much useful work on risk return has been developed in
what is known as portfolio theory (Lumby, 1984).
Unfortunately, the competitive world of construction
contracts prevents contractors adopting risk return
theories when pricing contracts, thus competitive
contract bids expose contractors to an inadequate risk
return relationship. When this is allied to a capital
structure which is often under capitalised we see how
exposed the contractor is to a cash flow haemorrhage and
a possible liquidation.

7 Contract cost time relationship

The cumulative cost time relationship of a contract can
be represented by the contract S-curve, as shown in
figure 2. The vertical axis is cost and the horizontal
axis is time. The bottom of the S-curve starts at the

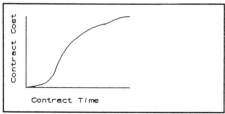

Figure 2 Contract S-curve

origin while the top of the S ends at the coordinates of
contract completion and contract sum. In bill of
quantities contracts, quantity surveyors have produced
these graphs from monthly measurement. In an effort to
reduce these monthly costs of measurement incurred by the
employer much work has been done on developing
mathematical functions to generate the S curve (eg.
Tucker,1988; Miskawi,1989). However, the concentration
on the determination of the S curve may be criticised
because:

    a A linear function in most cases would be a
    reasonable approximation of the cost time
    relationship. The error which will arise will be an

element of front end payment to the contractor thus reducing cash flow risk.
b   It does not tell us a great deal about contract risk.
c   It concentrates on the rate of payment rather than the range of likely values for contract sum and duration.

8 Determination of contract sum and duration based on uncertainty

A criticism of the fixed price building contracts is that their emphasis on contract sum and duration is too deterministic.   Construction projects are based on many activities.   Each of these activities will have a variety of risk factors yet traditional approaches to estimating tend to concentrate on a mechanistic determination of a specific value for activity cost, time and resources. From this, an overall project cost and duration can be obtained.   No wonder that if built on running sands the building may well fall down!
Perhaps as construction professionals we should look at the Uncertainty Principle of our physicist colleagues. In essence, Heisenberg the author of the Principle said that the deterministic model of the atom with a nucleus of so many positive protons with an equal number of negatively charged electrons orbiting the nucleus was misleading.   All that can be said is that the parts of the atom have probabilities for position and charge. Thus in physics measurements cannot be made with certainty.   If construction is viewed from the standpoint of uncertainty then it can be seen that project activities have a range of costs and durations. Thus when these activities are aggregated the resulting values for project cost and duration inevitably yield a frequency distribution giving expected rather than specific values for project cost and duration.
In order to arrive at these distributions the following procedure similar to that used by Bowers (1988) can be adopted:

a Determine project activities
b Determine project network in arrow diagram or precedence form
c For each activity produce the following matrix of activity cost time estimates.   It should be noted that three estimates should be obtained for each component. Although similar to the Project Evaluation Review Technique it is different.

Activity Cost Time Estimate Matrix

Activity	Optimistic	Likely	Pessimistic
Duration	Days	Days	Days
Variable Cost	£/day	£/day	£/Day
Fixed Cost	£	£	£

d. Using a computer simulation based on random values of these activity cost and time estimates, discrete frequency distributions for project cost and time can be produced. These distributions will probably be skewed and may even be bimodal.

Thus, by estimating possible values of activity cost, time and resources, the project cost and duration, can be predicted within confidence limits in terms of probabilities rather than unrealistic certainties. In addition, because cost is recognised as having fixed and variable characteristics, this technique assists with marginal analysis of projects. Similarly, a sensitivity analysis can be undertaken to determine those activities which cause the greatest change in either project cost or duration. However, the greatest potential in modelling project parameters lies with the application of Expert systems and in particular the representation of activity probabilities using fuzzy set theory (see Alty & Coombs,1984).

It may seem that this approach requires complicated computing. However, computer simulation of project parameters is much more straightforward than the computerised 3D visualisations or finite element analyses of structural and thermal performance which increasingly are becoming an accepted part of the design stage. Finally, it may be contended that computer simulation of the project parameters, apart from being easier to understand, are possibly far more cost effective than other types of design stage computer software.

9 Other methods to safeguard against project risk

Three other methods are possible to indemnify the employer against delivery of a project with unsatisfactory time, cost and quality parameters. These are:

Performance bonds
Professional Indemnity
Collateral Warranties

All of these are legalistic and based on deterministic
models of contract performance. The cost of these are
borne by the construction industry and thus ultimately
the consumer.

10 Conclusion

Construction projects are risk exercises involving the
management of uncertainty. They require considerable
manhours of organisational activity, decision making and
communication between an employer, designer and
contractor. The law of contract, rather than assisting
directly with this complex exercise, tends to offer the
promoter a basis for subsequent litigation in the event
of any default. As a consequence, it is argued, that
perhaps the current legalistic and often adversarial
framework existing between the promoter, designer and
contractor could be replaced by one which places emphasis
on ethics and uncertainty, rather than jurisprudence
based on certainty.

11 References

Alty & Coombs (1984) **Expert Systems Concepts & Examples**,
    NCC Publications, Manchester
Bowers J (1988) **Project Risk Analysis**, Paper to Institute
    of Mathematics and its Applications, Glasgow College
British Property Federation (1983) **Manual of the BPF
    System**
Burns C (1966) **Commercial Law of Scotland**, Hodge & Co,
    Edinburgh
Franks J, (1990) **Building Procurement Systems**, CIOB
Griffis FH, (1988) Case for Cost-Plus Contracting,
    Journal of Construction Engineering and Management,
    114, 83-94
Hildebrandt P, (1974) **Economic theory and the
    Construction Industry**, MacMillan
Horgan & Roulston,(1988) **Project Control** Spon, London
Jones GP, (1980) **A New Approach to the 1980 Standard Form
    of Building Contract**, The Construction Press,
    Lancaster
Lumby S, (1984) **Investment Appraisal**, Van Nostrad
    Reinhold, London
Miskawi Z, (1989) An S-curve equation for project control
    Construction Management and Economics, 7, 115-124
Perry, (1986) Dealing with risk in contracts, **Building
    Technology and Management**, April 1986
Sabbagh K, (1989) **Skyscraper the making of a building**,
    MacMillan, London
Tucker SN, (1988) A single alternative formula for
    Department of Health and Social Security S-curves

Construction Management and Economics, 6, 13-23

Constructability and the conceptual design

K.Th. Veenvliet and H.G. Wind
University of Twente, Civil Engineering for Technology and Management, Enschede,
The Netherlands

Abstract

Input to all project phases of both the ability to construct and the importance of construction, in particular
the conceptual design phase, is one of the factors which
leads to an optimal use of available knowledge, money, and
time, in respect of functionality, safety, durability (see
also Tatum, 1985). In order to be able to integrate
constructability in the design phase the present management
methods often fall short. Usually selection of alternatives
is based upon decision methods and decision techniques like
'rating and weighting' method, 'datum' method (Pugh,S.) ,
etc. The shortcoming of these methods is that
constructability is but one of many selection criteria and
allows constructability only partially to take into
account. The use of grouped criteria such as is the case
for the s-diagram, Kesselrings method, seems more appropriate for this aim.
In this paper an analysis is made of the proposed theoretical concepts and a study is presented of the conceptual
design process of seven large civil engineering construction designs. Particular attention is paid to the suitability of the proposed selection methods in design management,
as far as constructability is concerned. It is found that
in the conceptual design phase four steps can be envisaged:
selection of alternative designs, selection of feasible
designs, selection of promising designs, preparation of
conceptual designs. The decision methods applied in the
first three steps are rather simple. In the investigated
projects, constructability was assured, because of the
design and construct approach.
Keywords: Constructability, Conceptual design, Decision
methods, Decision techniques.

1 Introduction

In the (conceptual) design process of buildings and
structures use is made of various sources of information.
One of these sources is constructability. Jortberg (1984)

describes constructablity as 'construction knowledge and experience in planning, engineering, procurement and field operations'. This definition contains a management aspect and a constructive aspect. The management aspect deals with topics as project plan, major construction methods, lay-out of the site, logistic problems, entrances to the site etc. The constructive aspect is related to mechanical and material aspects of building. In a (conceptual) design process both management and constructive elements are important. This importance is highlighted in the study of Tatum(1985), where he finds that introduction of constructability in all phases of the design will lead to optimal use of available knowledge, money and time in respect of functionality, safety and durability.

In order to be able to achieve such high standing objectives, designers have various methods at hand. First, there are a series of management guidelines as outlined in Tatum(1985) to assure constructability input. Second, a wide range of decision methods, for instance the 'rating and weighting' method and the 'datum' method, is available for the designer to support the decisions he continuously has to make. A shortcoming of these methods in projects where constructability is a major issue, is that constructability is only one of many selected criteria and allows only partially to take constructability into account. In chapter two of this paper this topic is taken up again.

In 1990 a unique opportunity was offered to study the use of selection methods and the input of constructability in civil engineering design. The Minister of Public Works of the Netherlands invited five contractors to develop a competitive design and give a price for a storm surge barrier near the port of Rotterdam.

As one of the contractors presented two designs and the Public Works Department developed a 'shadow design'. A total of seven conceptual designs were presented.
In this paper an investigation is presented of the selection methods used by the various design teams. In chapter two an outline of these methods is given. In chapter three the storm surge barrier project is presented. The steps in the design process and the selection methods of the seven design teams are presented in chapter four, with particular emphasis on the input of constructability. Finally some aspects of the selection of the 'most suitable' design are given in chapter five and the paper ends with a discussion. This study confirms the statement that in order to realize the opportunities for constructability improvement, owners must insist on it and contractors must compete on it.

2 Theoretical framework

In the design process continuously decisions have to be taken. In 2.1 the steps in such a decision procedure are briefly recalled. A key issue in the design process are criteria and their rating scales. This topic is treated in 2.2. A birds eye view of decision methods in the design process is given in 2.3, followed in 2.4 by a discussion on the input of constructability in the decision methods discussed before.

2.1 Strategy of the evaluation of alternative designs
The importance of a structural description of the selection of 'the most suitable' design, in particular for complex problems is pointed out by various authors, e.g. de Boer(1989). He describes the following seven-step pattern to evaluate 'few-alternatives'.

0 Include 'ideal' and/or reference alternative(s) if needed;
1 Establish criteria, including their rating scales.
2 Establish weighting factor per criterion;
3 Determine the decision rule that will be followed;
4 Determine scores per criterion and total scores;
5 Examine the (sub-)scores of the alternatives;
6 Decide on one alternative (based on the decision rule).

In literature several selection techniques are prescribed for each phase except for phase 0 and 6 and are summarized in the appendix A.

2.2 Criteria for the evaluation of alternative designs
Application of the selection techniques mentioned in 2.1 to the conceptual design phase implies that both quantitative and qualitative criteria are required. Pahl & Beitz (1986) give a list of aspects, which are suitable to formulate criteria with accents on 'operation' and 'realization'. Table 2.1 shows these aspects and accents:

Aspect	Accent	
	'operation'	'realization'
1 Functional	x	
2 Effective	x	
3 Compilation	x	x
4 Safety	x	
5 Shape	x	
6 Manufacture		x
7 Control		x
8 Assembly		x
9 Transport		x
10 Use	x	
11 Maintenance	x	
12 Recycling	x	
13 Expenses	x	x

Table 2.1: Design criteria following Phal & Beitz(1986)

147

The criteria should be evenly distributed over 'operational' and 'realizational' accents. This grouping of criteria allows for highlighting constructability and, what is more important, improvement of constructability during the design process. If grouping is not applied, constructability is but one of the criteria and can easily be underrated. It is important to define not less than 8 and not more than 15 criteria based on the constructability concept in the conceptual design phase (Phal & Beitz(1986)). Each criterion should have the same importance and should be qualitative. The suggested rating scale should be from 0 to 4. The use of weighting factors in the conceptual design phase appears to be of little use.

The procedure outlined above seems to be rather straight forward, however the application of this procedure to the alternative designs revealed some drawbacks. In the discussion this point will be taken up.

2.3 Evaluation of alternatives

Decision methods and techniques based on grouped criteria, like the s-diagram (VDI 2225), are suitable to help recognition and consideration of constructability as an important means to achieve project objectives on evaluating concepts and alternatives for the conceptual design-phase. Each alternative is evaluated in two aspects. First, weak spots in the design are searched for by evaluating the subscores per group and per criterium. Second, each alternative is evaluated by comparing each group of criteria with the maximum score (the 'ideal concept'). In the following both methods of evaluation are briefly commented.

A well balanced valuable profile in respect to both 'operation' and 'realization' criteria is very important, especially in the conceptual design-phase. A concept with a high value score but with an unbalanced profile will be treacherous during the detailed design-phase. During the conceptual design phase it is often less risky to choose a concept with a less higher value but with a well balanced valuable profile.

The s-diagram is suitable to evaluate alternatives on grouped criteria. The technique is based on subscores per group of criteria. The subscores are displayed in a two-dimensional diagram, in which realization and operation obtain equal attention. The original s-diagram (by Kesselring) deals with 'technical' and 'economic' criteria. The technique is quickly to learn, easy to apply and appropriate for complex problems. When more than two main groups of criteria can be distinguished one can prepare an s-diagram for all combinations of two groups. It provides a useful way to visualizing the total scores per group of criteria.

The total scores for each alternative can be obtained for instance as follow's:

$W=\sqrt{W_1*W_2}$ (hyperbolical)   or,
$W=(W_1+W_2)/2$ (linear)
(W_1='realization'-value; W_2='operation'-value)

To decide on a more balanced alternative or concept, the hyperbolical decision rule is more appropriate.

2.4 Introduction of constructability in the design process

All the decision methods presume that constructability is introduced in the design process. However realisation of this objective is far from simple. Tatum (1985) has found at least three key constructability issues:1) the project plan,2) the site layout, and 3) major construction methods. Each of the three issues indicate important opportunities for meeting project objectives through improved constructability.

Introduction of constructability in the design-process, in particular the conceptual phase, requires several management actions (Tatum, 1985):

1) establishing a program(formal or informal);
2) identifying important issues and studies to focus activities;
3) completing necessary pre-construction planning;
4) building an interface with design;
5) reviewing the results;
6) resolving conflicts.

Tatum clearly points to both project management and to mechanical and constructive knowledge and experience as important aspects of constructability. The approach of Tatum and the suggestions of Pahl & Beitz link together on the point of application of grouped criteria as outlined above.

3 The storm surge barrier project

In this chapter a brief outline of the storm surge barrier near Rotterdam in the Netherlands will be given. The presentation of the selection methods and the role of constructability in the designs teams is presented in chapter 4.

3.1 The storm surge barrier: an innovative approach

As part of the protection of the surroundings near Rotterdam against a storm surge set-up, the Ministry of Public Works (RWS) in the Netherlands started in 1987 an extensive study on the construction of a storm surge barrier near the river mouth of the Nieuwe Waterweg shown in Figure 3.1.

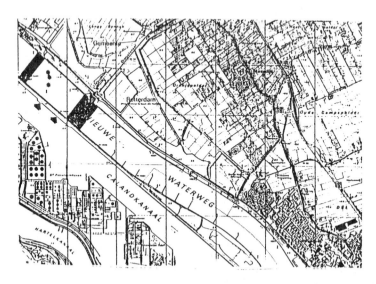

Figure 3.1: Position of the storm surge barrier.

The aim of the study was to find an alternative for the reinforcement and raising of the 354 km of river-embankments in respect of building costs, construction period and environmental consequences. In the summer of 1987, the Ministry of Public Works invited, by way of a competition procedure (design and construct), five consortia of contractors to submit a conceptual design for this storm surge barrier. The objective of the client was to obtain an innovative design for the lowest costs, in respect of functionality, reliability, safety and durability. To reach this objective the client selected design and construct as the contractual approach for this project.

As part of this design the design loads, ballasting system, probabilistic design and quality assurance had to be worked out. One of the design conditions was that the probability of structural collapse of the barrier had to be less than 1/1,000,000 in any one year. The plans had to be completed in a period of three month.

After that period a selection process into three phases followed over a period of 2 years. During this period the owner had to make a selection out of six concepts submitted by five consortia. To support the selection process the

Ministry also prepared a conceptual design. Figure 3.2a shows the clients concept and figure 3.2b the concept chosen out of six alternatives.

Figure 3.2a

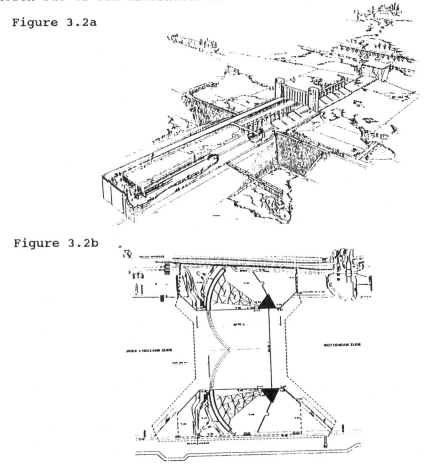

Figure 3.2b

Figure 3.2: Two conceptual designs for the storm surge barrier.

The design criteria, as formulated by the client, are presented in paragraph 3.2.

3.2 Design criteria presented by the client

The client formulated technical and financial criteria for the design of the storm surge barrier.
The main design topics are summarized in Table 3.1.

Aspect	Accent 'operation'	'realization'
1. Functional	x	x
2. Flexibility	x	
3. Constructability		x
4. Vulnerability	x	x
5. Quality control		x
6. Maintenance	x	
7. Disruptions for the shipping	x	x
8. Price		x
9. Price risk		x
10. Maintenance costs	x	
11. Operational costs	x	
12. Cost during construction		x

Table 3.1: Criteria of the client for selection of conceptual design

The selection criteria in Table 3.1 are quite similar to the list in chapter 2 mentioned by Pahl & Bietz. On some points, where needed, a further stipulation of the criteria and priorities was carried out during the execution of the project.

4 Selection methods and constructability in the storm surge barrier project

The investigation presented in this paper is aimed at the role of constructability in the conceptual design phase. As has been shown in chapter two, this role can to some extent be related to the selection methods and criteria used by the design teams. Information on these items was obtained by interviews and from reports produced by the design teams. The six teams, including the team of the client, have presented seven designs, hence one team produced two designs. All teams but one, were available for interviews. The resulting information on selection methods and criteria in the conceptual design phase will be presented in the following paragraphs.

4.1 Steps within the conceptual design phase

An analysis of the conceptual design phase, based upon interviews and reports, revealed more or less the same steps for all teams. These steps were:

a: selection of alternative designs
b: selection of feasible designs
c: selection of promising designs
d: preparation of the conceptual design

This implies that, although the time was very limited, the design teams went four times through a selection cycle, starting from a wide range of concepts and ending up with one or two promising conceptual designs. Alternative designs included all designs which could lead to the required objectives of the client. Feasible designs were those alternative designs which were feasible as far the constructive capability and capacity of the consortium was concerned. Competitiveness of the designs was particular important in the selection of promising designs. As shown in Figure 4.1., the uncertainty in the design reduced during each step.

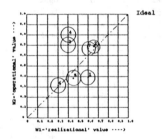

Step 1
many alternative designs;
large uncertainty

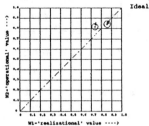

Step 2
a few feasible designs;
reduced uncertainty

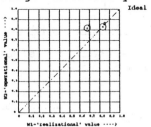

Step 3
promising designs;
reduced uncertainty

Step 4
conceptual design;
reduced uncertainty

Fig. 4.1 : steps in the conceptual design phase

4.2 Methods and criteria used for selection of feasible designs

Each of the design teams generated in the order of ten to twenty alternative designs (see Table 4.2). These designs resulted from past experience and innovative ideas. Selection criteria were hardly used in this first stage of the conceptual design process.

The feasible designs were selected from the set of alternative designs. Information on the decision rules and the weighing factors is shown in Table 4.3. From this table can also be seen that all teams used a more or less similar approach. Selection of feasible designs took place based upon the maximum score. The scores were determined intuitively and the method applied was 1a: grouping.

Decision methods and techniques

De-sign team	Number of alternatives	Establish criteria	Number of criteria	Establish weighting factors	Range of weighting factors	Determine decision rule	Determine scores	Examine scores	Number of feasible designs
A	20	1a: Grouping	3 groups Total 12	2b: Equal	-	3a: Max. score	4a: Intuitive	5g: Weak spots	3
B	16	1a: Grouping	4 groups Total 22	2b: Equal	-	3a: Max. score	4a: Intuitive	5g: Weak spots	3
C	9						4a: Intuitive	Weak spots Strong spots	3
D	15	1a: Grouping	6 groups				4a: Intuitive	Weak spots Strong spots	3
E	1							Weak spots Strong spots	1
F	29	1a: Grouping	7 groups Total 32	2b: Equal	-	3a: Max. score	4a: Intuitive	5g: Weak spots	8

Table 4.2: Methods and criteria used for selection
of feasible designs.

From a comparison of the feasible designs follows that, although the teams used the same criteria of the client, the outcome was rather different. This was partly due to the knowledge and experience of the design teams and partly due to the liberty for innovative designs which was possible within the posed criteria. For the question, whether at this stage the competition in fact already was decided, is referred to the discussion.

4.3 Methods and criteria used for selection of promising designs

In the third selection round promising designs were selected out of the feasible designs. These promising designs were expected to be competitive and formed the bases for the preparation of the final conceptual design. The decision rules, the criteria and the weighting factors applied by the various teams are summarized in Table 4.3:

Decision methods and techniques

Design team	Number of feasible designs	Establish criteria	Number of criteria	Establish weighting factors	Range of weighting factors	Determine decision rule	Determine scores	Examine scores	Promising designs
A	3	1e: Rating	21	2c: Pairwise	1 - 14	3a: Max. score	Multi-crit.	5a: Relative Weak spots	2
B	3					3e: Min. cost		5g: Weak spots	1
C	3 -> 7	1e: Rating score 1-10	12	2c: Pairwise	1 - 11	3a: Max. score	Multi-criteria	5g: Weak spots	1
D	3					score/ costs		Weak spots Strong spots	1
F	8	1a: Grouping Score 1-5	6 groups Total 32	2c: Pairwise	2 - 6	3a: Max. score	4a: Intuitive	5g: Weak spots	1

Table 4.3: Methods and criteria used for selection of promising designs

In contrast to the first selection round, several teams applied in the second round somewhat more advanced decision methods. Some teams applied for instance multi-criteria analysis to determine the scores. Clearly the type of information in the conceptual design phase does not warrant the application of some of the advanced selection procedures outlined in the appendix A. Table 4.3 shows the use of a relatively great number of criteria and a wide range of weighting factors. In 2.2 Phal & Beitz stipulated that it has no use to take more than 15 criteria and a wide range of weighting factors.

4.4 Preparation of the conceptual designs

In preparation of the conceptual designs, more advanced selection methods will be used. Information on this step will be accomplished separately

4.5 Constructability in the conceptual design

In the design and construct approach, the option of constructability input in the conceptual design is guaranteed. The constructive capability and capacity in the design team was a determining factor in the selection of feasible designs.

The importance of the constructability input varies from team to team. Team A made a more or less systematic grouping of criteria on constructability aspects into 'operational' and 'realizational' criteria. The other design teams used constructability aspects implicitly in their list of criteria. Interviews with members of the different design teams learned that construction input was more or less implemented in all stages of the design process and most strong in team A.

5 Kesselrings method and constructability

Constructability was felt very important by all teams, but rarely selection methods were applied, which properly accounted for constructability. More appropriate methods such as the Kesselring method were not applied. In order to highlight the use of constructability in the Kesselring method, this method will be applied to the selection of the 'most suitable' design. In the storm surge project the selection of the 'most suitable' design took more than one year and included a very careful and detailed analysis of all the designs. Such a procedure can be supported but not be replaced by any selection method including the Kesselring method. As the objective of this paragraph is only to demonstrate the Kesselring method, all weighting factors for the selection criteria have been set to unity and the conceptual designs of the design teams A through F have been numbered at random from one through seven.

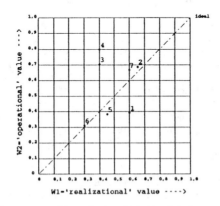

Figure 5.1: Conceptual designs of the storm surge barrier.

It follows from figure 5.1 that all conceptual designs ended up in the upper part of the Kesselring diagram. The differences between the designs result in the distribution of points in Figure 5.1. For a more realistic analysis of the conceptual designs again the Kesselring method can be applied, but then the real weights instead of unit weights should be applied.

5.1 Remark on the selection of the 'most suitable' design
It follows from table 4.3, that different selection methods are used. The 'seven-step' approach of De Boer completed with the work of Pahl & Beitz seems to be a rather straight forward method. Comparison of promising concepts could be based on the method just mentioned. The client could prescribe this method, not as a restriction of the room for innovative design, but to accomplish all the design concepts. The client should know that the selected 'most suitable' design still comprehends a certain extent of uncertainty.

6 Summary and conclusions

Constructability is one of the important sources of information available to designers. Tatum (1985) points to both project management and to mechanical and constructive knowledge and experience as important aspects of constructability. The link between the approach of Tatum and the suggestions of Pahl & Beitz (1986) is on the point of application of grouped criteria. The opportunity of constructability input in the conceptual design is strongly available in a design and construct approach.

An analysis of the conceptual design phase, revealed more or less the same steps for all teams. These steps were: selection of alternative designs; selection of feasible designs; selection of promising designs; preparation of the conceptual design. This implies that, although the time was very limited, the design teams went through a design spiral, starting from a wide range of concepts and ending up with one or two promising conceptual designs. In the second design cycle the feasible designs were obtained. All teams used a more or less similar approach. The selection were based upon the maximum score. The scores were determined intuitively and the method applied was grouping. In the third design cycle somewhat more advanced selection methods were applied. Some teams used for instance multi-criteria analysis to determine the scores. Clearly the type of information in the first three steps of the conceptual design phase does not warrant the application of some of the advanced selection procedures outlined in the appendix A.

A design and construct contract demands of the contractor to provide a structure for a fixed price with a prescribed performance. If the structure does not behave as expected and leads to small impacts with a high probability, simple arrangements can be made. Even high financial impacts with a small probability can be insured. However as soon as societal impacts with a small probability become immanent, this may touch at the responsibility of a government agency. This becomes even more clear if it is realized that small risks do not necessarily imply small uncertainties of these small risks. This makes clear the difficult position a government agency holds in a design and construct approach, where these large impacts with small probability are at stake.

The 'seven-step approach' of the Boer completed with the work of Pahl & Beitz in 2.2 seems to be rather straight forward. However application of the procedure to a set alternative designs revealed some difficulties. The method requires a well defined rating method for criteria such as functionality, safety and durability. Furthermore does the selection require that a trade-off can be made between the ratings of these different criteria. For non-monetary units this appears to be rather time consuming and only some support is found in the scientific literature. This comment places a question mark near the possibility to define ratings and weighting factors before hand, reducing the selection of the most suitable design to mere arithmetics. An additional disadvantage of such an approach is that the room for innovative designs will considerably be reduced, compared with the approach taken for the storm surge barrier.

7 References

De Boer, S.J. (1989) **Decision methods and techniques in methodical engineering design.** Thesis presented to University of Twente(Enschede, the Netherlands) at the Laboratory for Engineering Design in the Department of Mechanical Engineering,in partial fulfilment of the requirements for the degree of Doctor of Science.

Pahl, G. & Beitz, W. (1986) **Konstruktionslehre.** Springer-Verlag,1986.

Pugh, S. (1981) **Concept selection - a method that works.** Proceedings ICED 81(Rome 1981),Zuerich,Heurista,1981,p.497-506.

Sriram, D. .e.a. (1989) **Knowledge-Based system applications in engineering design:Research at MIT.** Research in Progress,Fall 1989,p.79-95.

Tatum, C.B., e.a. (1985) **Constructability improvement during conceptual planning.** Technical Report No.290, Department of civil engineering, Stanford University.

8 Appendix A

Results found by De Boer(1989): research on decision methods and techniques:

phase number and name technique number and name	tested	easy to apply	easy to learn	complex prob- lems
1.establish criteria				
1a grouping criteria	yes	+ +	+ +	+
1b objectives tree	yes	o	o	+ +
1c determine value functions	no	-	+	o
1d determining parameters	no	o	+	o
1e rating scales	yes	+ +	+ +	+ +
1f monetary terms	no	o	o	o
1g types of requirements	yes	+ +	+ +	+
1h reducing number of criteria	no	+	+	o
1i checklists	yes	+ +	+ +	+ +
2.establish weighting factors				
2a intuitive weighting factors	yes	+ +	+ +	-
2b groups of equal importance	yes	+	+	+
2c pair-wise comparison	yes	+	+	o
2d weighting factors in root structure	yes	+ +	--	+ +
3.determine decision rule				
3a maximum total score	yes	+ +	+ +	+
3b highest combined score	no	+ +	+ +	+ +
3c closest to ideal	no	o	+	+
3d profitability	no	o	o	o
3e minimum cost	no	+ +	+	o
3f majority rule	no	+ +	+ +	o
3g lexicographic ranking	no	+ +	+ +	--
4.determine scores				
4a intuitive scoring	no	+	o	o
4b evaluation against reference alternative	no	+	+	o
4c apply value functions	no	-	+	o
4d using parameters	no	o	+	o
4e dual comparison	no	o	+	-
4f costs-benefits	no	--	-	o
5.examine scores				
5a relative scores	yes	+ +	+ +	+
5b s-diagram	no	+ +	+ +	+
5c bar charts	no	+	+ +	-
5d pie chart	no	-	+	-
5e value profiles	no	o	+	-
5f estimating uncertainties	no	o	+	+
5g weak spots	no	+	o	+
5h differentiation	no	+ +	+	+
5i harris profile	no	+	+	+

Legend: -- : poor; - : moderate; o : fair; + : good; + + : very good.

Design and build – the role of a project manager

M.A. Cairney
E.C. Harris Project Management, London, UK

1 Introduction

Under the Design and Build form of JCT Contract there are three named parties – the "Client" – the "Contractor" and the "Employer's Agent". The key role of the Employer's Agent is to look after and protect the interests of the Client. Where in-house expertise might be lacking a professional adviser is a worthwhile investment to carry out this role.

The Employer's Agent needs to be sufficiently informed and knowledgeable to be able to rationalise the Client decision making process from outset to conclusion of the Project. He must administer the Contract and maintain both financial and programme control on the scheme as a whole. The extent of this service and responsibility tends to increase greatly as a Project increases in value – it is not as involved on a £2m simple warehouse on a greenfield site as it is on a £40million Headquarters complex for an owner occupier Client.

The key to the success of an Employer's Agent under a Design Build Contract can be summed up under three key issues:-

Trust between the Client and the Employer's Agent.
The generation of a Team spirit involving all parties with the Client's satisfaction in the finished product being the uppermost priority.
The clear understanding by all parties of the Contractor's proposals and up front decision making by the Client.

2 Management Structures

The priorities and need for Professional Advisers varies with the size and scope of Project if the Client's interests are to be realistically protected. Core to all of these management structures is the Client and his Employer's Agent. The Employer's Agent tends to be very much the central point of contact between the Contractor and the Client and therefore his role tends to be one of Project Facilitator. The professional training of a Project Manager might be from any actual discipline however he has to be able to deal with the Client, the whole Design Team and the Contractor. This therefore makes a Project Manager a strong candidate for the Employer's Agent Role.

Following on are four diagrams illustrating management structures worth consideration in a Design Build Contract scenario.

2.1 Diagram 1

Diagram 1 illustrates a typical management structure which might be employed on a simple small scale Project where only a superficial amount of change is likely to occur during the contract period. The cost advice can be limited to an overview at tender stage. It is suitable for Projects where the selected Contractor and his solution are established and schedule of payments calculated based on achievement of programme. This avoids the need for detailed valuations of the work.

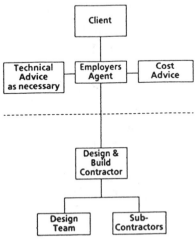

2.2 Diagram 2

This illustrates a structure applicable perhaps to a medium size Project with a higher level of Client intervention in the detailed issue and a need to influence matters throughout the construction process. Under such circumstances a more comprehensive advisory team is recommended. This will probably generate the need for more detailed cost advice and technical overview from specialist advisers related to complex issues of the Project in hand (eg. acoustic concerns, M&E concerns).

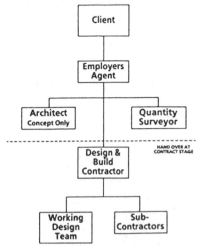

2.3 Diagram 3

Diagram 3 indicates an increasingly popular approach whereby the Design Team is employed in phases, directly by the Client in the concept stages perhaps including the obtaining of a Planning Permission. The Design Team's appointment is then novated or suspended during the Construction Phase and the Contractor establishes a direct appointment. This arrangement tends to ensure a better continuity of Design intent and clearly establishes that responsibility for the "Design" is not split between differing Professional advisors.

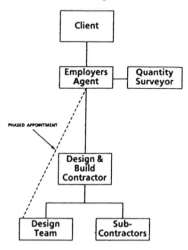

2.4 Diagram 4

Diagram 4 indicates adding to the Team further to afford a full audit capability to the Client independent of the Contractors design team. These advisers would be employed in the supervision of the scheme, to overview and comment in a technical manner on the detailed design and perhaps to provide a full site presence. This management structure would be recommended to a larger scheme to ensure that the quality and standard of the completed product conforms to the Employer's requirements at all times.

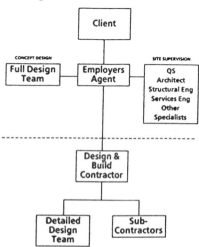

3 Employers Requirements

3.1 Format and Content

It is no secret that the key to Client's satisfaction in a design and build scenario relies on the Employers Requirements being accurately presented with no ambiguity. When preparing an Employer's Requirement document it is vital that the areas of key concern to the Client from a functional, a cost effective and an aesthetic viewpoint are properly quizzed and included.

Dependent upon the size and complexity of the Project in hand the Employer's Agent often needs to consult with specialist advisers and other consultants to establish the Employer's Requirement. This must be in a format that contains adequate specification criteria for the design and build team to produce a scheme that satisfies the Employer's needs.

When preparing the Employers Requirements the level and detail of information to be made available as the brief for the Design/Build Contract will vary. This might be a full working consultancy team preparing a concept scheme inclusive of all planning permissions which is handed to the Contractor for pricing and ultimate detailed design or a brief performance specification possibly related to a basic outline planning application.

3.2 Client Input

When debriefing a Client in order to prepare the Employer's Requirement document it is most important for the compiler to properly understand the Client's level of technical knowledge in respect of buildings. A full understanding of any standards that he currently employs must be reached which, in some ways, may be more onerous than industry norm. Due consideration has be given to any specialised facilities and their knock on effects (eg. kitchens or specialised manufacturing processes) and any strong views particularly in respect of image also needs to be quizzed and incorporated.

Often, if a Client is entering into an exercise for the first time for instance, effort will be needed to educate the Employer in options available and modern architectural solutions. When putting together the Employer's Requirement document it is all too easy to not fully consider the ultimate user or educate the Client sufficiently to ensure that there are no surprises when the Project is concluded.

3.3 The Concept Design Team

It might be appropriate on a project to appoint a complete design team to consider the concept design alongside the Client before the Contractors involvement. This is particularly relevant on the larger schemes which might warrant detailed or protracted planning applications to be carried out. The Client might also be very keen to visualise in considerable detail what it is he is asking the Contractors to price.

In these situations a traditional design team management approach can be adopted inclusive of a Quantity Surveyor who will produce estimates of cost. The detailed Employers Requirements are then formalised to sufficient detail to seek the Client's sign off prior to involving a Contractor.

With an agreed scheme in place the Project can be tendered to design build Contractors with design responsibilities very much restricted to the detailed elements. Alternatively the pre-selection of a Contractor can be undertaken and a negotiation carried out with regard to price.

There is an increasing popularity in novation and the passing over of the Design Team, particularly the Architect, as part of the enquiry. The Contractor should always be given due opportunity to raise objections, but this has a number of advantages. It includes the guaranteed continuity of Client Brief interpretation, clarity in respect of design warranties and the ability to influence and pre-agree site supervision levels as part of the Design Team fee structure.

4 Contractors Proposal Document

4.1 The Process

A most important and fundamental aspect of the Employer's Agent role is to check the contractor's proposal documentation against the Employer's Requirements once the price and details become known. If the scheme has been worked up in some detail by a full Design Team then it is usual to get what is in effect the Employer's Requirement document adopted lock, stock and barrel by the Contractor as a part of his Proposals. If the drawings and details prepared to act as the Employer's requirements are known to satisfy the needs of the Client, this obviously makes the process more straightforward.

However, if Contractors are to be given room for finding the most cost effective solution, the Employer's Requirement Document and appraisal process must be flexible enough to allow design development to take place during the pricing exercise. All such changes need to be carefully identified, audited and cleared with the Client as part of the checking of the Contractor's Proposals.

Other aspects which need to be considered during the appraisal of the Contractor's proposals is conformity with the Contract conditions, satisfaction with any proposed Collateral Warranties and a through check carried out to ensure that any provisional sums, provisional material selections or exclusions are identified and considered. Always a balance needs to be borne in mind during these exercises which acknowledges the commercial intent of the builder and is mindful to offer sufficient flexibility to allow him to engineer and develop the design, however, all parties must be very clear as to the quality and quantity that is contained in the offer.

Not yet tested in the Courts is the unwritten assumption the Employer's Agent must be mindful of - the Contractors proposals will probably take precedence over the Employer's requirements where these conflict. This again indicates the importance of checking these thoroughly. At the end of the day the key responsibility of the Employer's Agent is to ensure that the Client's ambitions and requirements are properly met and ultimately achieved.

The size, complexity and nature of the Project to hand will define the extent and depth of consideration to be given to the Contractor's Proposals. The more complicated or bespoke the scheme to a Client's particular needs and more important it will be to have independent professional advice to be satisfied the offer of the Contractor is appropriate. Late changes often prove far more difficult and expensive in this form of contract and any clarification or changes that are identified prior to it placing are likely to be more favourably priced.

If a competitive tender has been conducted then a series of in-depth technical interviews should be carried out with each of the Contractors and their Design Team. These should aim to identify any key differences in the alternate schemes particularly in quality or quantity.

Having identified the differences and considered them with the Client, it can be advantageous to carry out a balancing process between the competitors. Ask the question what the changes to their tender figure would be by adding or omitting elements identified as of different quality or quantity. After such an exercise one can expect to end up with a number of schemes that are technically similar and which represent the same functional facility. The only criteria for selection will then be the price and subjective issues; who the team feel the best Contractor for the job is and the Architecture.

When adjudicating on Contractors Proposals it is most important that the Contractor and the personalities are carefully considered alongside the scheme proposals and the price. Success on a design build contract relies very heavily on an open team approach by all parties and the avoidance of contractural stand off.

One further issue which shouldn't be ignored during the consideration of Contractors proposals is the question of running costs of the completed facility and, where appropriate, life cycle costing analysis. Some times the cheap option can prove to be much more expensive in the long run.

5   Contractor Control

Once the contract is let the role of an employers agent should become relatively straightforward. This assumes that all of the systems are properly put in place and the checks accurately carried out during the formation of the Employer's Requirements and the checking of the Contractor's Proposals. If the Project is set up properly at the beginning and all parties understand what is intended, then the administration, monitoring and control of these functions becomes fairly automatic.

It is vital that all documentation is in place on day one of the contract and the most important of these is the Contract itself. If the procedure for checking the Contractor's Proposals runs smoothly then in parallel the contract documentation can be prepared. Signature will avoid letters of intent brought about through pressure of programme. With the contract documentation there should be a comprehensive set of the Contractors Proposals attached for the avoidance of doubt.

Other matters to be included in the contract documentation is a detailed variation procedure, the forms of warranty, all legal requirements, copies of planning permissions obtained and all documentation in existence in respect of statutory authorities.

A feature of the Employer's Requirement document should be clear directive of the level of information required in order to satisfy the Employer's Agent of the programme logic and the information needed to monitor site progress. With the most comprehensive Employer's Requirements set down there is likely to be Client decisions wanted at various stages through at the contract. These need to be clearly understood and adhered to.

The Contractor will wish to retain the facility for change during the design development process and is likely to come forward with some proposals for change to the base specification after the Contract is let. The Employer's Agent will need to discuss and consider any such proposals with the Client to ensure that there is no reduction in the value for money achieved. Procedures should be clearly laid out for the Contractor to follow in order to highlight any such change proposals and for the subsequent adoption or rejection of them.

Whilst the Project is on site, regular monitoring of quality forms a central feature of an Employers Agent role. Necessary off-site manufacturing processes should be monitored and the Contractor's Professional Team should regularly be asked if they are satisfied with the quality being achieved. Regardless of the management structure the Employer's Agent should always insist at the end of a job that "the Architect" write a letter, (preferably direct but via the Contractor as a minimum) stating that in his professional view the building is in a state of practical completion sufficient to allow occupation and use. Within that letter also seek a statement on the overall quality achieved on site should be included.

As the building comes up towards completion a regime of handover sessions should be established to ensure the following:

That aesthetic, quality and quantity checks are undertaken and schedules of corrective action formulated and ticked off.
That detailed commissioning of the building particularly from a Mechanical and Electrical viewpoint is carefully monitored and recorded.

That the personnel who are to take over the building are properly educated in it's running and servicing needs. Detailed cleaning procedures, maintenance procedures and operational drawings, hand- books and information must be brought together at this stage.

It is a key responsibility of the Employer's Agent to ensure that these matters are properly covered.

During the course of the works the Employer's Agent will act as the central administrator between the Employer and the Contractor. This will involve the organisation and running of regular site meetings to ensure good communication and decision making. The Employer's Agent will formulate a comprehensive record of the scheme throughout it's life, he will process the valuation/payment function and generally act as the single point of reference for all parties. It is normal for the Employers Agent to report to the Client and he may also be required to supply information to other interested parties such as a Financial House or a Letting Agent.

6 Summary

The Employer's Agent has to make his first priority the translation of a Client's needs and ambitions into an efficient and functional facility. His remit, without doubt, must always be in the Client's interest. This position needs to be filled by somebody with a background knowledge of the building process, coupled with realistic management skills in discussing and resolving the questions and issues as they arise. Therefore, the position of a Employer's Agent on a design and build project is logically fulfileed by a Project Manager.
Inevitably, there are calls for some changes during the course of the contract period and the Employer's Agent has to be adept and even handed in negotiations with the Contractor during the Variation process. The Employer's agent should be flexible and open minded to the Contractors underlying desire to achieve programme and find the most cost effective way of fulfilling the Contractors Proposals. This emphasises the need to ensure that the quality and quantity required is fully defined in the Employer's Requirements and then into the Contractor's Proposals. My belief is that a Project Manager is ideally suited to the Employer's Agent role provided he has the right attitude to problem solving, understands the spirit of a design build contract and has sufficient background knowledge to offer balanced advice to the Client.
I would add, however, that a Project Manager can come from any professional background. It is the interpersonnel skills coupled with technical knowledge which is all important in these situations.

Note:

The views expressed in this paper are those of Michael Cairney, they are not necessarily those held by E C Harris as a Group.

CHAPTER FOUR

'There is a dearth of even the most elementary management techniques by those who own and run buildings. There are no adequate records, budgetary controls or estimation procedures. Some basic facts are unobtainable; other important pieces of information came, relatively easily, from quite unexpected sources. It is certain that no industry, owning capital equipment of similar cost to these buildings, could survive unless it had more data on its performance.'

T. A. Markus, et al.

Specification writing for preservation and maintenance works

D. Bosia
Dipartimento di Progettazione Architettonica, Politecnico di Torino, Torino, Italy
A. Ciribini
Dipartimento di Ingegneria dei Sistemi Edilizi e Territoriali, Politecnico di Milano, Milano, Italy

Abstract
This paper considers specification writing for preservation, rehabilitation and maintenance works from an exclusively methodological viewpoint.
Such a specification therefore is a vital document for introducing quality assured products and services into worksites and represents a means for communicating information between designers and contractors who often share the overall responsibility for specifications in a building project process.
The paper aims at proposing a methodological approach to this matter with regards to its technical section; part of the total documentation normally required to describe the rehabilitation work.
Contractor estimators, quantity surveyors, clerks of works and site agents must be offered a standard method of specifying for preservation and maintenance works, to avoid inadequacies and misunderstandings.
Providing a 'standard library' or selecting descriptive rather than performance specifications is for istance difficult, given the great variety of existing buildings. Investigating the relationship between technical drawings and technical specifications is also very useful.
Keywords: Quality Management for Rehabilitation Design, Technical Specifications, Preservation and Maintenance Works.

1   Introduction

The procedural and technical specifying phase is the most critical moment in a building rehabilitation project process, where role division (except for Design and Build procurement for instance) eliminates the need for an organic decision making centre to define not only materials and workmanship but also the exact analysis, diagnosis or conservation methodology or, better, the choice of equally proven surveying or conservation methods.

In traditional procurement situation, a specification is in fact the essential link for transmitting project documentation, graphic and alphanumerical data (which in turn translate into Client and
hopefully End User needs and requirements) to the Contractors responsible for execution of the work.

In this framework, the rather linear and sequential stages of a conventional building process model add to the more repetitive and interactive phases of the quality management model divided into: 1. briefing (including procurement); 2. designing; 3. specifying; 4. tendering; 5. constructing; 6. maintaining (including management) (Maggi, 1989; Cornick, 1991).

The specification therefore becomes the tool for setting the procedures and timing of control activity requested by the Client, in accordance with the design team, as part of activities closely integrated with constant feedback.

Since quality management in complex decision making procedures essentially means product or process quality related data management, the unambigous and non-redudant univocity of project document data becomes so important as to assimilate building to other production, industrial or service businesses. The specification becomes a technical/administrative document governing execution of the work and the contractual relationships between the Client who sets the conditions and the Contractors who undertake obligations.

Any one specification refers to one specific contract and is therefore prepared individually for each case. In order to set out the conditions for each work, its materials and execution procedures.

2 The role of technical specifications

The specification plays a vital role in the project building process since it fulfills both contractual and technical functions: «the purpose of a project specification, in conjunction with drawn, scheduled and measured information, is to define the quality of the systems, components, materials, workmanship and the finished work in such a way that the employer, contractor and professional advisers can have a reasonable degree of certainty that:
- the designer's detailed requirements will be met, compliance being judged on a definitive basis;
- the contractor's estimator can price the work with certainty and accuracy;
- the contractor can order materials and components correctly and in good time;
- the contractor can plan, execute and supervise the work in a controlled manner;

- the contract will be brought to a successful conclusion with the minimum number of misunderstandings and variations» (BPIC, 1987).

Contract technical specifications are the information that the Client transfers to the Contractor in order that the contract be a moment of continuity in the design, production, execution and management process.

The specification is part and parcel of the contract together with General Conditions and drawings in Italy, in so far as the procedural aspect is concerned. In the event of legal proceedings,the written text of the specification prevails over drawings, even when completed with written notes. Its exhaustiveness and univocity must be ensured in this case, also in compliance with European Communities Council Directive 440/89 of July 18, 1989. This Directive defines Technical Specifications as the set of technical provisoes mentioned in particular in the specifications defining the features of a work, material, product or supply so that they comply with the use that the Client destines them to. Such features include quality or usage properness levels, safety and dimensions as well as specifications applicable to the material, product or supply relative to the quality assurance system, terminology, symbols, tests and test methods, packaging, marking and labelling.They also include regulations on work designing and calculations, testing, control and receiving conditions of the works as well as building techniques or methods and all the other technical conditions the Client may prescribe by general or specific regulations, concerning finished works and with reference to constituent components or materials.

In so far as the design phase is concerned, the specification has a pre-eminent value; since it offers qualitative information, it represents an indispensable tool for indicating and checking compliance of the finished work with the Client's intention and achievement of the building's service life by means of contract clauses.The specification is therefore a document directed firstly at tenderers during the tendering phase; to the clerk of works, bidder, subcontractors, suppliers, site agent, technical inspector and quantity surveyor during execution and to post-occupancy assessors and maintainers during the management phase.

Due to the extreme articulation of the specification, many public and private bodies have prepared standard specifications capable of ensuring intrinsic low cost as well as the correctness of often repetitive procedural sections and the technical instructions set out on the basis of previous experience.

In the United Kingdom (Scott, 1984; Gardiner, 1991; Willis and Willis, 1991) and the United States (Lewis, 1975; Jellinger, 1981; Ayers, 1984; Meier, 1989; Lohmann, 1992) too, methods have been commonly adopted for writing specifications based on libraries of clauses (a system that approximates the standard italian specification) or combinations of coded and standard terms and sentences, although the fact of using «standard specifications is no guarantee of success unless they are rigorously reviewed for the particular situation of the design in question» (Cornick, 1991).

Interestingly, drawings (differentiated according to the purpose and project work in progress) are closely correlated to technical specifications, bills of quantities and the Standard Method of Measurement (SMM, 7th Edition) in Anglo Saxon countries, although often «specifications are not specific to the project, contain unachievable requirements and, more often then not, end up being ignored», because «in current building design practice the designers only specify the material and the workmanship - usually in rather broad general terms» (Cornick, 1991): «as a consequence Quality Assurance for design must encompass the development of the specification, and we must also be aware of the complex nature of the building industry» (CIB, 1989).

For Italy, we should like to mention the **Capitolato speciale Tipo per appalti di lavori edilizi** among the different standard ones. It was prepared by the Central Technical Service of the Italian Ministry for Public Works and has been revised recently to make it a dynamic rather than crystallized and static document as it had been so far.

It must however be recognized that certain experts hold that a standard specification should not be considered as a basis to be rather limitedly modified with a view to achieve the actual document; on the contrary, the logic of a guide to writing the specification should be followed.

This paper however only deals with the technical conditions of the specification, namely the set of the technical specifications that define the quality and types of workmanship upon which the contract is based; «specifications may be defined as written explanations delimiting the work to be undertaken and as written instructions regarding materials and methods that are to be used to acccomplish the work of the project» (Jellinger, 1981); «the project specification is defined as a document or part of a document, the main purpose of which is to define the materials and products to be used, the standard of work required, any performance requirements, and the conditions under which the work is to be executed» (BPIC, 1987).

Specifications should be written in a proper language «hand in hand with the preparation of the drawings» (Rosen, 1981). In the USA, discussions are in fact on preliminary or outline specifications. These ensure an adequate technological level of the information content, once they are refined through contacts with the decision making and operational systems coordinator and the many consultants who contribute to defining project documentation. They must be closely complementary with drawings and avoid overlappings or redundances since they are «a device for organizing the information depicted on the drawings» and «break down the interrelated informations» (Rosen, 1981) shown therein. One of the biggest mistakes made by many maintenance planning offices and conservation design practices is to postpone the introduction of the specification writer to the project until the working drawings are nearly finished.

Graphic representation of the project cannot be dealt with separately from the procedures of expressing the information of other contract documents, technical specifications included. Such documents concur together to define the contents of the communication to be transmitted to each party involved and must be made complementary and homogeneous, even though expressed in different languages. Technical specifications are in fact «written instructions to be used in conjunction with the drawings so that together they fully describe and define the work that is to be accomplished, along with the methods and quality that will be required» (Jellinger, 1981).

There are two ways of writing a specification: by description or by performance. The former - the descriptive specification or system method - has been commonly used in Italy so far. The writer, usually the designer or specifier in better organized design practices, indicates the exact specification of the materials and technologies to be used. This facilitates invitations to bid and instructions to bidders for contractors during the bidding phase as well as controls both during work under realization and final inspection by professionals appointed to do so. The latter - the performance specification or results system - is a specification written in a manner that sets forth all the requirements the installation or product must meet but does not state how.Performance specifications tend to offer definition and control tools independent of the building practice followed and the technologies used. They appear to follow the approach indicated in European Communities Concil Directive 440/89, modifying Directive 305/71 of July 27, 1971, that specifies the need to establish building contracts based on results instead of detailed technical specifications.

The performance approach, that was born with the advent of system building and the end of traditional "workmanship rules", however presupposes a vast structure of defining requirements and performance measurement and control. It is in fact very complex and sometimes technically impossible to establish a priori the exact compliance of "product concepts" as set forth in the framework of a performance definition with the "products" that physically make up the building and that as such are subject to mandatory morphological description when the specification is rated as a contract document.

The literature strongly suggests not to make too drastic a distinction between the two specifications, expecially in the presence of procurement routes expressly set to ensure avoiding the search for the best quotation by low bidder determination, but also using execution times, efficiency and technical value of the work as well as the life cycle cost. Some Authors hold that intermediate solutions should be explored by offsetting description of performance propensity based on the "share" of design activity performed directly by the Client or progressively delegated to the General Contractor or Subcontractors, i.e. according to the degree of project definition as set forth by the different procurement routes (Client Build, Design and Build, Traditional Consultant Design, Management Contracting, Construction Management). The structure of technical specifications therefore derives from the procurement system the Client chooses in setting contract terms and is gradually more detailed according to whether it is a preliminary, scheme, detail or working design.

The tender is sometimes formulated on the basis of the detail design or the final specification. In other instances, technical solutions are presented by the Contractors with reference to specification-programme included in the pilot project.
Specification technical conditions can anyhow be disaggregated into requirements of the environmental system, requirements of the technological system, building component and material features and use procedures.

From the viewpoint of its technical contents, the formulation of a particular specification on the basis of standard ones conceived as above will therefore consist of the level of detail for the above technical contents, taking account that the conceptual consistency of the three levels allows of non-strictly homogeneous structuring that features the simultaneous presence of elements belonging to the different levels.

The relationship between technical conditions and the schedules of work should therefore be clarified better. The latter is a descriptive document directed at finalizing bill of quantities which some experts believe could partially replace technical specifications, as it is pertaining to the design phases.

3 Rehabilitation and maintenance works specifications

A preservation and maintenance works specification presents certain special aspects, as in this sense the compliance of the finished work with design specifications must not only ensure proper works execution but also acts as a strong operational quality management tool (with reference to the conservation aims of the diagnostic and conservation design as well as maintenance management).

The peculiarity of the finished work also means that specification writing is more peculiar than normal. The comprehension of building logics must in fact become a specification in accordance with local procedures (Bosia, 1991; Ciribini, 1991).

The transfer of specific techniques for the new buildings cannot be automatic since the subject of the specification concerns treatment technologies rather than the assembly of materials, technical elements and components. The case of perharps essentially similar administrative clauses is different.

Recurrent doubts on the adequacy of standard specifications have arisen in this connection, because of the risk of the rehabilitation designer using standard clauses to absentmindedly apply specifications contrary to the interventions directed at the preservation of existing buildings. These documents also appear to be quite unsatisfactory from the technological viewpoint, since they hardly reach a high degree of precision, as the rehabilitation of buildings that differ widely as to year of construction, building materials and technologies cannot be summarized with rigid standard rules.

This would therefore lead to believe that using the descriptive form for writing the technical conditions for rehabilitation works specifications would be preferable in the present situation, also considering the advisability of preparing a diagnostic design specification separately from the rehabilitation design one. This would prevent the latter from appearing as a sort of document in progress, constantly under review, with the supplementary costs ensuing from the possible writing of an addendum caused by lack of design precision with the consequent interruption of works under way. In this scenario, there would be fewer variant under construction, that will anyhow continue to occur to a greater or lesser degree.

4 Conclusions

In order to reach correct writing of technical specifications for preservation and maintenance works in Italy, this paper has examined that **Standard Library of Description of Building Works**, prepared in the United Kingdom during the Sixties based on the standard phraseology for bills of quantities of building works.

This library is divided into sections like the SMM and is based on the mentioned standard method of measurement of building works. It offers standard terminology for the orderly description of the building elements and activity present in bill of quantities and makes the description of a rather wide range of operations possible.

Because of the method's extreme terseness and detailedness, this paper will close only by listing the contents of a technical specifications on a preservation works, for the following topics:

a) location of the work;
b) references to regulations and standards;
c) description of the operation;
d) materials: selection of qualified suppliers, characteristics, certifications and worksite acceptance criteria based on the method of supplier assurance;
e) description of workmanship, if possible certifiable against UNI standards similar to BS series 8000;
f) execution procedures, with reference to the possible presence of quality assured treatments and firms (general contractor, specialist contractor or subcontractor) with quality management certification against ISO series 9000;
g) plant and equipment.
h) environmental and local conditions;
i) operational planning;
l) preliminary operations;
m) safety measures;
n) inspections of work under realization;
o) final inspection;
p) maintenance facilities;
q) obligation to present historical quality data records to assess the reliability, maintainability and durability of treatments and products.

This checklist must of course be taken account of by the quantity surveyor or specification writer, the design team coordinator, the structural and services designers, the non destructive examination operatives, the chemical and physical consultants and the building pathologists especially when provided with a quality management system, that is anyhow mandatory to obtain formal quality assurance for the design practice.

The checklist could be used in codes of practice or in guidelines for rehabilitation works, that are particularly detailed for conservation treatments in Italy and act as a tool to check the technical correctness of design solutions.

5 References

Ayers, C. (1984, 2nd ed.) **Specifications for Architectiure Engineering & Construction** McGraw-Hill, New York

Bosia, D. (1991) **Il capitolato speciale di appalto per il recupero** Ph. D. Thesis, Università degli Studi di Genova, unpubl.

(BPIC) Building Project Information Committee (1987) **Project Specifications. A code of procedure for building works** NBS Services Ltd, Newcastle upon Tyne

Ciribini, A. (1991) **Per una teoria del capitolato speciale d'appalto nell'ambito delle discipline del costruito** Scholarship Report, ICITE - CNR (National Council of Research), Milano, unpubl.

Cornick, T. (1991) **Quality Management for Building Design** Butterworth, London

Gardiner L. (1991, 3rd ed.) **Standard method of specifying for minor works: as in the preparation of documentation for works of repair, improvement and conversion** Lewis Brooks, New Malden

Jellinger, T.C. (1981) **Construction Contract Documents & Specifications** Addison Wesley, Reading (Ma.)

Lewis, J.R. (1975) **Construction Specifications** Prentice Hall, Englewood Cliffs (N.J.)

Lohmann, W.T. 41992) **Construction Specifications** Butterworth, London

Maggi, P.N., Croce, S. et alia (1989) **Sinossi di fasi e controlli nel processo edilizio** Politecnico di Milano, Milano, unplub.

Meier, H.W. (1989, 2nd ed.) **Construction Specifications Handbook** Prentice Hall, Englewood Cliffs (N.J.)

Rosen, J.H. (1981, 2nd ed.) **Construction Specification Writing: Principles & Procedures** John Wiley & Sons, New York

Scott, J.J. (1984) **Specification writing: an introduction** Butterworth, London

Willis, A.J. and Willis, C.J. (1991, 10th ed.) **Specification writing for architects and surveyors** BSP, London

Building pathology and maintenance management: methodology and tools

M. Moroni
Department of Building and Territorial Systems Engineering, Faculty of Civil Engineering, Milan Polytechnic, Italy

Abstract
The maintenance planning and organization during the whole life cycle of a building is the way to optimize the technical-economical maintenance management of buildings, but, because of several reasons this goal is, nowadays, far from being reached. One of the difficulties is recognizable in the hardly knowable information concerning some time-related parameters. This paper illustrates how building pathology sciences, (studying the mechanisms of decay of building materials, components and systems), could allow the development of tools and knowledge that can be very useful to plan the maintenance process, and, closely, these tools make easier, profitable and more correctly usable two maintenance strategies: the emergency maintenance and the preventive maintenance. Maintenance planners need to be able to find out with a high certainty degree the failure causes in order to perform a correct maintenance intervention; this aim requires efficient methodologies and tools to investigate the decay process. Furthermore the detailed knowledge of the alteration mechanisms gives the possibility to obtain information about the steps taken by the components in their decay process, in order to recognize the different signals of an incipient failure. This recognition gives the possibility to act before the happened failure.
Keywords: Building pathology, Diagnostics, Maintenance, Performance decay, Service life.

1 The decay process

Diagnostic, which is the basic part of the building pathology discipline, requires, as introduction, the knowledge of the decay process suffered by the building components.

The decay process can be usefully represented by a model which consists of a flow chart.

This flow chart can easily show the stages of the building component evolving from a performance condition to a non-performance condition. This model is showed in Figure 1; a short glossary is related in the following Table 1.

On one hand, the pathologic decay is always started by one or more **errors** which might have been committed during different stages of the building process, whereas the natural decay is started by aging phenomena, of materials and components.

On the other hand, errors committed in the design or in the building construction cause **defects.**

These defects can either remain in a latent form or be started by the action of **external agents.**

Table 1. Terminology

Term	Meaning
Error	A wrong choice or decision or a choice that was not made during the design process; the consequence of uncorrect manufacturing or management.
Defect	The inadequacy or lack of one ore more elements constituting a system, to perform their functions. Defects are caused by errors. Furthermore the presence of a defect is not sufficient to provoke a failure, the presence of external agents is necessary.
Anomaly	An anomalous behaviour or phenomenon. The indication of a possible defect. The anomaly could be a symptom of one or more defects. It could be, itself, a light failure.
Failure	A decrease of physical structure or performance, more or less serious and evident.
Performance failure	The reduction, in value, of the performance offered by a product or a component or a system, dropping below the established acceptable limit. (This is the most important failure in the field of building pathology).
Damage	The economic consequence of a failure.

Interaction between external agents and defects is the necessary condition to cause a manifest showing up of the decay, that is of the **failure.**

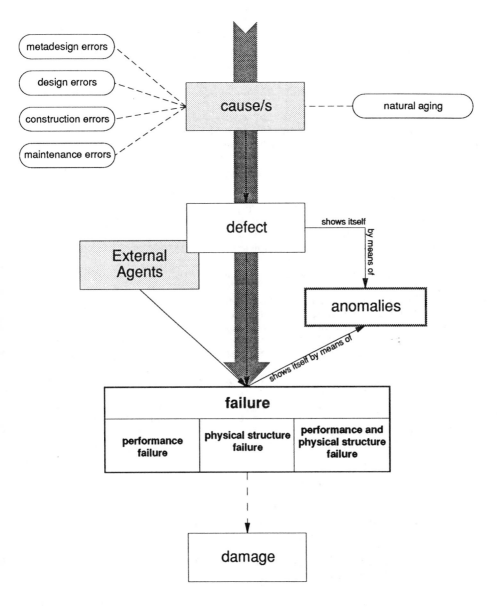

Fig. 1. The decay process

The failure in building components can either be structural, that is, concerning their physical, chemical and technological characteristics; or it can be a performance failure, that is, concerning the drop of their initial performance level below an established acceptable limit; or, finally, it can concern both aspects, which is the most common eventuality.

Certainly, the final user of the building object can be aware of the failure in a different way, according to its nature.

Under these terms, the showing up (called **anomaly**) through which the user becomes aware of a failure, can concern both the structure and the performance aspects.

The decay process anyway needs time to develop and it does not immediately cause components to pass from a performance condition to a failure condition; this is extremely important as to the possibility of planning maintenance strategies with a preventive purpose.

As a matter of fact, anomalies can show up even before the final failure occurs; when such is the case, anomaly becomes sort of symptom which points out one or more defects.

Therefore to study anomalies seems to be an easier way to set up a maintenance program disengaged from the knowledge of time dependent parameters of reliability, duration of service life, "mean time between failure" and so on, which are harder to obtain.

So, if on one hand the correct diagnosis of an occurred failure is an important condition to carry out an effective emergency maintenance strategy, on the other hand the possibility of a correct acknowledgement of anomalies, when the failure has not occurred yet, is fundamental for a preventive maintenance planning.

Finally, as the decay involves an economic damage, the estimate of this damage is included into the process model as the final stage of the representation: in fact the economic damage, although we cannot establish a strict relation cause effect between the failure and the economic damage, is, in the process flow, the direct consequence of the failure.

2 The diagnostic process

The diagnostic process starts from the observation of an occurred failure or from the acknowledgement of anomalies that point out the presence either of a defect or of a condition o an incipient failure.

The diagnostic process develops so as to deal with and methodically analyze all the diagnostic possibilities which may somehow be related to the failure itself.

The analysis of the anomalies that may be found in the building is a strategic passage of the diagnostic activity; i fact if we interpret them as symptoms, this will allow us a pre-acknowledgement of the defects which have caused the failure.

A following confirmation of the prediagnostic conjectures based on a more accurate instrumental/analytical survey and on a repeated elimination of the conjectures in contrast with

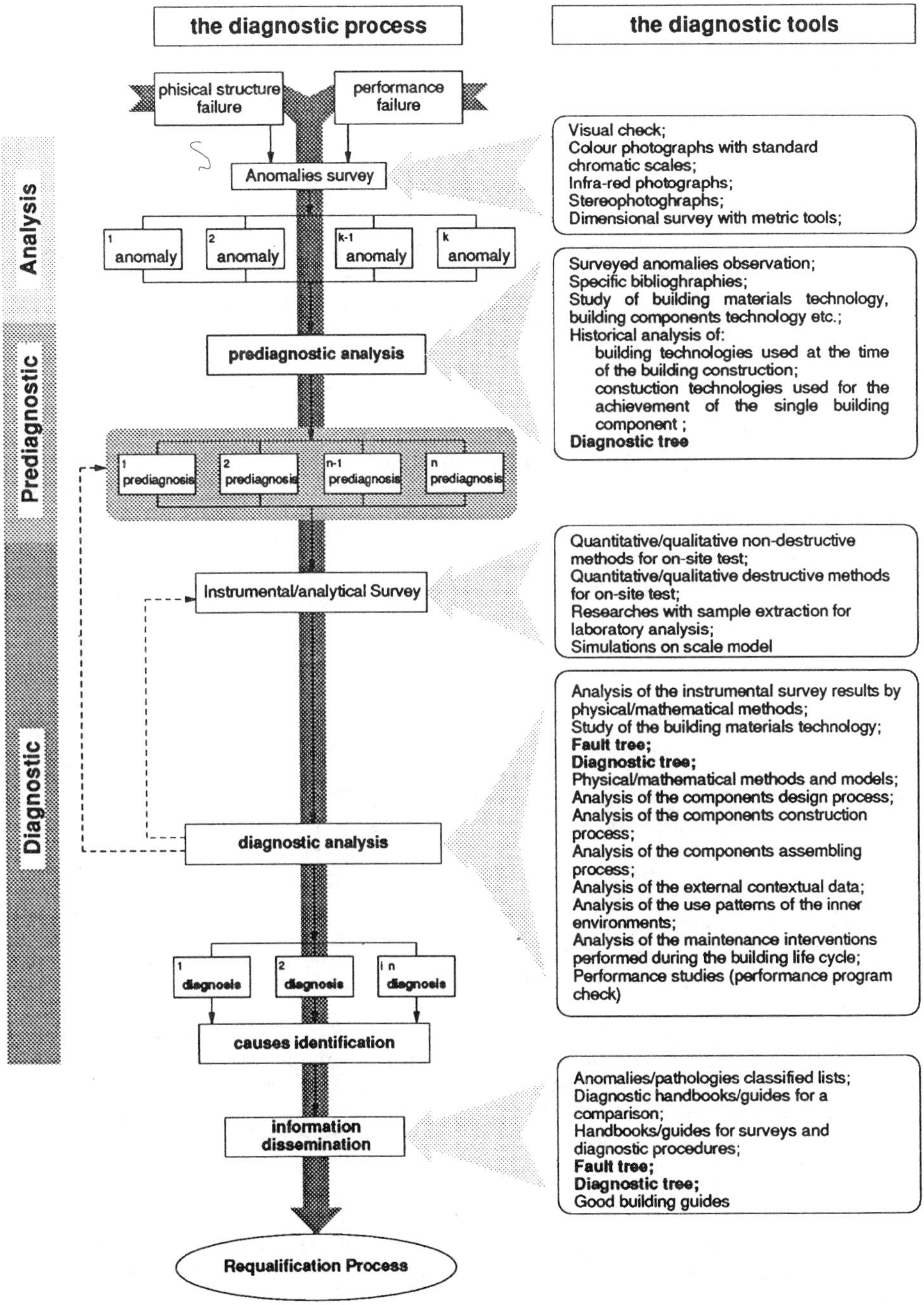

the diagnostic process

the diagnostic tools

Analysis

Prediagnostic

Diagnostic

phisical structure failure

performance failure

Anomalies survey

Visual check;
Colour photographs with standard chromatic scales;
Infra-red photographs;
Stereophotoghraphs;
Dimensional survey with metric tools;

1 anomaly | 2 anomaly | k-1 anomaly | k anomaly

prediagnostic analysis

Surveyed anomalies observation;
Specific biblioghraphies;
Study of building materials technology, building components technology etc.;
Historical analysis of:
  building technologies used at the time of the building construction;
  constuction technologies used for the achievement of the single building component ;
Diagnostic tree

1 prediagnosis | 2 prediagnosis | n-1 prediagnosis | n prediagnosis

Instrumental/analytical Survey

Quantitative/qualitative non-destructive methods for on-site test;
Quantitative/qualitative destructive methods for on-site test;
Researches with sample extraction for laboratory analysis;
Simulations on scale model

Analysis of the instrumental survey results by physical/mathematical methods;
Study of the building materials technology;
Fault tree;
Diagnostic tree;
Physical/mathematical methods and models;
Analysis of the components design process;
Analysis of the components construction process;
Analysis of the components assembling process;
Analysis of the external contextual data;
Analysis of the use patterns of the inner environments;
Analysis of the maintenance interventions performed during the building life cycle;
Performance studies (performance program check)

diagnostic analysis

1 diagnosis | 2 diagnosis | i n diagnosis

causes identification

information dissemination

Anomalies/pathologies classified lists;
Diagnostic handbooks/guides for a comparison;
Handbooks/guides for surveys and diagnostic procedures;
Fault tree;
Diagnostic tree;
Good building guides

Requalification Process

Figure 2. The diagnostic process and its tools

data obtained time by time, will finally lead to a sub-group of definitive diagnosis usually characterised by some degree of certainty.

The presence of different possible diagnosis must be taken into consideration at the moment of the requalification intervention. Diagnostic, if correctly applied and by adequat tools (operative and methodological) can carry out the function of optimizing the requalification procedures.

You will find the diagnostic process flow chart, with the tools which may be used to get all the necessary information, clearly in evidence, represented in Figure 2.

It is remarkable that the redundance of the survey stages, which considers the real difficulty of getting all meaningful data through only one initial survey, is justified by the essential difficulty of acquiring data and by the possibility to disregard them when it is not clear yet what we have to inquire into.

We propose to iterate the survey giving it the purpose to obtain, time by time, data which, from a quantitative and qualitative point of view, are rather limited; this allows u to involve, for each stage survey, small quantities of competencies and resources.

In fact, it will give us all and only those information which, time by time, are requested for a diagnosis confirmation.

3 The "Fault Tree"

Among the instruments that can be used for diagnostic there are two which are particularly useful as methodological and procedural guide in view of a systematic diagnosis formulation: the "Fault Tree" and the "Diagnostic Tree".

Both can also be used for a coordination of all surveys, analyses and formulation through the typical instruments normally used by the building pathologist such as non-destructive evaluation methods, computer simulations by physical/mathematical algorithms, infra-red thermography and so on.

The "Fault Tree" is the first instrument we propose: its purpose is to make evident the interaction logic between the acknowledged failures and their possible causes.

This instrument can be used to methodically represent all the data related to a certain decay phenomenon so as to introduce a global picture of the possible diagnostic conjectures.

As each acknowledged diagnostic conjecture closes, so to speak, one of the tree "branches", we can infer that the branch represents different evolution stages of a determined pathology.

In this way, the Fault Tree turns out to be a total representation of a certain decay phenomenon and, as such, it shows its utility during the planning phase and survey development for diagnostic, as its structure considers all the possible diagnostic assumptions and relevant pathologies (decay evolution logic).

Considering that the analyzed processes can be more or less complex, the Fault Tree structure can lead to sub-trees; in this case the starting event of a sub-tree usually belongs to the third level of the primary Fault Tree.

In Figure 3 you can see an example condensed for reasons of representation, of a Fault Tree conceived on purpose of analyzing problems of ceramics floor coverings detachment and raising. The Fault Tree structure can be divided into 4 hierarchic levels:

1° Failure level	This level represents the final decay event, that is, the failure (structure and/or performance failure).
2° Defect level	It represents the hypercritical condition which caused the failure.
3° Actions/Reactions level	It contains the list of the check parameters by which it is to be inquired whether the overcoming of a certain value has occurred or not; that is, the overcoming of a limit condition which starts the hypercritical condition.
4° Error level	This is the basic level which represents the possible errors that caused pathological situations to develop into a complete collapse.

4 The "Diagnostic Tree"

If, on one hand, the Fault Tree is useful for the representation of the critical sequences and of the possible diagnostic conjectures which lead from errors to failures; on the other hand it cannot support the diagnosis operator in choosing the branches related to the specific case, that is to say, it cannot help him in the diagnosis formulation.

The second instrument proposed, that has exactly this purpose, is the Diagnostic Tree.

The Diagnostic Tree is a sort of procedural guide for the development of diagnostic inquiry; it is used for the specific situation as a procedure tended to the choice of some of the Fault Tree branches: this choice is determined by answers to linked questions.

Like in the Fault Tree, there will be a correlation between the actions carried out by the context and the relevant component reaction capacity.

Generally, the diagnosis can tend either towards

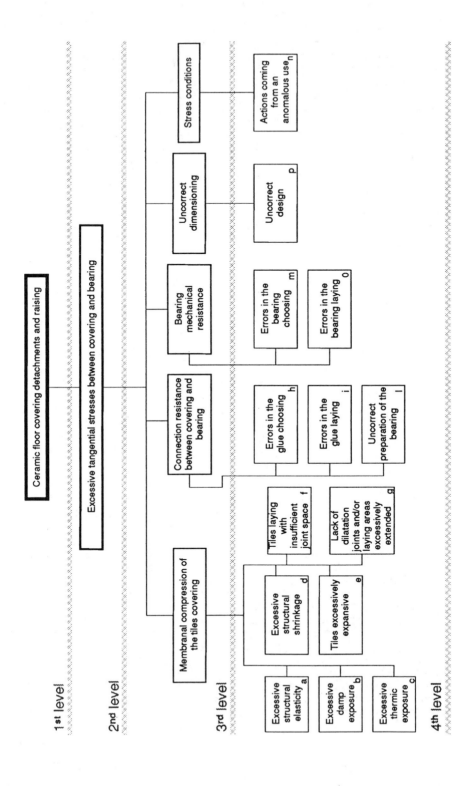

Figure 3. The Fault Tree

conjectures of exceeding stresses or conjectures of resistance defect.

Both these assumptions can lead to overcome a limit condition, as anticipated by the Fault Tree.

The elements necessary to form a Diagnostic Tree are the following:

1 - The failure.
2 - Questions which need an answer so as to proceed along the diagnostic tree branches.
3 - Decision instruments so as to answer the questions.
4 - The primary defects and the conjectural diagnosis.

In short, the two most meaningful advantages of the Diagnostic Tree are the following:

1 - It gives the possibility to order and systematize the diagnostic development.
2 - It prevents from neglecting some of the inquiry developments.

In Figure 4, as exemplification, you can see a part of the Diagnostic Tree concerning ceramics floor coverings detachment and raising problems related to the Fault Tree in Figure 3.

5 Conclusions

Therefore, instruments and methods of the Building Pathology are finalized to sustain the necessary decisions concerning the maintenance planning, and many researches and studies following this same direction are developed by national and international organizations, particularly inside the CIB Commission W86 "Building Pathology".

A further impediment which is the formulation of standard formats for the information exchange between the 'building pathologist and the 'maintenance managers'; other researches and studies follow this direction; particularly inside the Dept. Of building and Territorial Systems Engineering of the Milan Polytechnic, we are developing an Information Management System which deals with these topics.

6 Acknowledgements

This paper results from the research work carried out inside the Dept. of Building and Territorial Systems Engineering of the Milan Polytechnic;particular thanks to Prof. Sergio Croce for kindly allowing the Diagnostic Tree being published in Figure 4, of which he is the original author.

Particular thanks to prof. Giuseppe Turchini who has participated to the work and to the supervision of this paper.

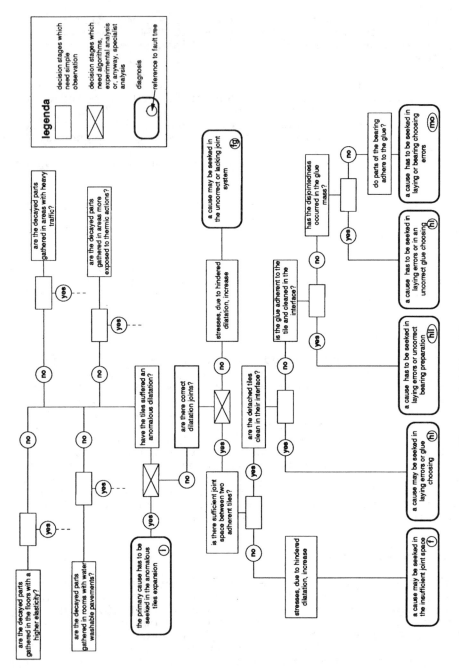

Figure 4. The Diagnostic Tree

7 References

Croce, S. Moroni, M. and Turchini, G. (1990a) The Diagnostic Tree. **Proceedings of the 6th Meeting of the CIBW86** Malaga.

Croce, S. Moroni, M. and Turchini, G. (1990b) Notes for a state-of-the-art report. **Proceedings of the 6th Meeting of the CIBW86**, Malaga.

Van Den Beukel, A. Moroni, M. et al. (1991) Building Pathology: a state-of-the-art report, second draft. **Proceedings of the 7th Meeting of the CIBW86** Malaga.

Molinari, C. (1989) Durabilità dei subsistemi e tipologia dei guasti: un inchiesta per interlocutori privilegiati, in **Manutenzione in edilizia** (italian), Franco Angeli, Milano, pp.161-211.

Post occupancy evaluation method for effective management of office facilities

H. Nakagita
Building Engineering Department, Nippon Telegraph and Telephone Corporation (NTT), Tokyo, Japan

Abstract
One of the effective methods that NTT developed for the office management is based on using a questionnaire for evaluation of office workers. This paper presents the construction of the questionnaire , the analysis program, and one of the interesting results in its application at NTT.
Keywords: Post occupancy evaluation, Questionnaire, Office, Renovation, Renewal

1 Introduction

NTT is a telecommunication company whose network spreads to every corner of the country and who owns more than 30,000 telecommunications buildings with a total floor area of about 20,000,000 square meters. Most of these buildings were constructed twenty to thirty years ago (**Figure 1**). Recent rapid innovations in information and telecommunications technology have brought major changes to the office environment, and the effective management of these building facilities has become a primary issue. The installation of heat-generating machines like personal computers, the recent concern for indoor air quality and the problem of building deterioration have prompted us to improve office productivity by renovating or renewing office space. When doing this, it is very important to quantify each prevailing conditions of each particular office environment. Based on this quantified assessment, it is possible to manage office facilities effectively and for office workers to work more efficiently in improved surroundings.

One method developed for assessing prevailing office conditions used as a tool for managing NTT's facilities is generally called Post Occupancy Evaluation (POE): in more specific terms, it is the use of a questionnaire. Significant data used to determine office design has been obtained by applying POE to our offices.

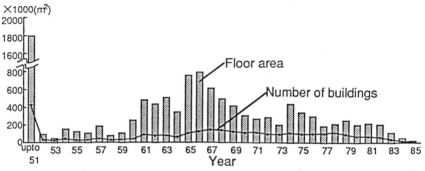

Fig. 1. Trends in the number of buildings constructed at NTT and their floor area.

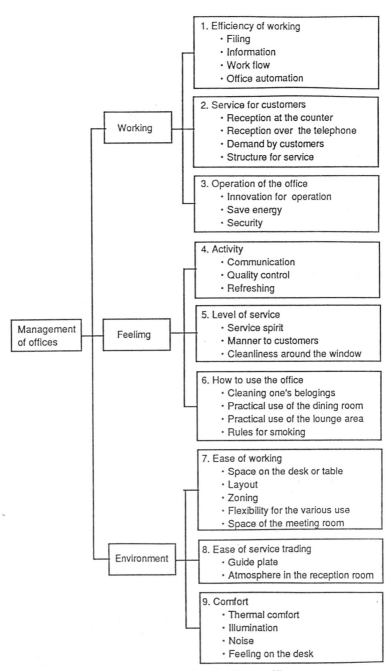

Fig. 2. Classification of elements in an office

2 Method for assessing the office

2.1 Post occupancy evaluation

Post occupancy evaluation is an effective way of determining the conditions prevailing in an office, and it has recently become popular to apply POE to office renewal in Japan. Most of these studies have been based on the results of questionnaires completed by occupants. NTT has developed an appropriate questionnaire and a personal computer program that can reduce the number of hours needed to analyze the questionnaire data.

2.2 Questionnaire

The purpose of the questionnaire is to reflect how occupants feel and to evaluate their office area and working conditions. There are many elements used to categorize an office (**Figure 2**), and the questionnaire NTT developed is constructed according to these classifications. To renovate or renew offices effectively and to work comfortably for workers themselves (office occupants), not only the office environment but also the workers' feelings and working conditions must be considered. The questionnaire NTT developed has 50 items. Five of these concern about respondent's profile. Another 15 items concern feelings about office facility management. Another 15 items concern work. The remaining 15 items concern the office environment. The response format is based on the semantic differential(SD) method. The six-point scales used for almost all the items on this questionnaire enable a precise analysis of and comparison between arbitrary items, (although three- or five-point scales are generally used elsewhere). Respondents can mark any of the six points, and because a six-point scale has no neutral point, each items must be rated good or bad. An example of this format is shown in **Figure 3**.

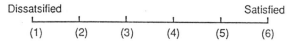

Question: "How do you feel about the comfort of your chair?
Please check the appropriate scale below."

Dissatsified   Satisfied

(1)   (2)   (3)   (4)   (5)   (6)

Fig. 3. Example of response format.

2.3 Evaluation

A mean response and standard deviation is calculated for each questionnaire. The mean response simply denotes the general tendency of the office occupants. The standard deviation is used to judge whether or not a cross analysis is required. For example, different distribution can be reflected in the standard deviation (**Figure 4**).

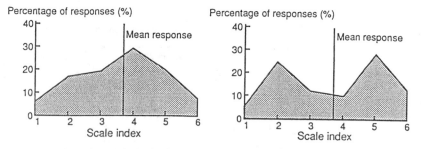

Fig. 4. Sample distributions of responses to questions.

For the overall evaluation, a deviation is calculated by using the mean response to each category's representative 9 questions:

office activity
Service for customers
How to use office
Ease of working
Ease of service trading
Comfort
Efficiency of working
Level of service
Office operation

Since there are many elements in an office, the results of this questionnaire are presented in the form of the following graphs:

Radar chart : Very effective for easy understanding and for comparison of each questionnaire. **Figure 5** is typical chart for analysis.

Bar chart: Shows the ratio of six-point scales' responses on each questionnaire, see **Figure 6**.

Cross chart : Shows two questions contrast. This is used to evaluate an characteristic of working, see **Figure 7**

Distribution map: Very effective for overall evaluation (**Figure 8**). The nation-wide average response is used for calculating the point that is shown as following equation:

$$\text{Point} = 50 + 10 \times \frac{\text{One assessment mean response} - \text{Nation-wide average mean response}}{\text{Standard deviation}}$$

According to the comparison between one assessment result and the nation-wide average response, the level of one assessment can be derived. A final overall evaluation is presented with the point that is the same distribution as that of an entrance examination to a university.

Fig. 5. Radar chart for evaluation

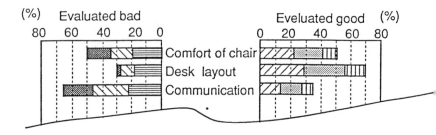

Fig. 6. Bar chart for evaluation.

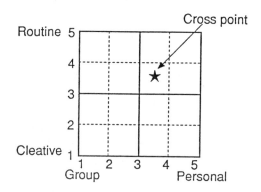

Fig. 7. Cross chart for evaluation of characteristic of working (5 scales).

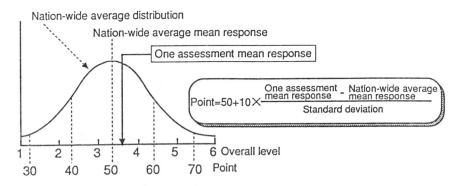

Fig. 8. Distribution map for evaluation

2.4 Personal computer

NTT Offices are located all over the country, and building engineers in each district are responsible for management of local buildings. To ensure that the same office evaluation occurs in every district, a personal computer program has been developed. This program provides the following functions:

Editing and printing of the questionnaire
Input of replies to the questionnaire
Statistical evaluation of responses
Graphic display of evaluation charts
Input of the nation-wide mean response and standard deviation for calculating the deviation of each assessment

Examples of this program's display are shown in **Figure 9**. It is possible to cut the required evaluation time to 20% of that previous required.

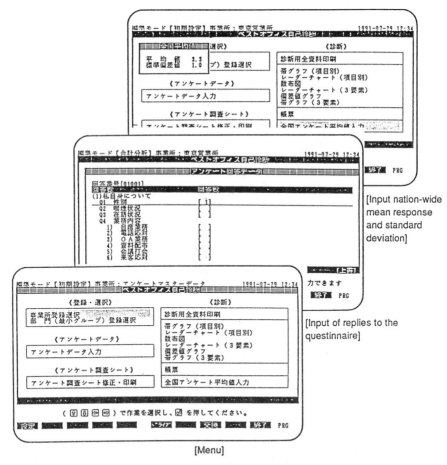

[Input nation-wide mean response and standard deviation]

[Input of replies to the questinnaire]

[Menu]

Fig. 9. Example display of the personal computer program

195

3 An example at NTT

The development of this method was completed in April 1991 and the personal computer program had been distributed to each district in June. To spread this method efficiently, an explanation note that shows how to evaluate had been made out and distributed. Before distribution of the program, this method had been used with representative workers who had been selected from each district and their evaluation results were used as the nation-wide mean response. Since then, this method has been used in each district, and this paper presents an example of the results.

Most NTT offices are relatively small with an average area of 100 to 200 square meters. On the average, there is about 1 personal computer for every 2.5 persons in these offices.

The example compares results before and after renovation. The renovation was that desk layout was modified and carpet and partitions had been installed (**Figure 10**).

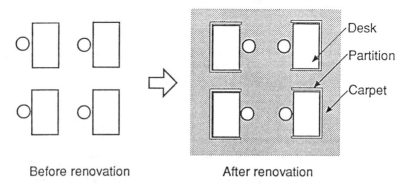

Before renovation   After renovation

Fig. 10. Desk layout modification.

3.1 Profile

The profiles that show sex, smoking or nonsmoking,and period working in present office is presented by using bar charts.Profiles are the same in both assessment (**Figure 11**). The ratio of smoking is nearly 50%, which is the remarkable characteristic at NTT.

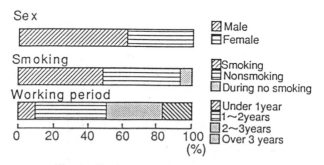

Fig. 11. Evaluation example of profile.

3.2 Evaluation of each category

The evaluation in each category is presented by using a radar chart: the rating of each category was slightly improved after renovation (**Figure 12**)..

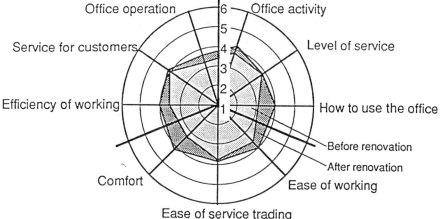

Fig. 12. Evaluation example in each category

3.3 Overall evaluation

The deviation value after renovation advanced 3 points and the mean response also advanced 3 points (**Figure 13**). The result in this office was higher than the nation-wide average even before renovation. Moreover, this renovation was appropriate for this office and its effectiveness was revealed by the POE method.

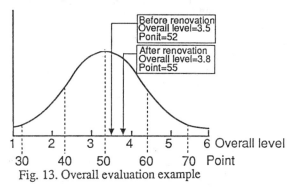

Fig. 13. Overall evaluation example

4 Conclusion

The post occupancy evaluation method developed at NTT and based on a questionnaire has been presented. Building engineers has been continuously using this method in NTT's office until now. For effective management of office facilities, it is necessary to continue such an assessment and to base the renewal or renovation of offices on the evaluations obtained from office occupants.

5 Reference

Yoshimura.M (1990) Post occupancy evaluation of telephone offices
    Environmental quality 90, England
Yoshimura.M et al (1991) A study on evaluation of corporate office environment level,
    Proceedings of annual meeting of the AIJ (in Japanese), Japan, pp. 207-208

Optimising premises performance through pro-active premises management

B.J. Varcoe
BWA Premises Management, Bromley, Kent, UK

1 Introduction

Premises are a largely unavoidable and integral part of any business or organisation that can have a fundamental effect on it's success. Whilst often representing a significant financial asset, their primary role is that of meeting the business needs of their occupier's core functions. The intensely competitive 1990's demands premises that are managed pro-actively, anticipating changing requirements and having the flexibility to absorb their effects without detriment to those they serve.

This paper seeks to place premises in their true business perspective, and from that basis present an approach to premises management that provides a way of creating pro-active flexibility, and thereby the potential for optimised use, in what is by nature a somewhat rigid and slow-to-adapt entity.

2 The Needs of Modern Business

Who, five years ago, would have successfully predicted and made provision for the vast changes that are taking place in Eastern Europe. Who fully appreciated the potential of the largely untapped market place it represents? Similarly, which organisations three years ago correctly identified the depth of the current downturn in the economy and prepared accordingly? These examples, like countless others, show that business life in the 1990's is arguably predominantly about the business of change. No matter how well one plans, something is bound to happen that upsets the 'status quo' requiring a reactive approach and solution.

Modern businesses demand people and systems that not only survive the change thrust upon them, but are able to take business advantage of it. In achieving this advantage, speed of response is critical, for success invariably means appreciating the new opportunities, and responding with the right products and services, ahead of the competition. Being first is what counts. There are few prizes for coming second.

The response to change, and the time that response takes is not the whole issue, though. Before a response to change can be made, the change needs to be identified in terms of extent and context. It is very important to have a knowledge of all the issues at a strategic level. Specialist abilities are then put in their correct context and can be reviewed accordingly. The modern economy, in requiring businesses and organisations to appreciate the strategic and respond rapidly to the specific, therefore demands businesses and organisations that are flexible.

3 The Business Response

The business response to the requirement for flexibility is perhaps typified by British Petroleum. In April 1990, the Chairman of BP announced a corporate restructuring eliminating six tiers of management in reducing the existing eleven to a streamlined five. The flatter structure moves decision-making authority nearer the business interface, creating an environment more conducive to providing the flexibility and speed of response necessary.

Business is therefore seeking to streamline the operational procedures of its most valuable asset - its people.

4 The Significance of Premises

Staff usually represent the majority of a businesses' or an organisation's cost of operation. The analysis that is summarised in Figure 1 compares the staff costs of a leading financial services company to that of the premises they occupy, in terms of its capital, operating and replacement costs.

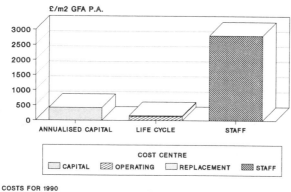

FIGURE 1

This comparison tends to suggest that premises are relatively unimportant, and this often manifests itself in corporate attitudes that regard premises as an overhead cost to be kept as low as possible. Such an approach does not give due regard to two important facts however. Firstly, business premises often represent more than 30% of an organisation's total asset value, as illustrated in Figure 2. Secondly, and perhaps more importantly, premises have a fundamental effect on the people that occupy them - the business's most important asset. The primary role of business premises therefore has to be that of supporting at all levels, from the individual to the strategic, the goals and aims of the businesses and organisations that occupy them. They must be as ready for change as any other business component, if not more so, being able to adapt to or absorb its effects with speed and efficiency.

TOTAL ASSETS v PROPERTY ASSETS
I.T.COMPANY plc

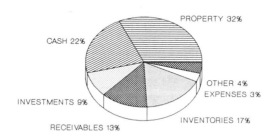

FIGURE 2

Just as the market dictates flexible businesses, so the businesses in turn need to demand flexible and efficient premises. They cannot afford to do without them.

5 Current Practice

Having identified the need for flexible premises that effectively meet the needs of their occupiers, premises are, as stated previously, unfortunately all too often only seen to be a cost centre that has to be minimised. 'Value-for-money' is all too often identified as being the achievement of the lowest spend possible. The service that the premises provide as a result of that level of spend, and how that relates to the real needs of the business, are not considered. Typically, all decisions in respect of the premises are reactive, items being replaced when they break, or when complaints from staff reach an intolerable threshold, and relocation options are considered when the staff car park can contain no more 'Portakabins'. Similarly, budgets are set year-by-year based on what was spent previously, as adjusted by the Board taking into account what they consider necessary. Overspends are commonly only identified at the point of occurrence or, worse, three or four months later when the accounts department has processed all the orders and invoices.

6 Pro-active Premises Management

Premises today need to be managed pro-actively. Those that react to events are not flexible and do not serve the business interest. For business premises to offer optimum performance through pro- active management, a good starting point is a written premises policy. Such a document states all factors of company policy and standards that relate, or should relate, to its building stock. Each and every company and organisation is unique, and therefore every premises policy will likewise be unique, reflecting different policies, requirements and considerations.

7 The Premises Policy

The main board of a business exists to ensure the success of the mainstream business function or functions. As a matter of course, therefore, they imply the basic premises policy by way of the Business Plan. The premises policy produced by the premises or facilities department needs to support and be derived from this, and should not itself be a source of influence.

The premises policy, although unique to each occupier, will nevertheless have a common core of factors that should be included. Typically, these are as follows:

7.1 Location
Location policy should be considered in terms of at least two aspects:

(a) *The 'Macro' policy*, identifying, if necessary, regional, city or town location requirements or preferences.

(b) *The 'Micro' policy*, stating locational requirements or preferences within the 'macro' centres such as prime sites, secondary, out-of-town, etc.

These two aspects can be considered at whatever level is suitable for the organisation, ranging from the 'Group plc' overview to individual departmental requirements within individual companies.

7.2 Real Estate
Policies and constraints in terms of real estate considerations need to be identified. Given the proportion of total asset value property typically represents, this is a very important aspect. The lease/buy mix needs careful appraisal in the light of factors such as liquidity requirements, lengths of tenure, financing capabilities, market trends etc.

A wary eye also needs to be kept upon the disposability of those premises that have a limited timespan of use to the organisation, particularly if the standards required of the premises by the occupier fall significantly short of those generally expected by the market. Short term savings on specifications and standards can lead to long-term costs as premises prove difficult to pass on, particularly in a 'bear' market as is prevalent today.

Throughout all real estate policy, however, the primary purpose for acquiring interest in property - namely, that of being a piece of plant that serves the core functions of the business - must not be overlooked. It has not been unknown for a business's real estate dealings to consistently contribute more to profits than the supposed core function, to the latter's long-term detriment.

7.3 Space Management
Effective space management in terms of budgeting and control cannot be carried out without defined space standards. Ideally, these will be established using principles based on user need and not status. The standards can be determined at departmental level by way of target averages per head, but preferably will be set at a more detailed level that considers individual job functions within departments. Use of Computer Aided Design facilities makes the application of such detailed information in planning less of a time burden than it might otherwise be.

Once standards are set, a further refinement is the design and incorporation within the premises policy of workstation footprints, identifying the furniture system components that comprise each module as well. Such a modular approach if nothing else, should significantly cut down the effect and cost of 'churn' and help to ensure that use of the space resource is maximised. Putting the importance of efficient space utilisation in context, reducing a maintenance spend by 5% is insignificant in cost terms compared to occupying 5% more space than is necessary, as shown in Figure 3.

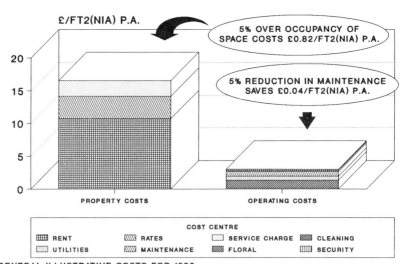

PREMISES COST ANALYSIS
- PROPERTY COSTS v OPERATING COSTS -

GENERAL ILLUSTRATIVE COSTS FOR 1990

FIGURE 3

7.4 Spatial Quality

The standard of spatial quality provided is the synthesis of many issues, and can vary by function within the corporate structure. Areas with a high customer profile may,for example, warrant a more generous overall quality and quantity of space than data-processing functions. Care has to be taken to ensure that the standards are consistent and relate across the organisation, though.

Aspects that ought to be considered when establishing policy in respect of spatial quality include the following:

(a) *Information Technology* (I.T.) can have a fundamental effect on premises. The full future implications of I.T. in respect of the business or organisation needs to be fully understood and established. To be safe, premises should be flexible enough to accommodate as a minimum a workplace/terminal ratio of 1:1, linked by a Local Area Network (LAN) or multi-user system with communications links to other remote facilities. This typically demands generous vertical and horizontal service routes to accommodate cable runs, and air-conditioning systems able to cope with the large heat emissions such systems generate. Indeed, in such circumstances, buildings are usually faced with the problem of year round cooling, not heating.

(b) *Premises Standards* over and above legal requirements in respect of health and safety, fire regulations etc, should be defined. A company may deem it prudent to standardise on a minimum level of fire protection measures in excess of the requirements of the fire regulations. Lighting standards are another area that ought to be identified for the different generic types of space use relevant to the organisation concerned.

(c) *Office Decor* can benefit from being standardised to a set of co-ordinated schemes. These should include statements in respect of matters such as floral densities and passive fabric protection, as well as the more obvious colour scheme boards etc.

(d) *Image*, and other subjective concepts that reflect the company style, are difficult to establish, but benefit from an attempt at definition. They will, of course be reflected in the specifications and standards identified elsewhere in the premises policy, but specific statements can help mould technical solutions and requirements to more accurately reflect corporate needs in this area. For example, 'conservative' and 'flamboyant' immediately conjure up completely different images and styles (and probably cost levels as well!) that will render a good selection of properties in any premises search immediately inappropriate.

For each of these aspects of spatial quality, and any other category or matter that is identified, specific attention should be paid in respect of high profile areas, such as receptions and foyers, primary circulation routes, demonstration and customer training facilities, and any other type of space likely to have an interface with customers or those of business influence.

7.5 Asset Management

An 'Asset' is defined variously as

  (i) an item of property

  (ii) something advantageous or well worth having

  (iii) the property of a deceased or insolvent person, considered as chargeable for all debts.

Asset Management seeks to maintain the first definition in the condition of the second, thereby hopefully avoiding the onset of the third.

Policy in respect of asset management needs to be fully integrated and co-ordinated with every other aspect of the accommodation provision. Maintenance standards therefore need to reflect and take account of spatial standards, for example, so that an organisation trying to 'squeeze a quart into a pint pot' recognises and provides for the fact that the wear-and-tear associated with such intense use is high, thereby demanding a more intense, and expensive, maintenance regime to match.

Perhaps the most important statement of approach that can be made at this level, however, is that the management of assets will primarily relate to the premises' natural life cycle, as illustrated in Figure 4, and not to annual, or even quarterly accounting

THE NATURAL LIFE-CYCLE OF PREMISES COST

TEN YEAR PLANNED MAINTENANCE PROGRAMME

BUILDING A	1988	1989	1990	1991	1992	1993	1994	1995	1996	1997	1998	1999	TOTAL
	£	£	£	£	£	£	£	£	£	£	£	£	£
SUBSTRUCTURE	0	0	0	0	0	0	0	0	0	0	0		0
SUPERSTRUCTURE:													
Frame	0	43293	25318	5761	12753	8193	24990	21159	4752	12753	7912	0	166884
Upper Floors	0	15813	0	0	0	100	0	0	0	0	2178	0	18091
Roof													852038
Stairs													0
External Walls													316183
Windows and Ex													3707
Internal Walls an													263284
Internal Doors													90260
INTERNAL FIN													
Wall Finishes													124854
Floor Finishes													375300
Ceiling Finishes													48494
FITTINGS/FUR													106563
SERVICES:													
Sanitary Applian													13753
Services Equipm													0
Disposal Installat													1408
Water Installation													0
Heat Source													0
Space Heating/Ai													221980
Ventilating Syste													0
Electrical Installa													268800
Gas Installations													0
Lift and Conveyo													44000
Protective Installa													53935
Communication Installations	0	0	0	0	0	0	0	0	0	0	3500	0	3500
Special Installations	0	350	0	0	79200	1667	0	0	21420	0	0	0	102637
EXTERNAL WORKS:													
Site Works	0	0	0	0	0	0	0	0	0	0	0	0	0
Drainage	0	0	0	0	0	0	0	0	0	0	0	0	0
External Services	0	0	0	0	0	0	0	0	0	0	0	0	0
Minor Building Work	0	0	0	0	0	0	0	0	0	0	0	0	0
TOTAL (£)	0	1080294	448322	128181	105483	554389	72510	113073	58148	145838	369433	0	3075671

FIGURE 4

requirements. Whilst overall business affordability cannot be overlooked and ignored, effective management of premises will only take place if that management, as a basic principle, identifies itself to, and plans, monitors and controls, relative to overall building life, and the many individual component life cycles within that. Pro-active management over this time period will provide the opportunity for the correct macro-decisions to be made, which in turn will lead to the right micro-decisions to meet the desired business requirements, particularly in respect of budgets.

General policy requirements can be established in a number of ways, ranging from the identification of target task response times to outline planned preventative maintenance structures and procedures. Alternatively, or in addition, standards can be established and monitored by way of pre-set staff complaint levels.

Asset management policy will also specify standards in rather more detail in certain key areas. Amongst these are security and cleaning. The level of cleaning provided in particular needs careful alignment with corporate requirements and policy. By way of example, a standard specifying a clean of all worksurfaces and desk tops every night is not suitable where there is no clear desk policy. The performance level specified, and probably paid for, in such an instance, in all likelihood will not be possible to deliver.

7.6 Staff Facilities
Special staff facilities warrant clear identification as policy. Clearly a policy to provide all staff with the facility of a subsidised hot meal at lunchtime, or a car parking space within five minutes walk of their building, can fundamentally affect premises decisions and costs.

7.7 Cost Control
A formalised system of pro-active cost control as a policy is a very important pre-requisite for effective facilities management. There are three main factors that must be present for the proper control of costs to be achieved - budgetary control, competitive procurement and value engineering.

Budgetary control involves the process of estimating, planning, checking and reporting costs at all stages, from inception to completion, with the object being to ensure that planned budgets are never exceeded unless approved prior to the event actually occurring. Carried out successfully, it is anticipatory in nature, and provides the opportunity to consider a range of options to a problem or task, affording sufficient time for a carefully considered decision to be made.

Having established the right budget for a given task, the next step is to procure the work in the correct manner. In this respect, it is always important to ensure that the market is consistently tested to obtain the best possible price for the performance required. Where this is not directly possible by competitive tendering eg: with a direct labour force, check quotes should still be obtained at strategic intervals to provide a monitor. The tax implications of the chosen procurement path should also be borne in mind. Where, for example, VAT cannot be offset against other business activities, the 17½% charge on a contract maintenance gang might make the direct labour alternative appear financially more favourable.

The third component necessary for effective cost control is value engineering - the elimination of redundant performance. Procedures to test every solution and assumption for more efficient alternatives must be built into the cost control function, to ensure as far as possible that the right level of service is provided, in the most efficient manner, and not too much or too little.

Effective cost control demands all three facets - without one, the other two are seriously impaired to the point of being ineffectual. For example, a carefully budgeted task that has been thoroughly value engineered, and thereby represents the right performance level for the operation, might cost 10% or 20% more than it otherwise need to if let on a sub-standard contract based on an inappropriate 'negotiation' ....all cost control is lost.

With all facets of the policy drafted, each then needs to be rigorously interrogated and challenged. All redundant performance has to be identified and eliminated, and all aspects of the document need to fully co-ordinate with each other to provide a cohesive and consistent premises statement.

8 The Pro-active Tool

With the premises policy established, the premises department has a tool it can use to substantial benefit.

Ideally the premises policy, or an executive summary of it, needs to be ratified by the Company Board, or their equivalent. The document will contain many aspects of policy fundamentally affecting the business or organisation in terms of how effectively it will operate and how it will be perceived by the outside world. As such it merits a portion of their time.

The premises policy, by establishing levels of premises performance, even if only generically, will represent a budget level of premises cost. This needs to be identified and reviewed in respect of general business affordability, and other measures such as expenditure/profit ratios etc. It is a very fortunate and probably unique premises department that finds that it's budget cost level will be within perceived affordability strictures. The premises policy will provide the means of making the correct value judgements, however.   Decisions can be made as to whether policy performance and standards can be eased and refined in certain areas to reduce cost levels, or conversely whether they need to be maintained or even increased where the derived benefit outweighs the expense.

The next logical extension beyond deriving an indicative budget level for premises is where real pro-active premises management is established, however. The premises policy needs to be the basis for the generation of a number of business scenario models that reflect possible and probable avenues of future development and events, as illustrated in Figure 5. Once defined and established, they need to be checked and updated on a continual basis to reflect changing business or organisational requirements, as well as market conditions.   Incorporated with the premises policy into the centre of the premises or facilities department's existence, the models form the basis of any action plans and are valuable for disseminating a general understanding of the theoretical base.

With a system of premises management established along the lines described in this paper, change is managed on a daily basis, and provision of the premises resource is

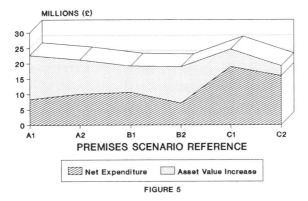

BUSINESS SCENARIO MODELS
EXPENDITURE v INCREASE IN ASSET VALUE
- COST SUMMARY -

MILLIONS (£)

PREMISES SCENARIO REFERENCE

Net Expenditure   Asset Value Increase

FIGURE 5

continually monitored and adjusted as required to meet business needs. The premises policy, in identifying the real business or organisational needs, in turn inherently provides premises with the necessary short-term flexibility required of them, whilst the strategic models exist to identify, plan, action and meet fundamental requirement changes before their accommodation needs arise.

The establishment of an agreed premises policy, and its use in building and maintaining business models, provides the vehicle for pro-active management of property. Corporate premises requirements are established in a manner that promotes the optimisation of the property resource, and instils management disciplines that predict change and are ready to accommodate it, rather than react hastily to it in an unco-ordinated ad-hoc manner that is unlikely to meet the constraints of time, quality and cost.

With a fully developed and utilised premises policy, the pro-active premises department has a heart that beats.

CHAPTER FIVE

*'Value engineering is an organised creative
approach which has for its purpose the
efficient systematic identification of potential
cost savings and the elimination of unnecessary
cost. Value engineering has the greatest effect
on savings during the preconstruction phase.
It includes operability and maintainability; a
higher investment cost may be prudent when
evaluated against future operating costs.'*

*The Construction Management
Committee of the Construction
Division, compiled and edited by
George Stukhart.*

Development of models and methods for the management of the building process and design

R. Vinci
Sub-Project 3 'Quality and technological innovation' of the CNR's Progetto Finalizzato Edilizia, Milan, Italy

Abstract
In the world of construction the necessity of dealing with buildings not only as objects to be built, but as a complex system to be managed over time has recently becomes evident. The concept of a finished product is replaced by that of a building as a dynamic object, which might undergo different processes: changes of its uses, changes in its purposes, management of its different functions, ageing management, etc.

Thus it is important to obtain buildings not only flexible on the basis of predetermined solutions, but also buildings able to modify the management parameters as well as to fulfil further technical requirements which cannot be determined during the first and well-known design stage.

Hence comes the interest in the management. The paper intends to present a scientific undertaking of the National Research Council of Italy, named Progetto Finalizzato Edilizia, both in its details and as a whole.

The main aim of Progetto Finalizzato Edilizia is to set up a link between researchers and producer in order to trigger off a course of actions leading to modifications and innovations in the building field which can strengthen national experts on the European market.

Keywords: Design, Research, Management, Information.

1 Foreword

To face the topic of Architectural Management it is useful to start by saying that the subject is presently being completely reshaped throughout all the industrialized Countries and that such a process is gradually, but steadily changing and that it must rely on two basic considerations:

- first, the awareness of the role of the final user is changing and he is not willing anymore to delegate completely the management of the building process to the designer, so, being more aware and "instructed" as concerns the building technology, he looks for new opportunities and forms of direct decision-making intervention.

This attitude does not just aim at improving the control - and sometimes, the cheapness - of the process, but also at affecting - at the beginning just to improve his own technical knowledge and awareness - the choices and the possible alternatives for what concerns the definition of space, and mainly the technical and technological definition of the plan;

- secondly, in the world of construction the necessity of dealing with buildings not only as objects to be built, but as a complex system to be managed over time has recently becomes evident. The concept of a finished product is replaced by that of a building as a dynamic object, which might undergo different processes: changes of its uses, changes in its purposes, management of its different functions, ageing management, etc.

Thus it is important to obtain buildings not only flexible on the basis of predetermined solutions, but also buildings able to modify the management parameters as well as to fulfil further technical requirements which cannot be determined during the first and well-known design stage.

This implies abandoning the classical planning schemens and, sometimes, making all the requirement of a building fit in a "management" of its own over a period of time which does not expire with the "end of the building works", but going on for several decades, thus requiring the application of those forecasting attitudes that so far have been widely employed in the economic and financial field.

2 The problematic area

Hence comes the interest in the management. The subject matter of Architectural Management seems to be destined to free itself from a too obedient and monotonous reference to the mere building and architectural sphere, and imposes to the operators of the process more differentiated competences and a stronger and stronger disposition to co-operate with the others, so, many of the possibilities of creating an actual operative synergy will be based on the improved attitude of the individuals to communicate with one another and, first of all, on the actual availability to understand each other.

Such a process of re-adaptation has been, for instance, completely assimilated (in the most advanced production sectors) by the industrial sphere, where the capability of foreseeing the change of the production activities and their consequences, seems to be economically more important than the simple initial definition of the activities themselves and, as a consequence, implied the fulfilment of new competences for a more precise preventive evaluation for what concerns the planning and the management.

However, the main "link" between the users' demands and the building process is still the designer, but this profession is becoming more and more complex according to a series of factors that, while contributing to further differentiate the process and the relationships between the operators, has not so far identified new intermediate professional roles able to cope with it. So, the designer is still the main point of reference for the whole process, from the identification of a "need" to its solution from the building point of view.

For instance, the designer is the main link between the technical standard and the building process, the main operator for the transmission of the information related to the greatest part of standard contents - in particular the ones concerning the environment and technology - and still this peculiar professional figure has the task of ensuring the achievement of those results that some time ago belonged to the rules of practice.

This exacting task gives this traditional figure of the process a new and different importance, based on new and different responsibilities requiring articulated competences, extensive references and continuous specialistic investigations (town-planning, architecture, technology, ergonomics, economy, finance and programming, study of molecular structure, plant-engineering, etc.) in order to mediate the technological development on the one hand, and the transformation of the social and cultural needs of the territory and of users on the other hand, forcing him to acquire and manage suitable instruments of analysis and evaluation.   The designer is often induced against his will to forget obvious and simple factors because they are considered to be already solved, or easy to be solved.

So there arise new needs as concerns the disposition towards the Management: also the designer, if he wants to realize his own ideas (for instance the "architectural quality"), must find out solutions implying and enabling the attainment of others' goals; this consideration leads to the need of knowing the other operators of the process and to understand their problems, co-operating to solve them.

A plan can be considered as good when everybody can identify with it in order to provide the highest contribution to its achievement; in other words, it is a problem of synergy, whose possibility of being realized and whose efficaciousness are widely demonstrated by experimental applications of the physical science.

So the designer must show good dispositions to the dialogue and a firm will to co-operate, as well as a patient awareness about the fact that his role can be realized only if he takes part together with all the others in the building process.

Nevertheless it is to be considered that planning, even if characterized by independent and specific methods and instruments, can not be completely affected by the presence and the action of the other operators of the building process. Planning originates as an interpretation of cultural, social, political (and red tape), economical, geographical, production and technological components of the space-time context in which it takes place, but it must always be an "interpretation" and not a mechanical outcome of these process components, since each of them can be taken and used more or less frequently, according either to the designer's will or to his ability to act as an "intermediary" with reference to the specific needs of the other single operators.

This way of thinking is a primary element for the comprehension of the designer's role and it is certainly independent from what is planned: this means consciously taking on a correct method and ethical behaviour as to the planning action, that must be able to be extended beyond the limits of the "construction action".

If this way of thinking is correctly interpreted it becomes clear that it can be seen as the core of the management required by the building sector in the short term.

However, if any pattern of traditional building process is carefully considered, it becomes clear that it shows many faults with reference to the stillness of the sequences between the various stages of the planning approach:
- the provisional planning, including technological and economical decisions;
- the comparison with the market production reality and the consequent correction of the initial technological choices;
- the final stage of planning definition and construction, that is meant to be a final synthesis between the planning will and the production reality, but generated - and often heavily conditioned - by economic problems.

So there is the need to bring together these aspects, to modify consolidated procedures that nevertheless are no more an economic solution as to the planning Management that must try and reduce the negative effects of the excessive breaking up of the process and, particularly, of the "disconnection" between planning and construction.

In other words, the function of planning must be defined again in the light of an industrial logic, not as an alternative or a contrast to the traditional way of working, but as a more rational operative instrument giving a suitable answer to the complexity of the problems to be faced using more effective criteria and in view of better qualitative results.

So the plan must evolve, actively involving all the operators of the building process whose activities are however conditioned: in my opinion, the importance and timeliness of Management are to be found in this apparently little difference between a passive behaviour (typical of the so-called "mass-production" sequence) and the acceptation of a "sharing" role.

This topic is to be interpreted as an optimization of the relationships between the operators of the process and, through the interpretation of the designer, it becomes the object of the research Program - in some of its research and study aspects - that will be briefly introduced in the second part of this short contribution.

For a better comprehension of the extent of this compelling task, it will be more useful to refer to the available program and final documents.

3   The building goal-oriented research programm of CNR

Progetto Finalizzato Edilizia (PFEd), a scientific undertaking of CNR - Italy's National Research Council - is a 5-year goal-oriented research programme designed to financially support building organizations by allocating funds up to a total amount of 115 billion lire (82.14 million dollars). PFEd has been offically launched in May 1989 and it has undertaken and partly completed now its second Executive Program.

PFEd's aim is to act as a link between the research field and the production field in order to foster actions and processes leading to changes and innovations in the building field and able to forward the national operators on the European market.

PFEd is divided into three Sub-projects, each involved in specific research trends:
- Sub-Project 1 - "Process and procedures": aims at improving the building process status and its relevant procedural stages organization.
- Sub-Project 2 - "Design innovation": is meant to provide the grounds for developing tools and cultural skills that can help designers cope with and manage the design process in building.
- Sub-Project 3 -"Quality and technological innovation": is addressed to develop innovatory technologies and to support standardization, experimentation and control.

In particular it has been leading the research programmes to achieve innovatory goals, which in turn can assure the growth of quality in the building production and construction sector.

The transferability of the results is an important aspect which will undoubtedly affect the Project's further choices.

It is no use to try and detect, in the latter phases of the research programs, only the ways to transfer knowledge, just as it seems as much difficult to expect that this transfer acts outside the research units that have worked within the field of the Project.

So the transferability is to be ensured during the working-out phase of the programs and achieved by a part of the operators, within their specific field, which is with no doubt the most fertile as concerns either scientific or technological receptivity.

The first theory is, in fact, that only through a co-ordinated intervention and through strategic and even international choices it becomes possible to establish research trends for the solution of many-sided and complex peculiar aspects, which would otherwise only poorly affect individually the coherent development of the building field, especially in this moment in which, due to the opening of the European Market, quality and qualification are going to play a more important role than in the past. In this sense, this Congress represents a very stimulating and useful chance for a further confrontation.

3.1 Some of the main expected results
Sub-Project 1 "Process and procedures" mainly aims at clarifying,

simplifying and innovating the main procedural phases of the process, for instance the relationship between operators and their relevant tasks, the technical management and the economical and financial management.

As concerns Sub-Project 2 "Design innovation", the main goals are to obtain specific results in the area of the methods and of the instruments for the planning as concerns both the innovation of the contents and the planning organization, and the integration of information technologies in the working practice.

As particularly regards Sub-Project 3 " Quality and technological innovation" all the efforts focus on setting up a series of innovatory building components and systems in order to improve the qualitative aspects. Another goal to be achieved consists in the improvement of the organization for the management of quality, by dealing with the subject-matters related to the technological transfer and to qualification.

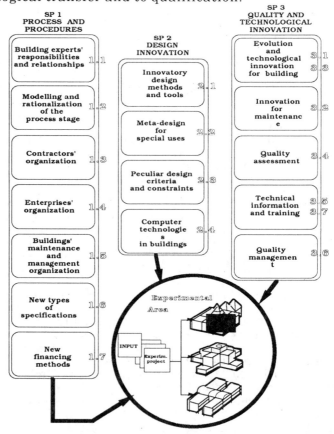

Fig.1. Generalconfiguration of the Executive Program
as a handbook for the understanding of
Progetto Finalizzato Edilizia

The scheme in fig.1 points out the thematic contents of the research Areas included in the three Sub-projects as well as the Experimentation Area (AS), a study for the construction of 3 intelligent buildings in a 5-years period which is to be interpreted as an outstanding result of PFEd's research activity. These buildings are to be used as a test-bench of the project as a whole.

B - management instruments (technical/structural and economical), concerning the organization of criteria of knowledge and proposal as regards:

- management of preventives and final evaluation (especially as concerns rehabilitation);
- technical and managerial training for the people involved in the process (new professional figures, programs and structures, contents and reliability, etc.);
- assessment of production processes and goods (technical certification and standardization as concerns the innovative and traditional aspects with a view to the future European accomplishments);
- co-ordinated action for the rehabilitation, the recovery and use diversification (for parts of town-scale, for single buildings or for classes of use destination, etc.).

Generally, SP 3's main goals concern:

- as regards management instruments (B), the goals range from the feasibility studies and the critical verification of the existing instruments, to the suggestion of experimental methods and activities which are outlined in the contents and which can depend on the technical and building sphere, rather than on the economical and formative one.

Besides, it should be taken into consideration that the evolution trends of the building sector are not structurally uniform and they have to be approached in a different way by the various operators of the building sector; it is, nevertheless, through this research activity that a sector is able to sense and to foresee the changes: this is the reason why inside SP3 some elements have been found, acting as general reference instruments for the achievement of the specific research goals within the Project and the sector; these elements are:

- innovation, meant as a process for the promotion of reviews or new solutions, by introducing new systems and criteria;
- organization, meant as a process for increasing the functionality and the efficiency of structured and systematic operations.

The main goal, however, remains quality, which is a basic concept, especially during the important period of transition which will lead to the effective internationalization of the markets and that will also turn, as a consequence, into an increase of competition on the national market.

In any case, quality, is not only a goal to be accomplished, but a "philosophy" and to comform to it, means to witness the level of maturity reached by a sector. If this philosophy is fully understood by everyone, it leads to a great emphasis of the overall results: in this connection, research is one of the best available tools and it gives a very qualitative chance.

Looking at the building sector, it can be noticed that the

Looking at the building sector, it can be noticed that the analysis of the quality of the technological and scientific changes and the interactions existing between them and the strategies of the enterprises, as concerns the production, allows to underline how science, technology and practice can be considered as a "whole" representing a single "composite" resource able to develop individual effects on economy and society.

However, this happens in the building sector to a lower extent than in other industrial sectors.

This consideration underlines the discrepancy between the need of intensively using a resource that becomes more and more essential and expensive - as know-how is - and the evident impossibility of attributing to its development and to its evaluation the economic rules that belong to the contractors activity, bearing in mind that its development is made possible by the contributions of science, which stands out by virtue of its meaningful and peculiar aspects of self-propulsion and substantial autonomy.

Anyway, as it has for a long time been underlined, technology is an intermediate moment between the area of the theoretical knowledge (science) and the area of the practical knowledge (technics). In this way, technology has an important part to play; it has to orient the scientific efforts toward very precise targets, and then it has to organize these efforts into a system, programming the use of the results in order to limit lacks of balance as well as undesired consequences, resorting to rationality and to the multitude of disciplines. These latter characteristics are, as a matter of fact, the most meaningful features of technology.

Contractors (which, as a matter of fact, are most interested than all the other different operators of the building process, in obtaining the results of the research carried out by this Sub-Project) have to face several practical problems, in order to manage this type of relationship. These practical problems are generally related to:
- the involvement, which does not always mean real will to provide a practical contribution, which is often limited to passive interventions;
- the accessibility, which is the equivalent of the available and applied degrees and levels of transferability of scientific, technological and technical know-how;
- the possibility of getting the results, that is to say, the interest of the individuals to use the results in an exclusive way by wielding a monopolistic defence.

These aspects can be solved, whenever the general interests are correctly protected by the public institutions, through the "information management", that has a large system of definitions which all share the peculiar characteristic of flexibility.

It is already known that research, except for few sectors, is a field with no other barriers but knowledge. It is also known that the technological and scientific community has always been an "open" system that, by virtue of this characteristic, continuously gets new resources and *stimula* for the improvement of the acquisitions, through the comparison of the ideas, leading to innovation through an iterative process of reviews and new solutions, which have been started off by using new systems and criteria.

So, we believe that researchers must undertake to open the "way" as concerns the expectations, the goals and, obviously, the interests of the various operators involved in the building process in the field of technological knowledge which, still at present, is a partially unexplored field, but very attractive and potentially rich as concerns the various applications and the developments of the research activity.

One of the problems that SP3 had to be faced with, during the introductory phase and during the first year of activity, was to compare with the heterogeneous category of the operators involved in the research program (producers, contractors, researchers, professors, experts, etc.). As a matter of fact, each of these categories has its own peculiar competences and specific criteria to be adopted in order to approach the research activity, and all these criteria are highly differentiated as concerns both strategy and the concreteness level of the results that can be obtained.

All these different contributions are moreover very important and useful for the growth of the sector, and under this principle, it has been tried, as far as possible, to start an Executive Program concerning the first three years of activity, taking into account all the needs and values, while privileging the proposals aiming at:
- the actual realization of innovation,
- the experimentation on new technologies,
- the increasing of the working capacity of the structures having a key role within the process,
- the critical analysis of the instrumental areas,
- the pointing out of new contents and tools to be employed for training.

A particular attention was paid to those research goals that could have provided strategic and instrumental contributions that were already looking forward to 1993 European Common Market. Within SP3 these contributions have been interpreted in a synergic way with reference to the procedural backslidings that were assumed in SP 1, and they have been proposed by the producers and by the bodies concerned with research, experimentation, certification, standardization and technical training.

So, at the end of the day, the main aim of Progetto Finalizzato Edilizia is to improve the technical knowledge in the building sector, but also to set up links between researchers and producers in order to trigger off a course of actions leading to modifications and innovations in the building field which can strengthen national experts to better "manage" quality on the European market.

Value management enhances professional development

J.E.S. Dale
The Polytechnic of Huddersfield, School of Architecture, Huddersfield, UK

Abstract
My aim is to show how Value Management sandwiches together
Accountability, Buildability, Creativity, Coordination, Communication and
Teamwork in a positive, constructive and organized methodology, and that it is
an **additional** (rather than an alternative) expertise which all professionals
involved in the design and construction of buildings would find an asset in
respect of their professional development.
Keywords: Value Management, Teamwork, Communications, Creativity,
Professional Development, Architecture.

1 Introduction

"Success" (or, in a depressed market, "survival"), in business is not based on
any single issue. It is a combination of factors that includes the harmonious
integration of time, cost, and quality; and coordinated management, teamwork
and productivity, with highly trained and dedicated people working together,
led by skilled and creative managers. In other words, to achieve both success
and progress, it takes a disciplined approach, an operating methodology, and a
work ethic supported by a committed management/1/. However, "Progress"
often means "Change" - a change in the way one thinks and a change in habit
patterns. This is the biggest obstacle to overcome.

The aim of this paper is to show the key elements of Value Management
which contribute to the overall improvement of the design and building
procedure, and how a knowledge of the philosophy and methodology of Value
Management can enhance the professional development of the Architect,
Engineer or anyone involved in the design of buildings.

The above hypotheses contains a number of components which form the
parameters of this paper, namely:-

- Value Management - the key elements
- Design and Construction process and procedures
- Value Management related to contract procurement
- the integration of the above factors

2 Value Management - an overview

The generally accepted definition of Value Management is :-
"Value Management is a Function-Oriented, Multi-disciplined Team and Systematic Approach to provide Value in a product, system or service"
Value Management is not a single initiative, or even a group of multiple initiatives. It is a methodology that embraces those initiatives and management skills that make a business successful. It means "the ability to **manage value** ," and the word **VALUE** is a marketing term - not an architectural or engineering term/2/. Only the Client/User/or Customer can determine the ultimate Value of any facility or product.

Value Management relies heavily on teamwork, good communications and coordination. It has, as its core, a structured, multi-disciplinary team who are committed to achieving a common goal. It has a proven record of success. In the design and construction field, it has been proved that the Value Management Team can produce more ideas, better solutions and better "buildability" requirements than the individual disciplines working alone.

A brief description of the key elements of the Value Management approach is set out below:-

2. 1   Function Analysis
This is a specific technique or methodology used to establish objectives and to eliminate uncertainties. It is a means to an end, and not necessarily an end in itself. It focuses the mind on the precise task in hand, and sets targets for the creative problem solving techniques to follow. It is often described as the **"heart"** of Value Management.

2. 2   Creativity
Value Management uses Group Creativity as a means to solving problems. It is a recognised fact that "the use of a multi-disciplined group has been shown to yield from 65-93% MORE IDEAS than from individuals working alone"/3/. The Creative phase is often referred to as the **"backbone"** of Value Management.

2. 3   The Multi-disciplined Team
This is not just the design team. It is a team which is flexible, and can extend to incorporate the Client, the end User (operations and maintenance operators etc.), and the Contractor. This team does NOT meet for just a few hours once a week in the usual way. It is virtually "locked together" for an extended period of time - conventionally known as the 5-day 40-hour Study. No other system contains this concentrated "togetherness" through which a rapport is established between the members of the team resulting in a "thinking alikeness". This is the **"brain and nerve centre"** of Value Management.

2.4 Value Criteria

This incorporates techniques such as Cost:Worth Analysis. The use of the multi-disciplined Team plays an important role here, because each discipline has a different perception of Value. and it is necessary to evolve a **"common value criteria"** if communications and coordination are to improve. The value management team's goal is to establish this common value criteria.

2.5 The Job Plan

This represents the discipline or structure of the system, similar to the Plan of Work which architects uses. The VE job plan is universal, and although there are slight variations, the principle elements and procedures are always present. This is the **"life blood"** of Value Management which runs through the whole process linking all the elements together.

From the above we can see that the Multi-disciplined Team plays a fundamental role in Value Management since the rapport that develops between the individual members throughout the Study improves; hence communication and coordination skills also improve, due to the structured nature of the job plan. The Value of these skills, once learnt, will extend beyond the Study itself - they become an ATTITUDE of MIND.

3 The Design and Construction Process

Now it is necessary to examine briefly the essential elements contained within the design and construction process.

3.1 Changes in the Building Process

The building industry as a whole has little corporate identity. There are many features which set it apart from other process industries and which accentuate the need for professional management. Every project is a "one-off-custom-made" product. The team which produces a building is in existence only for the duration of that particular project, and the members of that team are drawn from a diverse background of professions and skills.

The NEDO Report /4/of 1988 stated that :- "of the changes and new trends which now influence the procurement of commercial buildings, the most important is **the increasing fragmentation of the design and construction process,** as more and more specialist inputs are required and employed......The industry is not only fragmented in terms of separate businesses, but also by the diversity of professions and trades, and by the increasing numbers of self-employed people.......**The proliferation of organisations and specialisms has aggravated the existing problems of coordination, communication, motivation and control, both within the industry itself and in its relationships with the customer**....... the research has shown plainly that **management was all too often inadequate**".

However, it is interesting to note that a similar situation existed back in 1963 when the Tavistock Publication was commissioned/5/. The "instability and lack of definitions of responsibility for members of the building team resulted in a general anxiety among all concerned". It was this report that highlighted the communications aspect - "Communications of many kinds constitute the energising and controlling factor in the development of the building team. It is through communications that it is conceived, developed and directed in the service of the building process"/6/. It appears that 25 years later, despite the fact the industry has grown and expanded, the same situation remains.

3. 2   Identifiable components

The two most identifiable tasks in the building process are that of design and construction. Traditionally these were allocated to the Architect and the Main Contractor, each separately employed by the Client.

In its simplest form, it can be expressed as follows:-

---

the Client
the Instigator of the project, without whom it would not exist. This component incorporates the financial element, and also extends to the user/occupier components.
the Architect
traditionally the leader of the design team - this component incorporates ALL the people involved in the design of the project
the Contractor
the Builder - incorporating the materials element and all those who are involved in the construction of the project.

Fig.1 Basic Components of the Design and Construction process

In earlier times the Architect felt technically and contractually secure enough to perform an overall management function on behalf of the Client. "The growth of new technology and greater prevalence of court action on professional liability have together reduced his readiness to manage and take responsibility"/7/. Over the same period, the work of the contractor has been similarly curtailed in scope. He is finding it impossible to encompass within his organisation all the technical know-how, and is becoming increasingly dependent on specialist firms to ensure that the work is done properly.

Figure 1 however, is very simplistic - and is true for possibly less than 20% of all construction work   (one-off houses/small extensions etc). In all but the simplest of projects: -

- the Client - is not the end user of the building;

- the Architect - is not the sole designer of the building;
- the Contractor does not build the project entirely from his own resources.
Today - THIS (figure 2) is a more realistic diagram of the manpower required to design and construct a project - and even this does not fully encompass everyone!!

The TEAM has not only EXPANDED, but also DIVERSIFIED. What's more - this diversification is increasingly taking place at an earlier stage in life - namely in **training** and **education.**

visiting user	infrequent user	occasional user
	CLIENT	
main user	resident user	main user
	geotechnic engineer	
civil engineer		quantity surveyor
structural engineer		landscape architect
	ARCHITECT	
mechanical engineer		interior designer
electrical engineer		acoustic specialist
	lighting specialist	
site agent		cost estimators
domestic subcontractors		domestic suppliers
	CONTRACTOR	
nominated subcontractors		nominated suppliers
project manager		quality control managers

Fig. 2 Interface between Client, Design and Construction

The change has stemmed partly from new market pressures, with the switch to commercial customers motivated by the need to compete. For them, early completion, attractive designs, user satisfaction and low running costs were essential. Accordingly, several of them set about improving the management of their own building projects. At the same time, an increasing number of professionals and builders saw the market need to provide management services which would enable the modern building industry to perform better/8/. In the UK,the changes to the Code of Conduct for Architects in 1981 made it possible for the Architect to take on the role of Developer as well as to become Directors of building companies. The profession, already in a dilemma since the report by Lord Esher and Lord Llewelyn Davies, became even more divided. The proverb "divide and conquer" would have been an appropriate epitaph, for the Architect as leader of the team was reaching a crisis point. The new role of Project Manager was being introduced in the capacity of team leader and coordinator of the building process on many of the larger scale and faster construction projects. This seems to have created even more confusion, especially with regards to control and liability. Hence, not only was the leadership aspect in question, but also the range of contracts available, was also changing and expanding.

4 Value Management related to Contract Procurement

In the UK there are, basically, 3 forms of contract procurement:-
- **Traditional; Design & Build; and Management procurement.** Each form has inherent advantages and disadvantages, and the final selection depends on what is "Right" for the individual project. i.e. Choose the **contract** to suit the **job**: NOT make the **job** fit the **contract** !!

In the traditional forms of contract used for building projects the Contractor has no contact with the Architect until the documents are released for tender purposes. The introduction of Management Contracting has not only opened the door for contractor participation in the design process, but it has also insisted contractually that it shall happen/9/. Similarly, the development of the Design and Build Contract meant that the coordination of the design process and building procedure could take place at a much earlier stage than it would in the conventional type of contract. Finally, the introduction of the North American form of Construction Management contract saw yet another way of integrating the skills of all the design-construction team. Whilst the increased pressures of time (i.e. the need to design and build faster) influenced the growth of the new forms of contract, it is the "buildability" factor that has made them work. Detail design cannot be divorced from construction without major cost and time penalties /10/.

Now let's look at procurement and procedure together, in terms of the application of Value Management.

First, the **DESIGN & BUILD** Procurement method - here, all parties (Client; Architect; Contractor) are known at the beginning of the project. Hence, Value Management studies can make the best use of a totally multi-disciplined TEAM - with representatives from all parties. In fact, it would be to the Design & Build **Contractor's** advantage to promote Value Management, since, under this method of procurement, he is the party who carries most of the risk.

With the **MANAGEMENT** Procurement method, the situation is slightly different. (This refers to Management Contracting as opposed to the other forms of Management procurement, such as Construction Management). Whilst the Client and the Architect/Design team are known at the start of the project, the time of the appointment of the Management Contractor can vary - though it is usually recommended to appoint one at an early stage of the design. Secondly, it is the job of the Management Contractor to MANAGE the project, NOT to BUILD it - i.e. he does not CONSTRUCT the building. Finally, the various contract packages (often numbering over 100), which represent the parties who actually BUILD the project, are not usually known at the outset, but are released continuously throughout the construction period.

Nevertheless, it would be to the CLIENT'S advantage to consider the use of Value Management at the stage when the Management Contractor has been appointed, thereby involving the 3 principle manpower components - as an aid to strategic planning as well as an aid to the design and buildability aspects - since, (in this form of procurement), it is the Client who carries the risk. Value Management could also be used at both later stages of the contract, and for individual packages, since these projects tend to be both extensive and often complicated.

Finally, the **TRADITIONAL** form of procurement - when only the Client and the Architect/Design team are known initially. The Contractor is usually appointed after Tender stage, by which time the design of the project has virtually been completed. Whilst, Value Management can be used during the construction period, with participation from the contractor, it is more cost effective at the pre-tender stage, when it can be used to coordinate the design team with the client/user components.

Value Management, therefore, can be applied to any of the procurement methods.

5 Teamwork and Communications

The entire subject of Teamwork, Communications and Coordination within the Construction Industry covers a vast area. In the United Kingdom, numerous articles and Reports have been written about this topic - not only recently, as per the NEDO Report/11/ of 1988, but as far back as the Banwell Report /12/ of 1964. WHY? - The answer appears to be because, even after all the recommendations, the surveys, analyses and proposals, **there is still a lack of Teamwork, a lack of Communications, and a lack of Coordination within the Construction Industry.** The situation has not yet been resolved.

I have spent 17 very enjoyable years working as an Architect in practice. Like most Architects in the UK - when you are given a project, you are with it from start to finish - that is, you do the design, then you produce the working drawings (if you are lucky - you may get some assistance, but not always) and then you supervise the work on site right up to the end of the job. The same is true, I think, for most Engineers and Quantity Surveyors. Being part of this gigantic, multi-disciplined TEAM is stimulating, it's fun, - and yes, of course, at times it's chaotic - but it's still enjoyable!!!

Last year I moved into the academic world - teaching architecture. The first thing that I noticed was the fact that I was surrounded, almost entirely by other architects (students and staff), and the second thing was the realisation that these students spend 5 years training to be architects, surrounded only by other architects, doing one-off projects on their own. Since I am the 5th year tutor - by the time they have reached this stage of the course - they don't even like doing a group project amongst themselves, let alone going to the lectures given by the engineers and quantity surveyors!! **TEAMWORK does NOT EXIST.**

So Figure 2 - should really look like THIS.

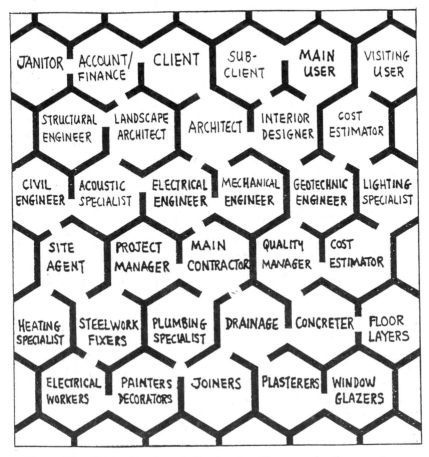

Fig. 3 The Client: Designer: Contractor: Communications system

I have deliberately chosen the honey-comb - for several reasons: -

First, although the individual disciplines are trained in isolation of each other, they are taught the principles of the other professions. There is an awareness of what "the Team" consists of. Hence, they do not appear in little boxes - there are routes of access to everyone else - however tortuous it may appear.

Secondly, like the bees producing honey, we are all working towards the same end - to produce a building that satisfies the customer. We are all building the same honeycomb. Unfortunately, there is a tendency to stay within one's own "cell" - and, as you can see - communication between the cells is sometimes difficult. The lines of communication are somewhat obscure!!

Also, the bees carry out their work in a set sequence - they have a Job Plan, a plan of work which is both structured, and **very well coordinated**. We have a plan of work - but the COORDINATION often leaves something to be desired.

Finally, the bees have a common set of "VALUES"- we all have Values - the problem is, we all have **different VALUES** - Often, because our education is in relative isolation, we **assume** that everyone else's "VALUES" are the same as our own - and this is not the case.

TEAMWORK relies on good COMMUNICATIONS and COORDINATION - NOT on ASSUMPTIONS!

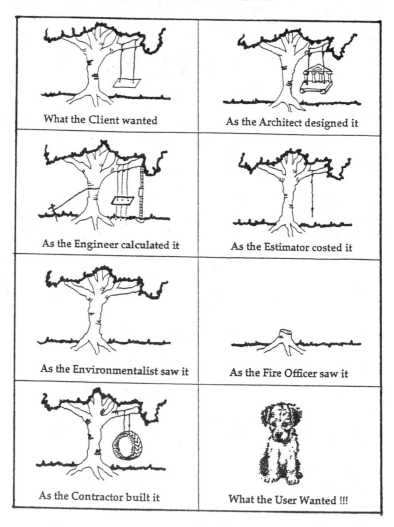

Fig. 4 Communications - "The Birthday Present"

This popular cartoon has appeared in various forms over the years., but I have made one slight alteration at the end. I call it **"the Birthday Present"**.

1.   The **CLIENT**.- in the goodness of his heart, wants to give his 6 year old boy a specially designed Swing for a birthday present. You can almost HEAR the reasoning, the philosophy, the **value** put on each design by the various parties involved:-

2.   the **ARCHITECT** - " it is a statement of the grandeur of a momentous occasion, reflecting the divorce from post-modern, de-constructive asymmetry to the neo-classical revival".

3.   the **ENGINEER** - "well - how old IS the tree ? it could fall down any time, and I can't take any chances".

4.   the **ESTIMATOR** - " you just said "a swing" - I didn't think you meant THAT sort of a swing"

5.   the **ENVIRONMENTALIST** - "a tree is a living thing - which should be allowed to keep its own natural beauty, without human ornament!!"

6.   the **FIRE OFFICER** - "That tree is a fire hazard - 2hr fire rating- you must be joking! You won't get an certification of occupation. ."

7.   the **CONTRACTOR** - (one of the most "creative" persons in a project) - "I thought of a more buildable solution at no extra charge - and NO, it did NOT fall off the back of a lorry!!"

Seven people with seven valid reasons -

- UNLESS they COMMUNICATE with each other;
- UNLESS they establish a COMMON VALUE CRITERIA:
- UNLESS they act as a TEAM;
   - you COULD finish up with 5 swings and no tree!!

And there is one more person who should be considered - one who is frequently left out of the design and construction process - that is - the **END USER** - what did **he** actually WANT for his birthday?

It is this Team effort approach which needs to be encouraged - an attitude of **"our project"** as opposed to **"my project"**.   The value in experience alone, of attending a Value Engineering Study must contribute towards an appreciation of the advantages of working as a team over that of each discipline working independently.   Encouraging groups of professionals from disparate backgrounds to seek out answers, to go beyond the obvious, is one way of allaying our natural prejudices.

Two other Art forms rely on this aspect, namely Music and Drama. The orchestra works as a team to produce the harmony in the desired form under the leadership of the conductor who, in turn, interprets the score of the composer. The Director directs the actors, actresses and stage technicians; coordinates the costumes and scenery; and interprets the script of the author to produce a play or film. Teamwork, communication and coordination are an accepted part of these activities /13/.

Finally, in 1971, the American Architect William Wayne Caudill, (winner of the AIA Gold Medal for his contribution to Architecture) wrote /14/, - "The day of the prima donna approach to designing buildings has passed. The new

way is by team.". He summarizes by adding that: -   "Almost any team can produce mere shelter, but **to produce buildings which possess architecture takes a new kind of team - one sensitive to human needs and values**. The idea of architecture by team has three underlying ideas: -
1. The team is a genius,
2. The client / user is a member of the team, and
3. The team is an ever expanding unit, not limited to the design profession".
and to the above I would like to add a fourth idea, that:-
4. Value Management as a concept can contribute to the team approach.

6   Accountability, Buildability and Creativity

6. 1   Accountability
"All designs have unnecessary costs". Value Management ensures that all possible solutions to a design have been investigated, and that the areas containing unnecessary costs are removed. The Function Analysis phase of a VE Study ensures an in-depth understanding of the project. No other technique encompasses this methodology in such detail. The recommendations of a VE Study are given to the Client and the Design team in a fully detailed, unbiased and comprehensive Report which indicates the advantages and the disadvantages of accepting a recommendation - it is therefore giving the Client all the facts from which to base his decision.

Architects may argue that they are "accountable" for their designs. Certainly in terms of "legal liability" this is true. However, with respect to giving the best "value" in terms of the Client's requirements, this can only be a subjective opinion. Value Management offers an objective opinion; it gives alternatives; and it sets down reasons why those alternatives have been proposed. The Client can then be assured that all possible solutions to the problem have been investigated before he makes a decision.

However, the accountability factor also extends beyond the design and construction of a project. To whom is the Client "accountable"? If the Client is a private concern (i.e. self-financing the project) he is only accountable to himself - so long as the building remains within his domain. If the Client is, for example, a Developer, then he should be accountable for decisions which effect the future Life-cycle costing, Energy efficiency and Maintenance of the building. Finally, if the Client is a Government (Local or Central) Body, or a Limited Company, then the Client must be accountable to the tax-payers, rate-payers or shareholders for all aspects of the design - present and future. The public who see the building in passing should also be considered. Nothing else can offer this degree of "Accountability" except Value Management/15/.

6. 2   Buildability
Buildability has been defined as "the extent to which the design of a building facilitates ease of construction, subject to the overall requirements for the

completed building"/16/. The means to achieve this is through teamwork, coordination and communication. The result is not only "ease of construction" for the project, but it is also a means to achieve better quality control and at the same time, a means of avoiding adverse relationships, since everyone is working together on the same team. McGeorge writes that "designs are not produced just by draftsmen or engineers, but by a system of resources working together as a balanced team...the engine which drives the design system is the brainpower of its members, and the fuel which powers it, is information"/17/. In his writing, concerned with design productivity in relation to the problem of quality, he concludes that "Better and earlier communication with the contractor is needed"/18/.

It was in 1977 that Barrie and Mulch recorded that, "one of the advantages of successful Construction Management is the absence of adversary relationship often present between the Architect/Engineer and the General Contractor....everyone benefits when discrepancies are talked over internally and straightened out prior to finalization of construction contracts.....this same concept can be applied to the Value Management effort......the emergence of Construction Management, and the early involvement of the contractor in the design process has fostered the use of Value Management"/19/.

It is part of the job of the VE team to determine the facility with which a design can be constructed and, should this aspect pose a problem, it is their task to investigate alternative ways of overcoming the difficulty before construction takes place. Often, due to lack of time in the design period, the actual 'buildability' of certain details are not realised until they are about to be constructed. The Value Management approach in particular highlights the advantages of using the combined knowledge of the design team and the contractor to create designs which are not only "fit-for-purpose" but also practical and efficient to build.

It is sufficient to state here that, through a combination of creativity, teamwork, coordination and intensive analysis, Value Management can contribute towards the improved buildability of a project.

6. 3   Creativity

The overwhelming advantages of Group Creativity are well known. Unfortunately, the education, training and practice of Architects and other Professionals favours singular effort rather than group effort, and certainly avoids multi-disciplinary group effort.

Architecture is often regarded as an Art. However, the Artist / Designer, given a project to design, commences the design with sketches which are then worked into a final drawing - after which he /she then makes the object. In this way one becomes familiar with the material in which one is designing - be it clay, copper, silk-screen, wood or leather. One learns, very quickly, of both the limitations of the materials and their potential capacity. Consequently, one learns to design the object taking these factors into consideration. At an Art College, one builds or makes in three-dimensions the designs which one has created in two-dimensions. There is an awareness of what can and what cannot be Created, and there is an element of satisfaction in carrying ones ideas through to completion. **Creativity is linked with Buildability.**

The Architect produces drawings in two-dimensions, which somebody else then uses to create a three-dimensional building. The architecture / building is produced by a multi-disciplined team. In this respect the Architect has the frustration of not actually creating anything, but merely being the instigator of ideas which rely on other people to complete. **Hence Creativity and Buildability are not linked.** Therein lies the dilemma.

Value Management gives the opportunity of creating buildable ideas through the means of a multi-disciplined team. Hence, the magnitude of the creative solutions which can be generated is measured, not in arithmetic or even geometric terms, but in logarithmic terms/20/.

7   Summary

Every Saturday, hundreds of people watch sporting events, such as football.
THEY all have a Common Interest - but THEY are a CROWD.
It takes hundreds of people to create a building - THEY all have a Common Interest; - but They CANNOT be a Crowd; THEY must be TEAM.

Good COMMUNICATION and COORDINATION results in Good TEAMWORK -

Value Management creates a Common set of VALUES - by establishing the Value Criteria; through Function Analysis, it eliminates the uncertainties, encourages conciseness, and greater depth of thought. Function Analysis improves communications by identifying the individual's perception of what is wanted, and the Team then builds on this to establish a "commonality of purpose" or single goal. And the Job Plan acts as the focal point for coordination and direction.

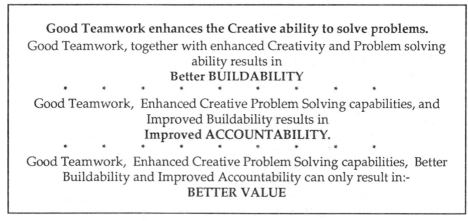

Fig. 5 The Result of Good Teamwork

It is evident that Value Management has much to offer both the Architect / Designer and the Construction Industry in this country. However, its acceptance will depend on those professionals already involved in the design and construction of buildings. First, they need to be educated in the entire philosophy of Value Management, so that they understand it is not a threat to either their professional integrity or their design ability.

It is the duty of the Architect to provide "good value" in terms of design irrespective of budget. In Value Management, aesthetics and appearance can be rated in terms of Value. The fact that Value Management is committed to determining "good value" rather than "cost reduction", should therefore be an encouragement for Architects to promote its development. Seen either as a way to think about design or as a formalized procedure that helps the Designer to do something he is always trying to do - give the Client the best possible value - Value Management can be an essential asset. As Senator Jennings Randolph stated/21/, "it will not solve all the problems of the construction industry" - but it should go a long way to resolving the dilemma of the lack of communications and teamwork which currently exists.

Value Management sandwiches together Accountability, Buildability, Creativity, Coordination, Communication and Teamwork in a positive, constructive and organized methodology.

It is a philosophy and attitude of mind which anyone involved in the design and construction of buildings would find an Asset.

8 References

/01/ Kaufman, J.J., "The Direction and Growth of Value Management - a Strategy for the 90's". *2nd European Conference on Value Management,* AFVNA , France 1990

/02/ Ibid.

/03/ Dell"Isola, Alphonse J., *Value Engineering in the Construction Industry.* New York, Van Nostrand Reinhold Inc., 1982, p.47

/04/ NEDO., *Faster Building for Commerce.* National Economic Development Council, London, 1988.

/05/ Higgin, Gurth, and Jessop, Neil, *Communications in the Building Industry.* London, Tavistock Publications, 1965, p.52

/06/ Ibid., p.89

/07/ NEDO., Op.cit., p.10

/08/ Ibid., p.11

/09/ Illingworth, John, "Buildability - Tomorrow's need?" *Building Technology and Management.,* 1984, Feb. Vol.22 (2), p.16

/10/ Ibid.

/11/ NEDO., Op.cit., p.10

/12/ The Banwell Report, *The Placing and Management of Contracts for Building and Civil Engineering Work,* HMSO. 1964

/13/ Dale, Julia E.S., "Value Management Improves Communications and Teamwork in Design and Construction", *3rd European Conference on Value Management,* VDI Berichte Nr. 918, 1991, p.190

/14/ Caudill, William Wayne, *Architecture by Team.* U.S.A., Van Nostrand Reinhold Co. Inc., 1971, p.ix

/15/ Dale, Julia E.S., Op.cit., p.188

/16/ CIRIA, *Buildability: an Assessment,* CIRIA Special Publication 26, 1983, p.6

/17/ McGeorge, John, F., "Design Productivity: A Quality Problem." *Journal of Management in Engineering,* 1988, October, Vol. 4 (4), p.354

/18/ Ibid., p.350

/19/ Barrie, Donald,S.,and Mulch, Gordon,L., "Professional CM Team discovers Value Engineering." *Journal of the Construction Division (ASCE),* 1977, Sept., Vol.103 (C03), p. 431

/20/ Dale, Julia E.S., Op.cit., p.190

/21/ Macedo, Manuel C., Dobrow, Paul & O'Rourke, Joseph J., Op.cit. p.11

Value management – its relevance to managing construction projects

M.F. Dallas, Director
Hanscomb Value Management, London, UK

Abstract
Value Management is a well established discipline and provides a method
of addressing some of the most crucial areas of managing a construction
project to completion within time, to the right quality and at the
right cost. The most common grounds for failure to meet these criteria
stem from a number of well recognised sources, e.g., inadequate brief,
ill considered cost cutting, surprises and variations, poor performance
and inaccurate assessment of risk. Value Management, correctly applied
at the right time and involving the right people addresses all of these
issues, greatly assisting the project team in delivering a product
which is right for both the client and the end user. Value Management
does not seek to supplant traditional techniques of project control
but, rather, offer support and justification to them. To derive the
full benefits of Value Management it is necessary to follow some
essential principles which include senior management support, the full
enthusiastic involvement of a carefully selected team (including
client, project team and end user wherever possible) and to follow a
carefully structured method of working, normally referrred to as The
Job Plan. Value Management studies provide a rapid method of
addressing strategic or operational issues in a thorough and objective
manner and provide significant benefits for <u>all</u> parties including the
Client, the Project Team and the End User.

Keywords: Value Management, Project Management, Construction Cost,
Teamwork Value Analysis, Value Engineering, Function Analysis, Life
Cycle Costs.

1 Project Management Objectives

Project Management has been defined in numerous ways and is one of
these terms that tends to be debased by one frequent use, being applied
equally to the supervisor of telephone installation gangs or the prime
mover behind the Channel Tunnel project.

I prefer the definition in which Project Management is equated to
the management of change.

In recent years, due in no small way to the efforts of the

Association of Project Manager, Project Management has become increasingly recognised as a professional discipline in its own right and Management by Projects has evolved into an accepted management style.

As a generalisation, the Project Manager's task is to deliver a project within a number of, often conflicting, parameters set out by the sponsor at the outset and, frequently, subject to change during the evolution of the project. These parameters may usually be grouped under four main headings :

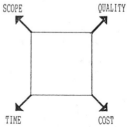

Scope - what will be delivered?

Quality - How well it will perform?

Time - When it will be delivered?

Cost - How much it will cost?

Fig. 1. The conflicting parameters of Project Management

During the evolution of the project the Project Manager will be subjected to conflicting pressures to maximise scope and quality while minimising time and cost.

To achieve a successful conclusion the Project Manager must be able to define clearly the priorities governing these conflicting pressures and then make decisions and exert controls to guide the project through a successful conclusion.

In fulfilling these tasks the Project Manager requires considerable diplomatic skills and understanding to communicate with and involve <u>all</u> the numerous disciplines involved in or affected by the outcome.

To assist him in the successful management of a complex project a number of powerful tools have been developed and refined over the years. This paper addresses what is possibly one of the less well understood but, nevertheless, much talked about tools in this armoury, **Value Management**.

2 Reasons for project failure

In order to consider fully how **Value Management** may assist the Project Manager it is necessary to dwell for a moment on some of the key reasons for project failure. These may, of course, be numerous and complex but the following, either on their own or in combination, probably account for most problems.

Poor concept   A poorly defined brief is a certain recipe
or brief   for disaster. Not only is the client unlikely
                   to get what he wants at the ends of the day
                   but the design and construction team are
                   likely to spend much abortive time and
                   resources in developing solutions which must

later be rejected (either because they are found wanting or because, more than likely, the brief changes). Misunderstandings will be rife and delays and over runs on costs almost inevitable.

Cost Cutting

Often estimates of project costs increase as design development proceeds to the point where they exceed the budget. Cuts, reducing the quality or scope of the project are simple to impose, however, since the deliverables have been reduced from what was originally envisaged, many of these items will now creep back in. Late introduction or re-introductions of an item usually cost more than if they had been included from the outset, leading to a double penalty and final cost overruns.

Surprises and late changes

These may stem from may causes, some more foreseeable than others. Some may be due to incomplete information at the outset, or may arise due to inadequate understanding or communications between different contributors to the project. In any event they will result in disruptions to progress causing both cost and programme overruns.

Poor Performance

Poor performance by key contributors affects not just the area of responsibility of the poor performer but will often have significant knock on effects to others. The results can be very costly in terms of quality, progress and cost. Poor performance may arise for many reasons but inadequate time and budget, coupled with poor selection and briefing procedures, may be contributory causes.

Over Design

Over design can result from allowing for excessive risk due to misunderstandings or lack of clear instructions as to clients' requirements. The result is over expenditure (both of money and resources) in one area, often resulting in cut backs in other, lower risk, areas.

Value Management, correctly applied at the right stages of the project, can address all these points, greatly assisting the development and management of the project to the benefit of all contributors and, not least, the client and user.

3 Value Management

3.1 Definition and origins

Like Project Management, Value Management has been the subject of many definitions, however the essence of the discipline is summed up in the following paragraph.

Value Management is a **creative, organised, intensive teams** effort directed towards the analysis of **functions** and focuses on the **elimination or modifications** of anything that **adds cost** to an item **without contributing to its function.** Put simply Value Management addresses the elimination of waste.

Credit for the evolution of Value Management is generally given to Larry Miles, working for the General Electric Company in the U.S.A. in 1947. Larry Miles was charged with maintaining production of components in the face of severe shortages of traditional materials and evolved a technique of analysing the functions performed of a component and then seeking alternative ways of fulfilling those functions. The technique was so successful that frequently components and/or productivity were not merely maintained but improved.

Over the years the techniques have been refined and usage widened to include almost all areas of industry business and commerce.

Terminology includes Value Analysis, Value Engineering, Zero Option Analysis and other expressions. All, however are based of the same fundamental techniques. Commonly Value Analysis is the term used for the application of the techniques to improve an existing product, process or organisation.

Value Engineering, on the other hand, is applied to the use of the techniques to improve the design and development of a project which has not yet been implemented. Value Engineering is thus the more commonly used term when applied to a construction project.

The above terminology is however not universally used, particularly overseas. I therefore prefer the term Value Management which embrace all the above. This is consistent with the Value Analysis Glossary, recently published by The European Community Programme for Innovation and Technology Transfer (SPRINT).

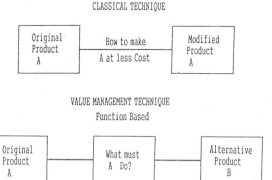

Fig 2. Problem Solving Techniques

3.2 Function based problem solving technique

Value Management is essentially a powerful problem solving technique which differs from classical techniques in that it is based on the analysis of function. It asks the question "what does it do?" rather

238

than "what is it?" before seeking alternatives.

This functional rather than elemental approach offers a new dimension of freedom to the enquirer often resulting in an entirely new approach to a problem rather than simply a modification to the original product.

3.3 Structured Team Activity

Value Management is not, as so often suggested, merely a brainstorming session for generating alternative ideas. Certainly creative techniques such as brainstorming play a vital part in the technique, but Value Management is much, much more than this.

Along with the function base, the concept of a close knit and carefully chosen team working to a well defined and carefully structured job plan lie at the heart of Value Management. Without this structure the full benefits of the technique are unlikely to be realised.

4.0 The role of Value Management in Project Control

There are numerous very effective means of controlling projects. I outline below merely some of the more frequently used, to demonstrate that **Value Management does not seek to supplant these but offers support.**

4.1 Arriving at the brief

The traditional means of arriving at the project brief is generally an iterative process of meetings between the key contributors during which an initial outline of requirements is honed into an acceptable form. All too often key contributors, eg the builder or end user, are not party to this process and their views may therefore only be represented through a third party.

At the same time the brief often sets out what the client thinks he **wants** which may, in fact, not present the true **needs** of his business.

The structured Value Management approach provides a technique for validating and defining the project objectives with the minimum use of time and resources including all key contributions.

Similarly, The use of Value Management leads to a better understanding of the project objectives by all team members and helps to ensure all elements are considered from the outset, thereby minimising surprises and variations and improving design solutions.

4.2 Achieving Quality

The standards of required quality are generally defined in a specification developed by the design teams in response to the brief. Attainment of the desired level of quality in the final product is ensured by an appropriate system of inspections supported where necessary by tests and or certification.

Frequently difficulties may arise because the standards of quality demanded are unrealistically high (or low) and unattainable within the budget or do not represent what the client expects or needs.

Value Management offers a means of establishing the right level of

quality consistent with the budget and the clients expectations at the outset of the project. Better team understanding assists the development ofetter solution, simplifying over complicated designs and reducing the scope for error.

4.3 Programme Control

There are numerous software packages available today which, given the right input, assist the Project Manager in controlling progress (they do not, in themselves, control the project !). A Project Manager will use one of these packages to help him monitor and predict the achievement of certain milestones and deliverables throughout the duration of a project. Ability to predict problem areas enables him to take appropriate remedial action.

Value Management assists Programme control in a number of ways.

The involvement of <u>all</u> contributors in the early stages of a project, avoids unrealistic or over generous targets being set. The identification of Value Management workshops at strategic Milestones within the programme assists in the definition and quality of the information which needs to be available at those milestones.

Improvements of understanding and quality reduces the incidence of variations and delays which can have such a disastrous effect on progress.

4.4 Cost Control

The setting of an initial budget may result from a number of processes. Once set, however, it is the project manager's primary tasks to ensure the budget is not exceeded.

Various established means of cost control exist, including carefully
prepared contract documentation and tender procedures, regular cost reporting systems and the more sophisticated computer based Cost/Schedule Control Systems Criteria in which Actual Cost of Work Scheduled (ACWP) is measured against Budgeted Cost of Work Scheduled (BCWS) and Budgeted Cost of Work Performed (BCWP).

Powerful as may of these control techniques are, none of them addresses the fundamental question of whether the right budget was set in the first place.

Nothing is easier than to bring in a project within budget if the budget was overgenerous at the outset.

Too low a budget on the other hand can give rise to insuperable difficulties and a strong temptation to cut scope and quality.

The use of Value Management techniques enables the project team to ensure that the <u>right</u> budget is set for the client's needs. It also ensures that project achieves the designed balance in short and long term costs.

5.0 The Essential Principles of Value Management

If Value Management is such an established technique and can achieve so much for project control, how is it that it is not more commonly used? The answer is, of course, that <u>parts</u> of The Value Management philosophy <u>are</u> widely used even if they are not <u>called</u>

Value Management.

To derive the full benefits of Value Management, however, it is necessary to employ <u>all</u> the stages in a carefully structured sequence, although, depending on the type of study and the nature of the project being studied, the emphasis on the various points of the technique will vary.

In the following paragraphs I outline the essential principles which must be followed for:

5.1 Senior Management Commitment

Full and enthusiastic support of Senior Management, from Board level downwards is essential if Value Management is to become part of corporate philosophy and be successful in its application.

5.2 Clear Objectives

Before any Study, at a strategic or operation level, can be undertaken, a clear statement of the objectives **of the study** needs to be agreed and information pertinent to those objectives gathered together. The information should be complete and consistent since any results can only be as good as the information upon which they are based.

5.3 Team Involvement

Careful selection and involvement of the right team is vital for the success of any study. The choice is important for four key reasons:

- Involvement of all parties who have significant influence on costs or are affected by them facilitates a balanced approach and, since this includes the client, gives authority and credability to the results.

- Willing involvement of key members of the incumbent project team (those who have to carry the project through to completion) is vital if ownership of the study results is to rest with those who are charged with implementing its proposals.

- The process of value management is a powerful factor in building team relationships and imparting better understanding of the project objectives. It is important that these benefits are carried through to the project team.

- Sensitive introduction of external consultants to the Value Management Study Team can enhance the objectivity of The Study and improve results. It is important, however, that the project team do not see the Study as an audit of their performance (which it is not).

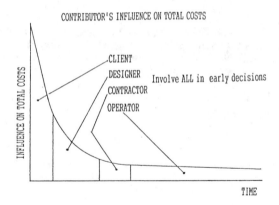

Fig. 3. Team Involvement

5.4 Structured Job Plan

The Job Plan is a well defined sequence of activities in carrying out a full Value Management Study which may be undertaken in three stages, Pre-Workshop, Intensive Workshop and Post-Workshop.

To ensure that best use is made of the resources available a specialist experienced Value Management team leader or facilitator is selected, who acts as chairman to the study team and conducts _their_ efforts to best effect - ideas for improvements come from the Value Management team not the Facilitator.

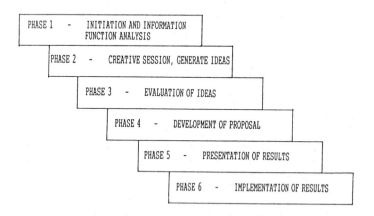

Fig. 4. The Value Management Job Plan

Phase 1, the information phase, undertaken mostly pre-workshop, involves defining the objectives of the study, agreeing a suitable timetable, selecting the study team members, identifying and assembling the appropriate information, analysing and distributing the information to study team members.

This information phase is completed at the beginning of the intensive workshop (see below) when the study team, in group session, undertake a detailed **function analysis** of the project components and attribute estimated costs to these functions (Function Cost Analysis). This analysis provides a powerful overview of project cost distribution and assists senior management to assess whether money is being spent in the right places.

Not until all this preparatory work has been completed can the study team be in a position to understand the full nature of the problem they are trying to address or select those parts of the projects which are most likely to benefit from the study. **Unless the problem has been properly identified it will not be possible to arrive at these best solution!**

Phase 2, the Creative Phase, involves the generation of alternatives to fulfil the functions identified above. There are many creative techniques available, of which the most commonly used is brainstorming. Here, the team, still in the workshop environment, generate random ideas, **without evaluation,** answering the question "what else will do the job?"

All members of the team are encouraged to participate, regardless of relevance of their discipline to the problem at hand – very often some of the best ideas can come from those with least experience (and therefore the least inhibitions!).

A typical creative brainstorming session may generate over a hundred ideas, and in a complete workshop – involving several sessions – 500 to 1000 ideas may be generated.

All ideas, regardless of merit, are recorded and displayed visually to the study team.

Phase 3, Evaluation: Many of the ideas generated above will have less merit than the original design and may well be downright crazy. In this phase the Team must evaluate the relative merits of each idea with a view to selecting the best ideas for further development. Ideas are evaluated against criteria which reflect the study objectives.

Phase 4, Development: Once a shortlist of the best ideas has been selected the team, still in workshop session, will develop each proposal in sufficient detail to enable the project team to decide whether or not to implement it or carry it forward for further analysis.

Phase 5, Presentation of Results: The study results are pulled together (usually by the Value Management Facilitator) into a detailed written report for presentation to the study sponsor and key project team members who may not have been present during the workshop itself. The purpose of the report is twofold - to provide a written record of the Study and to assist the decision makers within the project team in the implementation of its results.

Sometimes it may fulfil a third very valuable function in supporting an application for funds by demonstrating that the project represents value for money.

Finally, in **Phase 6 of the Job Plan**, the Project Team will **implement** those proposals that, after validation, are selected for inclusion in the final project. In common with all other activities it is important that the implementation of proposals is properly organised and managed.

5.6 Total Ownership Costs

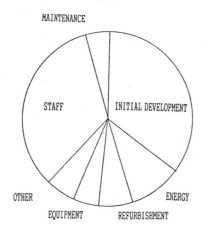

Leisure Facility
5 year life between refurbishment
Costs expressed as Present Worth

Fig. 5. Total Ownership Costs

An important feature of any Value Management Study is that **all** issues which may affect total ownership costs are addressed. These include not only initial capital costs and longer term maintenance and running costs, but also more strategic issues such as tax and marketing considerations etc. The relative weighting of such considerations will depend upon the project and study objectives.

5.7 Strategic and Operational Issues

As a project progresses, so the costs of implementing changes increases and the capacity for change decreases. It stands to reason, therefore, that the earlier a Value Management Study is carried out the greater is the opportunity for influencing the outturn costs

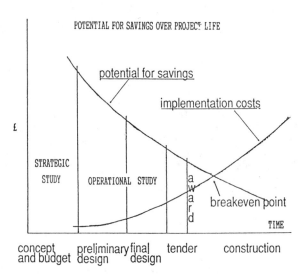

Fig. 6. Timing of a Value Management Study

Studies condusted at concept stage are generally of a strategic nature (eg clarification of the design brief), concentrating on the fundamentals behind a project. Information may not be very detailed or specific and the study duration fairly short (1-2 day workshops being common).

A study conducted at the end of scheme design (RIBA Stage D) will concentrate on more operational issues and will be based on much more comprehensive information. Due to the amount of detail to be studies, the workshop at this stage may well be longer, say 3-5 days duration.

6.0 The Results

The objectives of a Value Management Study may vary. A speculative developer may be looking to maximise the gross:nett ratio; an owner occupier will be seeking to optimise total ownership costs and create the best environment for conducting his business. In a corporate headquarters quality and aesthetics may be of prime importance in projecting the company's image to the outside world. Some improvements in **value** may require an increase in **cost**. It is, therefore, not always easy to quantify the imporvements resulting from a Value Management Study.

Our practice is to reduce all cost implications to Present Worth values for comparison purposes and typical savings measured in this way are frequently in the order of 10-20% of the total project cost. Typically, the total cost of conducting a Value Management Study may be recouped 50-100 times.

7.0 Summary

By focussing on alternative ways of achieving function, Value Management succeeds in eliminating or modifying only those elements which make no positive contribution and are therefore wasteful or unnecessary. All the **desired** attributes are retained and very often enhanced and there is no pressure to reintroduce those elements which may have been eliminated by thoroughly examining all aspects of a project at the outset and involving all those who will contribute significantly to it or be affected by it (ie the end user) a better product is likely to result, accurately reflecting the Client's needs, balanced to suit the conflicting requirements of sponsor client and end user and incorporating features to simplify procurement and implementation.

That same involvement of all key contributors helps build good team relationships and better understanding all round, leading to better solutions, fewer variations and less waste.

Proper consideration of costs on a functional basis highlights anomolies and provides the basis for identifying and justifying the **right** budget for the job.

The structured Job Plan ensures that **all** significant aspects are reviewed in an objective and balanced manner at the right stage of the project, within the minimum time and with the use of minimum resources, generally producing improvements in value which outweigh study costs many tens of times.

The ability to demonstrate that the project represents good value for money provides powerful support to applications for funding.

In short, Value Management should not be seen as an audit but as a means by which a project can be improved to the benefit of **all**, Sponsor Client, Project and Design Team, Builder and End User.

Modern value engineering for design and construction

H. Ellegant
Howard Ellegant Associates, Evanston, Illinois, USA

Abstract
This paper explains the essential elements of Modern Value Engineering and how they help clients with site selection, establish project criteria at the briefing stage, and reduce costs during project concept and detailed design. Recent studies are presented and the key Modern Value Engineering techniques used in each explained.
Keywords: Value Engineering, Value Analysis, Value Management, Function Analysis, Total Quality Management, Cost Control.

1 Introduction

Two years after hanging out my Value Engineering consultant's shingle, I was still struggling with what Value Engineering really is. I attended a wedding on my wife's side of the family, sitting next to a woman, a distant cousin by marriage. Our conversation turned to vocation after location. I explained that I worked with groups of people involved with building projects to help them identify and solve their problems, usually related to excess costs. To which cousin replied: "Oh, you're a therapist."

A therapist for buildings. More precisely for the group or team that designs and constructs them. An interesting concept. I liked it, because in a sense that is what Value Engineering is about.

Like therapy, Value Engineering is met with varying degrees of acceptance depending upon the experience of the participant during the process as well as the results achieved.

1.1 Modern Value Engineering and Total Project Management

"Modern" in the title of this paper suggests there is an "Old" Value Engineering. And there is. The old Value Engineering deals with symptoms. Modern Value Engineering digs deeper, like therapy, to identify the real problem and even further to find its root cause. In therapy, correcting the real problem requires understanding and commitment. Modern Value Engineering is the same, requiring understanding of the process and a commitment to use it. For many in the design and construction business, Value Engineering simply means suggesting a series of alternative materials and systems. For others, a Value Engineering study conjures up the image of a group of people drastically slashing costs from a design without regard to architectural objectives or client requirements. Value Engineering has too often been used as the tool of last resort when a project estimate (or tender!) exceeds budget.

But that is the "old" Value Engineering which concentrates on reducing costs of systems and materials. Modern Value Engineering helps manage total project cost, quality and performance by expanding the focus of the VE team to include all aspects of project design, construction and ownership through an emphasis on the way the project will be utilized rather than on how it will be built. Modern Value Engineering is a proactive tool to help architects, engineers and their clients identify and correct project performance/cost/quality imbalances from project inception through design.

First and foremost, Modern Value Engineering repairs communication breakdowns - the primary cause of excessive costs and unfulfilled project requirements. If used early enough, Value Engineering prevents the breakdown. The leader of a Value Engineering study is responsible for facilitating the free flow of open communication between study team members.

So Value Engineering is therapy for the building project and the Value Engineering study team leader a facilitator for the people who are involved in defining and carrying out the project. Value Engineering's power is its ability to clear away the surface debris, help people dig down to find the real problems needing attention and then proceed to devise ways to solve them.

1.2 Function Analysis: VE's Key Technique

The tool Modern Value Engineering uses to dig with is complete Function Analysis. Using it, project stake holders break down the design into functional performance elements. Costs and benefits are assigned to each element. The value of each functional performance element is measured by comparing its costs and benefits. Appropriate changes are made to balance project performance and cost.

2 Value Engineering Before Project Design Starts

2.1 Function Analysis Changes the Project's Site

The CEO of a health care management firm asked us to facilitate a top management discussion about which of three existing suburban buildings to relocate to. We asked the CEO and her top executives to define why they wanted to move the company. To "Improve Operations," was the consensus.

Next we had the team spell out how the new location was expected to help "Improve Operations." We gave the team an exercise to build a diagram on which they had to separate their criteria between performance requirements (functions in VE language) really NEEDED to Improve Operations and others WANTED to make everything work even better. The team also had to relate the requirements to each other using a How?-Why? logic. (Figure 1.)

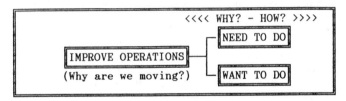

Figure 1. Function diagramming ground rules.

About one-half an hour into the exercise, the "Aha!" happened. The Human Resources Director suddenly exclaimed that the company did not have to move just to "Improve Operations." Operations could be improved at the current location just by rearranging offices, staff, and equipment. They were losing business when potential clients paid them a visit as part of proposal evaluation. The current location did not mirror their excellent capabilities, reputation and track record. Conclusion: a new site was required to "Increase Sales." The team agreed. The CEO was delighted.

With this changed focus for their work, the team completed the function diagram in Figure 2. and specified exactly how they expected the new location could help the company "Increase Sales."

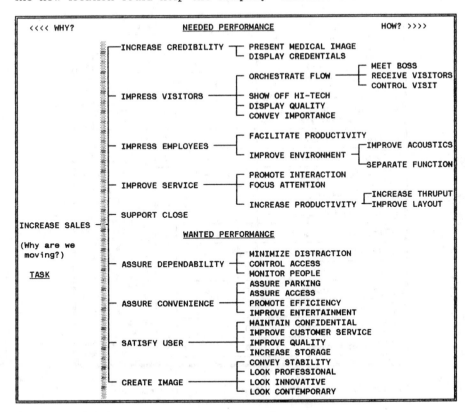

Figure 2. Function Logic Diagram of Corporate Move

The team compared and then ranked the importance of their primary performance requirements (functions) relative to one another. Using an evaluation matrix, they reviewed how well each site fulfilled each requirement and concluded that none of the sites were appropriate! The team decided to search for other buildings that could present a more positive corporate image of their company's professionalism and capabilities. A bad decision, based on a wrong assumption about why the company was moving, was avoided.

2.2 Generating Design Criteria Based on the Function Analysis

A secondary benefit of the exercise was development of guidelines to help the architect design each space and activity area of the new offices. The team created another matrix (a portion is shown in Figure 3.) They indicated which performance requirements (functions) should be fulfilled by the design for each major space or activity area, thus creating design criteria for the architect, who participated in the session, and quickly gained valuable insight into his client's project requirements and expectations.

After site selection, the team and the architect determine acceptable typologies of design solutions that fulfill the criteria for each space and activity area and their approximate costs. This establishes design and cost targets for the architect to work toward.

REQUIRED PERFORMANCE (Partial list)	Claims Preprocessing	Customer Service	Provider Relations	Direct Management	Reception
Present medical image		o		o	
Display credentials		o		o	
Receive visitors	o	o	o	o	
Control visit	o	o	o	o	o
Show off hi-tech	o	o	o	o	o
Facilitate productivity	o	o	o	o	o
Promote interaction		o	o		
Focus attention	o	o	o		
Increase thruput	o	o	o		
Support close				o	
Minimize distraction	o	o	o		o
Control access	o			o	o

Figure 3. Functions Allocated to Activities and Spaces to Create Design Criteria

3 "All Cost is for Function:" What Our Decisions Really Cost

The fundamental, underlying principle upon which Value Engineering's creator, Larry Miles, founded his discipline is that "All cost is for function." It recognizes that consciously or otherwise we spend our resources (time, money, etc.) to achieve our performance objectives (functions.) Identifying project functions helps stake holders understand client required performance. Determining what those functions actually cost is the first step in the process of helping the client decide if they are getting their money's worth.

During a Value Engineering review of a new Federal courthouse, the owner–user–architect team found the estimated cost of drywall partitions was $238,000. Just over $100,000 of that cost was for high sound attenuation walls enclosing the jury assembly rooms and offices for Social Security, probation officers, the U.S. Congressman, marshals and judges.

3.1 Clarifying the Client's Requirements
Before reviewing project costs, the team constructed the function diagram shown below in Figure 4.

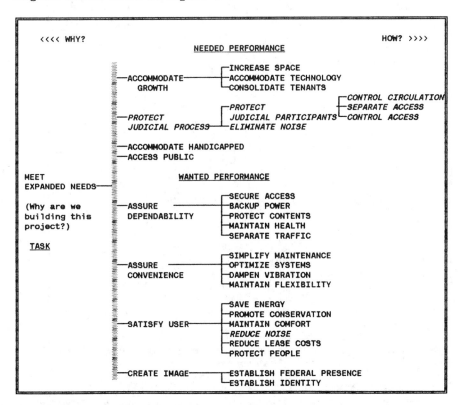

Figure 4. Function Diagram for a New Federal Courthouse and Offices

Using their function diagram, the team identified "Control Circulation," "Separate Access," "Control Access," and "Eliminate Noise" as performance requirements (functions) of the partitions. The sound attenuation capability of a wall directly relates only to "Eliminate Noise," a required function NEEDED to "Protect Judicial Process." By comparison, "Reduce Noise," is WANTED to "Satisfy User."

3.2 Compare the Design, Alternatives and Their Costs
There is a qualitative and quantitative difference between designing for the functions of Eliminate Noise and Reduce Noise. The quantitative difference, as shown in Table 1 following, ranges between $35.50 and $77.50 per linear foot of partition depending upon the qualitative level of sound attenuation specified.

Table 1. Comparison of Sound Attenuation Partition
          Construction, Costs and Function

RATING/ CONSTRUCTION	FUNCTION & PERFORMANCE LEVEL	PRICE PER LINEAR FOOT
FSTC 37 1 layer GWB each side	REDUCE NOISE Normal conversation audible; loud speech intelligible	$35.50
FSTC 42 1 layer GWB each side; insulated	REDUCE NOISE Normal conversation barely audible; loud speech audible but not intelligible	$51.35
FSTC 47 2 layers GWB each side; insulated	REDUCE NOISE Normal conversation inaudible; loud speech muffled	$64.20
FSTC 52 Double stud wall; 2 layers GWB each side; insulated	ELIMINATE NOISE Normal conversation inaudible; loud speech barely audible	$77.50

3.3 Select Systems Appropriate to Required Performance
Based on a discussion of attenuation required to "Protect Judicial Process," as well as where that protection was needed, the team agreed to revise the qualitative requirements for the partitions at the Jury Assembly Rooms, judges, marshall, U.S. Attorney, and congressman's offices from ones which permitted loud and normal conversation to be inaudible to a system which muffled loud speech, and kept only

normal conversation inaudible. Design criteria for partitions around the other spaces was also changed to allow loud speech to be heard but not be intelligible, and normal conversation to be barely audible, but not understood.

Estimated savings from matching appropriate systems with actual required performance levels of functions was just over $21,600, or nine percent of drywall partition direct costs.

In three days, the team followed four steps to balance total project performance and cost, saving an estimated $500,000, or 10 percent of estimated construction costs.

Step one, the client defined their performance requirements (functions) and the team diagramed them.

Step two, the team reviewed materials and systems and identified which functions and what performance level each was supposed to achieve and why.

Step three, the architect and engineers identified alternative materials or systems, and the costs of each, to perform the required functions.

Step four, the client selected the systems appropriate to actual levels of required functional performance.

4 Putting it Together: Functions, Function Costs and Function Acceeptance Helps the Owner/User Decide What They Really Need!

Before starting the Value Engineering study of a project in or at preliminary design, we conduct a round table session with project owners, architect and principal users, most of whom will not be VE study team members. We call the session an Owner/User Attitude Survey. During the session, we ask participants two open ended questions: What is important to them about this project (what should be there?), and what problems they want to avoid. We then ask them to rate relative to one another first the important features and then the problems to avoid.

The results are given to the VE study team after they have completed the Function Diagram and allocated construction costs to the functions. The team reviews each statement and indicates on the Function Diagram to which function(s) they agree the statement refers.

When this exercise is complete, the VE team has a total picture of project functions, function costs and function acceptance. Figure 7 is a photo of the architect project manager and the County Sheriff's jail commander in front of the completed function diagram for the new 752 bed, $30 million Ventura County California jail.

The Old Value Engineering selected targets for improvement by focusing on high cost project elements. Modern Value Engineering looks for value mismatches - where project functions, function costs and function acceptance are out of balance.

These may be high cost functions with little client acceptance, (so why are we spending the money to do them?) or they may be low cost functions important to the client but performed poorly (could we invest more money to improve performance?) The team may suggest ideas to improve systems, materials or even change the project baseline requirements.

Figure 7.   Seated in Front of the Completed Function Analysis
           Diagram, The Architect Project Manager (left) Discusses the
           Ventura California County Jail Project With Its Commander

In the Ventura County Jail study, the team defined the overall
purpose of the project as "Manage Sentenced Inmates." They further
identified "Receive, Classify, Release and Confine Inmates" as functions required to achieve that purpose.

Allocating materials and systems costs to specific functions
on the diagram, the team identified $3,142,000, or 10.5% of the es-
timated construction costs as the function cost to "Receive, Classify
and Release Inmates." As the team reviewed the project, additional
critical facts emerged. A significant amount of floor area was consumed by an inmate property storage room, designed to support the
requirements of "Receive and Classify Inmates." This space, associated circulation and other areas were being considered for redesign to
resolve space and budget problems. Because of a promise made to
the local community, all release and new inmate intake will be done at
the existing main jail, several miles away.

Armed with all the information, the jail commander reexamined the
decision to include inmate property storage in the new jail, and
suggested deleting it. Property of inmates confined in the new
facility could be stored at the main jail.

Within two days of the meeting at which the discussion occurred,
the construction manager toured the existing jail with a vendor of
property storage equipment. The vendor made a layout and estimated

costs for redoing the existing jail's property storage area to accommodate the additional requirements.

Estimated first cost savings of $500,000 were reported at the next team meeting. Life cycle cost savings from eliminating the property storage center staff position and avoiding property storage equipment maintenance are another $1.3 million. The architect was given direction to eliminate the property storage area from the new facility. Having the right people around the table speeded up the analytical and decision making process, helping to create a new jail which will conform to users and the publics requirements.

5 Conclusion

Modern Value Engineering methodology rigorously applied under the direction of a VE experienced facilitator helps overcome individual team member prejudices. The facilitator, like the therapist, makes sure the hard questions are asked and answered. The result is that the study team improves total project value by balancing performance and costs, and does not just reduce costs inappropriately.

Modern Value Engineering requires having the right people around the table. In each of the preceding examples, team members had specific project knowledge necessary to make decisions. Collectively the team had the responsibility, resources and authority to implement their ideas whether or not they had final approval of them. Each was a stakeholder in the outcome. A cooperative spirit was built by working together through the Value Engineering process.

Modern Value Engineering is a formidable project management tool from project inception through design. It helps clients articulate their requirements, creates total project understanding for the entire project team and insures cost effective decisions are made in harmony with the client's needs and desires.

Value engineering during design: new directions in research

S.D. Green
Department of Construction Management & Engineering, University of Reading, UK

Abstract
It is argued that the current practice of value engineering lacks a rigorous theoretical base. The essential characteristics of value engineering are identified and found to be in common with those which distinguish decision conferences. The connection between value engineering and design optimisation is also established. Decision theory is drawn upon in order to classify design optimisation models as either normative or prescriptive. Furthermore, it is suggested that the value engineering approach depends upon a decision model which is requisite in nature. Requisite models are distinguished from other forms of decision model in that they are produced by a process of group consensus in order to establish a common perception of the nature of the decision and the likely consequences of alternative courses of action. The necessary complexity of the model is dependent upon the requirements of the situation. The model would be continually revised until the point when no further insights are generated. Attempts to identify optimal design solutions are seen to be invalid, the purpose of requisite decision models is to establish a 'shared social reality'.

Existing approaches to value engineering are deemed to be successful in that they are requisite for the purposes of the workshop participants, i.e. they ensure that the decision-making process is explicit and, to some extent, rational. However, the increasingly sophisticated requirements of construction clients mean that more rigorous methods are urgently required. Several suggestions are made regarding possible topics for future research.
Keywords: Value Engineering, Building Economics, Design Optimisation, Decision Making.

1 Introduction

The origins of this paper lie in a research project which attempted to record the best of current value engineering practice. During the course of this research it became apparent that the theoretical basis of many of the approaches used in practice is alarmingly shallow. However, this did not seem to prevent value engineering studies achieving success. The emphasis of the research project was therefore changed and this paper represents the preliminary results.

The starting precept is that the majority of publications describing value engineering are theoretically naive. The primary objective of this paper is therefore to identify an alternative theoretical framework for value engineering. The secondary objective is to outline a research agenda which will establish value engineering as a bona fide field of study.

The scope of the paper is limited to the application of value engineering during the design of building developments. Furthermore, the discussion will be limited to the situation where the value engineering team leader acts with the existing design team in the role of facilitator. Whilst it is acknowledged that benefits can sometimes result from the use of a 'second design team', it is considered more important to concentrate research activity on improving design decisions in the first instance.

Initially, the essential characteristics which distinguish value engineering will be described. Secondly, it will be argued that the focus on 'function' is often a case of semantics rather than a distinguishing feature. It will then be suggested that value engineering is a form of decision conference.

The objectives of value engineering will be described in order to establish its relationship with the wider discipline of design optimisation. A number of different approaches to design optimisation will then be compared to the theory of decision-making. This comparison will lead to a reinterpretation of value engineering and to the identification of a valid theoretical base. Finally, several suggestions will be made regarding possible future research topics.

2 The Characteristics of Value Engineering

Value engineering is essentially a structured method of decision making. Whilst different sources (Dell'Isola, 1982; Macedo et al, 1978; Zimmerman and Hart, 1982) describe the stages of the value engineering job plan slightly differently, the essential procedural sequence is invariably the same. Firstly, the nature of the problem is analysed. Secondly, alternative solutions are generated and thirdly, the best solution is selected. It should be recognised that this staged approach is common to several methods of creative problem-solving and is by no means unique to value engineering (VanGrundy, 1988).

The conventional view of value engineering is that it provides a 'second look' at design decisions which have already been taken, however this interpretation is by no means universal. It is currently common practice within the UK for the value engineering team leader to play a facilitating role alongside the existing design team (Green, 1991). Whilst it remains customary for a study to be initiated in response to a projected cost overspend, it is also increasingly common for value engineering workshops to be built into the design programme in advance. Perhaps the key characteristic of value engineering is the group nature of the exercise. It is also distinguished by the way in which the group members are isolated from their normal activities for the duration of the study. Value engineering studies invariably involve the active participation of client and user representatives. This involvement often serves to satisfy the client's requirement that the decision-making process is both **explicit** and **rational**.

If the above features are accepted as being representative then it is possible to classify a value engineering study as a **decision conference,** an approach which is well described in the literature of decision theory. For example, Watson and Buede (1987) characterise a decision conference as:

'...the use of a structured process for dialogue and debate amongst the decision-maker and his experts during an intense, short-term conference. These conferences are best when held away from the workplace of the decision-maker since total involvement is critical. The objective of a decision conference is to focus attention on the problem in hand, to identify and evaluate a set of meaningful and practical options, and to synthesise a group consensus in favour of a single option.'

The only aspect of value engineering which is missing from the above description is the use of functional analysis. It is therefore meaningful to question the extent to which functional analysis is distinct from other methods of 'understanding the problem'.

3 Functional Analysis

It is commonly accepted that the concept of functional analysis is central to the discipline of value engineering. Indeed, almost every published definition is built around the word 'function'. Nevertheless, attempts to implement functional analysis in practice are often confused. This is particularly true during the earlier stages of the building design process.

Dell'Isola (1982) has defined function as the 'specific purpose or intended use for an item or design'. However, as Parker (1985) has pointed out, the interpretation of function is often dependent upon who is being served. This point has been well illustrated by Palmer (1990), who describes how a prison door was designed to keep people in, whilst a value engineering study revealed that the 'real function' was to keep other inmates out. It is therefore clear that function is dependent upon perception and cannot be considered to be an intrinsic quality of a design solution.

Given the dependence of function upon perception, it is perhaps misleading to talk of functional 'analysis' as if it were a totally objective process. It may well be more meaningful to refer to the **required** functions of a design solution. Whilst there is a danger of engaging in semantics, 'required functions' are clearly dependent upon, or even synonymous with, the design objectives.

It is also enlightening to compare the 'how-why' logic of FAST diagramming (Dell'Isola, 1982; Fowler, 1990) to the 'means-ends' analysis of objectives as described by Cooke and Slack (1984). The two approaches are essentially the same, the only real distinction is the use of different terminology.

Once the interdependency between functions and objectives has been established then it becomes difficult to argue that functional analysis is a unique characteristic of value engineering. There would therefore appear to be no reason why value engineering should not be classified as a form of decision conference.

4 Objectives of Value Engineering

Value engineering studies are commissioned for a variety of reasons. Early writers tended to emphasise the benefits in terms of improving productivity (Dunstone, 1973) or, more frequently, reducing costs (Mudge, 1971, O'Brien, 1976). Inherent in these early approaches was the assumption that all the alternative design solutions provide the same level of performance (Szoke, 1974). This assumption certainly applies to the case when value engineering is used to correct a cost overspend by investigating alternative component solutions. Indeed, it has been suggested that in this situation value engineering is little different to the traditional cost checking role performed by the quantity surveyor (Kelly and Male, 1990).

If value engineering is to be applied to the higher-level decisions taken during concept design then the assumption of 'equal performance' is rarely relevant. In these circumstances the design problem is open-ended in nature and the scope of the study is consequently much wider. It is clear that the assessment of competing designs will **not** be made on the basis of cost alone, other intangible criteria will also be taken into account. Whilst it is all too easy to claim that the objective of value engineering is to **maximise value**, major difficulties exist not only in the measurement of value, but also in its very definition.

The concept of maximising the value of building designs is not unique to value engineering, it has long been central to the wider discipline of building economics. A review of the relevant literature indicates that the notion of value maximisation has become almost synonymous with that of design optimisation. Szoke (1987) has argued that the prospects for using value engineering during building design are dependent upon progress being made in solving the general problems of design optimisation.

5 Design Optimisation

The impetus for the development of design optimisation was originally provided by the techniques of operational research. However, the difficulty with applying techniques such as linear programming is that they depend upon the existence of a single function which can be optimised. Wilson (1987) has suggested that 'the only true objective for design optimisation is value'. If this objective is to be achieved then it is necessary to establish an objective function which represents the design's value.

Building economists have often been tempted by the concept of utility theory, which is based on the use of numerical measures to represent the value of alternative courses of action. Warszawski (1980) has suggested the construction of a utility function for a building design which could, in theory, be maximised. However, there are a number of obvious difficulties with this approach. Firstly, it has to be established **whose** utility is being maximised. Secondly, it is necessary to adopt a rigorous method of measuring utility on an interval scale. Thirdly, the approach is dependent upon the assumption that the individual's utility function remains consistent over time.

The notion of utility maximisation has been heavily criticised, not only from the point of view of practicality, but also in terms of whether an optimal design actually exists. Many authors have followed Simon (1981) in arguing that an optimising approach is invalid due to the complexities of the building design process.

Design optimisation has also been used to describe the process of generating a limited number of alternatives and then trying to choose the solution which is 'best'. This interpretation clearly has more in common with value engineering than it does with the traditional techniques of operational research. Newton (1990) has classified this less ambitious approach as 'informal design optimisation', in contrast to 'formal design optimisation' which endeavours to identify **every** possible design solution.

Attempts at informal design optimisation have tended to centre upon the use of weighted evaluation methods (also known as weighted preference methods). These methods are well described within the building economics literature and are widely recommended for use in the context of value engineering. (Dell'Isola, 1982; Morton, 1987; Kelly and

Poynter-Brown, 1990).

The basic approach to weighted evaluation has three stages; firstly, it is necessary to identify the criteria against which the success of design alternatives are to be assessed. Secondly, the allocation of 'weightings' is necessary in order to account for the different levels of importance of the established criteria. Finally, each design option is rated against each criterion, the resultant score is then multiplied by the importance weighting in order to produce a weighted score for each attribute. A simple average is then calculated in order to produce a 'utility rating' for each design solution.

It is apparent that many of the difficulties associated with the utility maximisation model described above also apply to the use of weighted preference methods. However, the theoretical limitations of these methods are rarely discussed and, as Johnson (1990) has pointed out, the underlying assumptions are seldom validated.

It should be recognised that the brief review offered above is not totally representative of the considerable literature which relates to the concept of design optimisation. Nevertheless, it has served the purpose of providing a wider context within which to understand value engineering. The debate regarding the validity of design optimisation has been dominated by a number of controversial issues. Many of these issues can be clarified by reference to the classification of decision models which has recently emerged within the theory of decision-making.

6 Alternative Models of Decision Making

Current thinking within decision theory has identified the following four categories of decision model: descriptive; normative; prescriptive and requisite. An understanding of the nature of these different models is of considerable benefit in identifying theoretical frameworks for both design optimisation and value engineering.

Descriptive models are used in order to describe and understand how decision-makers function in practice. Descriptive models of the design process are therefore used to represent how clients and designers make decisions in real situations. The contribution of Mackinder and Marvin (1982) is essentially descriptive and forms a stark contrast with the maximising models of formal design optimisation.

The concept of optimising a design by utility maximisation is founded on the neoclassical assumptions of perfect information, infinite sensitivity and maximising behaviour. Decision models which are based on these assumptions can be classified as normative; i.e. they are concerned with the way in which idealised, rational, super-intelligent people **should** act (Bell et al, 1988). The overriding assumption of normative models is that an ideal solution exists which is waiting to be identified. Models based on utility maximisation clearly bear little resemblance to the way decision-makers operate in practice. The application of normative models to group decision-making processes (such as value engineering) is also severely limited due to the theoretical difficulties of achieving common measures of utility.

The third category of decision models consists of those which are prescriptive in nature. Whilst these models are still concerned with how decision-makers **ought** to behave, they do not depend on the unrealistic assumptions of perfect sensitivity and complete knowledge. Prescriptive models are essentially pragmatic in nature. They are intended to offer guidelines which can be followed, rather than idealised mathematical formulations. Prescriptive models also differ from normative models in that they recognise the limitations imposed by **bounded rationality.**

The concept of bounded rationality was originally described by Simon (1957). It is used to describe situations were decisions are made in the absence of perfect information by humans who possess a limited capacity for processing information. The recognition of bounded rationality in decision-making has raised doubts regarding the meaning of an 'optimal solution'. An optimal decision based upon the information which is available at the time may well appear to be much less then optimal in the light of subsequent information. In the context of building design, perfect information is clearly impossible to achieve. Even if all cost and performance data could be obtained with complete reliability, the intractable problem of predicting the requirements of the future (unknown) building users would remain.

Implicit in the notion of a prescriptive model is the realisation that the manner in which the decision is framed will inevitably influence the solution. Phillips (1984) has offered a further refinement by introducing the concept of requisite decision models. Requisite models are produced by a process of group consensus in order to clarify the decision objectives and identify possible solutions. The group would be guided in its deliberations by a facilitator skilled in the techniques of decision modelling. The model would not be intended to represent any sort of 'universal truth', but would attempt to establish a 'shared social reality'. The complexity of the model would depend upon the sophistication of the group members. Its usefulness would be judged by the extent to which it achieved: (i) a common understanding of the problem and (ii) new insights about possible solutions. The model would continue to be revised up until the point when no fresh insights are generated. The model would then be considered to be requisite and would form the basis upon which decisions would be made.

7 Reinterpretation of Value Engineering

The concept of a requisite decision model which is constructed within the context of a decision conference provides a new interpretation of value engineering. It also provides an explanation of why value engineering has proved to be so useful in practice despite the economic naivety of the literature. Practitioners have developed approaches which have proved beneficial to clients in illustrating the nature of the design problem and highlighting the implications of pursuing different courses of action. The only meaningful way to judge the success of a value engineering study is to assess how useful it was to the participants. If the stated objective of value engineering is to achieve value-for-money then it has to be recognised that the success of the end result is totally dependent upon perception. Value-for-money has more to do with psychological comfort than it does with objective economics.

The doubts regarding the theoretical basis of functional analysis also become less important when considered as part of a requisite decision model. Not only is function subject to perception, the validity of the adopted method of functional analysis is also subject to perception. The concept of requisite decision models implies that if an approach works to the satisfaction of its users then there is merit in that adopting that approach. However, as clients and designers become more familiar with value engineering they will demand an increasingly rigorous approach. The research agenda which is outlined below is therefore intended to ensure that more sophisticated techniques are available when they become required.

8 New Directions for Research

It was initially argued that the development of a meaningful agenda for research into improved techniques of value engineering is dependent upon establishing a theoretical framework. This paper has identified the connection between value engineering and the use of requisite models in decision conferences. It is now possible to draw on the extensive literature of decision theory in order to suggest a research agenda for the future development of value engineering. It should be stressed that the following discussion relates to open-ended design problems where issues of value preference are dominant. The recommended research topics are of little relevance to those whose interest in value engineering is limited to the identification of alternative component solutions.

It is suggested that the most suitable starting point for a research agenda is provided by the 'simple multi-attribute rating technique' (SMART), as described by Edwards (1977). This approach is sufficiently simplistic to be used within a two-day decision conference and yet the basic framework can be employed to incorporate recent developments within decision theory. However, it is important that participants appreciate that the purposes of the exercise are to help them structure their thinking and achieve a shared understanding. Decision models cannot be used to automate the process of decision-making. It must be recognised that the method of analysis will inevitably influence the client's preference structure.

Of particular importance in the development of a requisite decision model is the way in which the problem is structured and the manner in which importance weights are assigned to the identified attributes. Research is required into the possible application of the analytic hierarchy process (AHP) devised by Saaty (1980). There is also considerable potential in the use of value trees as a method of representing design objectives (Pitz and Reidel, 1984). It is interesting to note that value engineering practitioners who perform functional analysis by means of a hierarchial breakdown have inadvertently come very close to the value tree concept.

Whilst the scope of this paper has been deliberately limited to the theory of riskless choice, there is considerable potential for research into ways in which risk preference might also be taken into account. The application of venture theory (Hogarth and Einhorn, 1990) may prove to be of particular interest.

9 Conclusion

This paper has offered a reinterpretation of the theoretical basis of value engineering. It has been argued that the essential characteristics of value engineering are identical to those which distinguish a decision conference. The concept of function has been identified as being dependent upon perception and the uniqueness of functional analysis has also questioned. Furthermore, it has been suggested that the logic of functional analysis is indistinguishable from that displayed by the 'means-ends' approach to the analysis of objectives. It can therefore be concluded that although value engineering has developed its own distinctive terminology, it is not a unique discipline.

In common with any other method of decision conference, value engineering workshops can be implemented for a variety of reasons. Simple cost reduction is a valid objective if the workshop has been initiated in response to a projected cost overspend. However, there is an increasing trend for value engineering to be programmed into the design programme in advance. Sophisticated clients are demanding to be involved in key design decisions so that they can be assured that value-for-money is being achieved. The systematic process of value engineering offers reassurance by ensuring that the decision-making process is both **rational** and **explicit**.

The notion of optimising the value of a building design by

utility maximisation has been classified as a normative model of decision-making. It has also been suggested that the approaches to informal design optimisation which are described in the building economics literature are essentially prescriptive. Value engineering, however, is best understood in terms of a requisite decision model which is developed within the context of a decision conference. The sophistication of the model used should reflect the sophistication of the client and of the designers. Users are likely to react against a model which is too mathematical, they are also likely to be dissatisfied by a model which they perceive as too simplistic.

The concept of a requisite decision model discredits the notion that value engineering studies can be used to search for ideal, or optimal, design solutions. The primary objective of value engineering should be interpreted in terms of providing the client with 'peace of mind'. This is best achieved by demonstrating, to the satisfaction of the client, that the decision has been made on a rational basis. In the final analysis, value-for-money is more of a psychological state of mind than an economic target which is measurable in any objective sense.

The concept of a decision model being used to generate confidence in the decision process is useful in the interpretation of current value engineering practice. If the client is satisfied that the value engineering study has resulted in value-for-money, then it is difficult to criticise the approach adopted. If the users were satisfied with the model which was used then it follows that the model was requisite for that particular situation. However, practitioners should not become complacent. Clients are becoming increasingly sophisticated in their requirements. Whilst they may be satisfied with the value engineering services they currently receive, there is no reason to assume that this will remain the case. If practitioners are to continue to provide clients with a meaningful service then they must aim to increase the sophistication of their techniques. An important first step in this process is the adoption of the terminology and rigorous approach which has been developed within decision theory. The application of value trees has been identified as being particular appropriate for value engineering studies. Perhaps the major challenge for the future is to devise a workable approach which takes into account, not only value preferences, but also risk preferences. However, there is one statement which can be made with certainty; in the absence of an active research programme value engineering will inevitably fall into disrepute.

10 Acknowledgement

This paper is based upon a research project funded by the

Chartered Institute of Building's QE II Silver Scholarship Scheme.

11 References

Bell, D. E., Raiffa, H. and Tversky, A. (1988) Descriptive, normative and prescriptive interactions in decision making, in **Decision Making: Descriptive, Normative and Prescriptive Interactions** (eds D. E. Bell, H. Raiffa and A. Tversky), Cambridge University Press, Cambridge, pp 9-30.

Cooke, S. and Slack, N. (1984), **Making Management Decisions,** Prentice Hall International, Englewood Cliffs, NJ.

Dell'Isola, A. (1982) **Value Engineering in the Construction Industry.** 3rd edn., Van Nostrand Reinhold, New York.

Dunstone, P. (1973) **Value Analysis in Building** (eds G. H. Hutton and A. D. G. Devonald), Applied Science Publishers, London, pp 112-126.

Edwards, W. (1977) Use of multiattribute utility measurement for social decision making, in **Conflicting Objectives in Decisions** (eds D. E. Bell, R. L. Keeney and H. Raiffa), Wiley-Interscience, Chicester, pp 247-276.

Fowler, T. C. (1990) **Value Analysis in Design.** Van Nostrand Reinhold, New York.

Green, S. D. (1991) Value engineering during early design. **Facilities,** 9, (9), 10-13.

Hogarth, R. M. and Einhorn, H. J. (1990) Venture theory: a model of decision weights. **Management Science,** 36, pp 780-803.

Johnson, R. E. (1990) **The Economics of Building: a Practical Guide for the Design Professional.** Wiley-Interscience, New York.

Kelly J. and Male, S. (1990) A critique of value management in construction. **Proc. CIB 90 Building Economics and Construction Management,** 2, pp 130-139.

Kelly, J. and Poynter-Brown, R. (1990) Value management, in **Quantity Surveying Techniques: New Directions** (ed P. S. Brandon), BSP Professional, Oxford, pp 54-74.

Macedo, M. C., Dobrow, P. V. and O'Rourke, J. J. (1978) **Value Management for Construction,** Wiley-Interscience, New York.

Mackinder, M. and Marvin, H. (1982) **Design Decision Making in Architectural Practices,** Research Paper No. 19, Institute of Advanced Architectural Studies, University of York.

Morton, C. W. (1987) Value engineering and its application to the construction industry, in **Building Cost Modelling and Computers** (ed P. S. Brandon), E. & F. N Spon, London, pp 31-40.

Mudge, A. E. (1971) **Value Engineering in Design and Construction.** McGraw-Hill, New York.

Newton, S. (1990) Formal design optimisation and informal design. **Proc. CIB 90 Building Economics and Construction Management,** 2, pp 182-193.

O'Brien, J. J. (1976) **Value Analysis in Design and Construction,** McGraw-Hill, New York.

Palmer, A. (1990) **A Critique of Value Management,** Chartered Institute of Building Technical Information Service, No. 124, Ascot.

Parker, D. E. (1985) **Value Engineering Theory,** Lawrence D. Miles Foundation, Washington.

Phillips, L. D. (1984) A theory of requisite decision models. **Acta Psychologica,** 56, 29-48.

Pitz, G. F. and Reidel, S. (1984) The content and structure of value tree representations. **Acta Psychologica,** 56, 59-70.

Saaty, T. L. (1980) **The Analytical Hierarchy Process,** McGraw-Hill, New York.

Simon, H. A. (1957) **Administrative Behaviour,** MacMillan, New York.

Simon, H. A. (1981) **The Sciences of the Artificial,** 2nd edn., MIT Press, Cambridge, Mass.

Szoke, K. (1974) Introduction, **Proc. CIB W-55 1st International Symposium on Building Economics: Assessing the Economics of Buildings,** pp 1-6.

Szoke, K (1987) The 17-year old W-55 is still developing, **Proc. CIB W-55 4th International Symposium on Building Economics,** Keynotes, 13-22.

VanGrundy, A. B. (1988), **Techniques of Structured Problem Solving,** 2nd edn., Van Nostrand Reinhold, New York.

Warszawski, A. (1980) Evaluation of multiobjective ventures. **Proc. CIB W-55 Methods for Comparing and Evaluating Alternative Products and Designs,** IV, pp 159-165.

Watson, S. R. and Buede, D. M. (1987) **Decision Synthesis: the principles and practice of decision analysis.** Cambridge University Press, Cambridge.

Wilson, A. (1987) Building Design Optimisation. **Proc. CIB W-55 4th International Symposium on Building Economics,** Keynotes, pp 58-71.

Zimmerman, L. W. and Hart, G. D. (1982) **Value Engineering: A Practical Approach for Owners, Designers and Contractors.** Van Nostrand Reinhold, New York.

Value management from a global perspective

W.F. Lenzer
VEI, Inc., Dallas, Texas, USA
Society of American Value Engineers, Chicago, Illinois, USA
Lawrence D. Miles Value Foundation, Washington DC, USA

Abstract

The value concept is presented as a higher order thinking process which is innately ingrained in all humans. Using the Miles' method of defining and relating function to cost as a form of value expression can improve individual and organizational effectiveness. The system that Miles originated as "Value Analysis" has spread throughout the world. Specific variances have evolved in the Orient as a result of the East-West cultural gap.

Examples are presented from four widely differing areas: Product, Construction, Organization/Procedures and Overhead (Utilities).

The history and evolution of Demings' Quality Concepts and Miles' Value Concept and their integration into Japanese business is presented and the major similarities and differences are discussed.

The Miles' Value concept as a key communication tool is presented. It's use in improving cross cultural understanding is also discussed.

Applications of the value concept in Architectural Management, or any form of management, are discussed and the benefits identified.

Keywords: Function, Value, Value Analysis, Quality, Miles, Japan, Management.

1 Value Engineering as a High Order Thinking Process

The basic concept of **Value** has existed for a very long time. It has been addressed exhaustively in areas such as economics and philosophy. Larry Miles, however, was the first person in history to develop a method by which the previously abstract concept could be quantitatively expressed in a way which facilitated detailed analysis. He called his method Value Analysis. The key to Miles' contribution to our world society in this regard was his development of the "**function**" feature of Value and its relation to cost.

While written languages differ significantly between cultures, it would appear that almost all modern spoken languages use a combination of verbs and nouns to express an action performed or desired on an object. The use of a single verb and a single noun to express a "function" is the most important key to Value Analysis/Engineering in that it:

(a) forces people to express an idea (function) in its simplest and most basic two-word (verb-noun) form;

(b) forces people working together on a project or a problem to discuss the exact meaning of words and their relationship to each other and the particulars of the specific situation;

(c) dramatically improves communication and understanding.

As very young children learning to speak, we all expressed our needs in their most basic form, such as "want food," "need water," "go sleep." As we grew older, we learned to expand and elaborate on these basic expressions and something like "want food" became: "I am really hungry and would like to have a 1" thick, 16 ounce steak dinner with a baked potato."

The evolution of language in a civilization or culture certainly followed a similar development. Pre-historically, simple grunts and sounds developed into specific simple expressions such as "tree," "hunt" and "food." As time progressed, sounds and meanings were added and eventually evolved into our more complex modern day language systems.

The basic concept of "value" has been with all of our cultures since their earliest beginnings. For instance, when a prehistoric man became hungry enough he felt a need to eat food. In this case his function or objective was to "**Eat Food.**" In order to achieve this objective, it might be necessary for him to expend energy and resources to find and kill an animal. This expenditure or effort and resource to "hunt animal" was in effect his cost (personal effort) to achieve the function. His value system could then be expressed as:

$$\text{Value} = \frac{\text{Eat Food}}{\text{Hunt Animal}}$$

where...

"Eat Food" = Function   &   "Hunt Animal" = Cost in terms of effort

The value expression as derived by Miles is simply that: $\textbf{VALUE} = \dfrac{\textbf{FUNCTION}}{\textbf{COST}}$

The methods of defining functions and relating them to "costs" formulates a common basis for cross cultural communication. Furthermore, once the relationship and methodology is learned and understood, it can be expanded and applied to every aspect of business, products, systems and even one's own personal life.

In its highest order of perspective the Value concept can define the "purpose" and be viewed almost as a philosophy. When brought down to detailed and specific problems, the concept provides very effective techniques for detailed analysis/engineering and improved cost effectiveness.

Larry Miles observed that the individuals who appeared to gain most from learning his Value concept were those in the top 20% of "intelligence." The power of the concept compounds (see Figure 1) when imposed at any level of intelligence but increases almost asymptotically at higher levels.

Dr. Takehiko Matsuda of Sanno College, during an impressive presentation at the Lawrence D. Miles Value Foundation's 1988 Pacific Basin VE Conference, presented the concept that VE is an important element of increasing "Organizational Intelligence." He further stressed the importance to all businesses of increasing the organization's level of intelligence in order to meet the challenges of the future and to maintain a competitive position in the world marketplace.[1]

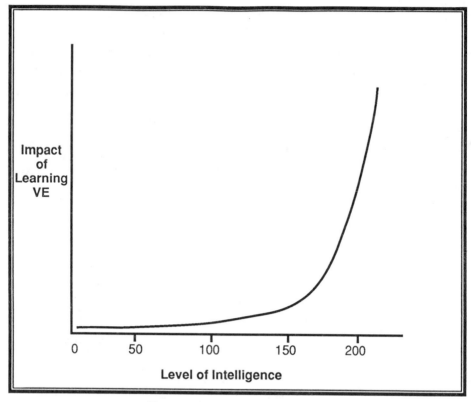

Figure 1: Intellectual Impact on VE

2 Some Basic Definitions

In the USA there are several slightly different definitions of Value Analysis/Engineering. The Lawrence D. Miles Value Foundation has published the following definition for "Value Analysis":

> **1. A method for enhancing product value by improving the relationship of worth to cost through the study of function, 2. A methodology using an organized approach [job plan] with an organized effort [multidiscipline team] to provide required functions at lowest overall cost consistent with achieving required acceptance or performance, 3. The determination of the value of product functions as perceived by the user/customer in the marketplace.[2]**

While Larry Miles first called his function thinking system **Value Analysis**, over the years other terms have been used to refer to the same basic process but with different areas of focus. For instance, in many (but not all) USA manufacturing organizations the following apply:

270

Value Analysis. The value process or methodology applied to something that exists or a product in the production stage.

Value Engineering. The value process or methodology applied to something that doesn't exist or is in the planning or design phase.

Japan and most other countries in the Orient have adopted the term "Value Engineering" as the key word to name the Miles methodology. When comparing Japanese terminology used in some USA manufacturing companies the following results:

USA	Japan
Value Analysis	2nd Look VE
Value Engineering	"O" Look VE and "1st" Look VE

Some other common differentiations used in the USA and their application meaning are:

Value Management (VM). The value process or methodology (1) applied to management systems, structures and procedures or (2) used by management in the conduct of their business.

Value Control. The value process or methodology used to "control" costs in any organization.

There are many other variations which surface from time to time. For instance, some recently used terms have been AVA (Activities Value Analysis) or OVA (Organizational Value Analysis or Overhead Value Analysis). The most comparable term to VM, AVA and OVA in Japan is Soft VE, which encompasses all aspects of VE which are not hardware or related to something physical.

The "VE Job Plan" is essentially the same worldwide. There are probably more variations used in the USA than anywhere in the world. The "VE Job Plan" is basically a step-by-step procedure by which a VE effort is performed. Some job plans have as few as three steps, others can have 20 or 30 steps and sub-steps. The more detailed Job Plans are very good for teaching, but may sometimes "stifle" individuality and opportunities for more creative approaches. In the Miles' Job Plan approach there are only five essential steps which are as follows:[3]

STEP	ACTIVITIES
INFORMATION	Gathering all data and information; asking questions and understanding the project from all aspects.
(FUNCTION) ANALYSIS	Identifying functions, relating functions to cost, evaluating worth and, in some cases (not necessarily all the time), developing "FAST" (Function Analysis System Technique) diagrams.

STEP	ACTIVITIES

**CREATIVITY
(or SPECULATION)** — Generating ideas (focusing on functions) without pre-judging, in mass quantities, without restrictions.

JUDGEMENT — Evaluating ideas and selecting those which appear to have the best features and opportunity for development.

**DEVELOPMENT
PLANNING** — Developing the selected ideas into specific proposals and recommendations. This phase also includes presentations, implementation and follow up.

These five key elements or steps are contained within all VE Job Plans everywhere in the world, from India to Australia to Brazil to Europe, China and Japan.

Most of the Western countries have adopted and modified the American value techniques with less modification than the Orient. Some of the peculiarities of VE in the Orient are:

"FAST" (Function Analysis System Technique):

(a) Diagrams are similar to function-hierarchy diagrams turned sideways;
(b) Maintain a rule that in moving from the "why?" to the "how?" (right to left) the number of functions must always decrease; and
(c) seldom utilize "when?" feature.

Team studies:

(a) always done as a group; and
(b) avoid "individual" ownership; and
(c) avoid conflict.

Human relationships:

(a) prevent loss of "face"; and
(b) maintain respect for society "order" and individual's position.

Creativity:

(a) cultural boundaries; and
(b) more methodical as opposed to spontaneous.

3 Examples

3.1 Example No. 1: Product

Project: Electronic section assembly for missile guidance/control: circuit board attachment to interconnect board. The original design (actually in production) required a special hand welded interconnect fitting. The special fitting was a sole-source item.

Current Cost:	£6.31
Quantity of Next Production Batch:	40,000 units
Total Production/Assembly Cost:	£252,400

VE Approach: A multi-discipline team of VE trained people from engineering, quality, production/ assembly, and purchasing along with a CVS team leader (all in-house) participated in a three-day concentrated VE study.

Results: A complete redesign resulted which:

(a) Reduced number of parts from 2 to 1;
(b) Eliminated need for hand soldering;
(c) Eliminated sole source;
(d) Improved reliability; and
(e) Reduced maintenance.

Initial Savings:	£4.90 per unit
Implementation Cost:	-0.44 per unit
Net Savings:	£4.46 per unit (71%)
Total Savings:	£178,400

3.2 Example No. 2: Construction

Project: A research and development complex of over 300 buildings on a site totalling over 3 million square meters (almost 700 acres) located in the western portion of the USA needed to prevent any accidental pollution of wastewater. A system was designed to divert the wastewater into temporary holding tanks upon detection of a hazardous condition.

Capacities of the project were:

(a) Maximum sewage flow:	5600 liters/minute
(b) Maximum storage capacity:	818,400 liters

Previous cost studies:

(a) A VE study had been conducted at concept ("O" step) by in-house people.
(b) A cost reduction effort had been completed two weeks prior to a scheduled independent VE study. The results were:

Cost Before Cost Reduction:	£1,352,000
Cost Reduction:	- 214,000
New Cost:	£1,138,000

Project status: 100% complete design.

Approach: A concentrated five day VE study was conducted by an **outside team** of VE professionals. The team consisted of a CVS team leader, an electrical engineer, a mechanical/process engineer and a civil engineer. The study was conducted on-site with substantial interface between the VE team, the owner and the design team.

273

Results: One hundred sixty-one (161) ideas and 20 proposals were generated resulting in doubled capacity (elimination of future expansion facility) and savings over £353,000 or 31%. Also eliminated 5 minute delay and relieved overloaded system.

3.3 Example No. 3: Management/Organization

Project: Patient medical records in a large hospital servicing more than 2500 patients per day were stored in 3 different locations - a total of more than 300,000 patient records. For each patient seen, the record had to be located, pulled, and distributed to the appropriate doctor. At the end of each day thousands of pieces of paper had to be filed in individual records and those records returned to their proper location.

Approach: A two week study conducted by CVS team leader, a CVS team member and a hospital consultant was performed. In depth analysis of patient record procedures was the primary focus.

Results: Sixteen (16) recommendations resulted, including a staff reduction of 69 positions and a 26% improvement in productivity due to new, computerized processes. An annual savings of £941,000 and life cycle 20 year savings of £15,300,000.

3.4 Example No. 4: Overhead

Project: Large synthetic material manufacturing operation, outside of USA. Facility included multiple process lines with enclosed spaces totalling approximately 300,000 m^2 and annual utility costs of approximately £17,650,000 per year. The VE study was focused on utility systems and costs.

Approach: The VE effort consisted of a mix of independent VE professionals (A CVS team leader and two VE trained mechanical/electrical engineers) and key representatives from client's engineering, utilities, process, quality and operation staff (a total of 12 individuals). The study spanned a six month period and consisted of:

(a) a ten day information gathering effort on site with a 45 day follow on/analysis effort;
(b) a one week on-site creativity and analysis session during which ideas were selected and assigned to individuals for development;
(c) a multi-month development effort and;
(d) a final review, report assembly and formal presentation to the plant management team.

Results: Three hundred and fifty-six (356) ideas were generated and ninety (90) ideas investigated in detail. Thirty-nine (39) proposals were presented for immediate implementation. Thirty-eight (38) proposals were accepted resulting in more than £2,060,000 in annual savings.

The proposals covered a wide range of areas such as:

(a) Changes in fuel type and quality
(b) Changes in methods of cooling, heating and piping
(c) Changes/additions to control systems
(d) Waste recovery and heat transfer
(e) Changes in process operation

4 Value & Quality

Dr. W. Edwards Deming and Larry Miles were contemporaries. Deming was born in 1900 and Miles was born in 1904. Both individuals and their developing methods were significantly influenced by World War II. In 1945 Deming made his first visit to Japan, and by the early fifties his quality concepts had been adopted and were being promoted as QC.

It wasn't until 1955 that Japan discovered Miles and the Value Analysis system. The development and expansion of the Miles' system began to bloom through the efforts of Dr. Ichiro Ueno and SANNO Institute of Business Administration in the early 1960's. This lead to the eventual formation of the Society of Japanese Value Engineering in 1965.

In the USA the Value Analysis/Engineering concepts of Miles were adopted and expanded by many industries in the 1950's and 1960's. Few in the USA knew of Deming and the Quality Concepts.

Today "quality" concepts of Deming and the related concepts of Juran, A.V. Feigenbaum and, more recently, Philip Crosby are well known and respected in both Japan and the USA; however, it has only been in the last 15 years that the value of some of these concepts have been recognized by USA industry.

How did they begin to "recognize" the impact of the quality concepts? By first recognizing that Japanese industries were doing something that they weren't and making a concentrated effort to find out why Japan was increasing its share of not only the American but the world market. This has led to what some people term the "Renaissance of American Quality."

As part of this Renaissance, American quality experts have been in excessive demand domestically as never before. A person like Philip Crosby can charge as much as £7100 per day for his time. This phenomena has not occurred yet in the USA in the area of Value Engineering in any of its forms. Larry Miles left this world in 1985, never fully recognized (like Deming) in his own country. Why?

The Value Concepts of Miles are used extensively in American industry. The big difference is that its use is considered almost a "company secret" and is not widely publicized. Those who do "advertise" their use of the methodology do so very cautiously and generally only indicate their results superficially.

The other problem in the USA is that there are many "Value Consultants" and for the most part these consultants are very protective of who their clients are and what they've done with VE. The individual consultants openly compete fiercely on every front. Because of the widespread awareness of the quality movement in the USA, many VE consultants have reoriented their practice towards quality.

Although the US Federal Government has been virtually the only government in the world to implement and promote VE in all of its agencies, some overshadowing has occurred in recent years by the popularity of the quality movement. There are movements now to push TQM (Total Quality Management) as the all encompassing system. This movement is being received with mixed opinions.

There are major differences between the Quality and Value concepts. Some of the value concepts which most significantly differentiate the two are that the value methodology...

(a) can be applied in a wider range of areas and to any subject.
(b) is a thinking process that helps bring abstract ideas into a manageable concrete form.
(c) is function oriented.
(d) creates a common language of function communications.
(e) can be used to clearly define "the purpose" of a system, product or organization at several different levels of abstraction.
(f) can produce measurable results in a relatively short period of time.
(g) can improve personal and organizational levels of applied intelligence.
(h) should be understood and actively used by the top levels of management.

There are also many common elements between the Value and Quality methods. Some of these are:

(a) Teamwork
(b) Involvement of and feedback from customers and users.
(c) Creativity and brainstorming techniques.
(d) Involvement of workers or employees.
(e) The use of appropriate mathematical techniques for analysis (such as SPC).

The ongoing and even worldwide arguments about whether Quality or Value Concepts are the most important have been answered in my mind long ago. It would appear that the "Value Concept" opens the human mind and provides a way to expand and improve everything. It addresses the issues of "purpose" but certainly does not contradict the value of examining "cause and effect."

From a VE standpoint the objectives of programs and movements can be defined but "Quality" concepts do not seem to be able to achieve the reverse. Figure 2 shows the end result of a multi-faceted "FAST" diagram which began with the examination of a single function **"Improve Profit."** The evolution shows the ability for VE to examine many aspects without limiting the thought process to a singular focus.

5 Communication Aspects of VE

Recently I had an opportunity to review a portion of a proposed text dealing with VE. The text was written originally in Japanese and translated into English by a professional translator. My review was for English understanding, not teaching concept or specific technical approach. The difficulty of language and culture became evident in two areas:

(a) Some "functions," when spoken in Japanese with two words (verb-noun), were translated by using up to six words.
(b) One translated expression of a "function," while literally correct, represented a socially unacceptable American expression.

The "Renaissance of American Quality" has resulted in perhaps many misunderstandings of how things really work in Japan. Perhaps the global ideas get across, but some of the finer points are certainly lost in the translation.

For instance, in bringing back to the USA from Japan the concept of Quality Function Deployment (QFD), the system has totally lost the aspect of defining function with two words. Those who are now the American QFD experts have no understanding of how Value and Quality techniques have been integrated.

Communication means getting across to another person an "exact" idea. Under any circumstances this can be a difficult undertaking. I've often been in large meetings and have found in subsequent conversations/consultations that different people heard different things. These were meetings where everyone was a native speaker of English. The problem of multi-lingual meetings is compounded by several orders of magnitude.

In my dealings with the Japanese Value Specialists, I have found that communications improve even if conducted through an interpreter. This has mostly resulted because we have a mutual understanding of "function" and how that is expressed in the verb-noun context.

The effect of forcing understanding and agreement between two or more people by defining "functions" and organizing them within a system can be beyond the understanding of anyone who has never experienced the opportunity. It can represent unlimited brain power and, as Larry Miles said, "creates clear thinking."[5]

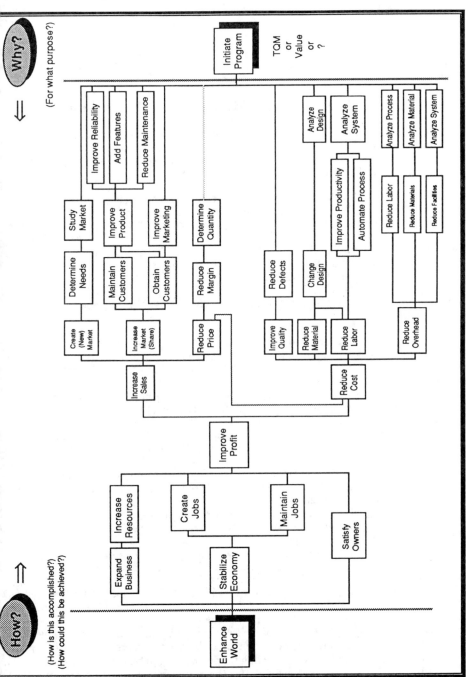

Figure 2: Improve Profit

6 The Future

Every person, company, culture, family and special interest group is motivated by different factors and to different purposes. The "purposes" may have some common aspects but the factors vary widely. A person or organization may have all the knowledge and ability possible, but if there is no motivation, performance is zero. This idea is expressed simply as:

$$(Knowledge + Ability)\ Motivation = Performance$$

The future of our world and its individual countries, companies and people holds much opportunity and challenge. Who will be successful? While only time will expose everything, I believe that there are a few basic ideas that will help any company, culture or individual succeed. These are:

(a) Try to know and understand yourself, your company, your client and your customer.
(b) Be willing to be flexible and accept new ideas and change.
(c) Improve the thinking abilities of yourself, family, company, country and the world in general.
(d) Improve "communications."
   • Understand self.
   • Understand organization.
   • Understand others.
(e) Organize and focus efforts to identify and resolve issues as quickly and efficiently as possible.

In my opinion the Value methodology is the key way to implement these ideas. The Value methodology does not preclude the use of any approach or technique, but complements them all as a means to identify, solve and/or resolve specific issues or problems.

While Deming has 14 specific principals for good management, I have only seven, the first four of which should be followed in sequence. The seven key concepts are:

1. OBTAIN FACTS. This means all facts, information, data, and input from every possible source. Questions must be asked/answered and the veracity of everything must be verified.

2. ANALYZE THE FACTS. Define "functions." Relate functions to costs. Consider "worth" of functions. Look at everything and compare with whatever "knowns" are available. Identify questionable items and areas.

3. GENERATE IDEAS. Use brainstorming and group idea generation. Produce quantity and ignore all restrictive parameters. This must be a distinguishably separate activity dedicated to the purpose.

4. DEVELOP & IMPLEMENT. Analyze ideas and select what appears to be the best for further development and implementation. Follow up on everything and be tenacious in your pursuit. Demand exacting feedback.

5. ALWAYS LOOK BACK. Never stop revisiting Steps 1 - 4. Facts and situations, as well as information, *may change daily*. Accept the fact that we are in an "information society" and the volume of data increases with each passing second.

6. INVOLVE OTHERS. While all of the steps presented above can be implemented by only one person, the effectiveness is increased by several orders of magnitude by having two or more people involved in the processes. (**Note: My experience indicates that five to eight people offer the optimum. Beyond that quantity the**

278

formation of sub-groups or teams is recommended.)

7. SEEK CATALYTIC AGENTS. Outside objective analysis and input can expand the dimension of any effort. Outsiders are not (or should not be) influenced by internal factors and should be able to bring a wide range of background and experience to the effort.

This approach does not preclude any specific technique, it only opens the door to consider all aspects. In other words, it fosters an "open mind" approach that can result in using the "best" way for any particular situation at any specific point in time. It offers an opportunity to balance -- the ying and the yang -- it will happen, so why not be a part of it and help it occur by using the Value methodology?

7 References

Matsuda, Dr. Takehiko (1988) Presentation on "Organizational Intelligence," The Lawrence D. Miles Value Foundation's 1988 Pacific Basin VE Conference.

Miles, The Lawrence D. Value Foundation for the Society of American Value Engineers (1988) **Directory of Value Analysis/Value Engineering Consultants**.

Miles, Lawrence D. (1989) **Techniques of Value Analysis and Engineering.** Eleanor Miles Walker.

Miles, Lawrence D. conversations with Bill Lenzer (1978 - 1985)

Walton, Mary (1986) **The Deming Management Method.** The Putnam Publishing Group.

CHAPTER SIX

*'There are many applications where computers
can take over tedious and repetitive tasks,
thereby freeing people to devote their minds
and more creative ability to more fruitful ends.
One of the important factors about the use of
the computers is the facility that they offer to
help extend man's natural capabilities.'*

David Campion

Data transfer – designs on the move

C.R. Coleman
Consultant, National Economic Development Office, London, UK

Abstract
The NEDC Construction Industry Sector Group is the only body that represents the entire scope of construction and related activity in the United Kingdom. It has identified and redressed the lack of leadership within the industry by establishing a Working Party to investigate CAD data and other information exchange.

The Working Party's findings show that the introduction and encouragement of CAD data and information exchange practices offers substantial opportunity to rationalise the way projects are managed to the benefit of all participants, and at substantially lower overall cost.

The background considerations and some of the practical measures implemented to assist the UK building industry come to terms with its future are described.
Keywords: CAD Data and Other Information Exchange, Project Organisation, Building, Construction, National Economic Development Office (NEDO).

1 Background

1.1 The role of the National Economic Development Office

The National Economic Development Council first met on 7th March 1962. Its objective is to increase the rate of sound growth by:

Examining the economic performance of the nation.
Considering what can be done to improve efficiency, and whether the best use is being made of resources.
Seeking agreement upon ways of improving economic performance, competitive power and efficiency.

The organisation comprises three main elements:

The National Economic Development Council.
18 Industry Sector Groups and Working Parties.
The National Economic Development Office .

For over three decades, the Council with support of the National Economic Development Office, Sector Groups and Working Parties has tackled problems facing British industry and sought to bring about beneficial changes to improve economic performance.

1.1.1 The National Economic Development Council(NEDC) comprises six Cabinet ministers most closely concerned with the economy, six representatives of the Trades Union Congress, six representatives of the Confederation of British Industry, the Governor of the Bank of England and a number of independent members appointed by the Chancellor of the Exchequer.

1.1.2 The Industry Sector Groups and Working Parties represent a unique national resource which have contributed significantly to the UK's industrial per- formance. Chief executives, top trade union officials, senior civil servants and distinguished individuals give their time freely to identify how things can be improved in their respective industries.

1.1.3 The National Economic Development Office (NEDO) provides the secretariat for the Council and its Sector Groups and Working Parties.

NEDO projects are tackled to a high standard and within a strict timetable with emphasis on overcoming obstacles to small and medium-sized companies. Furthermore, the completion of the Single European Market has added impetus to NEDO's role of enhancing the competitiveness of specific industry sectors. It is against this background that the initiatives in respect of CAD Data and Information Exchange have been undertaken.

1.2 The NEDC Construction Industry Sector Group
The NEDC Construction Industry Sector Group commissioned the CAD Data and Other Information Exchange in Building Working Party to make **practical** proposals that could be progressively adopted from the present time. The remit was to identify the information transfer needs between all parties in a building project, if design, construction management, maintenance and operation, and finally demolition is to be carried out effectively and efficiently.

The NEDO Working Party has tried to anticipate and pre-empt the emerging difficulties and offer leadership.

1.3 Terms of reference: CAD data and other information exchange in building
The NEDC CAD Data Working Party was established to define its own scope of work, perceived industry needs, and actions to be taken. Trying to accommodate all interests both inside and outside the industry and refining the definition of activities has been a challenging but worthwhile task.

The prime objectives identified in respect of data exchange were to:

Highlight areas of concern, commercial need and opportunity for action.
Raise awareness of both suppliers and users.
Provide means to rationalise existing problems.
Encourage wider adoption of best practice in the deployment of computer systems in building.
Prepare short and longer term guidelines for the industry.

In addition, supplementary and tertiary objectives are within the scope of the Working Party where they concern the implementation of new technology leading to a rationalised and more effective industry structure.

2 Towards fully mobile design information

The starting point for considering CAD data exchange in building and construction is to imagine the worst possible scenario for information technology in a fragmented industry.

'When computer technology is adopted by individual disciplines architects, structural and civil engineers, quantity surveyors, building services engineers, etc., on the existing project organisational model with little regard for the responsibilities of fellow participants. Hard copy drawings being checked and passed between job functions, then redrawn in a proliferation of non-compatible systems. A multitude of CAD derived drawings with no indication of the originating system or release number. Add to these complexities, the demands of the developer, purchaser, tenant and subtenants, not to mention security and maintenance considerations and the problem assumes immense proportions.'

From this potential nightmare, insight is given to an enhanced industry structure.

As building practice is not rational; simply to computerise individual responsibilities and maintain existing relationships is not appropriate as it will merely reinforce existing inefficiencies. Clearly, new approaches are demanded to meet more sophisticated and complex building requirements. It seemed realistic that heightened awareness of present difficulties and enhanced perception of the potential benefits of change would encourage some companies to seek an ideal 'model' for data transfer. After all, computers are only tools, and their application should support, rather than detract from the efficient communication between all participants involved in a building project.

3 Project organisation

Unclear and missing information is a major cause of problems
in building and construction. Fig. 1 illustrates the
significance of unclear or missing project information
compared to other causes and the effectiveness with which
they have been resolved.

Efficiency tends to be subjective, however, and
expedience for one discipline often leads to added costs and
delay for another. One of the main objectives of data
exchange is to reduce substantially claims against the main
contractor for variations to contract conditions by quality
assured information transfer in design, con- struction
management, maintenance and operation, and finally
demolition.

Difficulties tend to occur at the interface between
disciplines and project phases. In order to define the
quality assured regime required, it is necessary to define
the interfaces and the information that passes across them.
Therefore, it is necessary to have a clear and detailed
understanding of what is happening between any two parties
involved in the 'contract'.

3.1 The respective role of each contractor
As a mission it is essential to:

Encourage the widest adoption of best practice in the
deployment of all project resources including computer
systems.
Ensure that the supplementary and tertiary objectives of
using new techniques are understood where they lead to
rationalised or apparently more effective project
structure.

Clients, such as building developers and process plant
procurers have to be educated with regard to the 'requests'
to the main contractor and the main contractor must be able
to evaluate the ramifications of changes easily.

4 Understanding how things go wrong in construction

Things go wrong for one reason only 'human beings are
fallible'. The UK contemporary approach to tackling
problems is to regard all participants, client through to
sub-contract suppliers, as 'Partners' and that everyone is a
'Customer'. The client is the 'External Customer' and each
member of the project team is an 'Internal Customer'. All
'Customers' have the right to expect the highest standards
of quality control from the project management team. This
activity relates principally to the control and maintenance
of contract information.

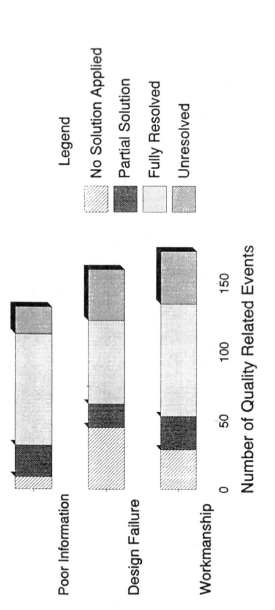

Fig 1 - QUALITY FAILURES IN BUILDING
The Causes of 500 Quality Related Events

Legend

- No Solution Applied
- Partial Solution
- Fully Resolved
- Unresolved

All Other Causes

Poor Information

Design Failure

Workmanship

Number of Quality Related Events

0   50   100   150

NEDC CONSTRUCTION INDUSTRY
SECTOR GROUP

A well organised 'Contract System' can substantially reduce if not eliminate the consequences of human failure irrespective of where it occurs. A poorly organised 'team' on the other hand exacerbates them. The principal difference between a well organised contract team and a poorly organised one is pivotal on the ability of individual members to organise, process and relay information correctly - not from their own perspective but from that of the receiving party and the use to which it will be put. Most problems arise because of:

Defective information.
Incomplete information.
Conflicts of information.
The use of non-authoritative information.
Multiple sources of the same information.
Use of information 'at hand'.

These problems are avoidable, however, and should be controlled by formal procedures. Thus the necessity of control procedures is defined. The task of formulating control procedures for a large building, however, is fraught with difficulty. This is because of the cumulative problem of a fragmented contract and pro- fessional structure based on traditionally adversarial relationships, ie. 'make a mistake and I'll see you in court!'.

4.1 Division of project costs
If the costs of design, procurement and construction of a building are considered as two distinct phases, then the typical division is:

Phase 1   Design Phase accounts for 15% of total cost.
Phase 2   Construction and downstream phase ie.,
           procurement commissioning etc., accounts for
           85% of total cost.

The dependency of the second phase, however, is highly sensitive to the quality of output from the first phase. A relatively small quality failure in the design phase has much more profound cost repercussions in the procurement and construction phases.

4.2 Project meetings
The design phase itself is susceptible to the greatest proportion of quality related events as a summation of pure design failure (8%) and information failure (34%). It is no coincidence that the majority of these dif- ficulties stem from the first project meeting when team participation is not fully mature. The procedures that are set at this first meeting, include:

Rules of procedure.
Roles within the scope of design responsibility.
Roles within the scope of construction responsibility.
Roles within the scope of commissioning responsibility.
Project management and reportage.
Continuous cost monitoring.
Methods of assessing risk.
Procedure for minimising risk.
Reliability.
Programme recovery.
Contingency provision.

The items lower down this list tend to compensate for ambiguities, potential failures and other information related issues further up the list. **As a consequence, the availability of agreed 'Quality Assured' information procedures at the outset of the project results in lowering risks, increased reliability, shorter programmes and smaller contingency provision.** Savings between 15 - 25% of total project cost are estimated if the potential benefits are fully realised.

4.3 Managing the issues
By taking the 'big problem' of achieving quality assured information exchange between participants and breaking it down into a series of smaller problems we arrive at the 'core issues' confronting the project team; these fall into three groups - Fig. 2:

Human and organisational issues.
Conceptual model issues.
Technical issues.

4.3.1 **Human and organisational issues** are principally concerned with quality, cost, time, professional and commercial objectives, classification of information, technical and non-technical information requirements.

4.3.2 **Conceptual model issues** are concerned with why the project resources and activities need to be modelled and the need for the development of Quality Assured information exchange between parties. By relating actual performance of previous practice and current working methods to an idealised 'project model', an assessment of potential benefits can be made.

4.3.3 **Technical issues** are concerned with the technology of the engineering itself. Adequate consideration must be given to the available methods of technical validation, data exchange, geometric and non-geometric information, the implication of standards and testing.

FIG 2 - CAD DATA EXCHANGE IN BUILDING
Categories of Problem

 Conceptual

Human

Technical

NEDC CONSTRUCTION INDUSTRY
SECTOR GROUP

The quality of the management of the information, data exchange media, and communication by definition is critical to each of these three issues.

5 Information and data exchange

Hitherto, the terms 'Information' and 'Data' have been used synonymously. Whether computers are involved or not it is good contract practice to regard these as separate quantities, thus **'Information is Data set into Context'**

An engineering analogy is to think of 'Information' as the vector equivalent of the scalar quantity 'data'. Unless, the party transmitting 'information' has a clear understanding of the 'context' as to how the data is to be used; then they are doing no more than sending numbers or words as 'characters' subject to many interpretations.

5.1 Implications for building and construction
Although each project tends to be executed slightly differently, the overall organisation is summarised in Fig. 3 - The Exploitation of Information by Contract Participants. The way in which information flows between participants during the design and construction process in the industry is illustrated by the matrix. Three stages of the exploitation of information are represented by:

I - Initiate information
D - Develop information
R - Read information.

Fig. 4 shows the main activities of participants ranked in approximate order of priority against three groups comprising the design team, constructors and suppliers. The list is intended to schedule typical information priorities, but does not claim to be either definitive or exhaustive, Note the diagram underlines the information exchange problems during the design stage when several different parties, usually in different companies, initiate design activity with strong added value content. The incidence of problems in coordination are high and opportunities for cost and time savings are worth pursuing.

5.2 Contract procedures for handling data and information
Contract procedures should recognise communication as being considered under one of the following categories - Fig. 5:

Read only data: one-way transmission.
Design iteration: two-way transmission and reception.
Archiving.

FIG 3 - INFORMATION EXCHANGE IN BUILDING

Three Stages of Exploiting Information

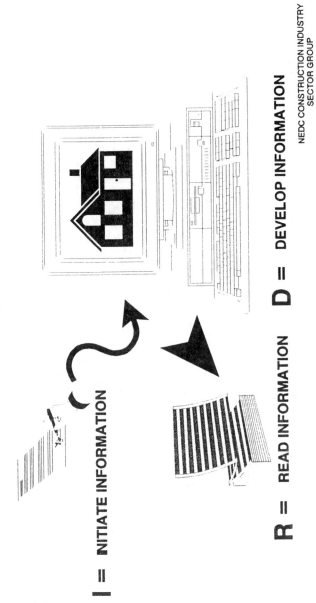

I = NITIATE INFORMATION

R = READ INFORMATION   D = DEVELOP INFORMATION

NEDC CONSTRUCTION INDUSTRY
SECTOR GROUP

FIG 4 - BUILDING: Information Interfaces.

ACTIVITIES IN ORDER OF PRIORITY

	Technical Brief (I)	Approvals	Plan & Programme (I)	Cost Controller (I)	Design Drawings (R)	Calculations	Specification	Bills of Quantity	Archive (R)	Construction Dwg.	Feedback	Maintenance (I)
Architect	R		R	R	—		D		—	—	R	D
Structural Eng.	R	—	R		—	—	D		—	—	R	D
M & E Eng.	R		R		—	—	D		—		R	D	D
Q.S.	R		R	—	R	—	—	—		R	R	R
Surveyor	R		R		—			—				
Planning Eng.	R	R	—		R							
Contract Check	—	R	R		R	R	R					
DESIGN TEAM												
Main Contractor	R		R		R	R	R		R			R
Sub-contractors	R		R		R	R	R		R			R
Specialists	R		R		D		R		—		R	R
Prop. Surveyor									R		—	—
CONSTRUCTORS												
Manufacturers	—			—		R	R		R			
Other Suppliers	—			—		—	R		—			
SUPPLIERS												

FIG 5 - CONTRACT PROCEDURES -
Handling Data and Information

READ ONLY DATA -
One -way transmission

ITERATION -
Two-way transmission
& reception

ARCHIVING -
Maintained Records

NEDC CONSTRUCTION INDUSTRY
SECTOR GROUP

Considerable simplification can be achieved and risks reduced if participants have a clear understanding of their responsibilities in this respect.

The highest priority must be given to looking at the contract as a whole and the methods by which quality assured information can be captured at an early stage. Contractors and suppliers have the crucial role to ensure that categorised data is used by designers for the purpose for which it is intended.

5.3 Opportunities for improved productivity: parts lists, manuals, schematics operating instructions and procurement schedules

There is a need and opportunity for developing supplier information at an early stage. Although some specific CAD databases of building products exist eg., RIBACAD; the majority of information about products used in building and construction is gained from paper catalogues and reference books. The specification of a part from a hard copy source into a CAD drawing may involve several draughtsmen performing the same task in different companies in ignorance of each other. Thus risk of errors occurring is ever present as described in Section 3 – Understanding How Things Go Wrong.

6 How CAD data and information exchange is achieved at present

At the outset of a building project the managing contractor is faced with a fundamental decision of profound gravity. How will quality assured and traceable information and data exchange be achieved all the way down to the 'place of work' at site level.

6.1 Available options

There are five options available regarding the transfer of information between participants:

Hardcopy	All communications initiated from controlled hard copy documents.
IGES	The initial graphics exchange specification.
DXF	The proprietary data interchange format originally specified by Autodesk.
STEP	Standard for the Exchange of Product Model Data.
	Dedicated database translators.

6.1.1 Hardcopy: Traditional practice perhaps, but now at considerable cost and time penalty. This means redrawing CAD originated drawings; re-entering computer processed numeric information and retyping text annotation. The greatest logistics problem is ensuring the correct issue of the drawing is available to all interested parties at the same time.

Use of hardcopy is not mutually exclusive of other information and data exchange techniques, but requires equal respect.

6.1.2 **IGES:** The UK contracting industry has had difficulty in exploiting IGES despite the success of this data exchange format in other industry sectors such as aerospace.

6.1.3 **DXF:** A partial solution and the preferred format adopted for widespread use of two dimensional data exchange. Industry specific layering conventions exist for more sophisticated data/information exchange.

6.1.4 **STEP:** Of the possible alternatives conceived at present, it is likely that STEP will provide the long term solution, but it is vulnerable to lack of support from the industry to provide sufficient resources to influence development specific to its needs. There is a lack of understanding within the industry as regards STEP, which is generally regarded as a future solution to problems as currently perceived.

6.1.5 **Dedicated database translators:** System specific CAD data translations can be achieved by the use of direct translators. Their application is most appropriate between two users with high volume or regular exchange requirements where the management of the exchange can be agreed and tightly controlled. They tend to have severe limitations for common use, however, as they are expensive and can require substantial human intervention.

Should 'New Technology' approaches be used, participants should be aware of the potential legal issues raised.

6.2 **Legal, insurance and copyright implications**
The pace of change in the use of CAD in the construction industry represents a challenge to the English and Scottish legal systems which usually look to precedents, rather than pre-emptive action. In CAD data exchange there are few, if any, well defined liability responsibilities.

7   **Recommendations**

The Working Party's combined wisdom can be delivered as a series of simple rules leading to the more profitable and effective exchange of CAD data and other information. These are to:

Establish the objectives of the data exchange exercise, giving this a higher priority than for the technical considerations.
Agree hardware media and communication protocols.
Agree data exchange format. The interim preferred format identified by the Working Party is DXF for 2D unstructured data sets; but STEP is seen as the long term solution to the industry's needs.
Structure CAD drawings observing a standard layering convention, ie BS1192 part 5.
Ensure your CAD vendor's DXF (or other) translator has been properly tested and is quality assured by an impartial authority. CADDETC offer both DXF and IGES evaluation services.
Agree the criteria to assess success or failure of the data exchange .
Define strategies in the event of failure and specify the corrective action necessary from the outset.
Test vendor commitment **prior** to purchase in respect of BS5750 - Quality Systems; BS1192 part 5 - Guide for Structuring Graphic Information; DXF translator evaluation.

'Exchange Agreement: guidelines for the successful exchange of product model data' is an excellent document available from the CADCAM Data Exchange Technical Centre, Leeds as a basis for a contract between any two parties wishing to exchange data.

Included with this paper is an order form for the various reports published by the NEDC Working Party upon which this paper is based.

8 **In conclusion**

Vendors and users alike should recognise the importance of dealing with all aspects of quality assured contract information at an early stage. Particular attention should be given to formulating a contract strategy in respect of exploiting computer aided design and other information exchange from the outset.
Competent and confident exploitation of quality assured CAD data and other information exchange based on new technology leads to innovative development, lower costs and reduced construction programmes, whilst minimising liability and maintaining copyright and other intellectual property.

Taking control of I.T.

M. Leith
KPMG Management Consulting, London, UK

Abstract
The recession in the construction industry has hit the business of the architect. The
traditional role of the architect is also under threat within todays evolving construction
industry. Information technology (IT) is playing and ever increasing part in the
construction process. To achieve success with IT implementation defining requirements
and selecting systems needs careful consideration. This paper sets out a strategic approach
for architects contemplating the introduction of IT or planning system expansion.
Reviewing business objectives, management and user involvement, and the process of
system selection are discussed. Finally, the paper raises the issues of benefits, commitment
and investment requirements.
Keywords: Information Technology, Architects, Business Objectives, Strategic Approach,
Staff Involvement, Planning, System Selection, Benefits, Investment.

1 Introduction

Until recently information technology (IT) has been slow to influence the business of the
architect other than, perhaps, in the areas of computer aided design (CAD) and word
processing. This environment is now changing with clients, contractors and other
professionals using more IT for both technical and management purposes. Under this
pressure and, in an evolving construction industry, architects must invest wisely in IT to
ensure that the systems they implement are usable and support their professional and
business activities.

Implementing any computer system must contribute to enhancing one or more of a
range of driving factors influencing most architects practices, these are likely to include:

- improving the running of the practice,
- delivering quality buildings to increasingly demanding clients,
- improving communications between all members of the building team.

The modern architect must assess the use of IT on the types of projects in which they
are engaged and how IT can help in the internal management of a modern practice. They
must assess investigate where IT can help improve performance of professional staff to
enable better quality buildings to be designed and specified, and how to reduce overall
costs in getting the buildings delivered. Clearly, the technology needs to be reviewed but,
more importantly, the human resource implications need careful consideration.
Unfortunately, there is a tendency to ignore this latter aspect to the overall detriment of
any IT implementation.

more importantly, the human resource implications need careful consideration. Unfortunately, there is a tendency to ignore this latter aspect to the overall detriment of any IT implementation.

The introduction of new technology has substantially rationalised the way in which projects are managed to the benefit of all participants. These benefits are only likely to be realised, however, if data and information can be more easily exchanged between the different participants in a given project. This is requiring the architect to use technology to enable not only their own business goals to be achieved but also to improve their relationships with other professionals, contractors and clients. But to simply computerise individual tasks and activities is not enough, existing relationships and working practices must also be revised in order to accommodate the improvements that the use of information technology can bring.

Unclear or missing project information has caused, and is causing, major problems with effective communication between contractors, consultants, suppliers of building components and feedback to clients. Computers and other modern forms of communication are only tools to enable this situation to be improved. The technology should support rather than detract from efficient communication between all participants involved in a building project. If the role of the architect is not to fall further, in relation to other professionals of the building team, they must be prepared to take technology on board and use it to influence the design and construction process.

This paper sets out a structured methodolgy to assist architects address the issues of IT implementation. The objective is to ensure that investment in IT has a positive impact on the business and improves the delivery of quality designs and buildings.

2 A Strategic Approach to I.T. for Architects

To implement IT successfully a broad view of the architects business needs to be taken. Various factors must be considered when assessing what the architect is trying to achieve in business terms.

Implementing IT to computerise isolated tasks has worked to a degree but it has resulted in "islands of technology" that are unable to communicate. In an era of open systems, and networked businesses, such a narrow approach to computerisation is no longer acceptable.

To avoid the technology trap architects must adopt a strategic approach to IT implementation. This will require a view of the business, the functions and information requirements matched by planned IT investment. The basic steps involved are:

- assess professional and business objectives,
- review existing information systems,
- determine management involvement and commitment,
- understand what users require.

This is illustrated in Figure 1.

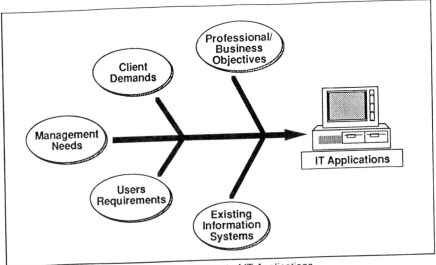

Figure 1 : Development of IT Applications

2.1 Understanding the Business

At the outset, the architect must assess the objectives of the practice, this will depend clearly on the size of the practice in the first instance, and the size and types of jobs that are undertaken by the practice. The architect must assess what he must do well to deliver a quality job, working closely with other professionals to achieve the client's objectives. In carrying out this assessment the architect must look at the functions within the business that are being carried out to achieve the end result of a building designed to meet the client's requirements. This should be followed by identifying the application areas for IT that need to be implemented to support the practice. It may be that word processing and computer aided design (CAD) form primary application areas. However, access to outside databases of building specifications and product information can often save time and money, when carrying out a design for a large store or office block.

The results of this exercise should include:

- a set of professional and business objectives (where do we want to get to, how will we get there?),
- a list of IT application areas that will benefit the practice.

2.2 Review any existing information systems

After identifying the IT opportunities, the architect must assess any existing information systems that are used within the practice and in connection with other members of the building team. This should include both manual systems and computerised applications. The resources used, the costs, the strengths and limitations of the different systems should be determined. This places a 'value' of any given system as it applies to the practice. It is also worth canvassing the opinions of users or intended users of any future systems. If there are any problems with the existing systems, identify them and list actions that may need to be taken. From this type of review additional IT applications are often identified, these should be added to the list for analysis.

2.3 What is the management involvement in IT?

Success in implementing IT will come from developing an effective management and organisational approach to using computers, not from the technology itself. It is the architects good judgement about using computers in the right place and at the right time that yields real benefits. (If necessary get advice from architects who have already moved towards a technology supported practice).

There are three factors that will contribute to success:

- Any effective computerisation effort must be led from the top - the Partners. Unless it is clear to others in the practice that the new system is important they unlikely to spend the time required to really make it work. The risk is subsequent failure and disenchantment.

- Challenge the way things are currently carried out, don't just automate existing procedures. Priorities for computerisation will vary from practice to practice depending on their particular markets.

- Don't be over ambitious. A major mistake is to try to do too much too quickly. Whatever is planned, do it incrementally. Break the plan into manageable elements, and make sure one aspect of computerisation works before the second is tackled, and so on.

Make sure everyone knows who is taking responsibility for IT in the practice. It is an issue that is often neglected but one that is a key success factor. Shouldering the responsibility shows management support and commitment.

2.4 Involve the staff, what do they require from IT?

Let others in the practice know that computerisation is being considered, get their ideas, and get their support for the idea of automation. Get them to learn about the ways technology can help, to separate fact from fiction. Without support, the best planned and most needed systems may sit, unused. Also, if others in the practice don't understand what computers can and can't do, their judgements about the system will be clouded. Computers can't work by themselves, after all. Some resistance to change is inevitable, but by involving and educating others in the practice will help to smooth the path to a more productive work environment.

3 I.T. Implementation to support the business

For any computerisation exercise it is important to understand why efforts towards automation are being considered. The driving factor for any architect has to be an improved service to clients and better relations with engineers and contractors, encompassed by overall business performance. To achieve this with the benefit of technology the architect will be subject to a number of pressures. These are illustrated in Figure 2 and discussed below.

3.1 Decide what to computerise first

There are always more opportunities than it is possible to pursue. Any of the following is a good place to start with computers in an architects practice:

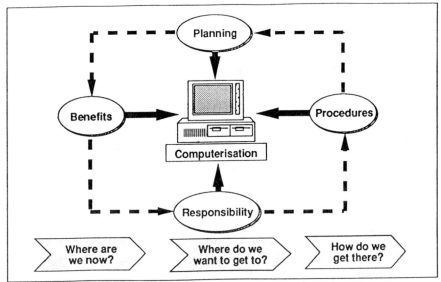

Figure 2 : Factors affecting computerisation

- Within the area in greatest need, such as word processing, CAD or even the accounts payable function, decide which has highest priority.
- Decide where the practice stands to gain an immediate advantage, such as generating a large number of detailed drawing for a major contract.
- Start by asking 'What information must be managed?' 'Where is the information?' 'In what format and with what frequency is the information needed?'

3.2 Identify the ways the computer will provide benefits
To get the value from computing the practice management must specifically decide what is expected from the computers and how they will help accomplish the business objectives. Identify measures of success that can be monitored as the systems begin to be used. There are many such measures, and the right ones for the practice depend entirely on the objectives for using computers. For example, if drawing revisions go out more promptly, in how many days? If contractor inquiries must be answered more promptly, within how many hours/days? Those and others can serve as measures of success. Many measures are difficult to quantify, estimates (not necessarily in financial terms) need to be set in order to enable system effectiveness to be monitored.

3.3 Develop a long-range technology plan
Once there is a good understanding of what computers can do, where they are needed most, what is wanted to automate first, and what benefits are expected to be achieved, a plan should be developed. The plan need not be lengthy or elaborate, but it should reflect the decisions about how computers and other technology are linked and to be used. Not everything can be done right away. Rather, the plan should set out the vision for the next few years. It should, for example, state what the practice wants to accomplish with technology, identify the technology to be used, specify software standards, and discuss issues related to adaptability. In short, the plan should serve as a

guide and provide a statement of direction. It should include a sequence of action-orientated steps, and identify the contingencies that may influence certain future actions.

3.4 Assign responsibility for implementation
Once the practice has set an overall policy direction and decided on a starting point, it may be time to find someone in the practice to handle the implementation. If this is possible, choose someone who is generally fluent (but not obsessed) with technology and who is a good negotiator.

Communication skills are often a key attribute for implementing change. No computer installation, no matter how small, goes as smoothly as originally planned. Negotiations will be inevitable with numerous people - hardware suppliers, software and perhaps communications salesmen, training resources, and other people in the practice. The practice management must keep the momentum going and reinforce the importance of the new computer; try to tap someone else's energy for the day-to-day system implementation. But make it clear that they have management support.

3.5 Develop policies and procedures
In the beginning, policies and procedures may be very informal, but several issues should be addressed. These include responsibility for maintenance of the hardware and software; back-up data (making copies of data periodically to assure work is not lost in the event of a computer problem; keeping a copy of data off-site, for example, in a safety deposit box); security of data (making sure only authorised individuals have access to sensitive information); and data integrity (making sure data collected is accurate and consistent eg. drawing standards in a CAD system).

4 System Selection and Implementation

Although the costs of computerisation are reducing there is clearly a certain level of risk associated with any implementation. The quickest and most cost effective approach for many architecture practices seeking to introduce new computer systems is to purchase well proven and widely used packages. This is particularly the case with CAD, word processing and accounting packages.

To make the task of system selection easier the practice should adopt a structured approach to the exercise. The steps involved are illustrated in Figure 3 and outlined below.

4.1 Statement of Requirements
A pre-requisite for any software selection exercise is a clear and unambiguous statement of user requirements. Such a document will enable alternative packages to be assessed objectively, and will also ensure internal agreement within the practice as to the nature of business requirements before commencement of the selection process.

4.2 Preparation and issue of a Request to Tender
The next stage is to incorporate the statement of user requirements in a formal request to tender (RTT) which should be issued to prospective suppliers. The RTT should also specify the criteria on which the tenders will be judged, and the information which suppliers must provide to enable tenders to be properly evaluated. The RTT should only be sent to suppliers who are likely to be able to provide a viable solution.

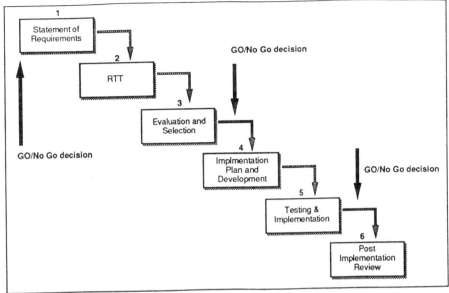

Figure 3 : System selection and implementation

4.3 Tender evaluation and selection

This stage involves assessing the proposals received against the agreed criteria. A weighting may need to be applied to the different criteria depending on the specific needs. Objective marking of the proposals should be carried out and full user involvement at this stage should be encouraged. At most two or three suppliers should be shortlisted for more detailed assessment and demonstration of their solution. Visits to existing users should be considered. Finally, the proposals from the shortlisted suppliers should be reassessed against all the information gained, and a supplier selected.

4.4 Implementation plan and development

A fundamental requirement for a successful implementation is a soundly based plan which sets out all the tasks involved, and assigns responsibilities and timescales for each task. Providing such a plan at the outset of the project gives a clear statement of the resources and time which must be committed to the project if it is to be successful. It also provides the basis for ongoing management of the implementation. As the project proceeds progress against the plan should be assessed, any slippage should be accounted for and the appropriate action taken.

4.5 Testing and implementation

With the system installed a test plan should be prepared with test data. The system should then be bench marked and the results assessed against the original expectations. A check on procedures, system manuals and operating instructions should be carried out. Management support and effective training are vital at this point so that momentum is maintained and the system can be integrated into the work of the practice.

303

4.6 Decision points and post implementation review

There are a number of decision points along the implementation path at which the practice can make go/no go decisions as to whether to continue with the project or not. Similarly, further development or system enlargement can be considered based on a post implementation review. This latter exercise is recommended so that implementation success can be measured against the original reason for considering computerisation.

5 I.T. Benefits,Commitment and Investment

5.1 Evaluate the benefits of technology

Are the hoped-for benefits being achieved? Are the documents, drawing and fee notes really getting out faster, for example? If not, why not? Are revisions being delivered within the promised time? If not, why not? Unless the practice realises the planned benefits of computers, all the time and effort may have been poorly spent. This evaluation process should be continuous, especially as more computer technology brought into the practice.

As a practice continues to grow, the partners direct involvement in technology-related issues may decrease. This will begin to happen as technology becomes more and more specialised and customised and as the business has enough resources to dedicate personnel to manage the technology. At that time, an organisational structure will emerge (or will need to be created) for managing technology on an ongoing basis.

5.2 Commitment

Most practices must maintain their computer systems without the benefit of on-site specialists. Not only does this fact demand that the systems themselves be simple and easy to maintain, but it demands that someone within the practice assumes an ongoing responsibility. The partners and others in the practice should have training and involvement in the computerisation process.

It is important to provide initial and ongoing training to current staff. Technology changes, and so do the ways it can be applied to solve various problems. Give personnel an opportunity to learn new ways that technology can help with the business of building design. If there are enough people, have an in-house seminar periodically. If not, send individuals to external training courses.

Be sure to provide training to new personnel. Don't assume that the right information will be passed on informally. Send new staff on training courses. Tell them what benefits are expected to be accomplished by using technology. Show them that their effective use of technology is important. Make sure they know that they need to do to get the most out of the investment.

Next, as noted previously, keep staff informed of the plans and goals for using computers. Get their ideas, too. Staff are one of the biggest assets - be sure to tap them.

Finally, to avoid a fatal mistake, make sure that more than one person in the business knows how to use the computer. The system manager/administrator should have a backup in the event of sickness or holiday. If all drawings are held on the system, and the assistant is in an accident, trouble could lie ahead if no support is available. This may appear to be a luxury that the practice cannot afford, but the cost to the business of system failure can be very large. Therefore, system support, maintenance contracts and helplines need careful consideration.

5.3 Investment

Often the first question many practice managers ask is, 'How much will all this cost?' The more appropriate question is: 'How much will it make for the practice?' Cost, in any absolute terms, must be weighed against the benefits that are expected from a new computer system. In this sense, a computer system must be treated like any other asset from which value is expected to be derived.

Only the practice manager, can identify the value hoped to be achieved from a system and the human resources who make it work. Evaluate the benefits expected to be obtained as part of the initial planning for computing. These benefits will be in addition to any financial ones. There is a balance between the value of all the benefits and the actual costs of obtaining them in arriving at a final decision about the software and hardware to use. This final decision also must take into account any other relevant financial factors, such as depreciation. In the final analysis, though, the decision should be based on the benefits expected from the new system, and not its absolute cost in terms of money or other resources.

6 Conclusion

Technology is now relatively inexpensive, but however small or large the financial investment, no cost can be justified unless, as a result of the investment, the practice runs more efficiently and more effectively in ways that can be measured. Planning carefully will assist in achieving the benefits from the use of technology to place the professional practice in better position to grow and profit. In turn, this will also enable higher quality buildings to be delivered and, in a cost conscious environment, help the construction process to be carried out more economically.

CAD utilization and issues at NTT – data coordination

T. Nishimura
Nippon Telegraph and Telephone Corporation (NTT), Tokyo, Japan

Abstract
NTT's CAD system and related application programs, developed for use in the design and management process, have now been put into practical use. However, as these systems were developed independently, data used by each process was not shared. The following points are being considered to enable these systems to interact effectively.

    Data coordination for each system and each process
    Complete equipment of overall system environment

This paper first gives an overview of NTT's CAD and CAFM systems. Second, we discuss the latest developments in integrating the CAD and CAFM systems and coordinating the data. Finally, the overall system environment is described.
Keywords: CAD, CAFM, Database, Data coordination, System integration.

1 Introduction

Nippon Telegraph and Telephone Corporation (NTT) has an obligation to deploy and maintain an advanced telecommunications network. NTT owns some 32,000 buildings, with a total floor area of approximately 21,000,000 square meters. The NTT Building Engineering Department, with 2,000 building engineers, is responsible for designing and maintaining NTT's facilities. To work effectively, computerization is actively promoted in planning, designing, maintaining, and remodeling, and particular importance is given to CAD utilization as the infrastructure of the FM.

2 CAD utilization

2.1 NTT's CAD
NTT has developed and uses an Engineering Workstation (EWS) based CAD systems, CADMARC, and a Personal Computer (PC) based CAD system, CADET. The outline of each program is as follows:

    CADMARC-A   Architectural design and drafting system which
                       produces general architectural drawings, such as a site

	plan, floor plans, elevations and sections.
CADMARC-P	Building planning system which caluculates space requirements based on height and sunshine regulations.
CADMARC-V	Perspective drawing system which produces exterior and interior views of buildings, using 3D datafiles.
CADMARC-CG	Computer graphics system which produces graphical images, using shading and ray-tracing methods.
CADMARC-S	An integrated structural design and drafting system which performs structural design and automated drawings, using the building structural database.
CADMARC-E	An integrated building equipment design and drafting system which makes electrical, mechanical, and plumbing drawings, mainly for building service engineering but also for making design calculations.
CADMARC-F	Facility management system which supports the planning and management of space and furniture.
CADET	Architectural design and drafting system which runs as subprogram of CADMARC on a PC.

2.2 Issues in CAD utilization

Important issues in CAD utilization fall into three categories, issues of the CAD system itself, issues caused by CAD utilization, and external factors.

Issues of CAD systems are as follows:

[Hard to operate as the user pleases] Since the input process demands numerical values, vagueness and incompleteness are not permitted. Since the design process is subjective work, it's hard to adapt the design process to a computer system.

[Not user-friendly] The operating procedure has many steps (command select, layer set, line attribute set, etc.). It's hard to understand the scale factor and position in a picture. It's hard to deal with changing orders. It's hard to check and manage the drawings. Since the system has too many functions without customizing, it's complicated and not useful.

[Data is not consistent] Since each system makes a new set of data for each process, the data is not used consistently in the cooperative work of the design process.

Issues caused by CAD utilization are as follows:

[Hard to estimate the effect] It's hard to show the effect of CAD utilization by numerical values.

[Hard to input as-built drawings] There are many drawings which need to be input immediately. (architectural drawings: 38,000; equipment drawings: 180,000)

External factors are as follows:

[Hardware environment] Since an EWS is expensive and hard to operate, the system environment for CAD utilization is not equipped sufficiently.

[Software environment] There are many CAD systems and application programs running on PCs and few systems on EWSs. It's desirable that the system runs on the same platform to improve data coordination.

2.3 Practical use of CAD

This section disscusses the following points in practical use of the CAD system at NTT, development, introduction, making materials for use, training, data input, user support, and applying to work.

[Development, introduction] CADMARC was developed to use as-built drawings in the design and management process. A EWS was adopted to manage the large number of such drawings, and some EWSs were installed in branch offices all over Japan. However the EWS is not spread enoughly for personal use, so CADET was developed for distributed processing on PCs. The CADET is described in Chapter 4.1.

[Making materials for use, user support] NTT wrote manuals on the basic operation, practical techniques, and reference, and produced a video manual to help users to learn the operation easily. Personal Computer Communication is provided for troubleshooting and file transport, and a Bulletin Board System (BBS) is provided for exchanging information and programs.

[Training] A short course in CAD operation is held twice a month to help architectural designers and building engineers to make immediate use of the system.

[Data input] When designing a new building, all data is input from the beginning, however, a case of existing facilities, the as-built drawings are input at the time of remodeling or in order of priority.

[Applying to work] It's necessary for business users to adapt their work style to the CAD system. Moreover, it's necessary to make the function of customaizing CAD system.

3 CAFM utilization

3.1 NTT's CAFM
NTT's CAFM systems are as follows:

Building Automation System (BAS) for building control
Bank control system for building supervision
Diagnosis system for estimating deterioration, environmental factors, etc.
Database system (inventory) for management
CAD systems for drawing management (CADMARC, CADET)
Presentation system for client persuasion
Other application programs running on a PC

3.2 Issues in CAFM utilization
Issues in CAFM utilization are as follows:

[Data is not shared] Many database systems and application programs are used in the management process. Hawever, they use databases independently and data is not shared. Accordingly, some original data is stored and copied many times and the data is not reliable.

[The amount of data is huge] The number of facilities is so large that it's hard to process the data.

[The concept of FM is not understood] Building engineers tend to restrict themselves to their expert field and have difficulty leaning new concepts of the FM.

Since the management process is mainly objective work, it should not be hard to adapt the management process to the computer system if the above issues are solved.

3.3 Practical use of CAFM

NTT has been attached importance to maintenance management and stored various technologies. The building engineers take charge of each facility using many application programs based on NTT's maintenance technologies. These technologies have been adapted to the FM.

This section describes the new methods of management using CADMARC-F. We adapted CADMARC-F to the following situations:

[Space management and planning] Designs the space layout, and outputs the total floor area, sorted by department and purpose, and calculates the cost of cleaning.

[Maintaining building equipement] Outputs maintenance information for building equipment (overhaul time, cost, etc.).

[Maintaining disaster control equipment] Outputs information on equipment sorted by floor and division (fire area, halon-gas area).

[Asset and furniture management] Outputs inventory.

The current trend is not maintenance but modernization, because of the changing purposes of facilities, so it's essential to integrate management systems and design systems (such as CADMARC-F) .

4 Integration and coordination

4.1 Approach to integration

To integrate NTT's CAD and CAFM systems and to coordinate the data, we developed two systems, CADMARC-F and CADET.

The CADMARC-F integrates CAD data made by CADMARC with FM data made by each CAFM system on an EWS. The advantage of this system is that the CAD data and FM data are referenced bilaterally because this system consists of two programs, CAD and DBMS (commercial relational database, UNIFY). Each program can also work independently. Thus, we can coordinate the FM data among CAFM systems by the function of relational database. The extensible database structure is shown in Fig.1.

The CADET coordinates CAD data from each system and each process. The CADET's data is compatible with the CADMARC's data and is on the same platform with other useful application programs and systems. The data flow in the CAD system is shown in Fig.2. The data flow in the remodeling process is shown in Fig.3.

4.2 Integrated CAFM system

FM work is classified into planning, design, utilization, estimation, analyzing current conditions (making a database), prediction, and presentation. We are planning to integrate these processes into an integrated CAFM system. The data flow in the integrated CAFM system is shown in Fig.4. We are now extending the database of the CADMARC-F to take building control data from the Building Automation System (BAS) and bank control system, and extending the function of directly access to management data of each CAFM system's database.

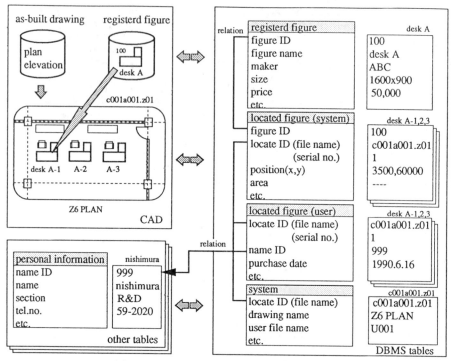

Fig.1 database structure of CADMARC-F

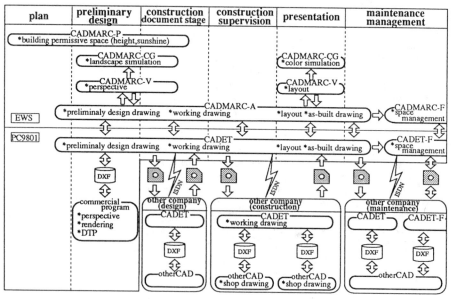

Fig.2 data flow in CAD system (architectural design)

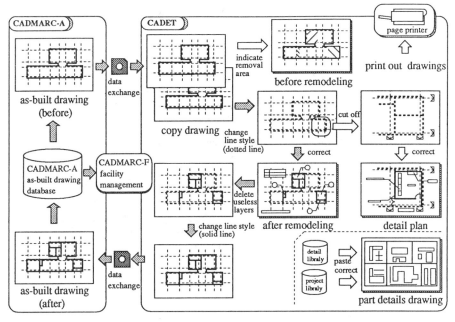

Fig.3 data flow in the remodeling process

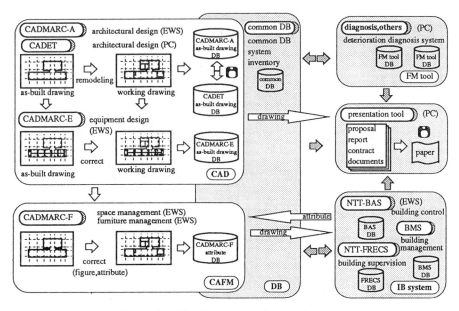

Fig.4 data flow in integrated CAFM system

5 Complete equipment of CAD system environment

5.1 Complete library of figures
Architectural standard figures are registered and used to make drawings effectively. There are three other libraries as follows:

[Standard detail library] NTT has published a standard detail library including 150 items with about 1,000 drawings. The most useful items are input to the CAD system and customized for each building.

[Standard facility library] Recently, some makers of furniture and sanitary fixtures have prepared libraries of their own products. These libraries include figures and other information, and will be used not only in the CAD system but also in quantity surveying and in the execution process.

[Project library] The drawings of complete projects are refered to by other projects.

5.2 Common use of data with other CAD system and DTP software
CAD data is used more effectively if it can take in drawings and figures made by other CAD systems. CAD data can then use unique function of other systems.

DXF is a common format for a data exchange file in architectural fields. It's necessary to enhance the CAD system to extend the number of files that can be exchanged with DTP software.

5.3 Data communication by ISDN
To transfer drawings between the design office and the construction sites, the head office, and branches, we usually use post, FAX, or Personal Computer Communication. Additionally, we are experimenting with ISDN (Integrated Service Digital Network) for more comfortable data communication. (See Fig.2) ISDN can transfer the data on a floppy disk, which includes six or seven drawings of intermediate buildings in three minutes. We are also experimenting with remote operation of the CAD system.

6 Conclusion

The most important point in using CAD and CAFM systems effectively is to share data between systems and processes, although each system does work independently. In this concept, the system is used flexibly in the work of user's responsibility and the data becomes valuable and reliable.

7 Future research

The following points about CAD systems are now being studied:

Three-dimensional modeling with attributes
Decision support tools for design process
Data standardization
Compatibility with multi-media data

8 Reference

K.Yoshida,
   OUTLINE OF COMPUTER APPLICATION IN JAPAN'S BUILDING INDUSTRY
   Proceeding of CIB 7th Congress, 1977, Edinburgh
N.Iwatsuki, K.Yoshida, and K.Moriya,
   CAD IN NTT ARCHITECTURAL AND BUILDING ENGINEERING FIELD,
   Proceeding of CIB 10th Congress, 1986, Washington

Coding for computerisation of building maintenance data

Professor A. Spedding
Bristol Polytechnic, Bristol, UK

Abstract
This paper briefly considers some of the work which has been
undertaken on information systems for the construction industry and
also considers some of the essentials of coding systems and brings
these concepts together with some comments on the use of information
systems and coding for the recording of expenditure on building
maintenance. The author has been involved with colleagues in the
Research Unit of Bristol Polytechnic on major projects funded by the
Hong Kong Housing Authority and the Science and Engineering Research
Council of the United Kingdom both of which projects deal with the
acquisition and the use of maintenance cost data for management
purposes.
Keywords
Building Maintenance, Maintenance Coding, Computerised Data, Built
Asset Maintenance.

1   Introduction

There are a number of information systems in existence for the
purposes of recording construction information but these usually
have been aimed at classifying new construction. The 1964 Report of
the Working Party on the costing, management and maintenance of
local authority housing suggested that it would be an advantage if
there was a standard classification of costs of maintenance
according to certain characteristics of buildings. They specified
nine groups which were largely elemental within which costs could be
held but the groups also included some functional aspects. However,
development of comprehensive codes for the computerisation of
maintenance records progressed very slowly and eventually the
Building Research Establishment of the UK commissioned the Research
Unit at Bristol Polytechnic to develop a coding system for
classification of building maintenance costs in relation to housing.
Subsequent to this, a different research project on the costs of
maintenance for school buildings, which was commissioned by the
Department of Education & Science, led the research team to devise a
coding system which would be more comprehensive and this was
published in 1985. (1)

Work done by the research team for other clients has resulted in the development of a more sophisticated approach to coding systems and this paper reviews some of the background to these developments.

2 Classification of Data

The author has looked at many systems currently used for the classification of maintenance cost data, and a characteristic of most of the systems in operation is that they were devised at other times for other purposes. Therefore when one is devising a new system, the first problem is to identify precisely what are the data to be collated, at what level of detail and how the data are to be combined. The system must be as comprehensive as possible within the limits of the storage and retrieval system. Inevitably a compromise must be made between recording considerable data on each item and the number of items in total which are to be recorded and their relative value.

In any large organisation there are inevitably a number of interested parties and when these people come together in committees to advise on the production and implementation of coding systems, they inevitably tend to ask for more information rather than less and they frequently lose sight of the fact that information has to be collected in some way or other and this has a cost.

There are some principles which should be borne in mind in the design of a system, from the management point of view. For instance, it is useful to relate the level of information output to the level of responsibility of the participants in the system so that a senior officer is not weighed down with day to day minutiae but similarly the operational surveyor will receive feedback on the items of performance in which he is interested. This requires the output of information to be matched with the input at various levels. Our experience has shown quite clearly that if the people who are putting the information in do not feel that they are getting out useful information, then they will not ensure that the input information is accurate, because they will take shortcuts such as allocating data to a "dustbin" code, such as day to day unspecified maintenance.

It is useful to try to build into the systems some means of checking the input and this should be as easy as possible but of course it will depend to a large extent on matters such as the code itself and the staffing which may be needed for such checking. Naturally one needs to bear in mind that staff change jobs, and that new staff will be brought in to use the code, without any previous knowledge of it. This therefore means that the implementation and upkeep of a computer system needs appropriate training manuals, explaining the logic of that system. As in every authority there will be in existence a system of some sort, it is probably going to be more efficient to implement a system in stages which means that the system should ideally be hierarchical, and devised in such a way that it will relate to other sub-systems, as it is installed.

In another context, a working party (2) analysed problems of data flow in construction into three elements: procedures or operations performed on the data, storage of data, and flow of information in processes. They recognised that although procedural rules are needed for the generation of data, there may be different rules for different purposes, and they felt that a preferred vocabulary was an essential part of the syntax for information flow. Of course we have systems available such as the SFB system and the Building Cost Information Service form of cost analysis. Additionally there is the National Building Specification and Co-ordinated Project Information which is particularly useful for specifying work. Thus, a logical coding system should enable changes to be made at a later date if needed and also provide for correspondence between other systems as long as their basis is reasonably similar; and here classification based on building elements seems to be a useful framework. This is particularly true where one is looking to the future for a quality assurance system where information on maintenance costs and failures is fed back to the design team in an attempt to improve the design of future buildings. The principle of using the elemental classification for coding maintenance data is sensible as the elements are generally those which are in place once the building is complete and one can begin to examine possible relationships between quality of specification, workmanship, maintenance policy, condition and life of elements.

Of course it must be remembered that the recording of data in an elemental classification raises the same problems whether it is a manual or a computerised system except that the computerised system can be made to work much more effectively and more quickly, and retrieval of data may be made much more efficient.

A problem that often arises in many large organisations is that work is ordered on schedules of rates which are usually trade based in their origin, and difficulties tend to arise because boundaries of classifications are different in many cases from the elemental. Also, works orders often don't carry enough descriptive information, relying perhaps on estimates based on build-up of items from the schedule of rates which don't actually appear with the order. Such orders frequently cross elemental boundaries, for example where an order to make good finishes and re-decorate an entire interior involves several elements. In such a case comprehensive decorative improvements might be coded as one operation under the decorative element, or alternatively the costs of the work might be separated into floors, ceilings, walls and windows, if such separation is needed. If this type of separation is requested, one must ask why this is so because both estimates and final accounts must be broken down into the appropriate sub-groups, which does involve quite a lot of extra work unless the whole of the schedule of rates is computerised and related to the maintenance cost data recording system. The efficiency of this process will depend to a large extent upon the compatibility of the schedule of rates and the maintenance data systems, and it may be that schedules of rates need to be adjusted to suit maintenance classifications.

3   Comprehensiveness of the System

The purpose of using codes is to compress information for economy of
storage and to increase the ability to manipulate data, and
therefore only relevant information should go into the code, whilst
accepting that a relatively uncomplicated coding system will result
in some loss of accuracy. It is certainly not outside the bounds of
possibility that natural English descriptions could be used by a
computerised system which would then translate the items into a
comprehensive code but the problem quite often is related to
programming for such a use and also the amount of storage space
which is needed. Some coding systems are based on mnemonics but this
can lead to ambiguity if similar but different words lead to the
same or very similar mnemonics. At one time punchcard input was
generally used and the codes were stored in books which operators
had to become familiar with. Although menu driven systems were
possible it wasn't until the late 1970s that time-share systems were
available in bulk, and over the last ten years increased speed and
capacity of affordable computers means that the processor can keep
well ahead of key strokes. Thus, menu driven input can be used by
less technical people because it prompts the answer from a limited
range of questions rather than requiring people to look up the
coding in a complex data base. It also means that quite long codes
can be stored if they are required because they don't require acts
of memory on the part of the user. By menu driven I mean that as
soon as a system is entered, a series of questions guide the user
from the broad elemental groupings such as "is it plumbing" or "is
it air conditioning system" right through to whatever level of
detail is required. In each level the system only requires one
answer to be chosen from a limited set of questions, the answering
of such questions automatically recording the code in the machine.
    There are probably two ways in which the coding system might
be listed. The first is to list all facets of the data in an
hierarchical table, and the second is to use an hierarchical listing
selecting only the necessary combinations of characteristics at the
levels of elements, sub-elements and so on. To take a very
simplified example, for service installations we might list all of
the characteristics or facets relating to each item of cost with
materials listed at level 3 as in Table 1.

Table 1.

CODE LEVEL					
1st digit		2nd digit		3rd digit	
Type of System		Component		Material	
Code		Code		Code	
1	C.W.	1	Pipe	1	M.S.
2	H.W.	2	Valve	2	S.S.
3	F.F.	3	Pump	3	Plastic

There are 3^3 or 27 possible combinations of data and, for
example, a cold water pipe in stainless steel would be coded 112.
However, many codes will not be needed such as fire fighting pump in
plastic 333. A more practical solution would be to use a system
where only the useful items are listed, based on the most likely
order in which the data might be required. Such a system might look
like Table 2.

Table 2.

CODE LEVEL					
1st digit		2nd digit		3rd digit	
Code		Code		Code	
1	C.W.	1	Pipe	1	M.S.
				2	S.S.
				3	Plastic
		2	Valve	1	M.S.
		3	Pump		
2	H.W.	1	Pipe	1	M.S.
				2	S.S.
		2	Valve	1	M.S.
		3	Pump		
3	F.F.	1	Pipe	1	M.S.

Thus, although a cold water pipe in stainless steel is still
coded 112, only 10 likely combinations of data and thus 10 codes
need to be considered. Table 1 however includes 27 - 10 = 17
potentially redundant codes which refer to non-existent items. Of
course, any system should have some redundancy in order to be
capable of allowing for a certain amount of expansion or even
contraction of categories of data. In modern computer systems the
difference is not material unless the system is to be deliberately
limited. The main difference in practice is that Table 2 will reduce
the likelihood of erroneous coding because choices are limited to
those which are to be found in the maintenance data.

4   Codes

Sometimes one might consider numerical or alphabetical codes, or a
mixture of the two. In a numerical code, one has ten alternatives in
a single digit from 0 to 9 whereas an alphabetical code has 26
alternatives, in a single letter from A to Z. If we choose a three
digit code from 000 to 999, this gives us 1000 items which could be
in ten main sections denoted by the initial number, each section
having up to 100 entries. An alphabetical code however for at least
the same number of items, if expressed in separate letters, would
need 7 letters and would yield 7 main sections, whilst the use of
the whole alphabet in each position of a three letter code gives 26

sections, each section having nearly 700 items, giving a total of about 17,000 items. In practice, of course, there could be a very large amount of redundancy, using a simply alphabetical code. There is a possibility of combining numbers and the alphabet into alpha numeric codes so that a three position code where the first position is alphabetical and the other two are numeric, would give 26 sections each with 100 items or a maximum of 2,600 listed items. Taking into account that codes should be as consistent as possible in their logic and length of constituent parts we chose in our research to use numeric codes because of their flexibility.

5   Typical Coding Systems

Many coding systems that we have examined are numerical and are based on three digits, tied in some way or other to financial systems so that the whole range of numerical possibilities are not available. One might find, for instance, that only 300 to 699 is allocated to the maintenance department and that anything in the 300 series deals with ordinary building work, anything in the 400s deals with special programmes of improvement, 500 series might be general services, and the 600 series might electrical and special services.

The difficulty about such a system is that the codes have often been chosen in a rather idiosyncratic way and don't relate to each other so one might find, for instance, code 363 would be external wall rendering and 364 would be installation of suspended ceilings. When one then realises that 347 might be the laying of tarmac surfaces to roads, it can be seen that the system lacks an internal logic which allows easy recognition of the work.

The problem also about such a system is that as a new item has to be recorded for whatever reason, it has to be added on the end, and in the 300 series there will only be 100 possible items. Therefore, if all the spaces have been taken up in the code, the only way to insert another important item would be to go through the list and drop something out which would mean that all of that data classification would be lost and also would not be collected in future. Thus the use of an expandable hierarchical system ensures that data, once collected, have a place and can be retrieved.

6   Uses of Maintenance Data

Of course there is a variety of uses to which maintenance data may be applied and much depends upon budgetary and staffing levels. These two are related and both tend to be rooted in precedent. Of course the monitoring of spending has to be undertaken for audit purposes and it is well known that the financial department's computerised recording of costs is more to do with monitoring who is charged with what than with examining patterns of failure and remedial works in building elements. This tends to mean that existing systems are not particularly suitable for the recording of maintenance data and in trying to change the system, the finance department will usually find a range of reasons why they should not change their classifications. In practice, there almost invariably will have to be some changes in order at least to achieve correspondence between the maintenance data system and other departments' needs.

If we assume that the maintenance budget is not unreasonably restricted (which it often is), much of the attitude of the maintenance department to cost data will depend on the type of stock, its standardisation and volume of work both in maintenance and new build. In respect of the budgetary process, it is important for maintenance management to be able to highlight an increasing number of failures, say in purpose-made joinery or pressed steel boilers, or concrete of a certain age, exposure and material content. For quality assurance purposes and for feedback it is also useful to be able to highlight those failures. Also, in equipment which may be installed in many dwellings or buildings, it may be important to establish what is causing failure in order to modify specifications or buying policy. Thus where specialist design departments, such as the engineers, specify components, the maintenance department's records can be a valuable source of data for them.

Therefore it is a matter of concern in designing a data system to establish not only the primary users, but also secondary users, and their legitimate purposes. In one study which we have undertaken for a large housing authority, there was considerable interest not only in the recording of failure of elements under particular service conditions, but also in the recording of the use of alternative remedial processes. This introduces another aspect of a coding system in that one has to be clear whether it is failure of a component which is being recorded or the remedial work being undertaken or both. In practice, most codes currently in use for maintenance data recording tend to contain aspects of both such as "strip off existing defective felt roofing and replace with new; to Type A as described in standard specification". This means that the first part of this sentence may be a frequent job but the specification may vary from time to time and monitoring may require a greater level of detail to be coded. This is easily catered for by extending the code as required and it is quite possible for, say, a four digit code on the main system to pick up the first part of the item whilst a subsidiary linked code perhaps held on intelligent micro based terminals by the building surveyors' department can hold the additional details.

The cost data therefore should carry enough coded information to enable identification of problems and it is likely that four or five digits will be needed for an adequate hierarchical recording system. Even so, this will only be adequate for identifying the particular element or sub-element under consideration and it has been suggested elsewhere (3) that the additional information on causes of failure, and processes used in remedying of failure, and so on, can easily be added on a menu basis to the elemental codes. In respect of the elemental codes, anything less than four or five digits is quite possible, but the logical elemental and sub-elemental basis would be difficult to follow through unless only a limited number of failures were to be classified. Generally speaking, as described above, the hierarchical system can be designed with gaps in it which reduce the options to be coded whilst leaving plenty of room for insertion of additional information as it becomes necessary. If the hierarchical logic is disturbed, then subsequent alterations to the code can be rather idiosyncratic and confused. After all, the astonishing increases in relatively cheap computing power are likely to continue for some years and a "complicated" code is easily generated from lists or menus displayed on the screen. Using the code developed at Bristol as the basis for an example, the first menu will be the main elemental headings, so movement of the cursor and depressing the return button against the fifth item (plumbing) would produce a second level menu with only three items, the third one being sanitary fittings, so a similar operation will bring up the third level menu of 9 items, of which the fifth, for instance, is WC. Therefore a code 535 is generated almost as quickly as the keys can be depressed and an order may be issued against that code entry without the operator having had to remember any of the codes.

Many authorities are looking for easily installed systems which will link to other functions such as keeping stock records, keeping records of labour and materials in direct labour organisations, recording costs for charging up of tenants in right to buy situations, and so on. It is our experience that the differences between organisations and the differences in information flow within those organisations do require systems to be modified to suit the individual authority. The devising of such links can introduce complexities into the system but it is quite clear that, with care, a menu system can be devised to cater for virtually all of the requirements of a maintenance cost recording system.

7   Conclusion

Increased computing power has meant that quite sophisticated data flows may be obtained as long as the data are input in accordance with a logical system. However, the computerisation of the system does not automatically provide information or analysis which could not be obtained by manual means. Therefore the problems of what level of data to record and the decisions as to how to deal with complex or multi-element orders still have to be taken by management before the system can be designed. Having said this, although sound technical knowledge is needed in order to write work orders, it is completely feasible for maintenance cost data to be coded at the time that orders are written without the need to remember complex codes. Indeed, the processing of the orders and coding may be undertaken by staff who have received only limited specific technical building training, and this may be the most significant factor for the future.

8   References

1.   A Coding System for Building Maintenance - R. Holmes et al
      CIOB Technical Information Service No. 47   1985

2.   An Information System for the Construction Industry - DoE
      HMSO 1971

3.   What You Want to Know About Causes of Failure of Building
      Elements
      Spedding A.   Proceedings CIB W70 Seminar   Edinburgh 1988

CHAPTER SEVEN

*'Perhaps the most valuable result of all
education is the ability to make yourself do the
thing you have to do, when it ought to be done,
whether you like it or not.'*

Thomas Henry Huxley

Development of a distance learning MSc in construction management

R.F. Fellows
Construction Study Unit, School of Architecture and Building Engineering, University of Bath, UK
T.D. Bilham
Director, Centre for Continuing Education, University of Bath, UK

Abstract
This paper examines the development of a Distance Learning
version of an existing, successful MSc course. Attention is
paid to initial marketing, internal factors which prompted
attention to distance learning and the anticipated
advantages. As with many novel ventures, the full
implications were not realized at the outset.

The course incorporates workbooks, readings, textbooks,
video tapes and audio tapes as the major distance learning
materials, all of which are supplemented by a one week
residential school requirement for each of the four taught
modules.

There now exist 3 modes of study of one single course.
As a single course, the continuous assessments, case studies
and examinations are common throughout although the periods
of study required by students vary depending upon the mode
of study adopted. Under distance learning, the speed of
study is dictated by students with the overriding
stipulation that the maximum duration required to complete
the course is 5 years.

To date, the distance learning mode has attracted over
100 student registrations, all of whom must meet the
stringent entry requirements for any MSc course offered by
the University. Results of students assessments has been
very encouraging, manifested by the complementary comments
afforded by the external examiner.

1 Introduction

Whilst working at Brunel University in West London, the
three academics who comprised the Construction Study Unit
(CSU) developed an MSc course in Construction Management.
The course began in 1980 with students studying by part-time
mode - this involved their attending the University for one
day per week for an intensive lecture and seminar programme
over a period of two years at the end of which they were
required to submit a dissertation to complete their MSc

studies.   Shortly afterwards a full time mode of study was launched to cater for market changes and to facilitate study by students from overseas.   Throughout the 1980s the course attracted some 20 full time students and around 8 part-time students per year.

As the course seeks to aid participants' personal development as well as their academic development, a management-oriented outward bound field course of one week's duration was introduced during the first few weeks of study.

This initiative has been a major success in aiding integration of students and staff and, we believe, has made a significant contribution to participants' success.

Following financial pressures on British Universities during the early 1980s, Brunel University decided, at first, to reduce and later to curtail its provision of degrees for the construction industry.   However, due to contact between members of the CSU and the School of Architecture and Building Engineering at the University of Bath, the University Grants Committee (now University Funding Council – UFC) agreed to effect the transfer of the academic staff of the CSU to the University of Bath; this transfer took place in October 1987.

Having settled in at Bath, the members of the CSU were conscious of the opportunities to expand their academic activities.   The market for conventional full time and part-time MSc courses was becoming increasingly competitive from both other universities and polytechnics, and the normal sources of funding for major research activities – notably the Science and Engineering Research Council (SERC, in application to whom the CSU had been very successful) were subject to quite severe financial cutbacks thereby being forced to make major reductions in the availability of money for research.

Discussions and analyses of education needs, opportunities and available progammes at postgraduate level in the construction industry indicated that MBAs were popular programmes and major competitors of Construction Management MScs.   Fortunately, the nature of the MSc which had come to Bath with the CSU was quite similar to an MBA course but within the contextural requirements of the construction industry; indeed several graduates from the course had labelled it the "MBA for the construction industry".

Due to the links between Brunel University and Henley, the Management College, the CSU had been instrumental in the launch of a joint MSc in Project Management between Henley and Brunel in which the Henley MBA programme was used to provide the basic management input and members of the CSU were responsible for providing the project management input and applications.   That course had been extremely successful and had been offered by full time, part-time and by distance learning; by far the largest cohort of participants studied by the distance learning mode.

As the construction industry has a tradition of
day-release and short-block release, so that people can
maintain full time productive employment whilst undertaking
education to obtain higher qualifications, it seemed clear
to the members of the CSU that extension of the existing MSc
course in Construction Management into the distance learning
mode of study was appropriate and desirable.   That members
of the Centre for Continuing Education (CCE) at the
University of Bath had considerable experience of preparing
distance learning study materials, through their experiences
with the Open University, was a real bonus.

2 Initial Development

Having decided that the development of a distance learning
mode of study was opportune, before major commitments of
work and resources were made, the necessity for some market
research was clear.   Hence, a "corner-flash" was added to
the advertisements placed in January 1988 for the MSc by
full time and part-time study indicating that a distance
learning version of the course was to be launched and
requesting anyone interested in studying that course to
contact the University.   Response was rapid and enormous;
within a few weeks some 425 enquiries had been made of which
about one third were from overseas.   By the end of the year
the number of enquiries had risen to over 1000.   Clearly
there was a large potential market for the course both in
Britain and overseas.

Fortunately, the UFC was seeking to promote new
developments in the field of continuing education.   An
application for financial support to develop the distance
learning version of the course was successful; £30,000 was
obtained for the year 1988/89 and a further £20,000 for the
year 1989/90.   Correctly, a part of that funding was
earmarked for the training of staff, both academic and
administrative; to enable academics to investigate and
acquire skills to produce materials sutiable for the special
learning needs of students studying by distance learning and
to inform and aid the administrative staff in setting up and
operating the extensive and complex systems needed to ensure
the proper operation of the course.   Short courses, run by
the Open University, were taken and there extensive meetings
and discussions with people from other institutions who
already offered courses through distance learning.   The
information obtained and advice given proved invaluable but,
despite quite extensive warnings and predictions, the time
and effort needed to develop the distance learning materials
was still under-estimated to a small degree.

3 Academic Acceptance

As this course was the first of its kind to be developed at
the University of Bath it involved setting a considerable
number of precedents. Further, it constituted an academic
"trail blazer" and, in consequence, was subject to a high
level of scrutiny by academic boards.

A problem which was encountered early was convincing
members of the School's Board of Studies that it was not
merely a "correspondence" course but was an extension of
existing academic activities, at a proper postgraduate level
and would incorporate a variety of study mechanisms and
materials to facilitate students learning at a distance,
that is without the everyday contact with academic staff
which takes place in a conventional university environment.
Resistance to this novel development may have been
exacerbated slightly by the view of certain members of staff
that the School was, in essence, a design school, that
construction management was rather peripheral and that
major developments of this nature would dilute the primary
thrust of the School's activities, namely design.
Fortunately one of the professors (who was designated to
take over as Head of School after some months) lent strong
support to the proposal.

An essential element in securing the agreement of the
academic boards (Board of Studies of the School and Senate
of the University) was that the proposal comprised the
development of a new mode of study for an existing,
successful Masters course. That the Scheme of Studies
(Syllabus) was in place and that all assessments of
students (continuous monitoring assignments, case studies
and examinations) and criteria for passsing were to be
commonacross all three modes of study. Two other deciding
factors were that the entry requirements would be common
across the course and that the distance learning mode of
study would incorporate compulsory residential schools
(complying with the University's attendance requirements
for part-time students) at which there would be intensive
study through more conventional techniques (lectures,
seminars and tutorials) and close personal contact
between the students and staff.

4 Adminstration Acceptance

In tandem with obtaining acceptance of the distance
learning version, acceptance of the project by the
University's Administration had to be obtained. After
preliminary discussions in which the principals involved
were considered in outline, the application to develop the
distance learning mode revolved around the business plan
which was produced jointly by the CSU and the Director of
CCE. Analysis of the Scheme for the full time

and part-time modes yielded a schedule of the study materals which would be produced. The study materials are noted under 'Course Structure' and shown in Figure 1. Having determined the necessary study materials, the next stage was to apply costs to their production. A major issue involved the video tapes for the course. Employment of commercial producers of video tapes, who would produce scripts from notes and produce the videos using actors, was estimated to cost between £1000 and £2000 per minute for the video tapes which would be produced – this option was discarded as being far too expensive! The outcome was the decision to produce the course workbooks, video tapes and audio tapes in-house.

It was established early in discussion with the University authorities that the development and offering of the distance learning version of the course was over and above the normal workload for academic staff; in consequence a schedule of payments was drawn up to reimburse authors, tutors etc for the various activities necessary to develop the course materials and, subsequently, to operate the course.

The business plan which emerged was sensitive to assumptions made about student numbers. Hence much attention was paid to the projected numbers recruited, how they would progress through the course and drop out rate. It was assumed that recruitment would build over approximately 5 years to a steady state of 60 new entrants per year, that the normal period of study for each of the 4 taught modules would be 6 months and that the drop out rate would average at 10% per module. It was assumed that students would take their dissertation during the third year of the course.

Essentially the business plan was prepared on the basis of marginal costing. The plan indicated that, due to the considerable costs of developing the course materials, the course would be in deficit for the first 3 years from commencement of its development. By the time the business plan was ready for presentation to the University, the UFC had agreed to provide a grant of £30,000 to assist with developing the course; taking that grant into account in the business plan, the cumulative figures showed that it would be necessary for the University to underwrite approximately £40,000 for one year. The business plan predicted that the third year of the course would earn a surplus sufficient that by the end of the third year the course would break even on a cumulative basis and that it would proceed to earn increasing surpluses over the fourth and fifth years by which time it was anticipated that the course would settle into steady state operation.

The business plan was presented to the high level planning boards of the University and was accepted by them as the basis on which development of the distance learning mode of study for the MSc could proceed.

5 Pre-Requisites

By the time at which academic and administrative approval
for the development of the distance learning mode of study
had been obtained, it was clear that four elements, all of
which were fundamental to the success of the project, had
come together.   Those elements were:

> Enthusiastic and highly committed academic staff in
> the CSU.
> Distance learning expertise and course administration
> skills in the CCE.
> A sizeable market.
> A successful bid for pump-priming money to help fund
> the initial development expenditure.

If any one of the four elements had not been present, it
is highly unlikely that development of the distance learning
version of the course would have been undertaken. (Indeed,
the proposal would have foundered much earlier in the
gestation period of the project.)

6 Main Development

Project Management

In order to develop the distance learning study materials
speedily, efficiently and effectively, a course team of 5
was established comprising the three members of academic
staff of the CSU, the Director and Assistant Director of the
CCE.   Each member of the course team was allocated primary
responsibility for several functions.   Broadly the
distribution was:

> CSU 1 - Author, academic course director, chairperson of
>   course team.
> CSU 2 - Author, admissions, residential schools.
> CSU 3 - Author, examinations and assessments.
> CCE 1 - Project Manager, Production Manager, Editor.
> CCE 2 - Marketing, administration, student support.

Naturally there were many other issues that had to be
dealt with; this was accomplished in a course team meeting,
by the member of the team using their particularly expertise
or by engaging an outside expert.   Generally the
arrangements worked very well due, in no small measure, to
the effort and enthusiasm of the team members.
Unfortunately, the level of interest and motivation to
develop the materials was not matched in the University more
generally which led to some problems in deciding the
appropriate systems to adopt, implementing decisions of the
course team and resolving issues which had major
implications for the University - notably financial matters.

Although many facets of the course were modelled on the Open University there were some major and fundamental differences:

All members of the course team were involved in the distance learning project in addition to their normal responsibilities.

Such part-time involvement put people under great pressure; especially to meet deadlines.

As none of the authors had any experience in the preparation of distance learning materials, it was necessary for them to undertake training and to develop the style of writing to be adopted throughout in a fairly ad hoc way. Fortunately, the use of experienced editors, with a knowledge of distance learning requirements, and the phasing of producing the materials eased the problem considerably.

Further expertise in the production of materials through other media had to be mastered – video tapes and audio tapes.

The lack of any distance learning courses within the University, meant that every aspect of the project set a precedent for the University, necessitating greater scrutiny of all decisions.

Although the total UGC pump-priming money of £50,000 was invaluable, along with the underwriting by the University (as noted in connection with the business plan), early recruitment of students and commencement of the course was considered to be essential to provide cash flow for development of further course materials as well as securing a leading place in the market.

7 Principles

From the inception, the course team adopted certain principles which it held paramount for the production of a worthy distance learning course.
Although adherence to those principles has been very difficult on occasions due to numerous changes which have taken place, adherence to them has been maintained vigorously.

Quality is paramount – both academic and presentational.

Entry requirements for the course are common across all modes of study.

All assessments and criteria for passing are common – assignments, case studies and examinations.

Attendance at the residential components is compulsory.

As far as possible all students taking the course by whatever mode of study and in whatever country should be

afforded the same opportunities and have equivalent
support mechanisms available.

The course fee must be at a competetive level but the
major factor to distinguish the course from others would
be its quality.

8 Course Structure

The course structure is shown in Figure 1. Students are
required to study and pass the 4 taught modules (Management
Principles - MT, Management Science - MS, Construction
Economics - CE and Management Practice - MP) and the module
comprising 4 case studies (one of which relates to each
taught module) before being permitted to proceed to the
dissertation stage. The University requires that the
residential requirement be met prior to the award of the
degree.

Each taught module contains the following study
materials:

Workbooks (1 per unit, hence 3 or 4 per module)
Textbooks (supplied to supplement, and referenced from,
the workbooks)
Supplementary readings (specialist papers etc, referenced
in the workbooks)
Video tapes
Audio tapes

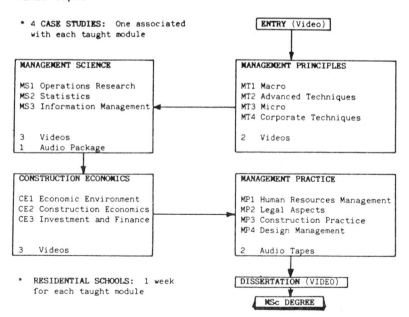

* 4 CASE STUDIES: One associated
  with each taught module

ENTRY (Video)

MANAGEMENT SCIENCE

MS1 Operations Research
MS2 Statistics
MS3 Information Management

3   Videos
1   Audio Package

MANAGEMENT PRINCIPLES

MT1 Macro
MT2 Advanced Techniques
MT3 Micro
MT4 Corporate Techniques

2   Videos

CONSTRUCTION ECONOMICS

CE1 Economic Environment
CE2 Construction Economics
CE3 Investment and Finance

3   Videos

MANAGEMENT PRACTICE

MP1 Human Resources Management
MP2 Legal Aspects
MP3 Construction Practice
MP4 Design Management

2   Audio Tapes

* RESIDENTIAL SCHOOLS: 1 week
  for each taught module

DISSERTATION (VIDEO)

MSc DEGREE

Fig. 1.Course Structure and Study Materials

Module MT contains 4 units, MS contains 3 units, CE contains 3 units and MP contains 4 units of which the students must take two (Human Resources Management and Legal Aspects) plus one option unit – either Design Management or Construction Practice.

As it is normal for students to take the modules consecutively (the order noted above is recommended), students performance in each of the 4 taught modules is considered by the Board of Examiners, including the external examiner, sequentially therefore, successful students accumulate pass credits for the modules studied as they progress through the course towards the dissertation. Having secured a pass credit in each of the 4 taught modules and the case studies module, students are permitted to progress to the dissertation stage; satisfactory completion of which is the final stage in their earning an MSc.

9 Logistics and Administration

The policy adopted of providing maximum flexibility for students within the 5 year maximum period of study permitted by the University has created a variety of challenging logistical problems, particularly for administration. All administrative support has been located in the CCE in order to focus control and facilitate monitoring and because the University's central administration has no experience of dealing with a distance learning programme. Further, students should have a clear focal point for contact with the University, preferably with a particular individual or small number of people. Therefore, the central administration maintains only basic records and carries out basic accounting functions, notably collection of fees. Examination arrangements and room bookings for residential periods at the University are dealt with by the School's administration.

Amongst the issues requiring particular, continuous attention are:

Entry twice early – May and November.
Students normally studying each taught module consecutively but may change their pace of study or defer for a period provided they complete the course within the 5 year limit.
Dispatching the multitude of course materials.
Ensuring efficient delivery of materials to overseas students, including custom clearance – especially for video tapes.
Organization of residential schools overseas
Organization of 18 individual residential schools per annum at Bath.
Establishing, maintaining and monitoring an extensive network of academic tutors.

Receipt of students work for assessment, distribution
to academic tutors, receiving marked scripts and
returning those to the students with associated
distributions of performance records.

A network of personal tutors and the provision of
counselling-type support.

Securing the production and delivery of all materials
on time.

Organizing examinations both at Bath and at overseas
centres.

10 Problems

The vast majority of issues which have been discussed
already have achieved satisfactory solutions.   However
certain major problems have emerged which, unless dealt with
speedily and effectively to secure satisfaction of the
people involved and, particularly to ensure that enthusiasm
and commitment is maintained by members of the course team,
could place the entire venture in jeopardy.

Unacceptable material from authors.   Only a few
instances and from externally commissioned authors
exclusively.   Such materials were of insufficient
standard; the probable best solution is to scrutinize
external authors rigorously and, after preliminary
discussions, to provide them with meticulous briefs for
the materials to be prepared.

Issues of copyright.   It is essential to determine who
owns the copyright in materials produced and to make
appropriate payments for the acquisition of copyright.

Use of the copyright symbol on course materials, with
the University's name appended, should discourage
potential plagerism.

What charges other than direct, marginal charges of
producing the course materials and operating the
programme should be borne, eg University general
overhead, school overheads.

Distribution of any surpluses earned.

Unfortunately some of the problems were not tackled
sufficiently early and, therefore, resulted in frustration,
anger and some, not inconsiderable, difficulties.

11 Impact on the Organization

The production of a distance learning course of the size and scope of the MSc in Construction Management is a major learning process for all concerned:

a)   Academically it is contributed to a reassessment of the content and structure of the full time and part-time modes of study for the MSc
b)   Organizationally it has required the University to amend some of its structures and systems to accommodate study by distance learning.
c)   Financially it has necessitated reappraisal of what are the implications of a major self-financing degree course.
d)   Contractually it has required clarification and amendment of the roles of various staff, notably academics.
e)   Professionally it has provided new skills and enhanced the standing of the people concerned.
f)   Opportunistically it has opened new markets world wide.
g)   Accessibility it represents a major opportunity for many people to gain a higher degree who, without such a course who otherwise would be denied access.

12 Current Position

To-date (July 1991) there have been several thousand enquiries about the distance learning mode, several hundred applications and registration of over 110 students.   The average drop out rate (people who have ceased to take the course apparently permanently) is around the 10% predicted. Academic success is high – so far no student has failed any module.   The external examiner has commented officially to the Vice-Chancellor of the high standards achieved by students taking the course by the distance learning mode of study.
Students from the first intake of the course (November 1989) are completing their final (MP) module and will be embarking on their dissertations in November 1991.   Hence the first graduates who studied by distance learning should receive their degrees in 1992.   Most students taking the course are UK based, around 20% are overseas.   The pattern of entry is that around 50 students join the distance learning mode in November (when both home and overseas students may begin the course) and approaching 20 students (UK only) enter the course each May. Thus, the course should achieve "steady state" student numbers in November 1991.

13 The Future

Amongst future developments under consideration and discussion is the possibility of joint operation of the distance learning mode between the University of Bath and Universities overseas which have a particular opportunity in the field of construction management.   The forms of such arrangements may vary but, at present, the overseas universities will, essentially, service the Bath course – it will remain a degree of the University of Bath but the overseas universities will share surpluses generated.

Further course contents are in development – currently, in the field of international construction.

Much interest in the distance learning mode of study has been generated within the University such that may other schools are persuing development of distance learning courses.

Perhaps use of high technology, interactive study media will be the next development for the MSc in Construction Management by Distance Learning.

Education in the role of management

G.M. Cairns
DEGW (Scotland) Limited, Glasgow, UK

This paper examines the role and responsibilities of the architect, with particular reference to the design and construction processes, and questions the current status of the profession with regard to this role. The primary role of the architect, as defined within the profession's own terms of appointment, is one of management and co-ordination of the design process. The profession promotes the architect as the lead member of the design team, a position which is, more and more, becoming the province of other professions.

The education system itself fails to support the primary role, being biased towards the promotion of the architect as designer and not of manager of a production process. Training in management of the design and construction processes is, at best, limited and, at worst, relegated to the position of an ill-considered add-on to the course of study.

The paper concludes that only through increased recognition of the importance of education in management techniques and of specialisation and teamwork will the architectural profession be able to justify and earn the right to leadership of the design team.

Keywords: Design Management, Education, Project Management, Primary Role, Teamwork.

1 The Role of the Architect

"The architect's primary professional responsibility is to act as the client's adviser and additionally to administer the building contract fairly between client and contractor". RIBA

The role of the architect is defined within the Royal Institute of British Architects' publication 'Architect's Appointment', the document preferred by the architect in determining his conditions of appointment and likely to be the least onerous in terms of responsibility and liability, where alternative conditions may be proposed by the client.

The primary responsibilities, as set out within the first few pages of this document, relate not to design but to management; the co-ordination of the elements of the design and the administration of the contract.

In setting out the architect's roles and responsibilities in relation to the design process the RIBA document clearly highlights his training for the role of assisting the client in understanding the process, for co-ordinating all the elements of the design and for administering the building contract.

Any prospective client presented with this document should, justifiably, feel secure in the knowledge that his architect has had a full and thorough training in the aspects of architectural management which are likely to affect the project.

2 The Reality of the Architect

Arising from the role implied in the introductory statements of the architect's terms of appointment, as manager and co-ordinator of the design process, the architectural profession has traditionally promoted its 'right' to a position of leadership of the design team.

The architect is charged, by this document, with overall responsibility for collating the client's requirements within the brief, of interpreting them in his design and of overseeing their implementation during the construction process. He is also required to advise the client on matters relating to contract, costs, programming and a wide range of other matters.

The appointment also bestows upon the architect the authority to co-ordinate the work of other professionals in incorporating them into his design.

It is likely, in these times, that any client willing to appoint an architect under the RIBA terms would, for the term 'have the authority to', expect the reality of the situation to mean 'accept the responsibility for'.

In defense of the design team leadership the architectural profession will vociferously attack others who attempt to usurp its position. It is doubtful, however, if many architects are adequately prepared for, or fully understand, the responsibilities which the acceptance of this appointment lays upon them.

The profession has, for a considerable period of time, permitted its members to abdicate responsibility for this role through lack of knowledge, understanding and, to a large extent, interest in the management of the architectural process.

The responsibilities which are accepted by the holder of the position of design team leader are those of management and control of the building design and procurement process. This management role must be clearly understood to be separate from the design role. It is unlikely, however, that many architects differentiate between the roles of designer and design manager and, thereby, they will readily promote the professions 'right' to be design team leader as arising from the role as lead designer.

The architect's role as team leader can be supported by the responsibility which he accepts under his terms of appointment, but cannot be based upon the the premise that, because he is the primary producer of the design, he must have control over the implementation process.

Logically there is no reason why the role of team leader should fall to the lead designer and, therefore, the position of design team leader is one to which the right must be earned and cannot be expected. Respect for the role of team leader can only be gained by demonstration of in-depth knowledge and understanding of the total project implementation process.

It might be argued that, in the past thirty years, the architect has allowed, through lack of interest, and subsequently been forced to allow, through lack of knowledge, some of his major roles in the fields of project and construction management to be assumed by others, losing control over their correct integration into the overall architectural process.

Reliance upon the quantity surveyor for cost information and control and, even, for specification writing has become commonplace, with the architect often taking little interest in the content and quality of the information provided.

The weakening of the architect's position in relationship to control of the design process weakens his overall authority and, therefore, his position in any argument relating to other aspects of the design process.

The architectural profession currently fights battles on the subjects of fee scale, aesthetic control and collateral warranties from a position of weakness, brought about by its loss of authority in the business of design production and procurement.

3 The Image of the Architect

The architectural profession, through its professional bodies and through the architectural press, has always willingly, if unwittingly, promoted the view of the architect as the 'whole person'.

Design architects are elevated to the position of 'gurus'; their works portrayed in glossy detail in the architectural press; the form, function and detail of the design displayed and dissected. Awards are bestowed upon the individual; gold medals, knighthoods and other plaudits.

There is little recognition of, and even less analysis of, the team structure and management process which lie behind the facade of design excellence.

Coverage of management issues in the press is not normally project specific or, if it is, it will most likely be limited to case studies of management failure, not of architectural success.

Technical studies of the construction, structure and detail are regularly presented for successful design projects, but the link which must exist between successful design execution and a knowledgeable design management team is not made. The pitfalls and obstacles to the procurement of good design are too numerous for the link not to exist.

The architectural profession promotes the image of the 'whole person' but fails to promote or foster within itself the understanding of the 'whole process'.

The segregation of product and process, along with the weighting of recognition in favour of product, follows through to the external image of the profession and into the profession's own teaching methods.

4 The Role of Architectural Education

"The education of architects prepares them to assist clients at all stages of a building project and to co-ordinate all the elements of the design and construction process". RIBA

Despite the clarity of the responsibilities set out within the first few pages of the RIBA document on the appointment of an architect, the majority of effort on teaching within the architectural education system is expended upon the process which the majority of architects in practice will never get the opportunity to effect on any major project; composition of the visual elements of design.

Other areas of the architectural process are considered secondary to this area and any form of management teaching which may be presented is frequently relegated to the position of being an add-on to the final year of the course, at a time when the final design project is viewed by teachers and students as the primary area of interest.

The teaching of architectural practice and management in schools revolves primarily around the building contract and its application and on legislation affecting the design process.

The education process should provide graduates with a level of understanding of the total architectural process which will prepare them for, and enable them to promote, the architect's role as lead member of the design team.

In reality, however, the major areas of project management, cost reporting and client contact are increasingly being controlled by others;

the quantity surveyor and the project manager.

The student's experience of management within the office environment, during the year out, is likely to be restricted by the nature of the work on which they will spend the majority of their time; on the production of information. The management of the office, its financial planning and resource planning, are areas within which the majority of practices are unlikely to grant the student access to information.

Within the field of architectural management, then, the teaching of entire areas of resource planning, financial planning, man-management etc are either covered in minimal outline only, or are omitted from the teaching process entirely.

At the RIBA conference on education, held in March 1991, Christopher Foster expressed the view that architects should be trained alongside other professions to fulfill their design and management role. The RIBA Journal subsequently reported that "this seemed to be a problem which the conference would not face". RIBA

Initial teaching of the basic principles of the entire architectural process and of the relationships with, and responsibilities of, other professions would assist students in determining those areas within which their particular strengths and interests may lie. It might also allow them to recognise and acknowledge those areas in which their own weaknesses should be reinforced by the contributions of others.

5 'Whole Person' or 'One Stop Shopping'?

It might be argued that the knowledge of all areas of architectural design and management cannot be known to the individual. This is undoubtedly true, but the acknowledgment of this truth should not be seen as a sign of weakness. Rather it should be seized upon as an opportunity to build strength.

It is noteworthy that the architectural profession stands almost alone in its promotion of the individual over the team in so many instances. In virtually all other professions the output of the process is acknowledged to be a team effort, even, as in the medical profession, where a degree of specialist knowledge in a particular field may be attributed to the individual.

Acknowledgment by the architectural profession of the need for team work and of the contribution of a number of different people to the design process would encourage greater specialisation within the profession; which might then accept that, instead of promoting the 'whole person' concept, it should promote a 'one stop shopping' concept.

Such a concept would involve the development of teams of specialists, able to promote themselves confidently as providers of the full architectural service; design excellence accompanied by the highest standard of design management.

6 Conclusion

It is only through full integration of the teaching of design and construction management into the education process that the student and architect will be able to understand the full architectural process and be able to establish their own strengths, interests and responsibilities within it.

Widening of the horizons of architectural education and recognition of the contribution of the purely managerial function to the successful implementation of good design would encourage the evolution of a new breed of architects.

This new breed of architects would encompass the fields of visual design, functional design, design management and design implementation within the term 'architect'.

The team responsible for the architectural process would have a full, but shared, understanding of the process and a mutually shared, rather than mutually exclusive, goal in its successful implementation.

7 References

Royal Institute of British Architects, (1988) **Architect's Appointment.** RIBA Publications Limited, London, p. 1

Royal Institute of British Architects, (May 1991) **RIBA Journal.** RIBA Publications Limited, London, p. 19

Open learning as a contribution to continuing professional development in British architectural practice

M. Hatchett
London School of Economics, University of London, UK

Abstract
This paper describes some of the developments that have taken place in open learning programmes during the last decade which may contribute to continuing professional development in British architectural practice.
Keywords: Adult Training, Open Learning, Continuing Professional Development (CPD), Architectural Practice, Post-Qualification Continuing Education, Life-Long Learning.

1 Background

In May 1990 Christopher Ball, in a report addressing the need for widening access to higher education in Britain, demonstrated a clear need to prepare for tomorrow's world because:

- the nature of work is changing and increasingly employers are calling for more people with professional, technical and managerial skills.

- fewer people are now able to rely on their initial education and training to provide them with the specific skills which will last a lifetime

- more and more people have discovered that lifelong learning improves the quality of life

2 Life-long learning in construction

Within the last 20 years many of the construction related professions have recognised a need for some form of post qualification continuing education. In 1978, a committee of the Royal Institute of Chartered Surveyors recommended that it should be compulsory for every chartered surveyor to devote some time after qualification to improving skill and efficiency, and by 1991 all surveyors, and by 1992 all British architects who are members of the RIBA, will be affected by the concept of continuing professional development (CPD).

The British construction related professions have adopted the following formal definition of life-long learning:

"The systematic maintenance, improvement and broadening of knowledge and skill and the development of personal qualities necessary for the execution of professional and technical duties throughout the practitioner's working life."

Such a definition has been adopted because it encourages a more coherent approach to continuing professional development. It also emphasises, to the employer as well as to the individual practitioner, just how important CPD is, and it acts as a catalyst to educational institutions and other course providers, to organise events specifically for qualified practitioners.

3 Attitudes of architects and other construction related professionals to CPD

In 1987 the RIBA participated in a survey to determine, among other things, attitudes to CPD within the construction related professions. Nearly 500 people, chosen at random and working in the construction industry, were invited to participate in the survey. Rather more than half the sample were architects and architectural students in practical training. The remainder were architectural technicians and other professionals.

The survey revealed that the majority of the sample were already participating, to some extent in CPD. It was also generally believed that CPD was "... a good ting..." and it was generally considered that the status of their professions could only be enhanced by participating in CPD.

However, there was some difficulty in reconciling a willingness to participate in CPD with an ability to do so in practice, lack of time was seen as the main constraint.

4 Methods of delivering CPD

In 1984 the British government asked the Manpower Services Commission to lead a campaign to raise awareness of, and influence attitudes towards, adult training amongst employers, training providers and individuals. The campaign was launched because research had demonstrated to the government that:

- high business performance was strongly and positively associated with high levels of adult training.

- many employers regarded training as an unwelcome cost and seemed unaware of the benefits training could bring to their organisations

- generally the providers of training, including educational institutions, did not respond flexibly enough to meet the needs of employers and individuals

- individuals often failed to appreciate the benefits training could bring to them, especially during periods of change.

One element of this campaign was the creation, in 1983, of an Open Tech Programme, funded until the spring of 1987 by the Manpower Services Commission as part of the government's adult training strategy. There are many ways of delivering CPD but the main purpose of this programme was to expand the range and flexibility of training opportunities available to adults.

Within this programme the principal characteristics of an open learning approach to continuing education were considered as:

- Providing an opportunity to learn at a pace, time and place which satisfies the user's and the employer's circumstances and requirements

- reducing or removing barriers of access to education and training and to progress through education and training programmes

- offering a choice of content to suit individual needs.

The British government favoured an open learning approach because:

- it was project based, and individual development projects with defined and acceptable objectives would be funded for an initial development period

- it was collaborative and involved the working together of employers, educational institutions, industrial training boards, employer's associations and professional institutions

- it was vocational and therefore was an employer-led activity.

5 Attitudes of architects and other construction related professionals to open learning:

The 1987 survey indicated that four out of five construction professionals were interested in the concept of open learning as a way of undertaking CPD. The flexibility of open learning was very much liked, particularly because it provided flexibility of time and venue.

Open learning emerged from the survey as a more popular way of undertaking CPD than the more "traditional" ways of educating qualified architects. There is, therefore, a large potential market in Britain for open learning materials which are suitable for use by architects in practice and by architectural students in practical training. Turning this large potential market into an effective open

learning programme is a challenge which now faces the RIBA and the other construction related professional institutions.

6 Two examples of open learning projects associated with the British construction industry

Since 1983 the author has been involved in the design and implementation of two open learning projects within the British construction industry

6.1 The Site Management Open Tech Scheme
This was one of the first construction related open learning projects to receive government funding. The scheme is linked with membership of the Chartered Institute of Building and registration is open to all who are more than 23 years of age with at least two years of general construction site supervisory experience. The scheme is sub divided into two stages:

A certificate programme, launched in 1986, in which a registered user selects 80 learning packages, in sets of 10, from the following modules of which the first six are compulsory. There are some 20 packages in each module and this gives a wide range of choice.

Industry and management
Communications I
Industrial relations and employment conditions
Safety, health and welfare
Contractual procedures
Planning and organisation
Productivity techniques
Management planning techniques
Services - technical
Levelling and setting-out

A diploma programme, launched in January 1990, in which a registered user selects a further 80 packages, also in sets of 10, from the following modules of which the first six are compulsory. Again there are approximately 20 packages in each module from which to make a selection.

Introduction to economics and cost control
Legal responsibilities
Communications II
Quality control
Estimating and quantity surveying
Personnel and industrial relations
Working with people
Services management
Maintenance management

Registered users of this scheme are provided with:

• a tutor led profiling exercise to establish principal areas of interest and to assist in the selection of appropriate learning packages

- programmed delivery of the selected learning packages

- tutorial support throughout the study programme

- assignments linked with each module assessed by tutors

- a range of short residential workshops linked with each phase of the programme

Non registered users may buy any number of packages for their own use but receive no additional support services.

The construction industry provides financial support for those:

- who are employed in companies who pay levy to the Construction Industry Training Board

- who are registered users

- who apply for financial support before embarking on an open learning programme

6.2 The RIBA Open Learning Programme

The RIBA Open Learning programme was launched in October 1989 with the publication of 46 packages associated with four topic areas as follows

Total project management
Architectural practice management
Building contract procedures, claims and arbitration
Building law, statutory requirements and legal responsibilities

The packages possess the following common features:

- subject matter presented in a way that is suitable for use by architects at work and by architectural students in practical training

- self assessment exercises supported by yardstick answers

- practice based assignments, so that users can relate the contents of each package to their own organisational and practice needs

- further study opportunities so that users can extend their interests in the subject matter beyond the limits of each package.

The packages have been prepared so that they are easy to enhance and update and new or enhanced packages have been added since the scheme was launched in 1989. One new topic area, in "practice exposure to liabilities, legal and insurance issues", has been added through external sponsorship, and new topic areas in lighting, the use of steel in architectural design - which has received external sponsorship - and in conservation are proposed.

The RIBA open learning packages have been prepared for use:

- in the larger architectural practices which have their own CPD programmes and programme organisers and which provide established programmes for architectural students in practical training

- in the RIBA's CPD regional centres as part of a nationwide network of CPD provisions

- in the recognised schools of architecture as part of the range of provisions available for architectural students in practical training and as part of the recognised schools' contribution to CPD and continuing education

- as part preparation for the RIBA's own examinations

7 The role of the tutor in open learning programmes

Open learning programmes do not make tutors redundant. There are several key tutorial functions that are necessary to make open learning successful. These include:

- pre-course counselling; open learning programmes are not suitable for everyone and there is a crucial role for the tutor to see that all potential users have the clearest possible picture of what is involved

- induction programmes; it is important that all open learning users make a successful start to their study programmes and the tutor may need to plan special induction programmes, particularly for those who have been away from structured learning for some time, so that users quickly become familiar with study methods

- on-line help and workshops; most open learning programmes provide for the users to have access to selected tutors by telephone or though regular tutorials or workshops

- selecting and marking assignments; tutorial guidance may be required in the selection of appropriate assignments and with the feed-back of results

- further study opportunities; many tutors become involved in discussions about the content and directions of further study.

8 Basic issues that arise from the development of open learning programmes

Open learning programmes provide:

- opportunities for sharing professional experience - writing open learning packages is a very real contribution to continuing education and CPD

- a means for disseminating knowledge regarding the more rapidly changing components of professional practice - the relevance and contents of topic areas and individual packages can be monitored

- opportunities for real collaboration between practitioners from different professions - several of the topic areas in the RIBA programmes have required considerable collaboration between members of different professions

- opportunities for more effective links to be developed between employers and professional and educational institutions - already some of the larger architectural practices have embedded open learning into their staff development programmes.

Open learning programmes need

- regular and continuing financial support from sources other than the income from sales - external sponsorship and the continual support of the professions through their education and CPD budgets are essential

- continued publicity and marketing so that practitioners are kept informed of new developments - if individual practitioners are to be encouraged to plan and implement part of their own professional development then they must know what opportunities are available to them

- regular and continued updating and enhancement - otherwise packages and topic areas will become dated and of limited value

- support mechanisms, such as user groups and tutors, are required so that packages can be incorporated into many different types of learning experience.

9 Some crucial concerns associated with the use of open learning within CPD programmes

There is an obvious conflict between the interests and needs of collaborative CPD programme and the interests and needs of individual practitioners. This conflict can be resolved by having a wide variety of CPD providers including employers, professional institutions, educational establishments and others working separately and in collaboration.

There is also a need for a wide range of CPD opportunities so that individuals can construct learning programmes that are relevant to their current needs and interests and to their future aspirations. Most busy practitioners in mid career need some help with the design and implementation of their CPD programmes. There will be a growing need for CPD counsellors, facilitators and tutors who are used to working with people in mid career.

At present CPD activities are grossly under funded and under
resourced. Therefore participation in CPD tends to be inadequately
supported, fragmented and uncoordinated. All participants -
employers, professional institutions, educational institutions and
individuals - will need to invest much more in CPD than is currently
envisaged for it to be successful.

10 References

Ball C (1990) **More Means Different** - widening access to higher
education, Royal Society of Arts, London
Clark A, Costello M, Wright T (1986) **The Role and Tasks of Tutors in
Open Learning Systems,** Industrial Training Research Unit, Cambridge.
RIBA Market Research Unit (1987) **Open Learning in British
Architectural Practice** - a market survey, RIBA for the Construction
Industry Training Board, London.

CHAPTER EIGHT

*'There is one psychological peculiarity in the
human being that always strikes one: to shun
even the slightest signs of trouble on the outer
edge of your existence at times of well-being ...
to try not to know about the sufferings of
others and your own or one's own future
sufferings, to yield in many situations, even
important spiritual and central ones - as long
as it prolongs one's well-being.'*

Alexander I. Solzhenitsyn

Managing change within the professional firm

P. Barrett
University of Salford, UK

Abstract

Change is a pervasive fact for the professional firm. This paper considers the positive and negative aspects of change. Ultimately a balanced view is suggested, although in the current climate it seems inevitable that firms should be open to change.

The driving forces for change and the factors that can be changed within the firm, namely: structure, technology and people, are considered with particular emphasis on people. It is argued that it is important to view change as a process rather than an event. Continued effort is required.

Keywords: Professional firm, construction, change, management.

1 What is Changing?

Professional firms in general, and those involved in construction in particular, have faced unprecedented change over the last decade and the rate of change appears to be accelerating towards the end of the millennium.

Major structural changes can be seen occurring in three main areas: the markets for professional services, the nature of client demand and, lastly, developments in information technology.

1.1 Change in Markets

A whole range of factors within the environment of the professional firm have changed over the last twenty years in such a way that the combined effect has been to push professional firms away from their traditional modes of operating towards a more business like approach. This is summarised in the force field analysis below.

In addition, there is the breaking down of trade barriers between the domestic U.K. economy and the remainder of Western Europe from the beginning of 1993.

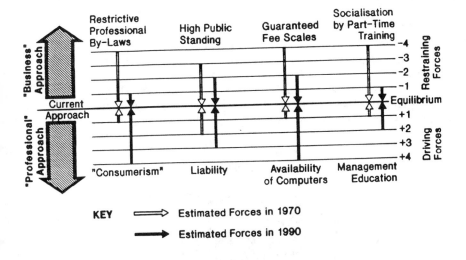

Fig. 1: Forcefield analysis of contextual changes
over the last twenty years (Barrett 1991a).

As the Lay Report (RICS, 1991) points out this will result in our local economy becoming a one twelfth part of a much larger economic system. This particularly noticeable change is in fact part of a trend towards globalisation and business with the EFTA countries is already building and so too are relationships with Eastern European countries as they move towards market economies.

1.2 Change in Client Demand

It is well known that many of the features of the "traditional" approach to construction used in the British construction industry can be traced back 100 years, and in some instances still further to the time of the Guilds. For all that, there have been significant changes over the last twenty years and many alternative procurement systems now available. This process of services being created, developing and then declining has been identified in the service management literature in terms of *service cycles* (eg Sibson, 1971; Webb, 1982; Foster, 1986).

This view stresses that the longevity of existing services cannot be taken for granted and professional firms, if they are to survive in the longer term, need a marketing orientation which makes them sensitive to changing client demands.

351

One major identifiable trend is the increasing demand for professional advice which takes a particularly broad view.

This is evidenced in the rise of the project manager in the case of construction and, in this author's view, a similar trend is emerging in relation to the use and adaptation of existing buildings as exemplified by the emerging discipline of the facilities manager.

Both trends imply a move towards a broad and balanced "world view" (W) of the issues involved. These trends are depicted Fig. 2 below, where the "construction system" and "client system" meet in the briefing process.

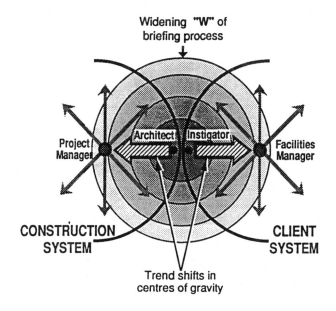

Figure 2: A holistic view of the briefing process (Barrett, 1991b)

In addition to these specific trends a demand for a broader view can also be seen in the increasing demand for construction professionals to take account of the environmental impact of their choices. This involves, among other things, the appearance of a building, the choice of materials, the energy performance and the quality of life that the building provides its occupiers.

1.3 Changes in Information Technology

There have been rapid advances in the availability of information technology which pose both threats and opportunities to the construction professions. On the one hand there is the danger that the professions will become deskilled as information technology makes expertise more widely available, possibly through expert systems.

On the other hand the same technology holds out the possibility for firms to greatly enhance the quality of the services they have to offer. In addition information technology can give firms great flexibility in terms of work patterns along with dimensions of time, place and content. Gone are the days when dictation to a short-hand typist took place in one's office and any corrections that had to be made demanded retyping. Now professionals can dictate work, make phone calls or link up with computers almost anywhere, leave work to be done by others at different times and very quickly manipulate existing documents by moving text, etc around. Thus, work can be made to fit in with the workers and quick accurate responses to client's request can be provided.

1.4 Summary

From the above it should be clear that the claim that the construction professionals are facing unprecedented change was not made lightly. In all of the above instances the changes are already upon us and affecting more and more firms within the industry.

The one factor which has not been mentioned so far is that of "people", that is, the individuals involved in the construction professions. The remainder of this paper will consider the effect of major changes on the people involved.

People cannot be seen as a side-issue if Lewin's (1947) suggestion is taken seriously, that if you dig deep enough into any problem you will come eventually to people! There is no point in firms making grand plans for change if they do not give equally serious consideration to how to manage the change process within their organisation. No change process is easy. It may appear blatantly obvious to the proponents, but it is likely to appear just as unreasonable to many of those affected. As a result the process is rarely comfortable.

The following sections will look at the reasons for resistance to change, techniques for overcoming that resistance and a model for producing lasting change. Lastly, the value of change compared with stability will be considered.

2 Resistance to Change

2.1 Levels of change

In managerial terms, although attitudes are interesting, it is behaviour, or people's *actions*, that matter in the end. Much of the resistance to change goes unnoticed because it is assumed that once a person is persuaded of the correctness of a point of view that they will in fact then change their behaviour as well. The process is more complex than this and Fig. 3 below shows the stages, from the changing of the person's knowledge base, which in time will have an impact on his or her attitudes and eventually result in changed behaviour patterns, provided peer pressure can be overcome.

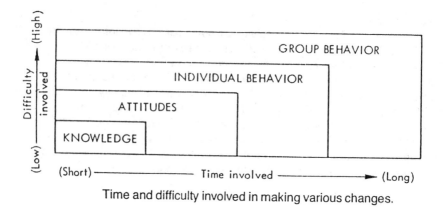

Time and difficulty involved in making various changes.

Fig. 3: Changing behaviour as well as knowledge
Kast and Rosenzweig (1978).

The effects of the model can be seen in the professions' response to computers. Initially people would readily admit that computers could lead to greater efficiency but still tended to have a negative attitude towards them. Slowly this attitude has changed as home computers have become the norm and it is now commonplace to find individuals within practices who are very willing to use computers to support their work, but it may be that in a (rapidly decreasing) number of practices the norms within the practice are still inclined towards hand drafting and so the individuals willingness is contained.

2.2 Social Resistance

The above model argues for a sustained approach to managing change which goes beyond merely winning the argument. A key stage in the process is to overcome group pressure which should not be underestimated. In the past many firms in different disciplines have sent individuals away on courses to change their attitudes and skills. When they have returned to the parent organisation it is common experience that they had little impact on the organisation as a whole (Argyris, 1962).

A measure of the potency of group pressure was provided by experiments carried out by Solomon Asch (1955) in which he created a situation where an individual being tested was put in a group of other people who had been told beforehand to give the incorrect answer to a very simple question which involved comparing lengths of lines on cards. The answers were patently obvious, and, on their own, the guinea pigs made no mistakes. When one other person was involved giving an incorrect answer it made no difference, but when in a group of three 14% of the "guinea pigs" gave the wrong answer to be in line with the other group members. In groups of four this went up to 32%. Those who did not fit in with the "group norm", that is the incorrect response, exhibited extreme signs of discomfort with sweating and stammering etc.

2.3 Conservatism

Another source of resistance to change has been termed "dynamic conservatism", which reflects the energy and innovation some people will put into maintaining the status quo. This is confirmed by Lansley (1985) who found that research is only well received by the construction industry if its suggestions are: familiar, focussed, self-contained and backed by people / bodies of high standing. Not a recipe for rampant innovation!

To a great extent this will be founded on sunk costs, that is the investment people have made in the past to produce the status quo. For instance, continuing our example of the use of computers, if individuals have developed hand drafting skills to a high degree then it is only natural that they should resist moves that will make this skill irrelevant. Similar arguments can apply to changes in structure where senior personnel with great power will be unlikely to support changes that will reduce their significance in the organisation of the future.

In addition to the above potential losses against past investments there is the question of costs attached to introducing further changes within an organisation.

Many of the adverse reactions to change will be rooted in a fear of the unknown and Fig 4 below gives a view on related changes in learning, confidence / confusion and anxiety springing from the introduction of change.

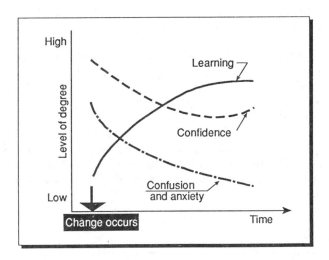

Fig. 4: Impact of Change on Confidence, Confusion
and Anxiety (based on Newman, 1975)

It can be seen that confusion and anxiety are likely to be high initially and decline as the learning curve rises. The diagram suggests that confidence will also be high initially, on the assumption that those involved thought the change was a good idea, but as time goes on the full implications will be realised and the discomfort felt will undermine confidence although it is anticipated that it will begin to rise again after a time.

2.4 Summary

The consistent message is that the change process must receive a sustained effort, over time, if it is to be successfully achieved. There is no point in saying "but you agreed to it, why are you backing out now?" It is better to be ready for this sort of development and to react positively to it.

It is important to appreciate the very real and potent resistance that there will often be to any change proposed. There is no point in just being right. It is necessary to overcome the resistance through a sustained effort if the initiative is to be successful. The next section considers alternative approaches to overcoming any resistance to change.

3 Overcoming Resistance to Change

Various facets will be considered: communication, involvement and power.

3.1 Communications

Clear communications are essential if the *process* of change is not to be blocked by misunderstandings. Those managing change need to (Adair, 1973):

o *reinforce* their message through repetition and using different media;
o *code* the message in terms, and using terms, that the receipients can readily understand;
o seek *feedback* and tailor the approach used to match the needs of those subject to change.

Canter (1983) stresses the importance of *how* a change is presented. She advises "change agents" to define initiatives in ways that make them sound: triable, reversible, divisible, concrete, familiar, congruent (with the rest of the organisation) and sexy.

3.2 Involvement

The question of involvement is important (Vroom, 1974). There are two main facets to this issue: knowledge and commitment. For simple problems, straightforward changes, the manager can simply make a decision on his own, but although this would meet the knowledge criterion, it would not create commitment. This may not matter if a firm decides to share an accountant with another firm in the same building, but if the everyday work of the firm is implicated, say by moving office location, then it would be well to involve staff, if only to increase the chances of gaining their commitment.

For complex, difficult changes, such as those typically produced by strategic planning exercises, it is wise to involve more people in order to create a greater pool of knowledge. It would be dangerous for an individual, or small group, to produce a solution alone. In addition to knowledge there is the additional benefit to be had from bringing a range problem-solving approaches to an issue (Belbin, 1983; Powell, 1991).

Obviously there is a cost attached to involving more people, but the potential benefits are rigour and commitment.

3.3 Power

However good a proposed change, however well presented, there is still likely to be a need to persuade some people. This introduces power as an important factor. Handy (198?) has suggested a continuum which could be said to range from "nice" to "nasty". He suggests that power is based on: personality (charisma), expertise, position, resource control or, lastly, physical threats. In managing a change process it is clearly better to use "nice" power sources first and "nasty" bases only if actually essential if longterm, self-maintaining change is desired. The less explicit the persuasion the more effective it can be. For instance, if greater team working is desired, arranging the spaces in the office to facilitate this is much more likely to succeed than telling or asking people to work in teams. Handy (1985) terms this *managing the ecology* of the organisation.

3.4 Summary

The above considerations are all important factors in achieving change. It is also desirable for changes to self-maintaining if at all possible. The next section will look at this aspect in more detail.

4 Achieving lasting change

The classic model in this area is the three stage model proposed by Lewin (1947):

o   unfreeze
o   change
o   refreeze

This model explicitly acknowledges the importance of making efforts before and after the change to achieve lasting results.

4.1 Unfreezing

The unfreezing stage is intended to prepare people for the change by breaking down their fixed views of the existing situation. Management consultants generally insist on a client survey which can provide a potent basis for change by undermining any complacency in the firm being studied. Similarly, a post occupancy evaluation of a building designed could be an effective way of persuading a design team that it should reconsider its approach.

The actions to unfreeze can be pleasant, such as removing to a country club to allow free thinking away from the office. They can be very unpleasant, such as sacking key people in the existing organisation, or bringing into disrepute the opinions of key opponents of the proposed change (Johnson, 1990).

4.3 Changing

In the actual change phase, symbolic actions and positive reinforcement are important. Johnson (1990) stresses various ways in which symbolic actions can make a massive difference. In one local authority the Chief Executive sat at the reception desk for an hour every Monday morning and dealt with the public to show the importantance he attached to a customer care initiative. Stories like these circulate the organisation and are very persuasive. At the other extreme, if there is any hint that top management is not fully behind a proposal it is almost certain to fail. The difficulty faced by managers is to:

> ... communicate meaning and vision in symbolic ways which relate to the 'mundane' reality of those in the organisation. (Johnson, 1990)

This has been one of the problems facing quality assurance. Partners can present it in a visionary way, but very often trivial procedures have simply not made sense to those doing the day-to-day work.

Positive feedback is also crucial to the process. Again drawing from experience in QA, the Norwegian Building Research Institute specifically looks for solutions to problems the *firms* identify in order to create quick gains in the initial stages of implementation. In this way enthusiasm for the process can be generated within the firms. Once this has been achieved a move is made on the overall system design.

4.4 Refreezing

If people have been involved in the change process and feel ownership it is quite possible that, at an individual level, the new norms and behaviour patterns will be internalised with no problems. At the organisational level there are two areas at which action can be taken to reinforce the changes: structure and technology.

In terms of structure the challenge is to move from a task force mentality to a "business as usual" frame of mind. However the firm is structured it should reflect the new mode of operating and the key personnel should be very carefully chosen to ensure that the momentum is maintained. Here the issue of "sunk costs" can be used to advantage. People who have invested a lot of time and energy in a change process are hardly likely to allow it to wither.

The technology developed, such as procedures and sources of encoded knowledge, again should be carefully set up to reinforce rather than undermine the change. This and the structure are key areas where the ecology of the firm can be designed to support and maintain the new social processes created by the change process.

5 Alternative approaches

5.1 Change v stability

So far the forces for change and positive ways to react have been stressed, but is change a "good thing"? Should it be accepted unquestioningly or treated with caution?

Some writers (eg Hurst, 1984) have argued that change is intrinsically good for organisations and have described firms that purposefully create turbulence in order to keep things fresh and dynamic. At the other extreme, it has already been indicated that it is quite normal for change to be resisted.

Louis and Sutton (1991) treat this issue in terms of how people think. They contrast "active thinking" with "habits of mind" and observe that the former are often thought to be better, *per se*. In contrast they take a contingency approach and acknowledge that for much of the time, for "business as usual", *habits of mind* are appropriate, whereas in conditions of novelty, discrepancy or for a deliberate initiative, *active thinking* is required. Their analysis focuses particularly on "switching cognitive gears" between the two modes and they suggest various barriers to switching from the automatic to the conscious mode of thinking. For example:

o   If the firm has rigid norms and values;
o   If the firm has experienced extended periods of success;
o   If the stimulus for change is minor or massive (not in between), "threat-rigidity effects" can operate in latter case;
o   If the required change is not incremental, but demands "double loop learning" (Argyris and Schon, 1978).

The authors argue that individuals need to be adept at both modes of thinking and that possibly the most important thing is to "... improve one's capacity to read the situation ..." so that the need to change one's approach is recognised. There is a danger that just when an organisation needs to change most it will be least able to.

5.2 Formal v informal approaches

A further issue is whether change should be formally planned or just allowed to happen. There has been a backlash against formal strategic management, for instance, rooted to an extent in studies of how effective managers work in practice, where a strong emphasis on informal measures has been identified (eg Mintzberg, 1973). Kotter (1982) has suggested that under conditions of uncertainty and dealing with a lot of people, managers need to develop personal "multifaceted agendas" which they seek to achieve through "networks" of people which are not based at all on formal hierchies and span many organisations. This approach is not instead of the organisation's formal plans, but operates in parallel with them, at the individual level of key decision-makers.

This complementary relationship between formal plans and what is really pursued is analysed by Dadfar and Gustavsson (1989) who summarise this aspect showing how the planned strategy is moderated by interpretation and incremental, day-to-day influences which *together* result in the actual strategy pursued (based on Mintzberg and Waters, 1985, p258).

5.3 Summary
It would be wrong to try to label "change" good or bad. It is appropriate in some circumstances and simply a distraction in others. Similarly formal change is not better or worse than informal approaches. They each have their place. Thus, sensitivity is needed to identify when change is required and then to choose, or facilitate, the appropriate way to effect it, probably involving some combination of formal and informal mechanisms.

6 Summary and Conclusion

Professional firms involved in construction are facing unprecedented rates of change in their environment. This demands a reaction, but change within the firm is often resisted. Overcoming this resistance is greatly aided by viewing change as a process, not an event. Further to achieve lasting change attention must be paid to preparing the ground and, afterwards, reinforcing the change.

Change within the professional firm is not good or bad *per se*, but in the turbulent environment currently faced it is likely to be appropriate. Given the conservative natureof the construction industry concerted effots are required to successfully achieve changes and formal and informal mechanisms should be used in a complementary way.

7 References

Adair, J 1973, Training for Communication, Gower, London

Argyris, C, 1962, Interpersonal Competence and Organisational Effectiveness, Tavistock Publications, London

Argyris, C and Schon D, 1978, Organisational Learning: A Theory of Action Perspective, Addison Wesley

Asch, S, 1955, "Opinions & Social Pressures" Scientific America, November, pp31 - 35

Barrett, P S, 1991a, Practice Management: An Emerging Discipline, Practice Management: New Perspectives for the Construction Professional, edited by P S Barrett and A R Males, E & F N Spon, London pp 3 - 12

Barrett, P S, 1991b, The Clients Brief: A Holistic View, Management, Quality and Economics and Building, edited by A Bezelga and P Brandon, E & F Spon, London, pp 3 - 13

Belbin, R M, 1983, Management Teams: Why they Succeed or Fail, London, Heinemann

Canter, R M, 1983, The Change Masters: Corporate Entrepreneurs at Work, George Allen and Unwin, London

Dadfar, H and P Gustavsson, 1989, Organisation, Environment and Strategy Part 2: Strategy and Strategic Decision, Working Paper 28, Umea University, Sweden

Hurst, D K, 1984, Of Boxes, Bubbles and Effective Management, Harvard Business Review, May - June, pp 78 - 88

Johnson, G, 1990, Managing Strategic Change: The Role of Symbolic Actions, British Journal of Management, Vol 1, pp 183 - 200

Kast, F E and Rosenzweig J E, 1981, Organisation and Management: A Systems and Contingency Approach, McGraw Hill

Kotter, J P, 1982, What Effective General Managers Really Do, Harvard Business Review, Nov - Dec, pp 156 - 67

Lansley, P, 1985, Putting Organisational Research into perspective, Construction Management and Economics, Vol 3, pp 1 - 14

Lewin, K, 1947, Frontiers in Group Dynamics, Human Relations, I, No 1, June, pp 5 - 41

Louis, M R and R I Sutton, 1991, Switching Cogniture Gears: From Habits of Mind to Active Thinking, Human Relations, Vol 44, No 1

Mintzberg, H, 1973, The Nature of Managerial Work, Harper and Row

Mintzberg, H and J A Walters, 1985, Of Strategies Deliberate and Emergent, Strategic Management Journal, Vol 6/3, pp 257 - 272

Newman, W H, 1975, Constructive Control, Prentice-Hall, N.J.

Powell, J A, 1991, Clients, designers and contractors: the harmony of able design teams, Practice Management: New Perspectives for the Construction Professional,, pp 137 - 148

RICS, 1991, Market Requirements of the Profession, RICS, London

Sibson R E, 1971, Managing Professional Services Enterprises; The Neglected Frontier, Pitman, New York

Vroom, V H, 1974, A New Look at Managerial Decision Making, Organisational Dynamics, Vol 15

The impact of cyclical trends on human resource requirements

J. Sommerville
Glasgow College of Building & Printing, Glasgow, Scotland, UK

Abstract
This paper discusses the cyclical nature of the construction industry in the U.K., the influences which may be perceived to act upon the industry and the ramifications in terms of human resource requirements brought about by the cyclical trends highlighted. Consideration is given to historical trends and the prediction of future industry workload. Strategic options available to management when seeking to source human resources are reviewed along with the efficacy of the various sources of referral utilised. The cyclical nature of the industry is clearly shown and management's attention is focused on key issues arising therefrom.
Keywords: Cyclical trends, Human Resources, Strategies, Referral Sources, Workload.

1 Introduction

The U.K. Construction Industry within which Architecture plays a vital role is beset by periods of rapid expansion or contraction. Many influences are seen to act upon the industry, some with beneficial effect, others with negative consequences, many will be well aware of the impact Royalty may have and also first hand experience of pressure groups. Each of the miriad of influencing forces will have impact upon the industry and modify its response to opportunities or threats. Those charged with the task of executing hard won contracts, be they design or construction, are faced with the challenge of ensuring that the requisite human resources are available as and when required, and with the appropriate basket of skills.

Experiences from within this industry and others, have shown the need to adopt longer term frameworks when considering human resource requirements and provision. Short termism is fine for the financial institutions who rely on "quick kills" to provide their income or growth but this industry, by its very nature, demands that lead and lag periods be an integral part of the overall process.

2 Cyclical Trends

Throughout the history of the modern U.K. construction industry booms and recessions have come and gone with alarming frequency. Parry Lewis (1965) in his painstaking analysis of the industry from 1700 through to 1963, clearly demonstrated the existence of a cyclical nature to the industry. The cyclical trends highlighted were found to be subject to influence from several major factors, namely:

population fluctuations;

shocks such as war;

credit.

The more important of these factors for the present period is of course credit, its availability and associated interest payment rates.

Successive Governments of varying political persuasions have sought to control the nation's growing inflation rate though restraining the provision of the built environment and hence the construction industry. More specifically the housing sector with its associated rise in capital values and hence perceived disposable wealth, have been targeted for special attention. Witness the present recession in the industry, primarily seen as being induced and driven by high interest rates. The view is held that whilst there has no doubt been a downturn in output from the early part of 1989 onwards, historically, and hence in cyclical terms, the downturn is perhaps best seen as a 'blip on the graph'. Annual construction outputs for the UK at constant 1985 prices are shown in Table 1.

Table 1. Annual output values

Year	Output Value in £ Millions	Year	Output Value in £ Millions
1963	24456	1977	26713
1964	27309	1978	28747
1965	28801	1979	29178
1966	29361	1980	27830
1967	31278	1981	25141
1968	31959	1982	25470
1969	31661	1983	26647
1970	30986	1984	27536
1971	31364	1985	27850
1972	31957	1986	28757
1973	32267	1987	31022
1974	28965	1988	33269
1975	27266	1989	34684
1976	26842	1990	35037

Analysis of the data clearly demonstrates the expansions in output, followed by the downturns which in turn are followed by a resurgence in output value. The period of 1963 through to 1968 saw a surge which was deemed inflationary and slowly brought back into line by use of the **interest control stick**. The resulting decline being shortlived and the boom continuing throughout the period 1971-1973. Many industry watchers will recall the 'crashes' of that period and the resulting collapsing organisations (RICS 1978). Similar cycles may be discerned for the periods from 1978-1982 and 1983-1990. Since we have had no major shock nor population fluctuation from 1963 onwards, then the principle influence which may be seen to be at work in the industry is that of credit and interest rates.

Correlation of year end interest rates with the value of construction output clearly demonstrates the effect interest rate has on the industry's output value. This relationship is illustrated in Figure 1 and Table 2. Analysis of this data shows that there is a correlation* with r0.09 when the output for each year is considered, which in reality is not what would happen since the interest rate increase will take some time to filter down through the various forms of operating mechanism; when a lag of 1 year is introduced into the calculations we see the value change to $r= -0.219$, this would in practical terms be a reasonable period within which we would expect to see some form of repercussion; and, if a two year lag is considered, then the value of r increases significantly to -0.387. Clearly demonstrating that interest rate does have a negative correlation with output values. The variability for this value of r shows that some 15% of the downturn in the value of output is directly attributable to the interest rate.

The Economists will no doubt point to the **Accelerator** and **Multipier** Principles when seeking to establish the clear link to cyclical trends and the swings in demand which the industry must take onboard.

The sample size given consideration within the analysis is, in statistical terms, considered to be small i.e. n is less than 30. None the less it serves to highlight the underlying cyclical nature to the industry. No doubt greater analysis over a wider timebase would provide a clearer picture of the emerging trends and correlations.

---

* Values for the periods considered are:
no time lag, $r=0.09$, S.D. interest rate=2.748, S.D. output=2749.449; 1 year lag, $r=-0.219$, S.D. interst rate =2.688, S.D. output=2629.082 and for 2years time lag, $r=-0.387$, S.D. interest rate=2.613, S.D. output=2641.406.

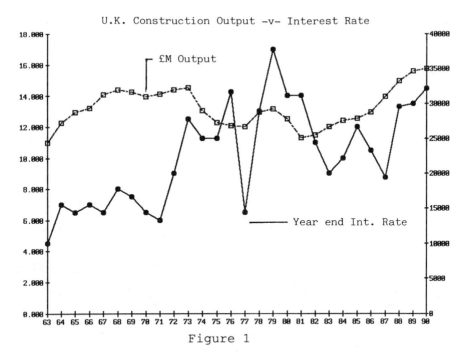

Figure 1

Table 2   Annual output value -v- Interest Rate

Year	(%) Int.Rate	* Output	Year	(%) Int.Rate	* Output
1963	6.000	24456	1977	9.500	26713
1964	6.000	27309	1978	11.750	28747
1965	6.750	28801	1979	15.000	29178
1966	7.125	29361	1980	14.000	27830
1967	7.125	31278	1981	15.000	25141
1968	7.625	31959	1982	10.000	25470
1969	8.500	31661	1983	11.250	26647
1970	8.500	30986	1984	12.000	27536
1971	8.000	31364	1985	12.750	27850
1972	8.500	31957	1986	12.300	28757
1973	11.000	32267	1987	10.300	31022
1974	11.000	28965	1988	12.750	33269
1975	11.000	27266	1989	14.500	34684
1976	12.250	26842	1990	14.500	35037

* £ Million constant 1985 prices, seasonally adjusted

3 Human Resources

Allowing for present high interest rates, it may be
forecast that the next major swing upwards in the industry
is not far off. Latham (1991) suggests sound reasons for
believing that the tide has turned for certain sectors of
the industry, "I believe that all the economic jigsaw pieces
are in place for a significant improvement in sales",
"Interest rates have been cut substantially, further falls
are imminent". Support for these statements is provided by
Hewes (1991) who sees the slump as being primarily related
to the housebuilding and property sectors, with the other
sectors escaping relatively unscathed. When the next surge
does arrive many of the problems witnessed in the early-mid
eighties will rear their ugly heads once again.

How many still recall trying to secure Technicians or a
squad of bricklayers in London, at the peak of the surge?
At what cost?

During the last boom many industry participants were only
too well aware of the shortages of skilled human resources
in particular geographic, as well as skill areas. Now that
the 'perceived' downturn is upon us the "Demographic
Timebomb" seems to have dematerialised. Has it been a case
of "Beam them up Spock"?

Employers seeking to recruit in the next rising current
will be faced with several problem areas:

    i)   Pressure on management to secure the requisite
            skills and skilled personnel.
    ii)   Induced stress on existing staff.
   iii) Increased recruitment costs.
    iv)   Restrictions on business take-up, through lack of
            Human Resources.

Management within the organisation will encounter many
others in the market-place, all seeking to recruit suitable
personnel. Competition will be fierce and therefore new,
and novel strategies will have to be implemented in order to
secure precious human resources, all of these activities
demanding much of the manager's valuable time.

Existing staff who have remained loyal to the
organisation (or have been retained) will face a two pronged
attack: the newcomers will perhaps command higher salaries
or benefits packages in order to induce them into joining
and the existing cohort will certainly have had to shoulder
a fairly substantial workload to enable the "lean and fit"
organisation to survive the downturn.

The search for human resources at a time when others are
trying to remove the same fish from the pool demands that
the recruitment methodology selected is fast, accurate,
reliable and cost effective.

The much heralded "Golden Hellos" of the city whizz-kids may well have to be applied to the industry's prima-donnas.

Much work will be put into winning tenders, but when it comes to executing the contract, human resources are everything - organisations basically comprise two components: people and jobs.

3.1 Strategic Options

Underlying and compounding the problem areas will be the reduction in the number of school leavers, coupled with the poor overall image of the industry. The poor image is demonstratively illustrated in the CITB Survey (1988) considering the occupational choices of school leavers.

The astute professional manager will of course be developing a full battery of strategic options to be implemented just prior to the upturn commencing. Likely options are illustrated in Figure 2, the majority of which may well have been exercised in the past and proven to be either acceptable strategies or those which have only short term effectiveness. Key areas associated with each of the strategic options available have been illustrated for further thought and consideration.

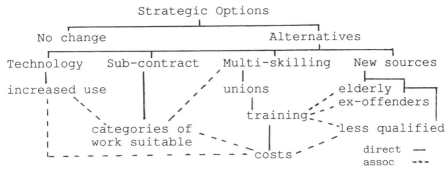

Figure 2   Strategic Options

3.2 Referral Sources

Gannon (1971) in his pioneering work considered the sources of referral utilised by one organisation and clearly demonstrated the link between length of employee service and the particular referral source.

If the employee is to be recruited and the associated costs are taken on board by the organisation, then it seems only logical that there should be a reasonable expectation of a considerable service period from the new recruit.

A variety of the recruitment referral sources open to management are illustrated in Figure 3. Whilst being indicative of the prevalent sources, Figure 3 is by no means exhaustive.

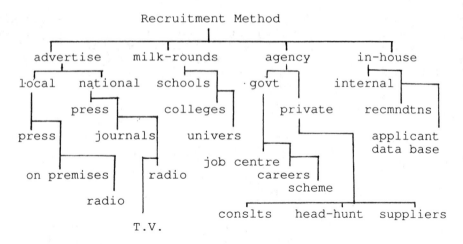

Figure 3 Referral Sources

Consideration of the referral sources utilised may well highlight those sources which are predictive of stable employees and also show where cost savings may be implemented i.e. why advertise if word of mouth is more productive and beneficial.

4.0 Workload

There can be little doubt that the upturn is coming, careful analysis of the impending industry workload, and consideration of the cyclical trends, clearly indicates that the next surge may be even greater in monetary terms than the last boom. The trends demonstrated by the analysis of the cyclical data clearly indicate that with interest rates falling, then the knock-on effect will begin to emerge. The effects may not be immense in the first year, but certainly by year two of the reduced rates, we should see a rise in the workload. The Accelerator and Multiplier effects should have begun to show through the system and work in-hand, and proposed, will perhaps have increased dramatically.
  Potential work areas include:
    The developing second wave in the North Sea Oil Areas.
    Harmonisation with Europe on 1st January 1992.
    The general need to upgrade the infrastructure within the UK, especially in light of EC Directives.
    Expansion of the UK Industrial and housing sectors.
    The potentially massive workload in the Middle East and ex-Soviet bloc satellites.

5 Conclusions

To secure and train the necessary human resources demands that time, effort, resources, and managerial expertise are focused on the issue now. Potential employees are immediately available in the U.K. market place, at what may be seen as discounted prices, waiting for the astute manager to make them an offer they cannot refuse.

Adoption of strategies with a wider timebase, towards human resources, can only prove beneficial in the long run. The image of the U.K. industry may be enhanced, the reputaion of certain employers may also be improved, and certainly the quality of work-life will undergo an injection of surety.

Trying to enter the market place when all others are trying to do the same can only lead to escalation of costs, reduction in effectiveness and loss of productivity.

6 References

The Construction Industry Training Board (1988)
The View of Young People and Their Parents.
Richmond, Surrey.

Gannon, M.J. (1971) **Sources of Referral and Employee Turnover**. Journal of Applied Psychology, Vol 55, No.1 226-228

Hewes,M.(1991) **U.K. Construction 1991**, Ravensbeck,London

Latham, M.(M.P.) (1991) in **Building**, 11 Oct 1991,pp25.

Parry Lewis, J. (1965) **Building Cycles and Britain's Growth** Macmillan, London.

The Royal Institution of Chartered Surveyors (1978)
The Property Boom 1968-1973 and its collapse.
London

Interdependent group activity in architectural management

R.A. Fraser
Miami University, Oxford, Ohio, USA

Abstract
As size, level of specialization and technology have
increased within our organizations, dependence upon group
activity has also increased. In order to get all the
facts, to analyze them, to decide and to act; more than one
mind is needed. The question is not whether to use groups,
but rather how and when they can be used most effectively.
The major purpose of this paper is to examine
interdependent problem-solving and decision-making
activities from two perspectives--the general case of
employee involvement practices and the specific case of ad
hoc team activity such as value engineering. Intelligent
use of these approaches requires understanding of the
mechanisms by which they work and the conditions under
which they will be most effective. Additionally this paper
discusses some of the operating problems that arise as
people work in groups. Ways to reduce such problems and
increase positive effects of assembly are discussed with
emphasis on issues of communication and leadership.
Keywords: Participatory Management, Team Development,
Interdependence, Organizational Change, Personnel.

1 Change in Organizational Management
Leadership of complex organizations has become increasingly
difficult due to the dynamic nature of the marketplace,
economic globalization, rampant geopolitical transitions,
and major changes in workforce demographics. Some of the
management responses to such changes represent wholesale
adoptions of "packaged" approaches to "new wave"
leadership. More often, management shifts are a function of
the cumulative nature of scientific knowledge that leads to
constant interpretation and revision of earlier
conclusions. More theoreticians and researchers are
studying aspects of management and organizational behavior
now than ever before. As our knowledge accumulates, it is
inevitable that interpretations of people's behavior will
continually change. For this reason, occasional "fads" in

management approaches are not necessarily evidence of confusion or lack of commitment; they may simply reflect the continual search for better management practice.

The changes we are experiencing today in leadership theory and practice go well beyond such incremental evolution. Present revolutionary views of effective organizational leadership reflect a major shift from conventional, bureaucratic (transactional) management to a new paradigm of open-system (transformational) leadership. The bureaucratic model characterized by division of labor, hierarchy of authority and a framework of rules and impersonality was viewed by the German sociologist Max Weber as the most rationally efficient form of organization. Fred Taylor's "scientific management" improved bureaucratic performance through increased specialization, standardization and efficiency of job design and training. Paradoxically, Weber's model with Taylor's improved management efficiences has come to symbolize the epitome of inefficiency. The pyramidal structure and concentration of power common to this form is best suited to stable environments and routine tasks. With increasing rates of change, bureaucracies are becoming immobilized by their own structures. Novel decisions must be made at a rate which cannot be met in a rigid hierarchical chain of command. More and more links in the chain are bypassed and decisions made by specialist staff members or the workers themselves. Over twenty years ago, Toffler (1970) suggested that "to live, organizations must cast off those bureaucratic practices that immobilize them, making them less sensitive and less rapidly responsive to change" (p. 141). In response to external and internal changes, organizations are beginning to become more dynamic and self-renewing. Rather than the relatively rigid, tightly organized bureaucratic design; we are experiencing the development of a new system of temporary "project team" groupings, called "adhocracies" by Toffler. Changes in the designs of our organizations must be accompanied by changes in the ways people experience life at work if we are to maintain our positions in the world economy. Structures and practices that reduce the effective utilization of human resources must be eliminated. Simplistic approaches provided in many "inspirational" management texts tell managers how to search for, be compassionate about, or even to invent excellence--hopefully in one minute or less. Many of the ideas espoused in such volumes are not bad ideas, but are less than management personnel will need in order to transform their organizations and their own behavior. Rather, managers need to carefully analyze the contingencies impinging on their practice and select from their management repertoire the approach or approaches that are most appropriate to increase effectiveness of available human resources.

2 Types of Interdependence

Three forms of interdependence described by J. D. Thompson (1967) can aid the understanding of employee involvement. The first, pooled interdependence. refers to a social situation in which two or more individuals render a discrete contribution to the whole, without any direct interaction with one another. Members are interdependent in the sense that unless each one performs adequately, the whole group outcome is jeopardized. Failure of any one member threatens the whole group and thus each of the other parts. Another form, sequential interdependence, refers to a social situation in which the work of one member must be carried out before the work of another member can be performed. Sequential interdependence involves pooled attributes with the additional aspects of direct interrelationship and order of the the relationship. The third form, reciprocal interdependence, refers to the situation in which the work of each member of the group directly permeates the work of all other members.

Work groups may be characterized by each of these types of interdependence at one time or another. For example, in the simultaneous detailing of specific areas within a given design by a number of detailers we see pooled inter-dependence. Frequently this type of interrelationship is a function of one manager who assigns the work to various employees who may not even be aware of the relatedness of others' work. Sequential interdependence may take place as the design is handed off to specification writers and again, when it is passed later to the construction organ-ization. Finally, reciprocal interdependence, the sort of relationship that occurs in well-managed project teams, occurs each time that members of the various subgroups meet to "iron out" transition problems. When we speak of problem-solving and/or decision-making teams, the interdependence is assumed to be reciprocal. Improved performance can be obtained in any of the relational arrangements through a variety of intervention techniques.

3 Participation in Decision Making

The call for transformational leadership generally includes aspects of employee empowerment and heightened employee involvement in decision making. In this approach, bureau-cratic hierarchy must give way to heterarchy; leadership attributes of control and command be replaced by coordin-ation and communication. Prominent theorists such as Chris Argyris, Warren Bennis and Rensis Likert have argued that employee participation in decision making is a necessary condition for the attainment of employee commitment, job satisfaction and overall productivity. Further, Sashkin (1984) asserted that the use of employee participation is an "ethical imperative."

On the other hand, researchers such as Edwin Locke

(1986) assert that participation is simply a managerial technique that, in some situations, can actually lead to lower employee satisfaction and performance. Overall, meta-analyses of studies of employee participation provide little evidence that interventions such as increased participatory involvement in decision-making, in and of themselves, will result in improved performance. Effects of such strategies as improved benefits, improved goal-setting and feedback to employees, and job enrichment have been demonstrably superior to participation in decision-making in some studies; especially in those situations involving pooled or sequential interdependencies. The merits of any given strategy seem to be realized only when it is judiciously applied in appropriate contexts.

Based on her own research, Rosabeth Moss Kanter suggests that authoritative (nonparticipatory) decisions are more appropriate when one individual has greater expertise on a subject than any others, if there is little time available, and if the individuals involved prefer and are capable of working alone. Kanter's data also suggest that participatory decisions should be used to develop new sources of expertise, when individuals are knowledgeable about the decision content, and when there are conflicting perspectives that need to be addressed. Similar contingencies have been suggested by Victor Vroom and Andrew Grove. As in Kanter's discussion, Grove identified the employees' abilities ("task-related maturity") as a key factor in the determination of the efficacy of participatory roles for employees.

In determining the nature of the participation desired, managers must consider the nature of the task itself, the nature of the employees, and the context of the task. Many participation efforts are based on team concepts and require significant organizational commitment. Managers must be willing to learn new skills and adapt to a role change. They must also be willing to take risks and to trust that employees will take responsibility for essential aspects of their job. Adequate financial and time resources must be provided to support team activity.

4 Improving Reciprocal Interdependence

As mentioned earlier, reciprocal interdependence is the structure related to "team" activity. Although the terms are frequently used synonymously, there are important distinctions between a number of individuals, a group and a team. Group members have a shared sense of identity and of the objectives they are trying to achieve. Teams have the additional characteristic of having developed and practiced effective strategies for meeting their objectives. Managed well, teams can combine the knowledge, skills and experience of many people to reach an optimum solution, increase commitment to support group decisions due to cross functional representation from throughout the organization, and provide for personnel development and opportunities for greater involvement and visibility of talented team members. If teams are not developed and managed well, they become a time-consuming, inefficient way to reach less than optimum decisions and poor solutions.

The effectiveness of the team approach has been clearly demonstrated within a variety of settings across a wide range of projects. To maximize team synergy, members should be selected from the major disciplines or functions related to the objective. The effects of group heterogeneity or homogeneity of some trait on overall group effectiveness have been extensively researched. The implications of such studies are clear. Heterogeneous, or mixed, groups consistently outperform homogeneous groups. In setting up a project team, then, it would be appropriate to select competent individuals with a range of experience, backgrounds, points of view, and talents. Individual differences are the primary source of the power and potential advantages of group activity. In addition to adequate expertise and functional representation, we must be careful to select members with effective interpersonal skills and positive attitudes regarding team activities.

4.1 Stages of Group Development

Before a group can accomplish anything as a group, rather than as a collection of individuals, it needs to get organized--to orient the group, agree on procedures and norms, and to get the group moving toward some objective. From the first time members of the group meet, they begin to develop systematically--to pass through a series of developmental stages, much like individuals develop psychologically. Groups can become arrested at any stage and not be able to carry on successfully. It is important to learn what these stages are, and how we can facilitate successful development through them.

The first stage, facilitating psychological membership, deals with development of interpersonal involvement and identity as members of a group. Although the time required to develop a general sense of inclusion differs from group to group; such factors as how much time they are able to spend together, previous relationships among the members, the ages, experiences with the content, and amount of diversity all effect the eventual resolution.

After the members become acquainted, build some security, and begin to feel that they are part of the group, issues of influence relationships become prominent. Each member needs to sort out what his or her position is relative to the others. For most effective synthesis of perspectives, each person must feel that his or her contribution is important. This doesn't happen simply because we are told we are important, but rather by being treated in such a way that we feel that both our ideas and ourselves are valued. The most effective teams develop very different "climates" from less effective groups and from most of our day to day interactions. If people have worked in highly competitive environments, there is considerable proactive interference to learning and using collaborative behavior. Competitive behavior, directed at obtaining a goal while keeping others from reaching it first, will doom team activity. If members have learned such behavior, significant early team development activity is required. The key developmental issue in this second phase is that members find their own niches in the group's structure. Until this has occurred, much of the group's energy may be siphoned off in power plays, bargaining, and hidden agendas.

Once the issues of belonging and influence have been successfully resolved, the group can directly and productively address its assigned task. Not that the group just sits around and "sorts out" its relationships for the first meetings. Some work, of course, is accomplished during the first phases; but not with the same effort and support that the members are able to provide in the third phase, pursuing group goals. By now, members know one another relatively well and have a good idea of how each one can aid in the pursuit of the goal. They have settled issues of leadership and are ready to move on to examine task issues, agree on approaches, and make decisions. If group members have developed skill in communication and decision making, the aspects involved in the early group development can be dealt with relatively easily. Unfortunately, too many groups have little opportunity to learn about and practice these skills. Training in effective interaction patterns should take place before and during the group activity.

During the third phase, members need a structured approach to their problem solving activities. There are many models available--including the "job plan" of value management, Delphi techniques, "nominal" procedures, cause-effect diagrams, and many other approaches. All to often, problems that are reasonably solvable look so difficult that people give up on them without an adequate attempt. Other problems that could be solved go unresolved because our attempts are random and the path to the correct solution becomes clouded over with fragmentary starts and stops. Using a set of shared guidelines for group activity, including an agreed-upon approach for dealing with the problem itself, vastly increases the probability that the best answer will be found. The system adopted by the group must provide for adequate information gathering, speculation about alternatives, analysis and evaluation of potential resolutions, and selection of the best solution.

Without a visible job plan, groups frequently start off well, but then get lost along the way. Training and/or facilitation in problem solving techniques can help group members use their resources most productively.

4.2 Communication

Cutting across each of these stages is the important issue of communication. If we think of human relationships as consisting of two or more individuals trying to satisfy their needs in the same situation, we can see the importance of communication. Only through communication can we let others know what our needs are, find out what others' needs are, and try to influence outcomes to achieve need satisfaction.

All communication includes components of content (both facts and feelings) and direction. Group productivity can be improved if members learn to use techniques such as active listening, paraphrasing, describing feelings and behavior, and giving useful feedback. Practice in such skills can reduce miscommunications--the discrepancies between what the sender intends and what meanings the receiver picks up.

Effective group problem solving requires interaction among members. Most of the time, our communications are of a coactive nature that places all the eggs in one basket. That is, a group leader or superior is the hub of the communication network. While this structure looks efficient since it takes less time; the morale, flexibility, and correctness of two-way or interactive approaches are much better. Careful team selection and development increase the probability that such interaction actually results.

4.3 Motivation

Group problem solving, like any other activity, is affected by issues of personal motivation. One of the most useful models of motivation is Lawler's expectancy approach, stated Effort--Performance--Outcomes. This includes and expectancy component ("If I try, I can do it") and an instrumentality component ("If I do it, good things will happen"). Breakdowns in the Effort-Performance relationship include any factors that we think will keep us from performing effectively: "If I try, I can do it. No I can't because _____". The ways people fill in the blank comprise the set of expectancy problems to be dealt with. These frequently include perceived or real lack of ability, lack of time, lack of direction, lack of authority, etc.. Thus, to provide for effective activity, we must be sure that those involved have appropriate instruction, sufficient time, and requisite skills and information available.

Breakdowns in the Performance-Outcome relationship

include any factors that reduce the perceived probability that improved performance will lead in turn to the attainment of valued outcomes. Instrumentality problems frequently involve lack of adequate reward, perceived or real lack of organizational value for the activity itself, and pressures to complete other work.

Many of the major rewards associated with team membership are inherent in the activity itself. In addition to the satisfaction that occurs when goals have been accomplished, people also feel rewarded by the security, affiliation, esteem, and influence that group membership may provide. When members have developed into an effective team with good communication skills and both personal and group needs are largely satisfied, a positive assembly effect has been achieved.

5. Conclusion

Organizational management is a complex and demanding task. There are many panaceas being offered in the literature-- techniques that purport to work in all places with all people and all times. Unfortunately, best evidence indicates that no such panaceas exist. With respect to participatory decision making, research results are mixed. Sometimes participation is useful and sometimes it is not. It is up to the manager to determine whether the task and personnel available are appropriate for this approach and then to provide the necessary environmental support. Increased opportunities for interaction will not necessarily improve performance. There must be a basic collaborative ability among group members and the absence of conditions creating serious conflicts of interest within the group, such as a reward system based on competition or the allocation of status symbols in a manner that impedes collaboration.

It has been said that if you dig far enough into any problem, you will get to people. While that may be the case, it is also true that people are the solution as well--especially if they are provided the skills and opportunities to develop high performance teams.

References

Block, P. (1987) **The Empowered Manager.** Jossey-Bass, San Francisco, CA.
Grove, A. S. (1983) **High Output Management.** Random House, New York, NY.
Kanter, R. M. (1982) Dilemmas of Managing Participation. **Organizational Dynamics.** 11, 5-27.
Sashkin, M. (1984) Participative Management is an Ethical Imperative. **Organizational Dynamics,** 12, 4-22.

Thompson, J.D. (1967) **Organizations in Action.** McGraw-Hill
   New York, NY
Toffler, A. (1970)   **Future Shock.**   Random House, New York,
   New York.
Vroom, V. and Yetton, P. (1973) **Leadership and Decision
   Making.**   Univ. of Pittsburg Press, PA.

AND TO THE FUTURE . . .

'The certainties of one age are the problems of the next.'

R. H. Tawney

Future organization of the building process

I.R. Wim Bakens
Bakkenist Management Consultants, Voorburg, The Netherlands
Coordinator CIB Working Commission W82 'Future Studies in Construction'

Abstract
In 1990 the CIB Working Commission W82 "Future Studies in Construction" started the
international study project "Future Organization of the Building Process". In this study
scenarios will be developed for future process organization in Building based on an
international confrontation of innovative ideas of experts on various aspects of process
organization and also based on an evaluation of trends and developments among others
on the building markets and in building technology.
Keywords: Future, Building Process, Building technology, Information Technology,
Building Market, Mega Trends, Procurement Systems, Project Management

1 Introduction

The results of the study will be presented at the W82 Symposium "Construction beyond
2000", June 1992 in Espoo, Finland.
Provisional results will be presented among others at the Symposium "Architectural
management" in Nottingham, U.K. In this presentation also an evaluation will be
included of the most important statements concerning architectural management that were
made during this symposium.

2 CIB Working Commission W82 "Future Studies in Construction"

The study project was initiated by and is executed under the supervision of the CIB
Working Commission W82 "Future Studies in Construction". The objectives of this
Working Commission are:
- to collect, create, evaluate and disseminate knowledge dealing with the development
  and the future of the construction filed on the medium and long-term scale;
- to analyse and interpret external factors (e.g. technological, economical, social,
  global, etc.) effecting the development and the future of the construction field;
- to analyse, develop and apply methodologies of future studies and forecasting (e.g.
  scenario writing, extrapolation, trend analysis, cross impact analysis, mathematical
  methods, etc.) in construction research and policy making;
- to formulate and evaluate future alternatives for the construction field and for its
  sectors (e.g. construction industry, housing, town planning, etc.).

To realise these objectives W82 strives for achieving synthesis of ideas and concepts of
future oriented and innovative experts with different cultural back grounds (e.g. people
from different types of countries and working with different types of companies and
institutes in the construction field) and from different disciplines (e.g. technical,
economical, social and managerial in policy making, planning, design, engineering,
contracting and maintenance).

3 Scope of the study project

In the figure below the scope of the study is summarized.

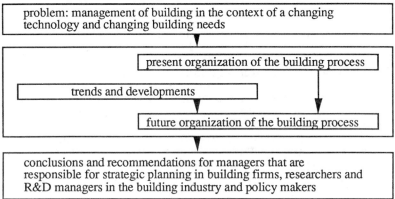

Scope of the study "Future Organization of the Building Process"

A basic assumption is that the traditional segmented organization of the building process no longer fits in the context of a fast developing building technology. In fact the traditional way of organizing the building process is one of the major hindrances for technological innovation and because of a non efficient use of new technologies the quality and the cost-quality rations in building are far from optimal. Also the traditional principles for cooperation in building projects often prevent a collective strive of all process participants for the top quality, that is needed to be able to compete with other industries. Also the traditional way of organizing the building process no longer fits in the context of a changing building market. For example responsibilities and liabilities are often unclear and clients no longer accept this as a given fact.

4 Trends and developments

Building process organization will be influenced among others by trends and developments in the following areas:
- building technology, with attention for topics like: industrialization of building, concentration of the supply sector and the use of robots in manufacturing companies;
- information technology in building, with attention for topics like: integrated CAD and CAD-CAM systems, computer integrated building, models for building information and communication, EDI, PDI and project data bases;
- building market, with attention for topics like: changing role of governmental institutions, professionalization of clients, changing structure of the building market, growing need for quality performance, declining market for extension of the building stock, changing planning principles;
- mega trends, with attention for topics like: labour market, environment preservation, individualization of building users, internationalization and even globalization of clients and of companies and changing appreciation of entrepreneurship;
- procurement systems, with attention for topics like:,post construction liability and insurance, new EC regulations in this area, various principles for tendering and Performance Specifacation.

In the study the possible effects on future process organization of these and related trends and developments are assessed.

In this context two categories of aspects of process organization are distinguished:
- legal aspects related to contracts and procedures in building projects;
- aspects related to project management, with attention for topics like: systems for coordination, logistical principles, systems for integrated quality management in building projects, etc.

Process activities and the responsibilities and roles of participants in the building process are a reflection of choices made with regard to both aspects.

5   World wide inventory of key studies

An important part of the study is a world wide inventory and selection of future oriented key studies in areas that are thought to be of importance. This inventory and selection has been made trough two channels:
- national inventory in countries participating in W82 (e.g. Austria, Belgium, Canada, Finland, France, Israel, Italy, Netherlands, Sweden, United Kingdom and USA);
- through selected CIB Working Commissions.

6   Preview on the study results

Some of the expected changes that will effect process organization in building in a more or less general way, are:
- better integrated process, with a more clear defined division of responsibilities and liabilities combined with a more effective and a more explicit method for coordination and with forms of cooperation based on co-makership;
- Information Technology based networks per project;
- project independent building concepts as a base for innovation and cooperation;
- integrated systems for quality management in building projects;
- standardized building components, combined with a system for flexible production organization, resulting in very individual and more flexible buildings;
- more client and consumer oriented attitude of all professional process participants.

However, there will not be one scenario for future process organization. Next to national and sectoral differences there will be differences in process organization per type of project (e.g. scale of technical and logistical complexity, type of financial involvement of process participants and financial risks, etc.) and per type of client (e.g. professional or non professional, profit or not profit oriented, etc).

It may be assumed that a stronger distinction will appear between on the one hand principles for building process organization for the execution of large and complex projects on behalf of more or less professional and often international oriented clients and on the other hand principles for process organization for the execution of more or less simple projects for non professional and mostly regional or local oriented clients. This distinction then will be a reflection of a parallel split in the building market. This split will force building companies more and more to make a strategic choice wether or not to specialize on acquiring and executing assignments in the top segment of the building market and to forget the rest of the building market.

Also concerning the future role of architects there will not be but one scenario. Next to national and other differences this role will differ per segment of the building market. Architects also may be forced more and more to make strategic choices concerning specialization in stead of being full service professionals.

Index of Authors

Index of Keywords